Sadao
Maou

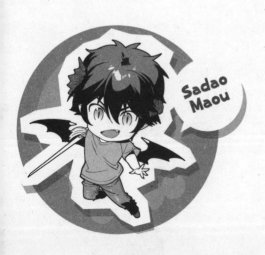

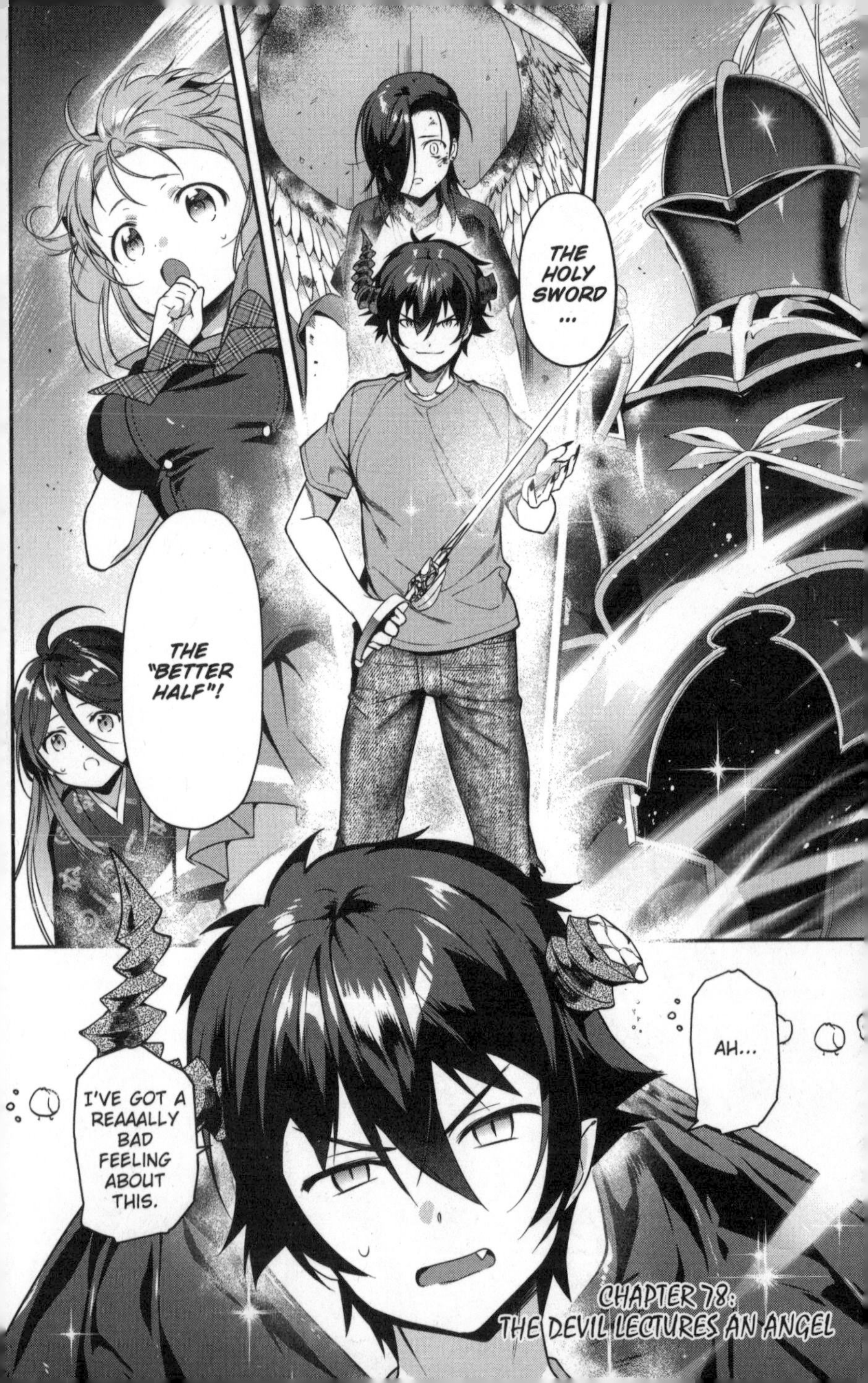
THE HOLY SWORD ...
THE "BETTER HALF"!
AH...
I'VE GOT A REAAALLY BAD FEELING ABOUT THIS.
CHAPTER 78: THE DEVIL LECTURES AN ANGEL

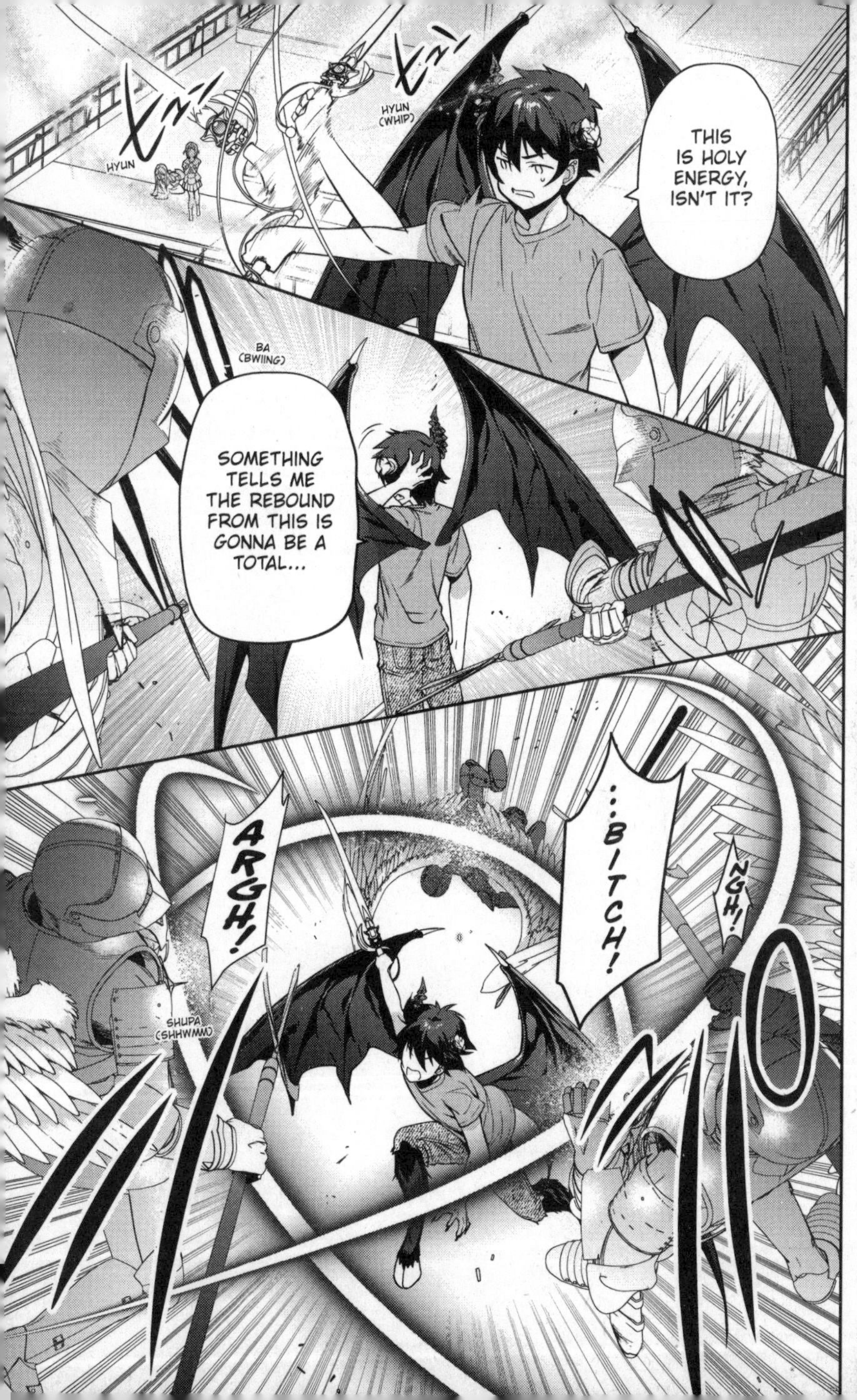
THIS IS HOLY ENERGY, ISN'T IT?
HYUN (WHIP)
HYUN
BA (BWIING)
SOMETHING TELLS ME THE REBOUND FROM THIS IS GONNA BE A TOTAL...
NGH!
...BITCH!
ARGH!
SHUPA (SHHWMM)

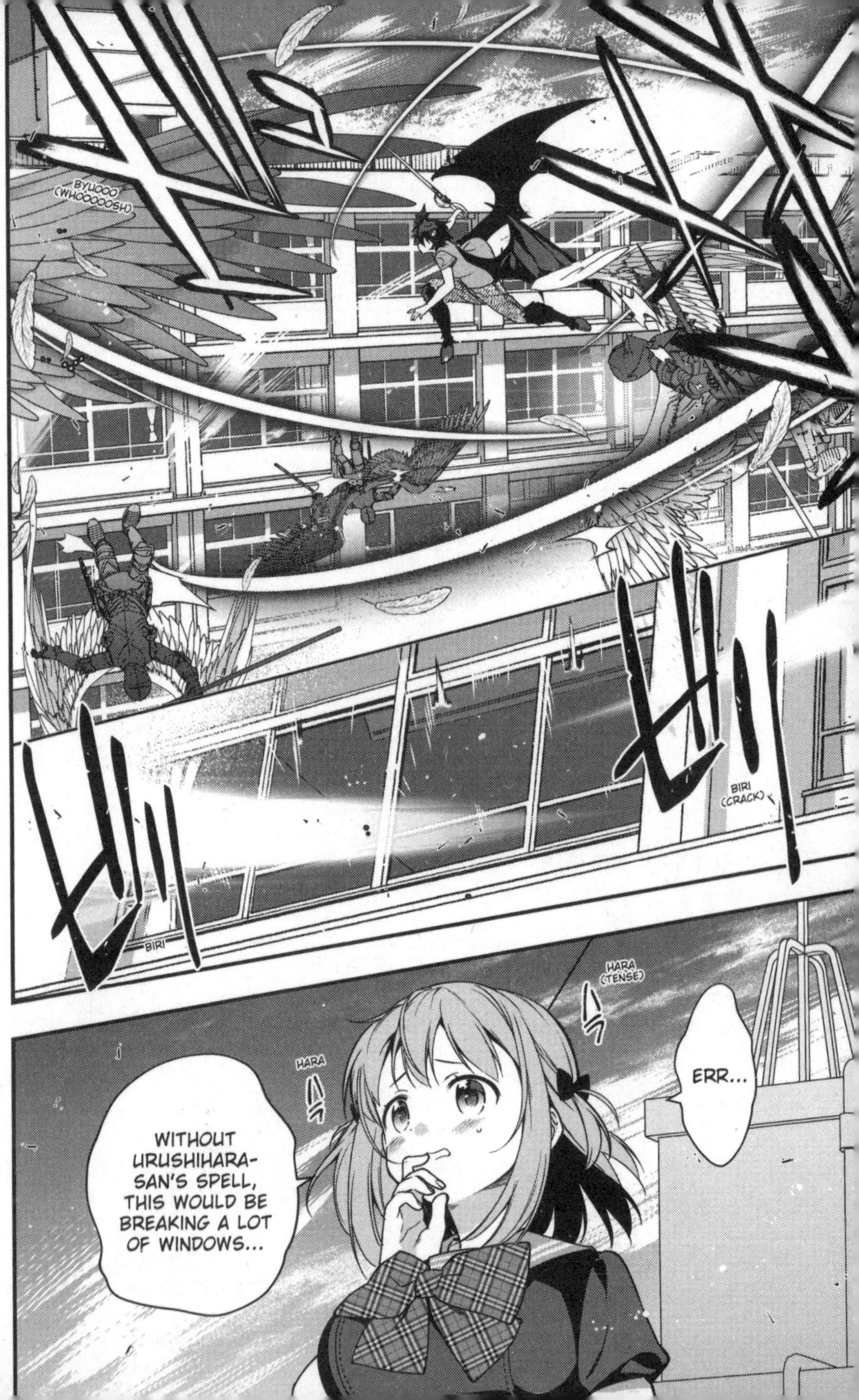
BYUOOO (WHOOOOOSH)
BIRI (CRACK)
BIRI
HARA (TENSE)
ERR...
HARA
WITHOUT URUSHIHARA-SAN'S SPELL, THIS WOULD BE BREAKING A LOT OF WINDOWS...

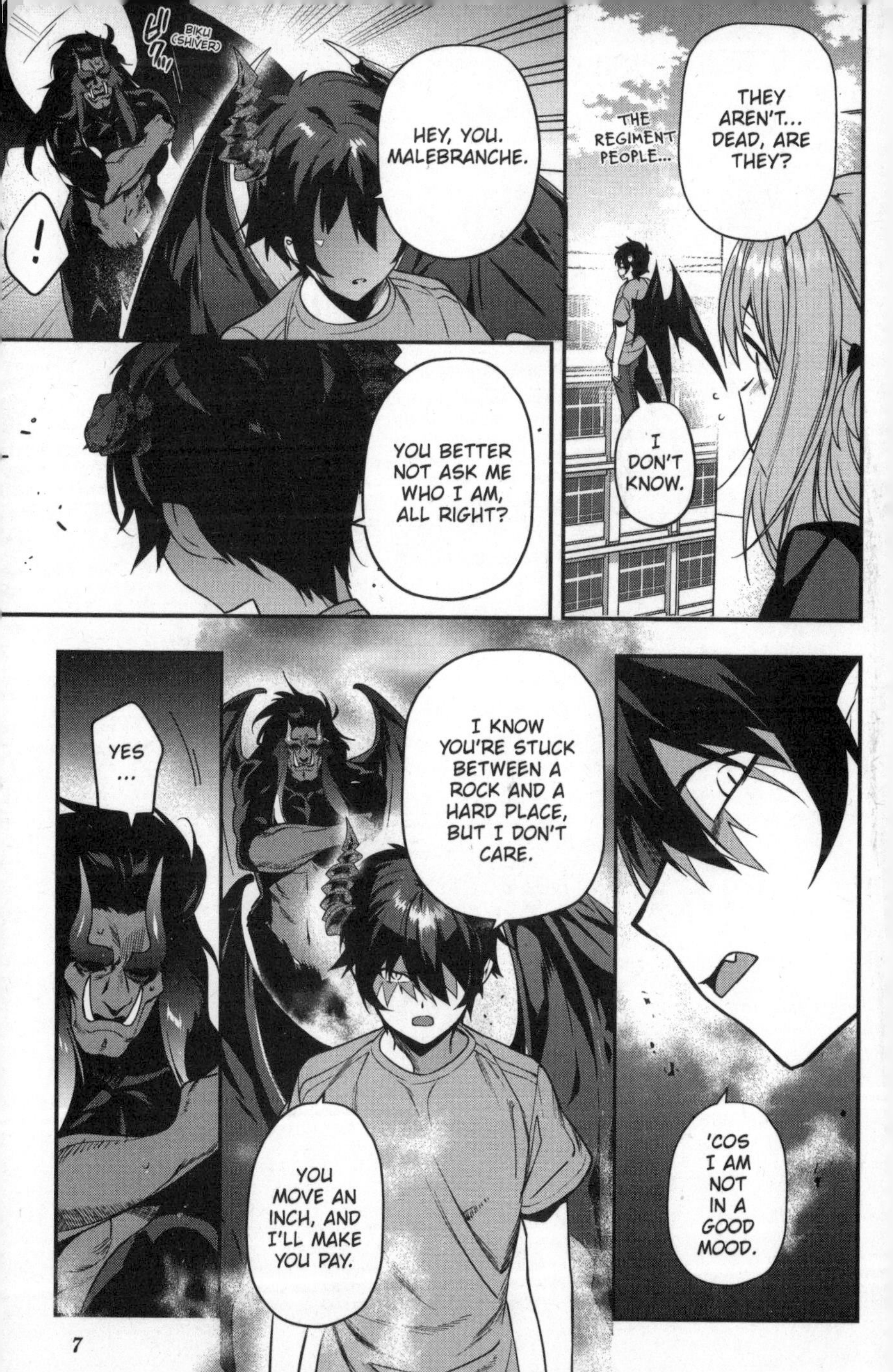
THEY AREN'T... DEAD, ARE THEY?
THE REGIMENT PEOPLE...
I DON'T KNOW.
BIKU (SHIVER)
HEY, YOU. MALEBRANCHE.
!
YOU BETTER NOT ASK ME WHO I AM, ALL RIGHT?
'COS I AM NOT IN A GOOD MOOD.
I KNOW YOU'RE STUCK BETWEEN A ROCK AND A HARD PLACE, BUT I DON'T CARE.
YOU MOVE AN INCH, AND I'LL MAKE YOU PAY.
YES ...

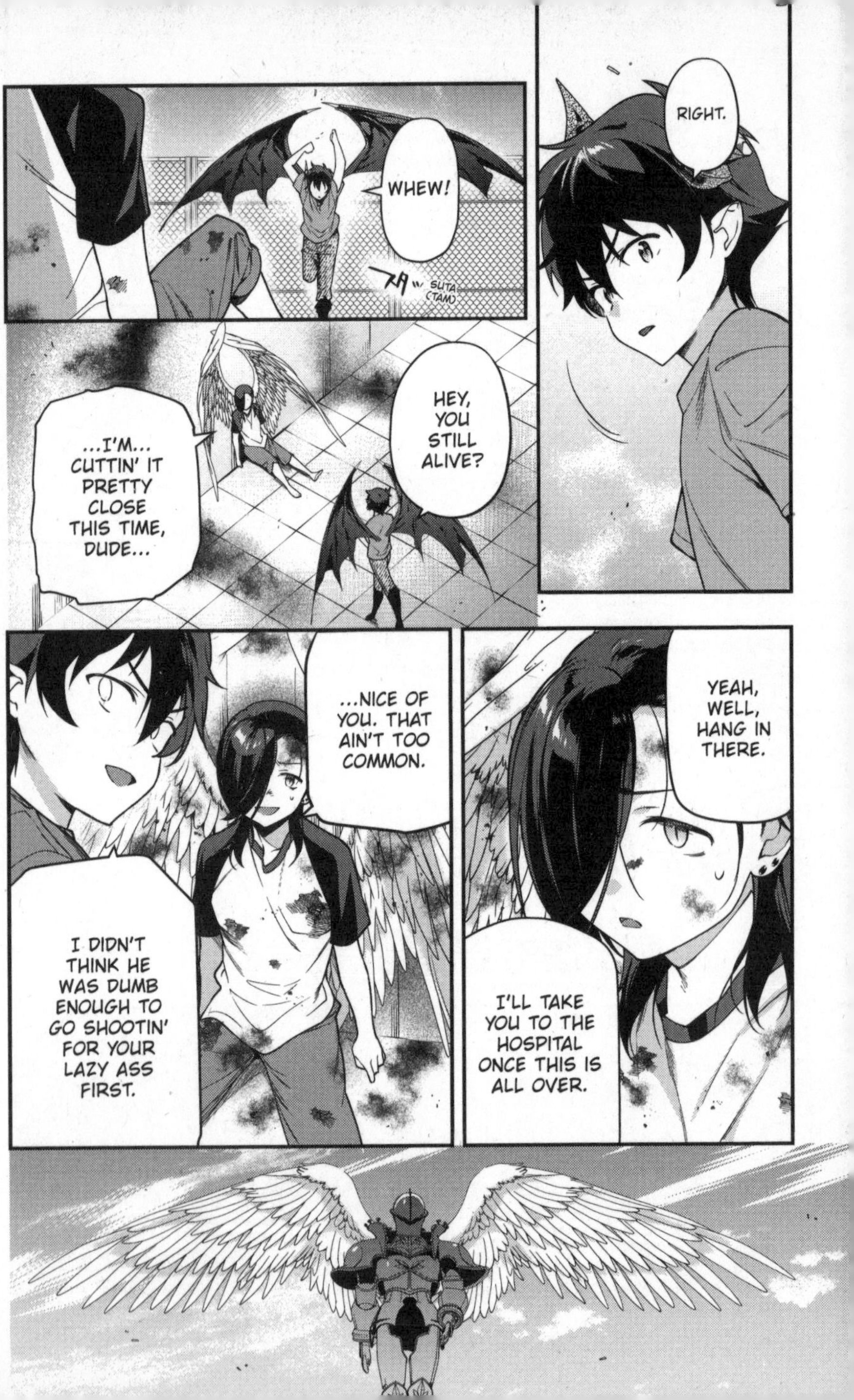
RIGHT.
WHEW!
スタ
SUTA (TAM)
HEY, YOU STILL ALIVE?
...I'M... CUTTIN' IT PRETTY CLOSE THIS TIME, DUDE...
YEAH, WELL, HANG IN THERE.
I'LL TAKE YOU TO THE HOSPITAL ONCE THIS IS ALL OVER.
...NICE OF YOU. THAT AIN'T TOO COMMON.
I DIDN'T THINK HE WAS DUMB ENOUGH TO GO SHOOTIN' FOR YOUR LAZY ASS FIRST.

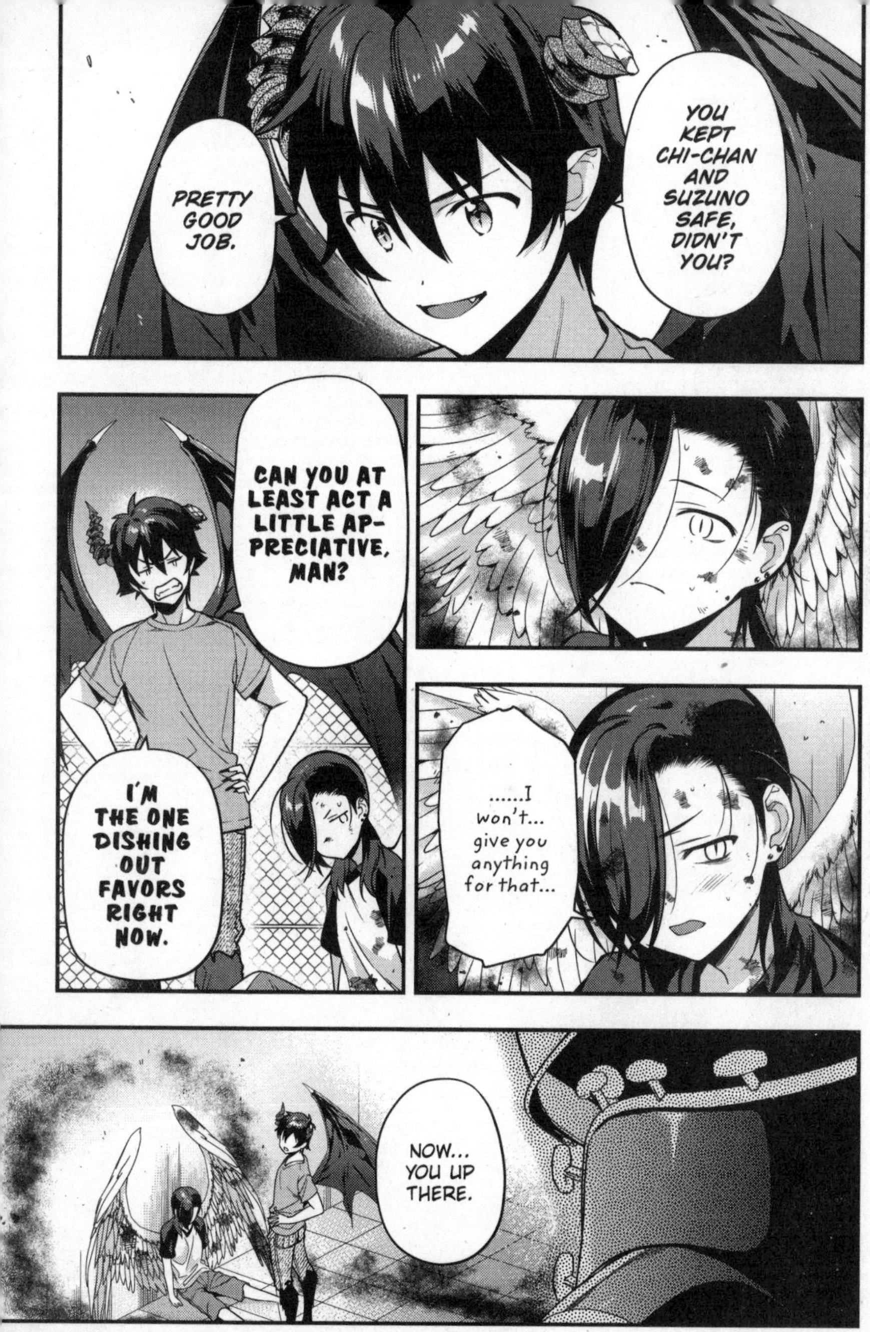
YOU KEPT CHI-CHAN AND SUZUNO SAFE, DIDN'T YOU?
PRETTY GOOD JOB.
......I won't... give you anything for that...
CAN YOU AT LEAST ACT A LITTLE AP-PRECIATIVE, MAN?
I'M THE ONE DISHING OUT FAVORS RIGHT NOW.
NOW... YOU UP THERE.

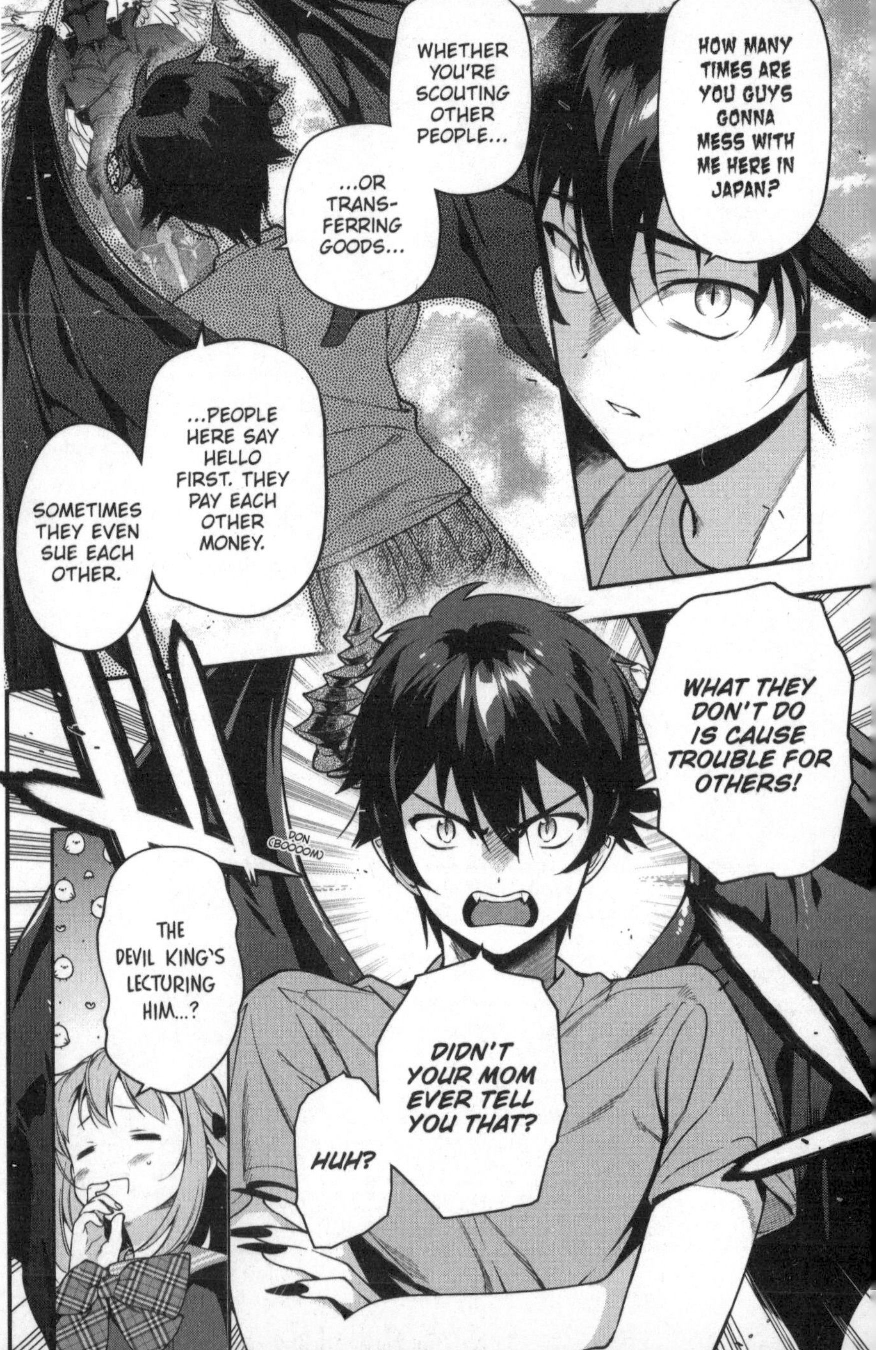
HOW MANY TIMES ARE YOU GUYS GONNA MESS WITH ME HERE IN JAPAN?
WHETHER YOU'RE SCOUTING OTHER PEOPLE...
...OR TRANS-FERRING GOODS...
...PEOPLE HERE SAY HELLO FIRST. THEY PAY EACH OTHER MONEY.
SOMETIMES THEY EVEN SUE EACH OTHER.
WHAT THEY DON'T DO IS CAUSE TROUBLE FOR OTHERS!
DON (BOOOOM)
DIDN'T YOUR MOM EVER TELL YOU THAT?
HUH?
THE DEVIL KING'S LECTURING HIM...?

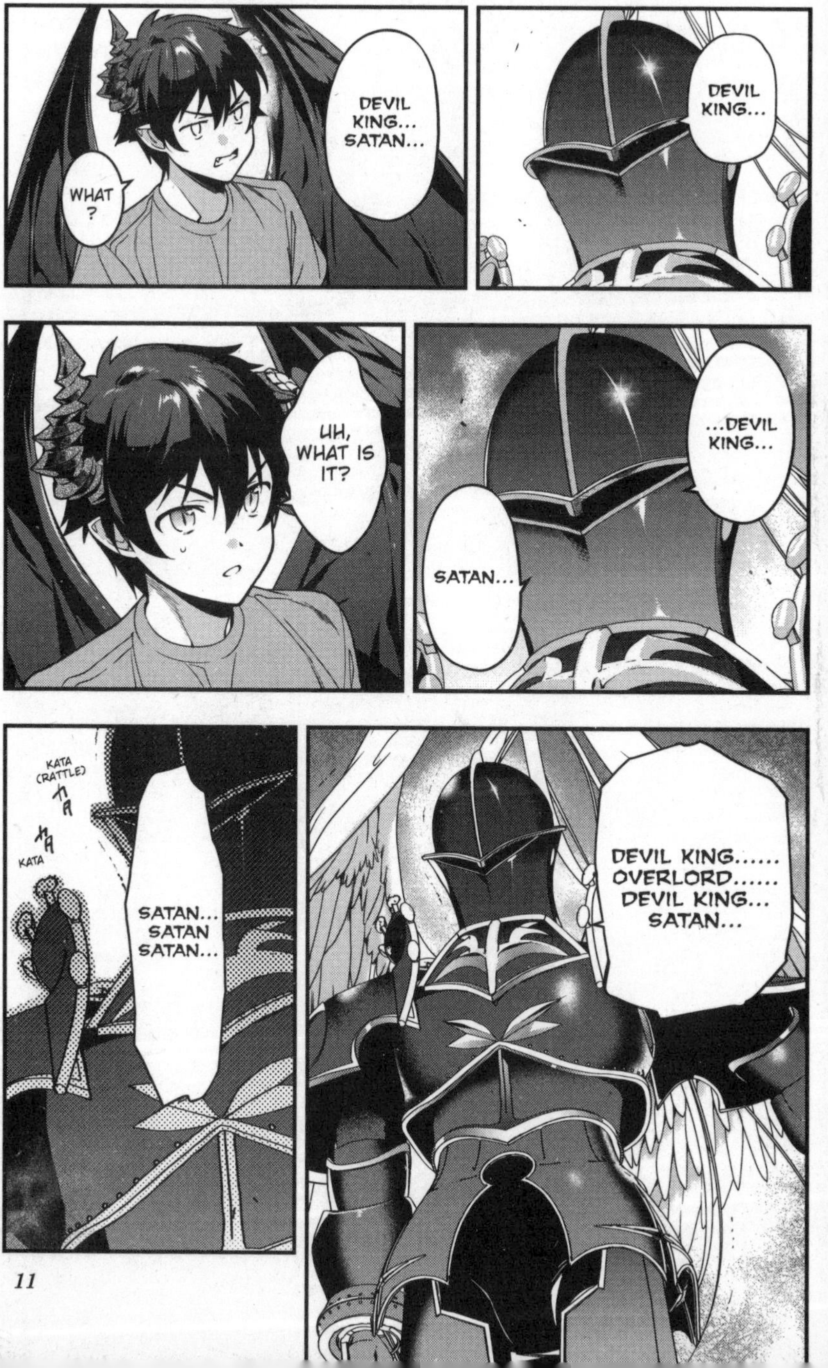
DEVIL KING...
DEVIL KING... SATAN...
WHAT?
...DEVIL KING...
SATAN...
UH, WHAT IS IT?
DEVIL KING...... OVERLORD...... DEVIL KING... SATAN...
SATAN... SATAN SATAN...
KATA (RATTLE) カタ
カタ KATA

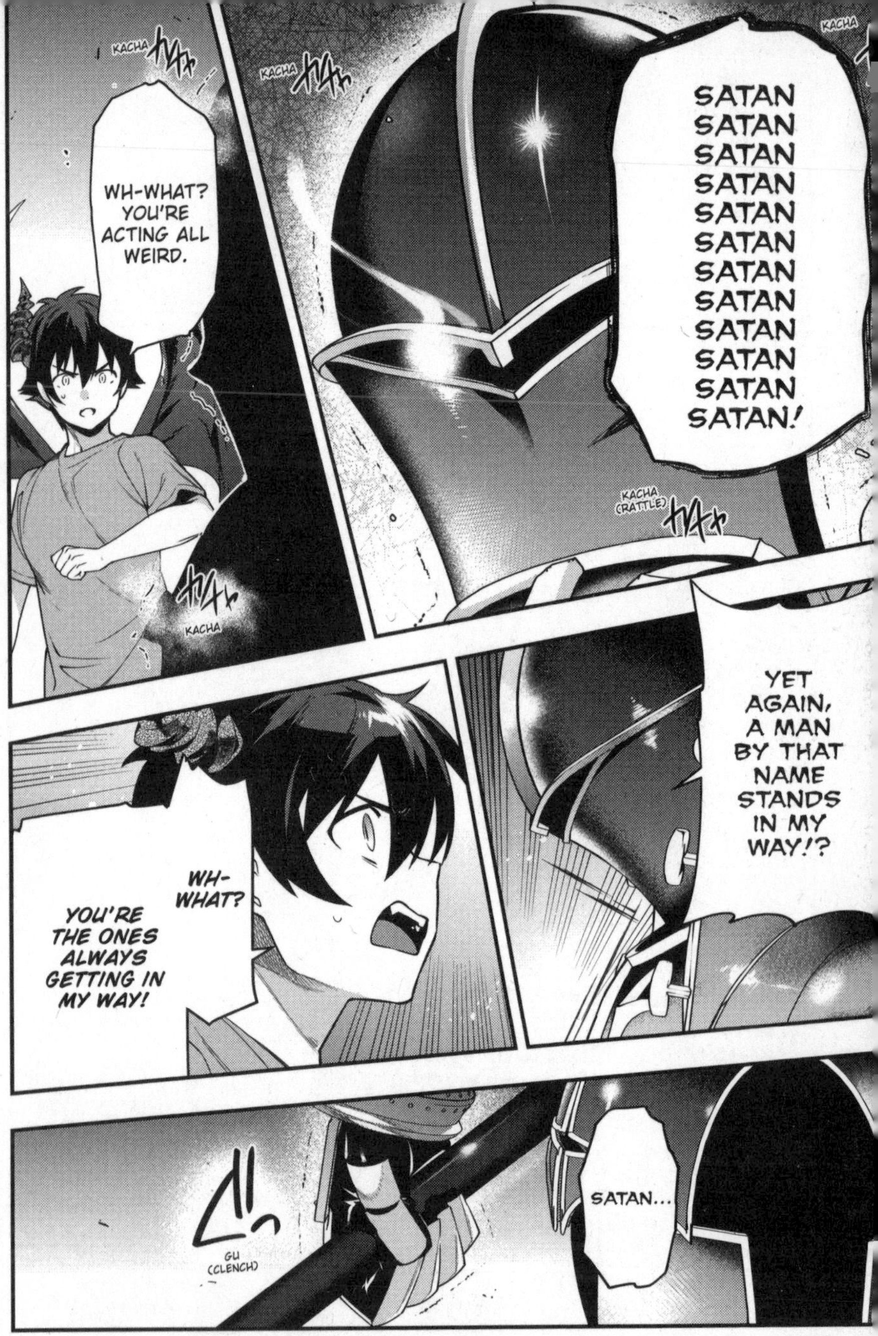
KACHA
SATAN SATAN SATAN SATAN SATAN SATAN SATAN SATAN SATAN SATAN SATAN SATAN!
KACHA
KACHA (RATTLE)
KACHA
WH-WHAT? YOU'RE ACTING ALL WEIRD.
KACHA
YET AGAIN, A MAN BY THAT NAME STANDS IN MY WAY!?
WH-WHAT?
YOU'RE THE ONES ALWAYS GETTING IN MY WAY!
SATAN...
GU (CLENCH)

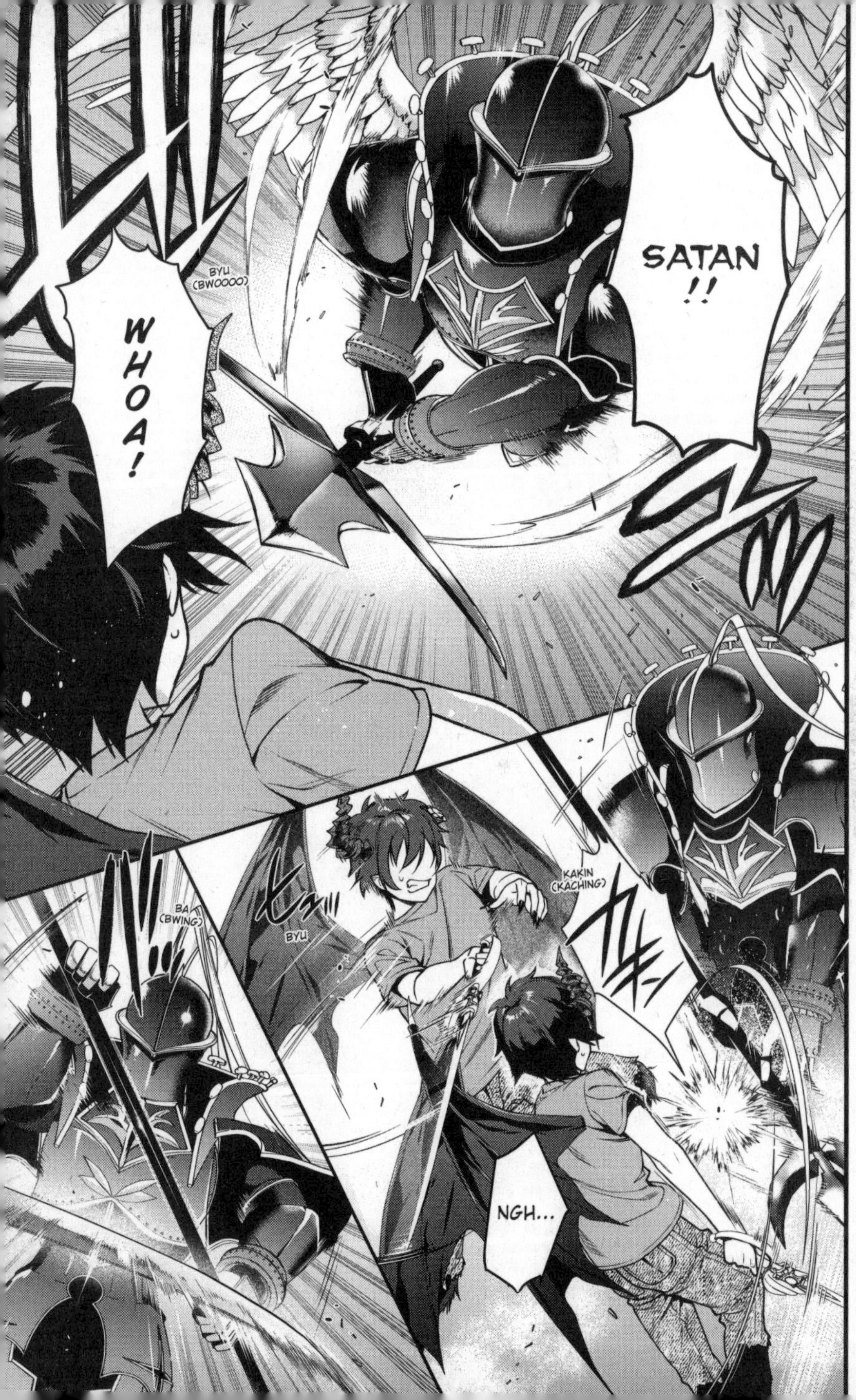
SATAN!!
BYU (BWOOOO)
WHOA!
KAKIN (KACHING)
BYU
NGH...
BA (BWING)

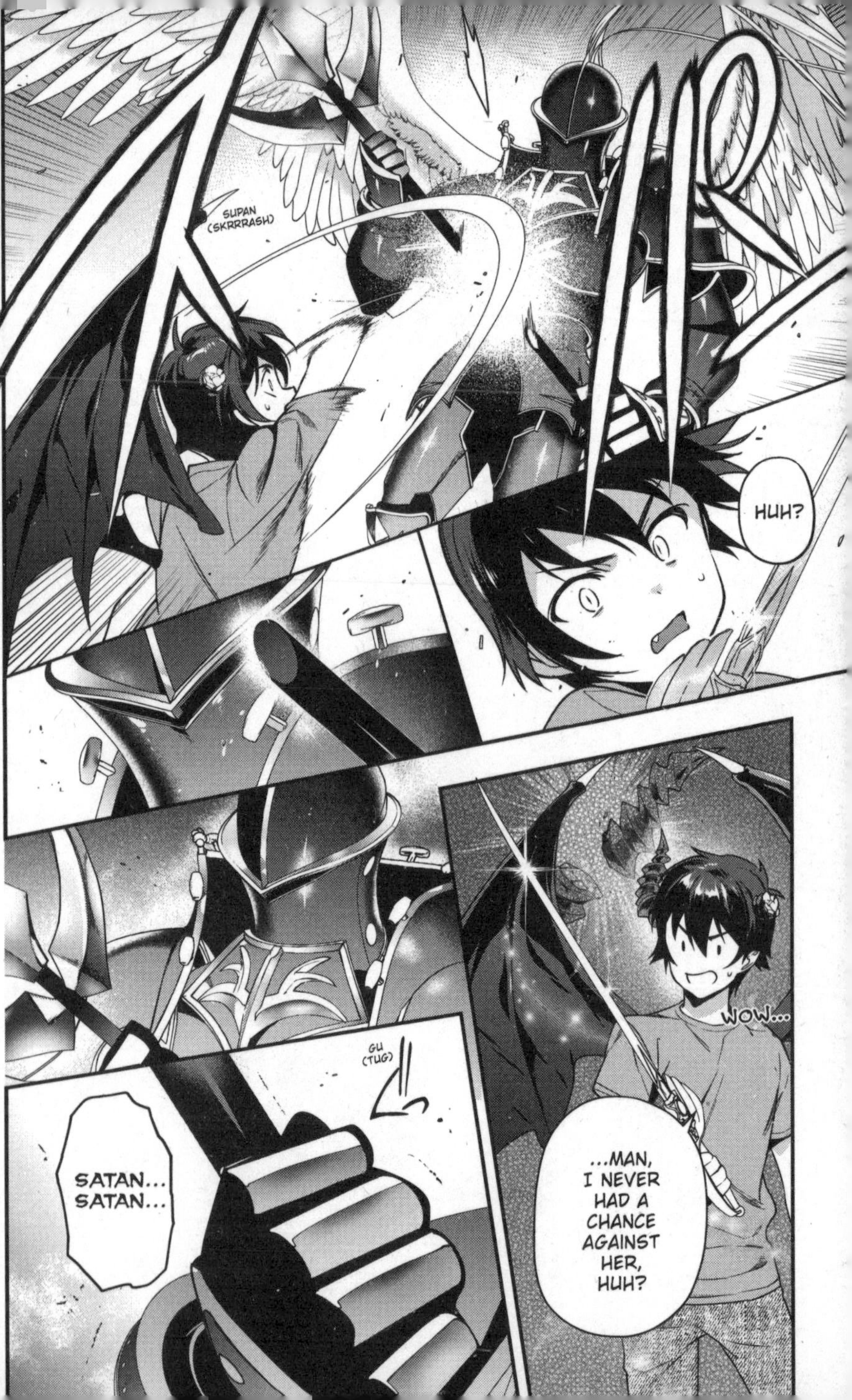
SUPAN (SKRRRASH)
HUH?
WOW...
GU (TUG)
...MAN, I NEVER HAD A CHANCE AGAINST HER, HUH?
SATAN... SATAN...

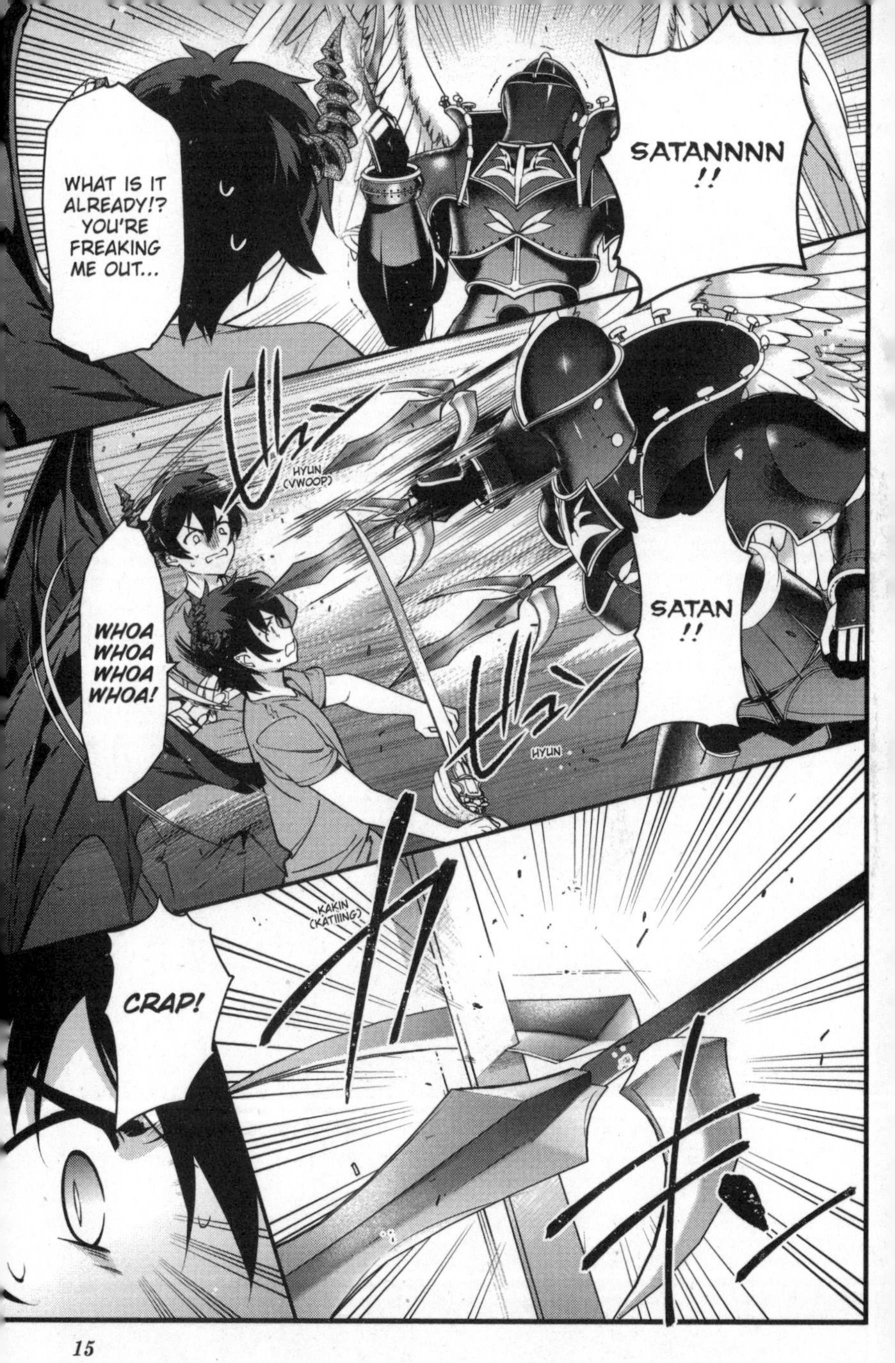
SATANNNN!!
WHAT IS IT ALREADY!? YOU'RE FREAKING ME OUT...
SATAN!!
HYUN
HYUN (VWOOP)
WHOA WHOA WHOA WHOA!
KAKIN (KATIIING)
CRAP!

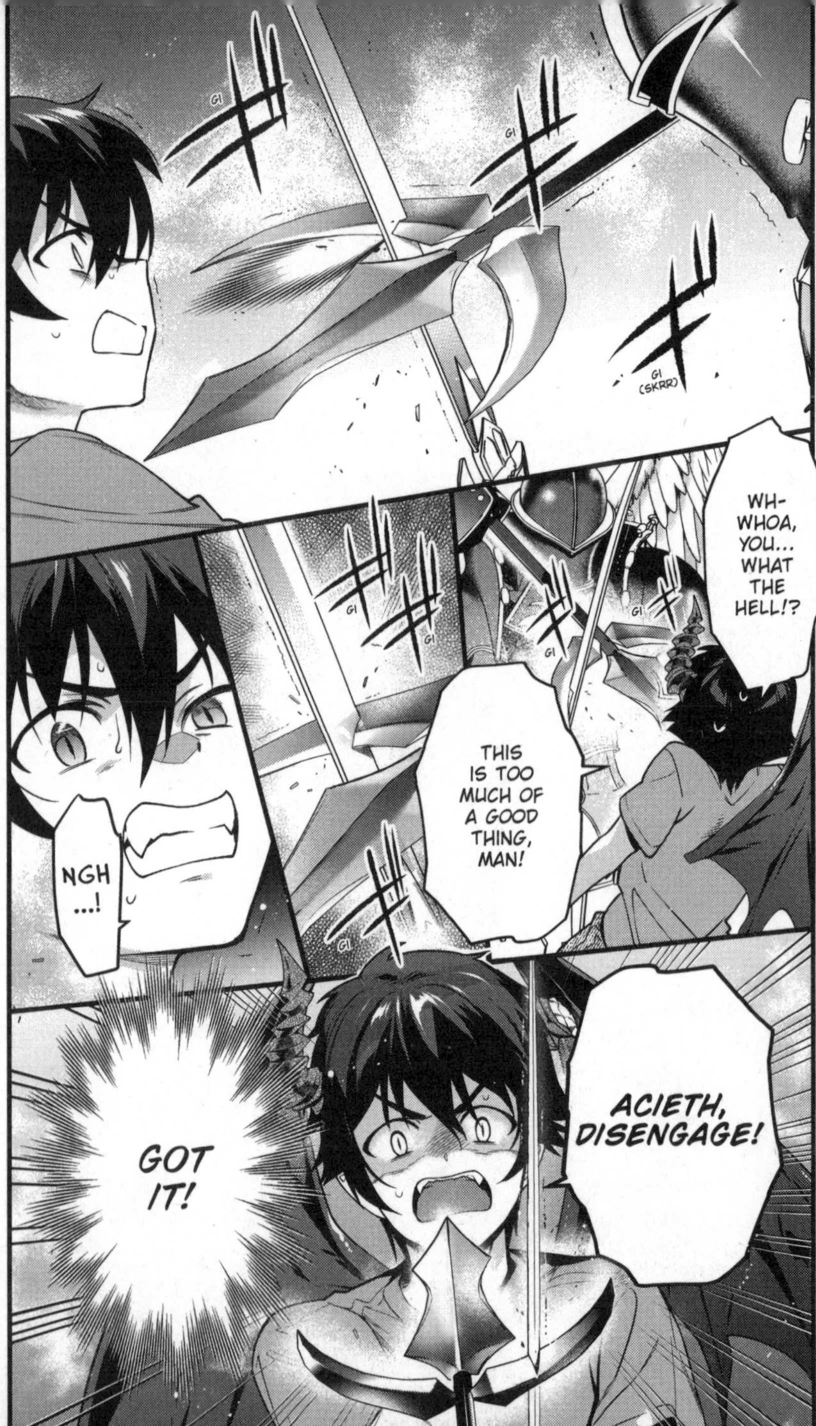
GI
GI
GI (SKRR)
WH- WHOA, YOU... WHAT THE HELL!?
GI
GI
GI
GI
THIS IS TOO MUCH OF A GOOD THING, MAN!
GI
NGH ...!
ACIETH, DISENGAGE!
GOT IT!

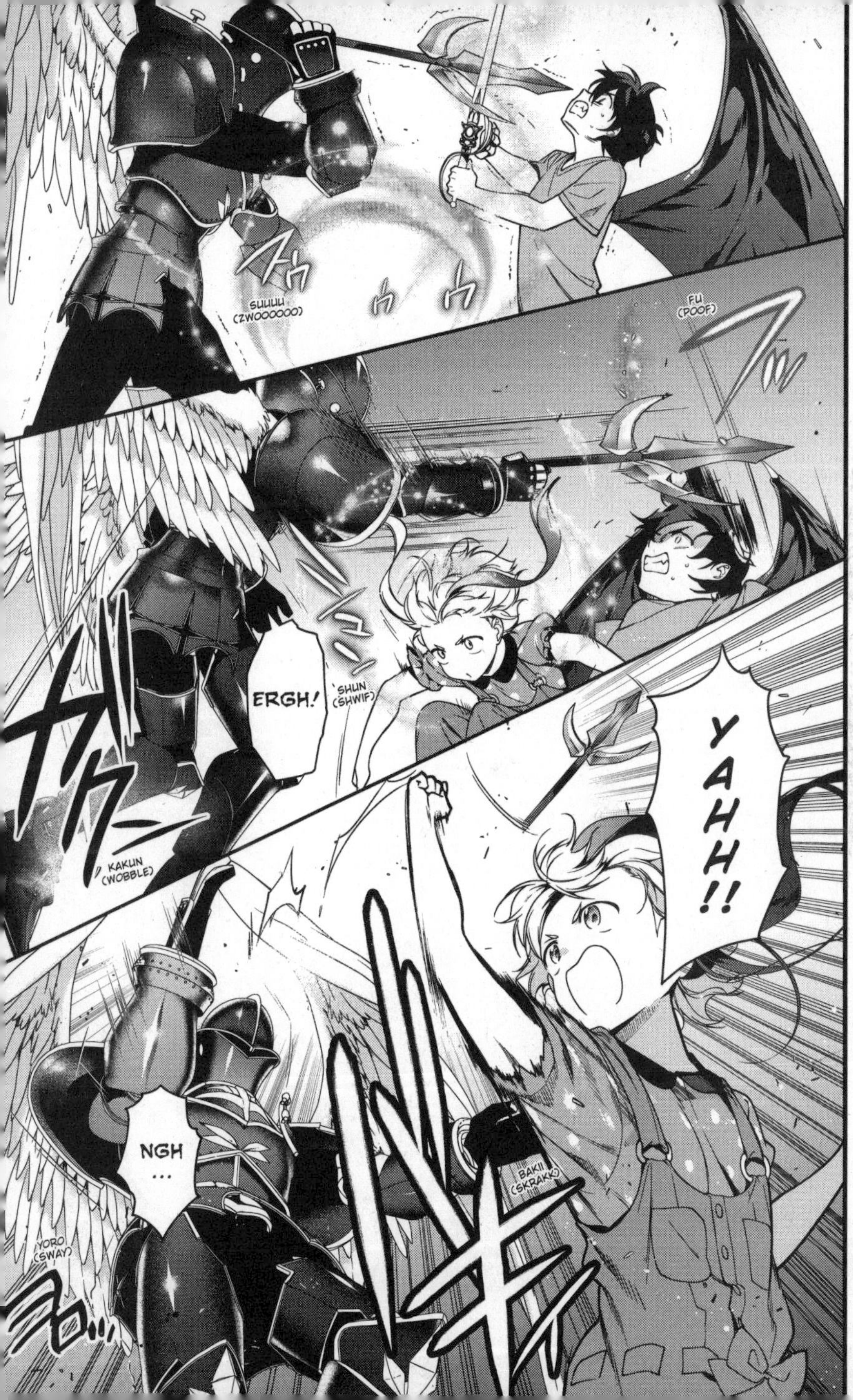

SUUUU (ZWOOOOOOO)
FU (POOF)
ERGH!
SHUN (SHWIF)
KAKUN (WOBBLE)
YAHH!!
BAKII (SKRAKK)
NGH ...
YORO (SWAY)

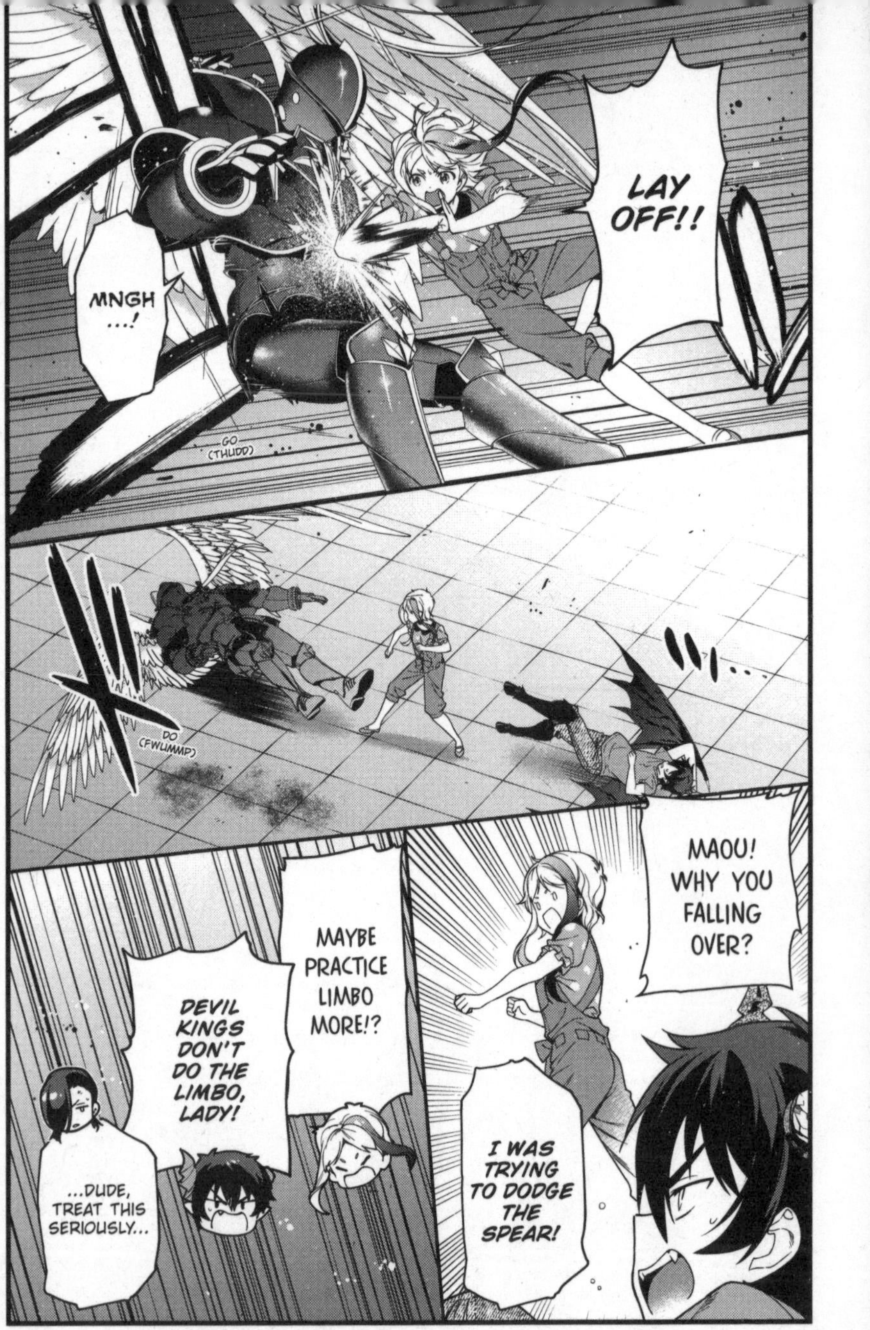
LAY OFF!!
MNGH ...!
GO (THUDD)
!!...
DO (FWUMMP)
MAOU! WHY YOU FALLING OVER?
I WAS TRYING TO DODGE THE SPEAR!
MAYBE PRACTICE LIMBO MORE!?
DEVIL KINGS DON'T DO THE LIMBO, LADY!
...DUDE, TREAT THIS SERIOUSLY...

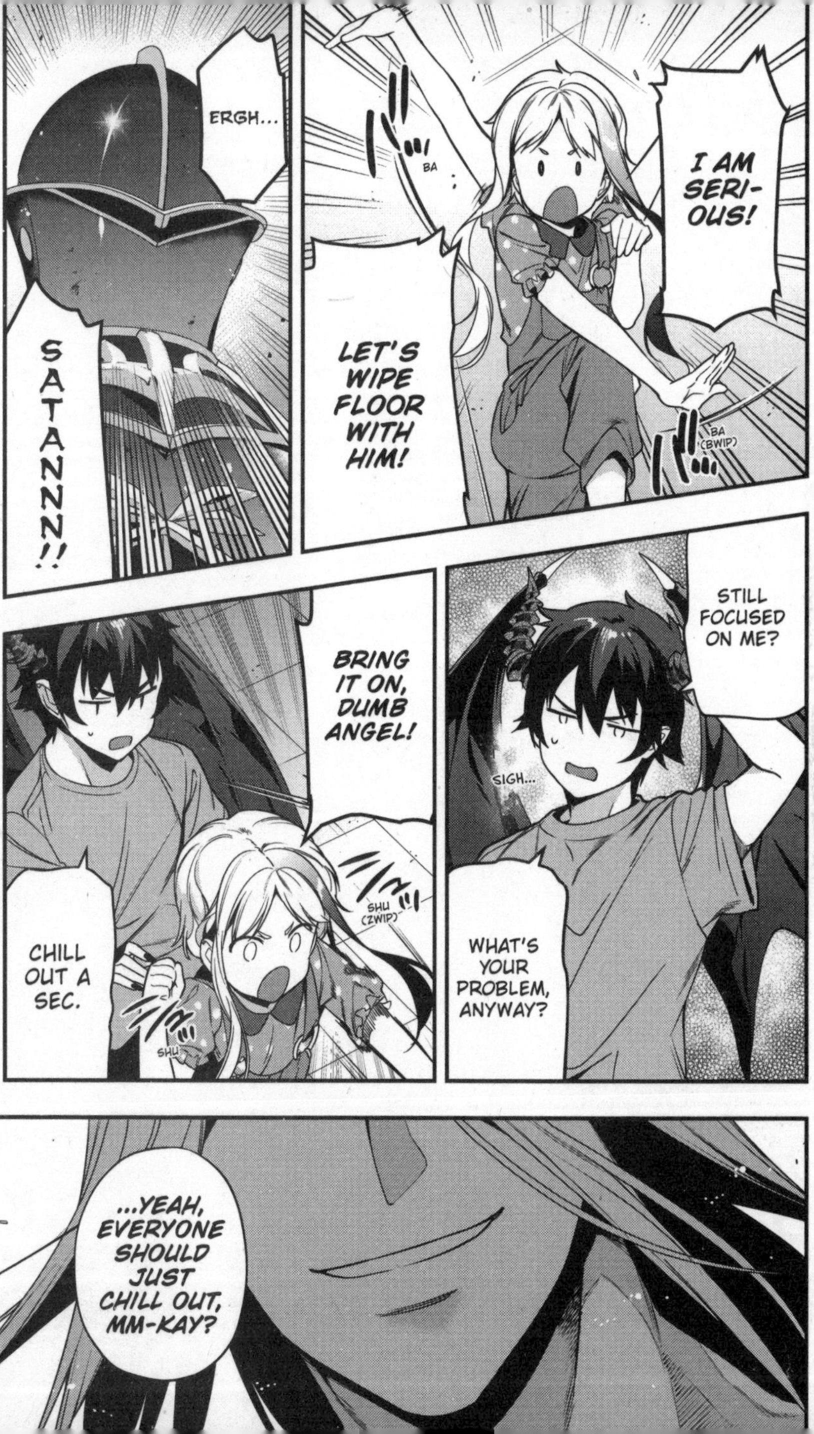
I AM SERI-OUS!
BA
LET'S WIPE FLOOR WITH HIM!
BA (BWIP)
ERGH...
SATANNN!!
STILL FOCUSED ON ME?
SIGH...
WHAT'S YOUR PROBLEM, ANYWAY?
BRING IT ON, DUMB ANGEL!
SHU (ZWIP)
CHILL OUT A SEC.
SHU
...YEAH, EVERYONE SHOULD JUST CHILL OUT, MM-KAY?

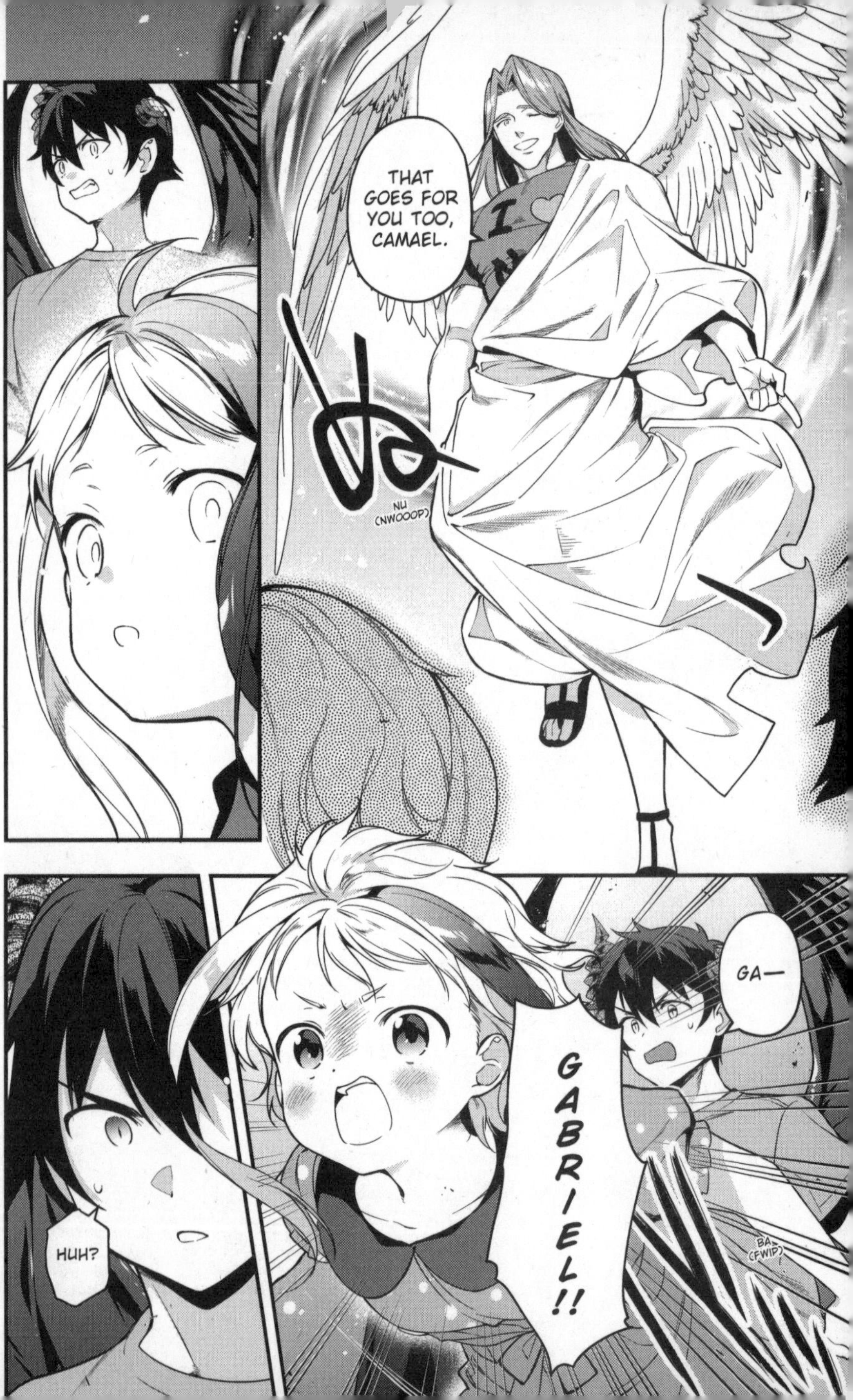
THAT GOES FOR YOU TOO, CAMAEL.
NU (NWOOOP)
GA—
BA (FWIP)
GABRIEL!!
HUH?

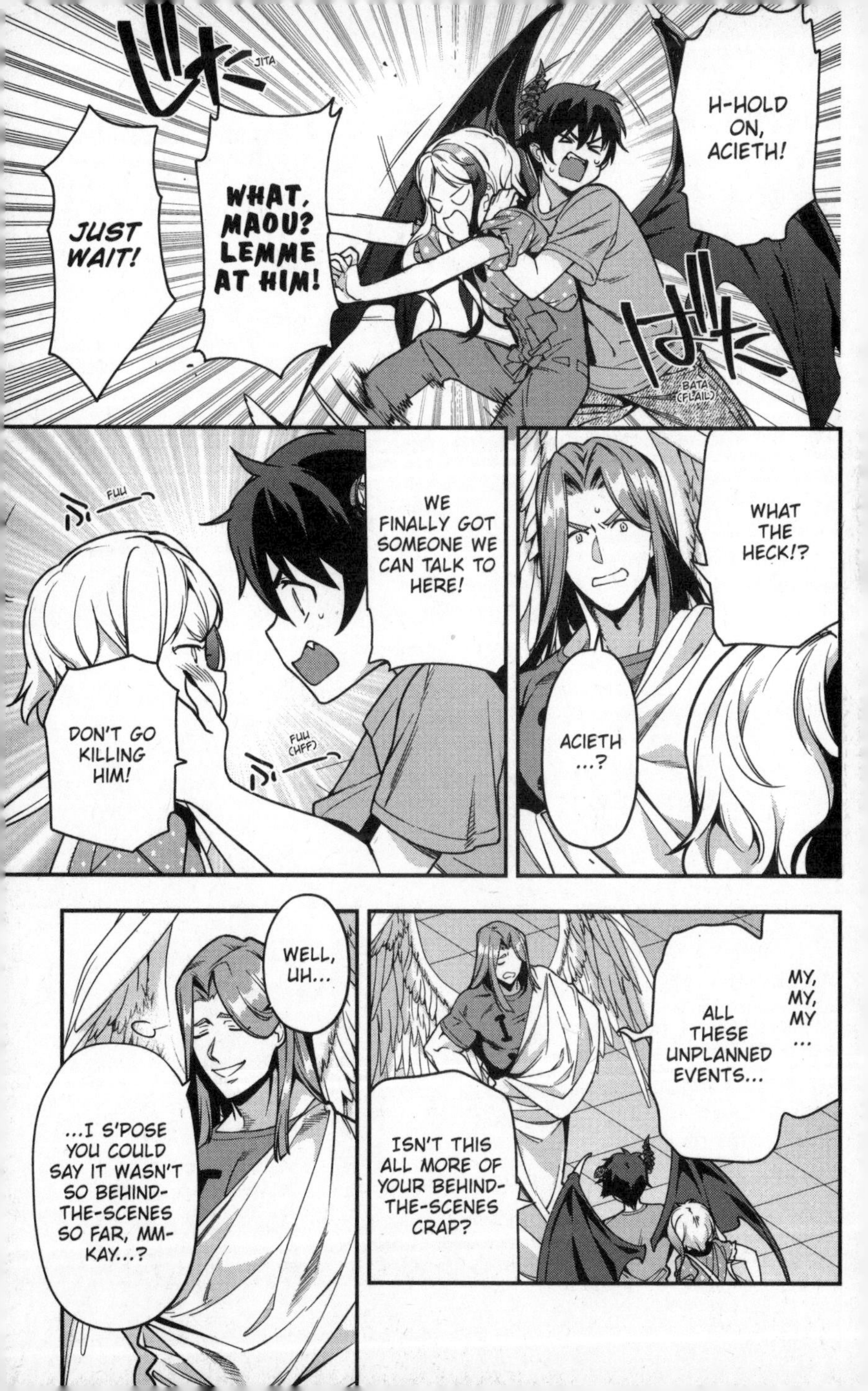
H-HOLD ON, ACIETH!
BATA (FLAIL)
WHAT, MAOU? LEMME AT HIM!
JITA
JUST WAIT!
WHAT THE HECK!?
ACIETH ...?
WE FINALLY GOT SOMEONE WE CAN TALK TO HERE!
FUU
DON'T GO KILLING HIM!
FUU (HFF)
MY, MY, MY ...
ALL THESE UNPLANNED EVENTS...
ISN'T THIS ALL MORE OF YOUR BEHIND-THE-SCENES CRAP?
WELL, UH...
...I S'POSE YOU COULD SAY IT WASN'T SO BEHIND-THE-SCENES SO FAR, MM-KAY...?

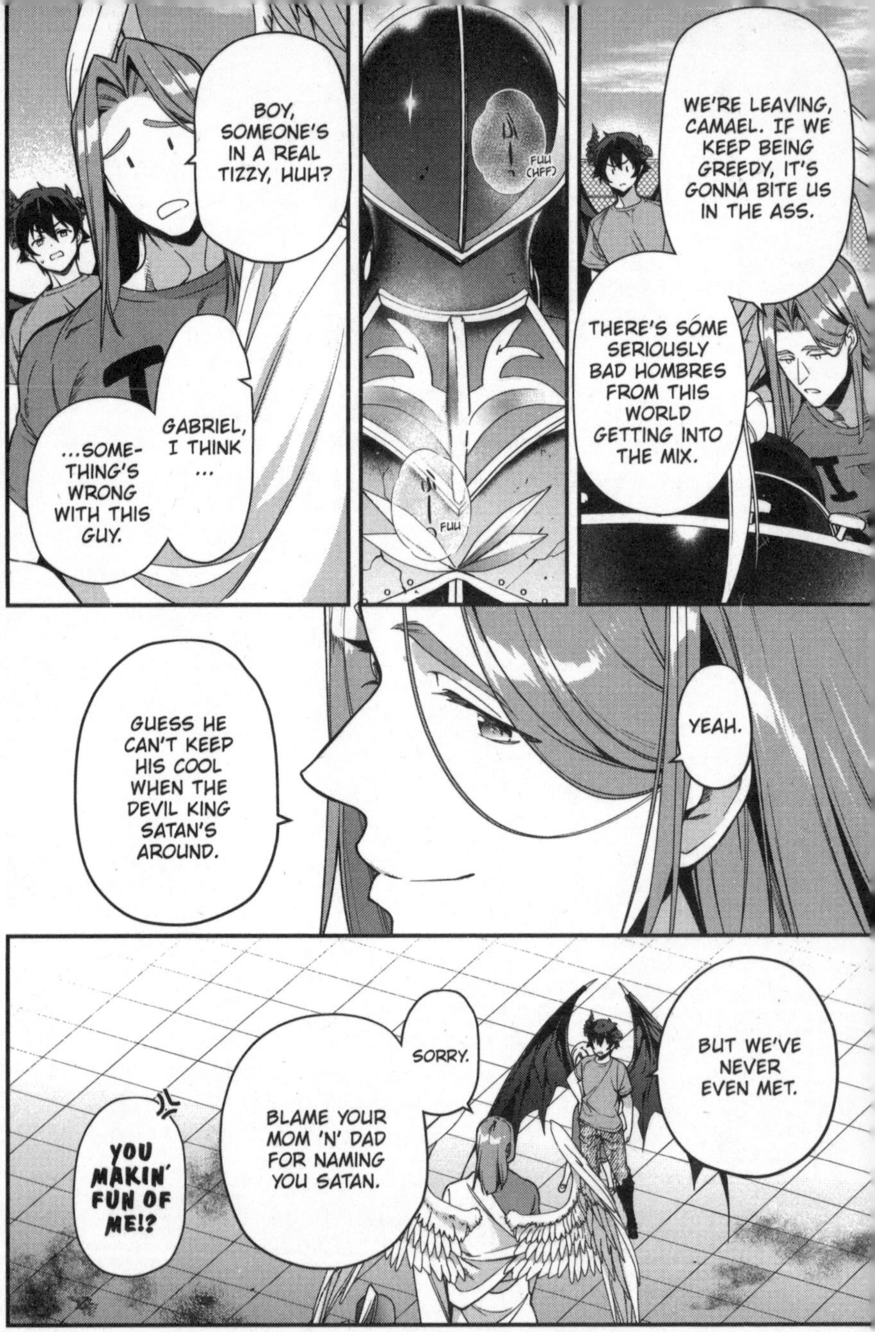
WE'RE LEAVING, CAMAEL. IF WE KEEP BEING GREEDY, IT'S GONNA BITE US IN THE ASS.
THERE'S SOME SERIOUSLY BAD HOMBRES FROM THIS WORLD GETTING INTO THE MIX.
FUU (HFF)
FUU
BOY, SOMEONE'S IN A REAL TIZZY, HUH?
GABRIEL, I THINK ...
...SOMETHING'S WRONG WITH THIS GUY.
YEAH.
GUESS HE CAN'T KEEP HIS COOL WHEN THE DEVIL KING SATAN'S AROUND.
BUT WE'VE NEVER EVEN MET.
SORRY.
BLAME YOUR MOM 'N' DAD FOR NAMING YOU SATAN.
YOU MAKIN' FUN OF ME!?

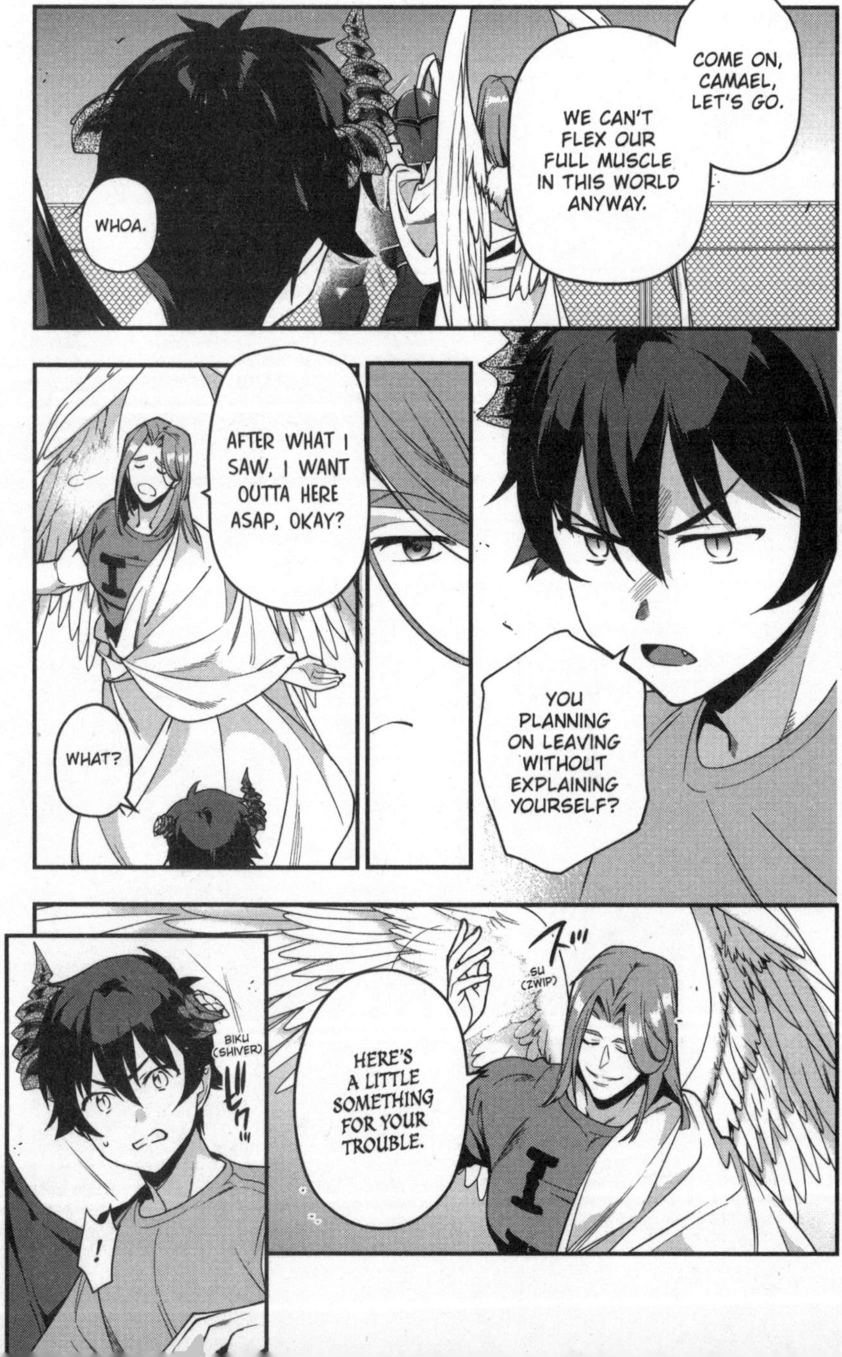
COME ON, CAMAEL, LET'S GO.
WE CAN'T FLEX OUR FULL MUSCLE IN THIS WORLD ANYWAY.
WHOA.
YOU PLANNING ON LEAVING WITHOUT EXPLAINING YOURSELF?
AFTER WHAT I SAW, I WANT OUTTA HERE ASAP, OKAY?
WHAT?
SU (ZWIP)
HERE'S A LITTLE SOMETHING FOR YOUR TROUBLE.
BIKU (SHIVER)
!

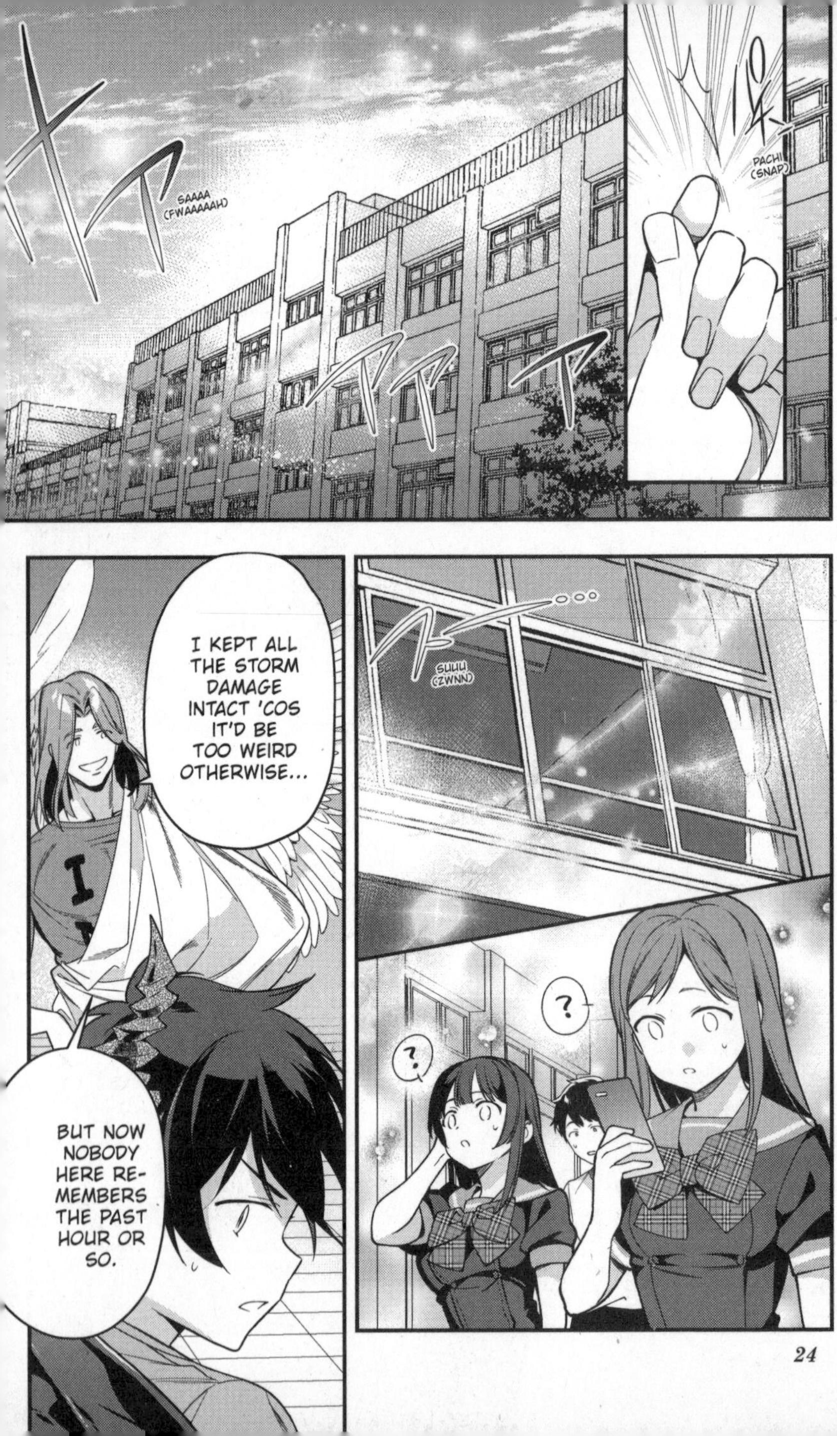
PACHI (SNAP)
SAAAA (FWAAAAAH)
SUUU (ZWNN)
?
?
I KEPT ALL THE STORM DAMAGE INTACT 'COS IT'D BE TOO WEIRD OTHERWISE...
BUT NOW NOBODY HERE RE-MEMBERS THE PAST HOUR OR SO.

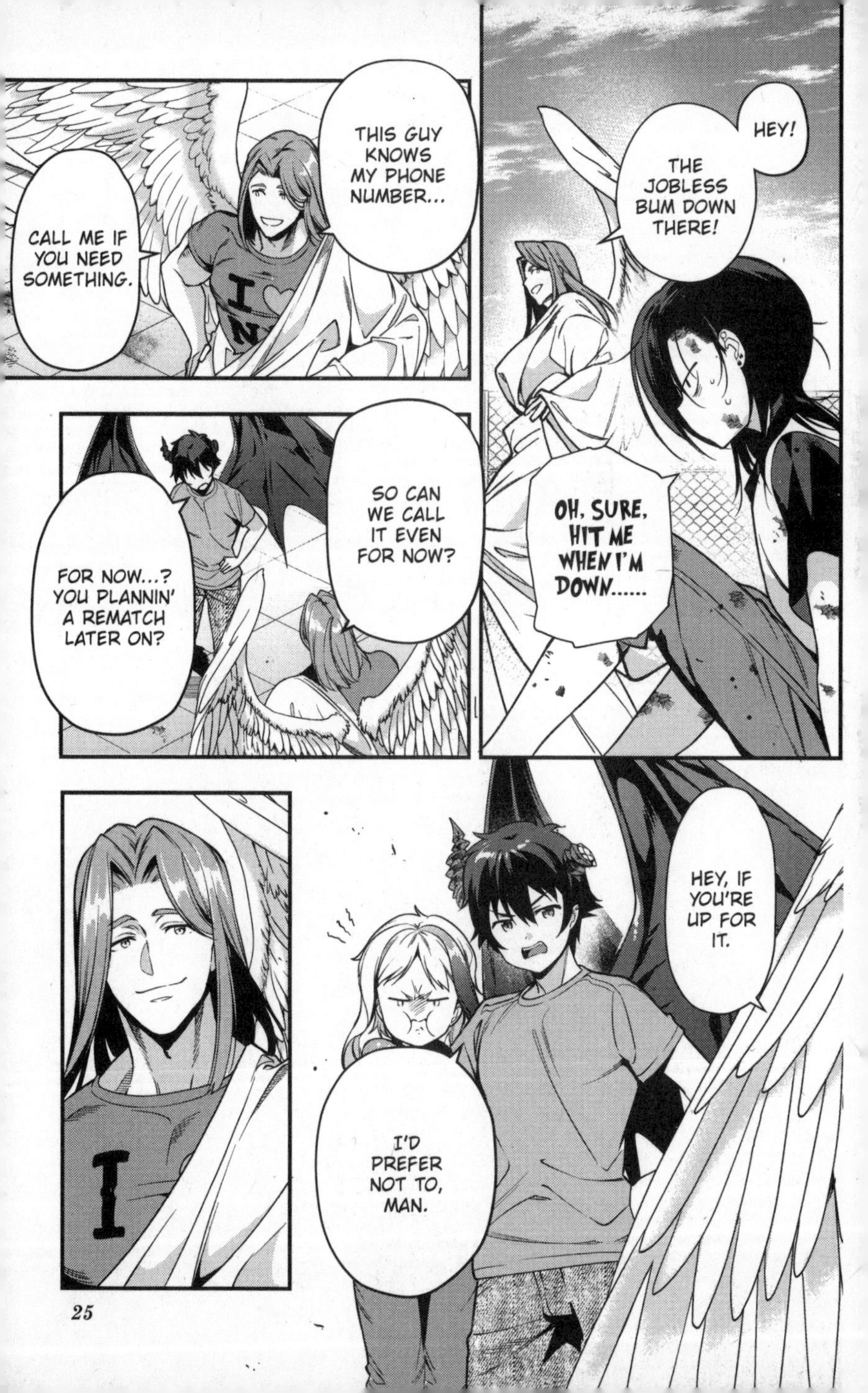
HEY!
THE JOBLESS BUM DOWN THERE!
OH, SURE, HIT ME WHEN I'M DOWN......
THIS GUY KNOWS MY PHONE NUMBER...
CALL ME IF YOU NEED SOMETHING.
SO CAN WE CALL IT EVEN FOR NOW?
FOR NOW...? YOU PLANNIN' A REMATCH LATER ON?
HEY, IF YOU'RE UP FOR IT.
I'D PREFER NOT TO, MAN.

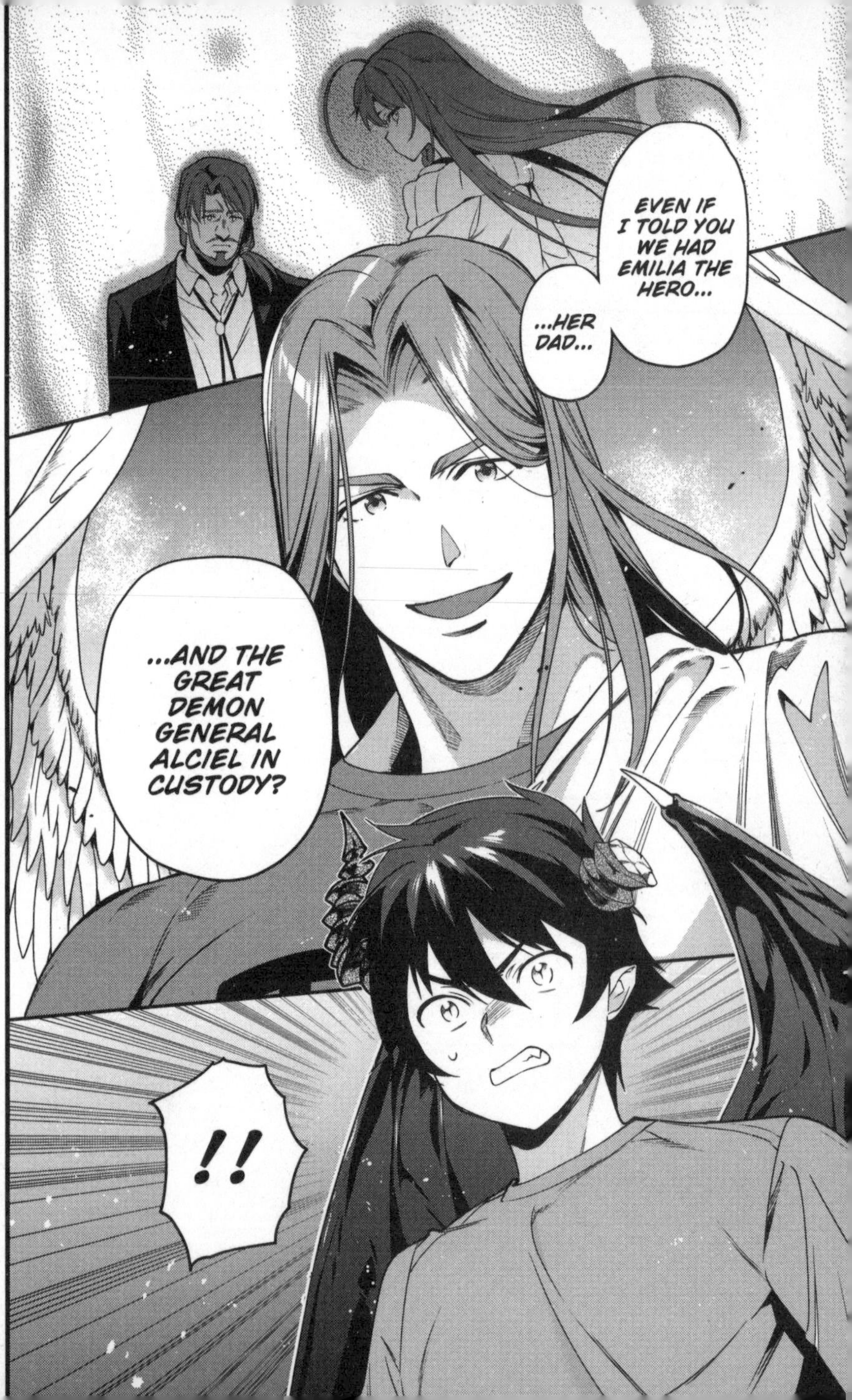
EVEN IF I TOLD YOU WE HAD EMILIA THE HERO...
...HER DAD...
...AND THE GREAT DEMON GENERAL ALCIEL IN CUSTODY?
!!

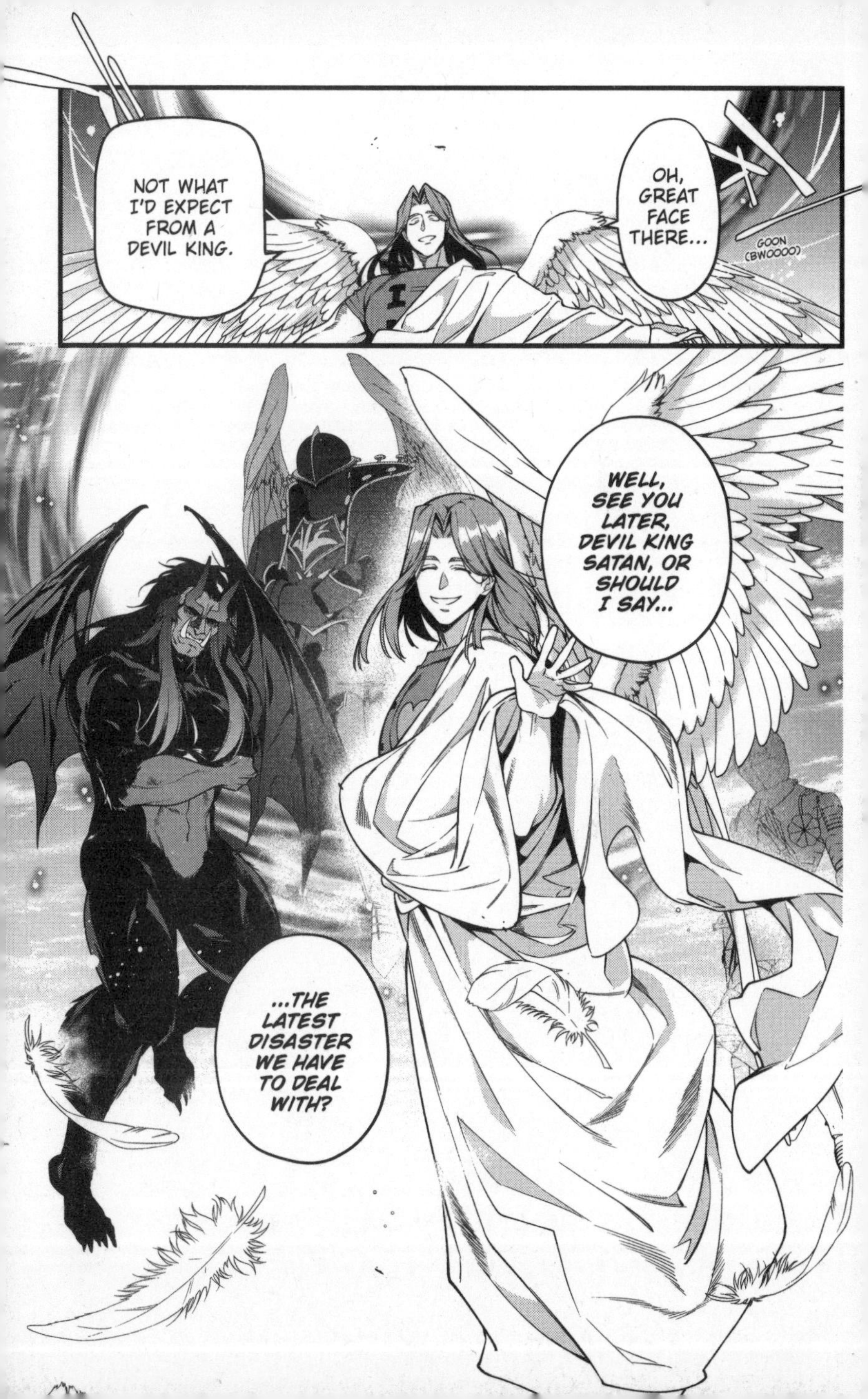
OH, GREAT FACE THERE...
GOON (BWOOOO)
NOT WHAT I'D EXPECT FROM A DEVIL KING.
WELL, SEE YOU LATER, DEVIL KING SATAN, OR SHOULD I SAY...
...THE LATEST DISASTER WE HAVE TO DEAL WITH?

THE DEVIL IS A PART-TIMER!

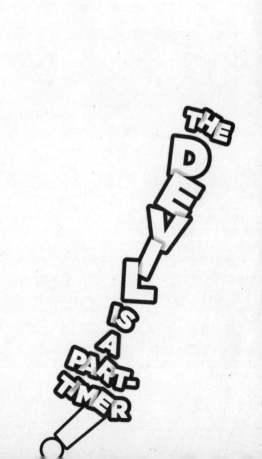

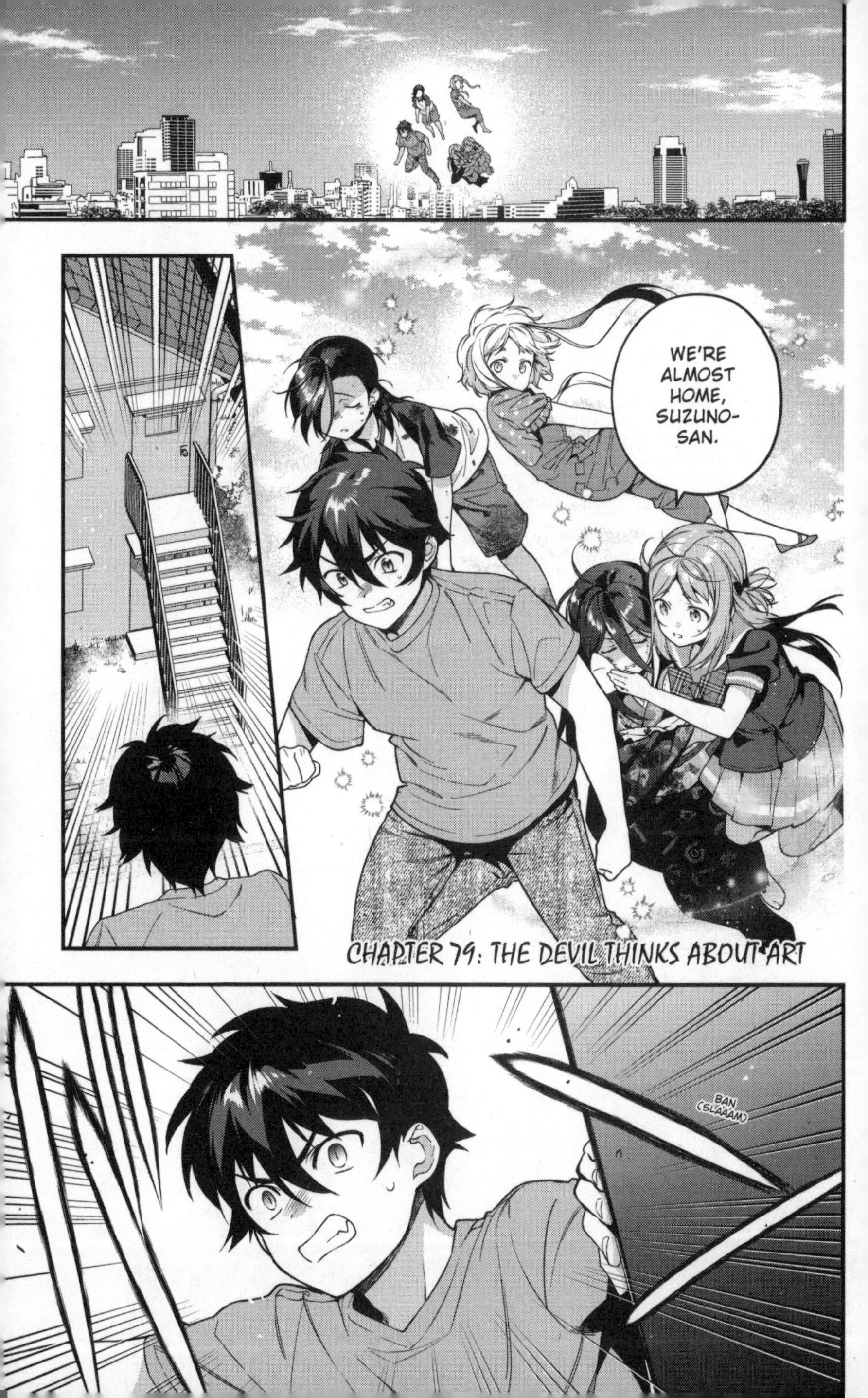
WE'RE ALMOST HOME, SUZUNO-SAN.
CHAPTER 79: THE DEVIL THINKS ABOUT ART
BAN (SLAAAM)

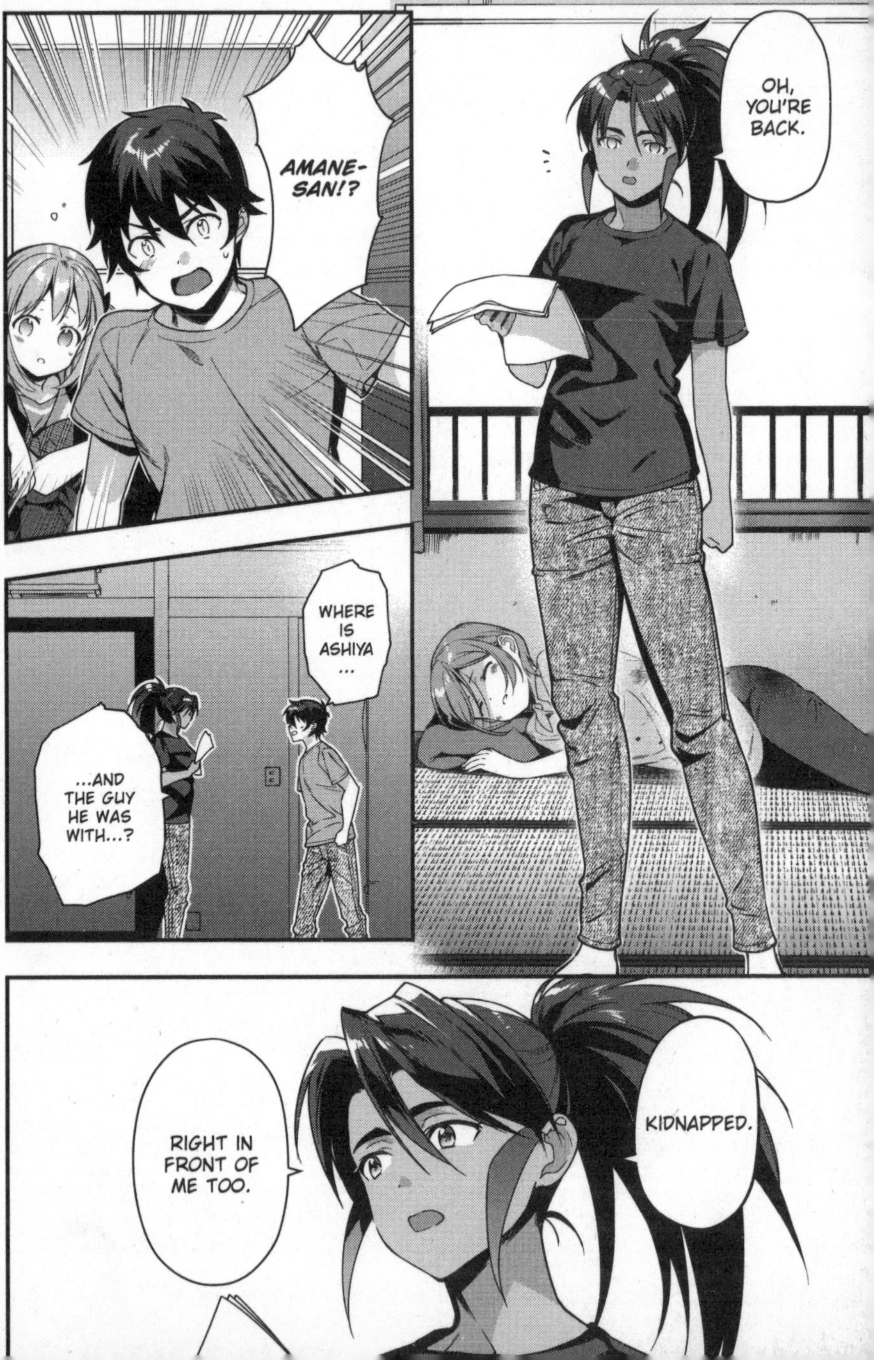
OH, YOU'RE BACK.
AMANE-SAN!?
WHERE IS ASHIYA...
...AND THE GUY HE WAS WITH...?
KIDNAPPED.
RIGHT IN FRONT OF ME TOO.

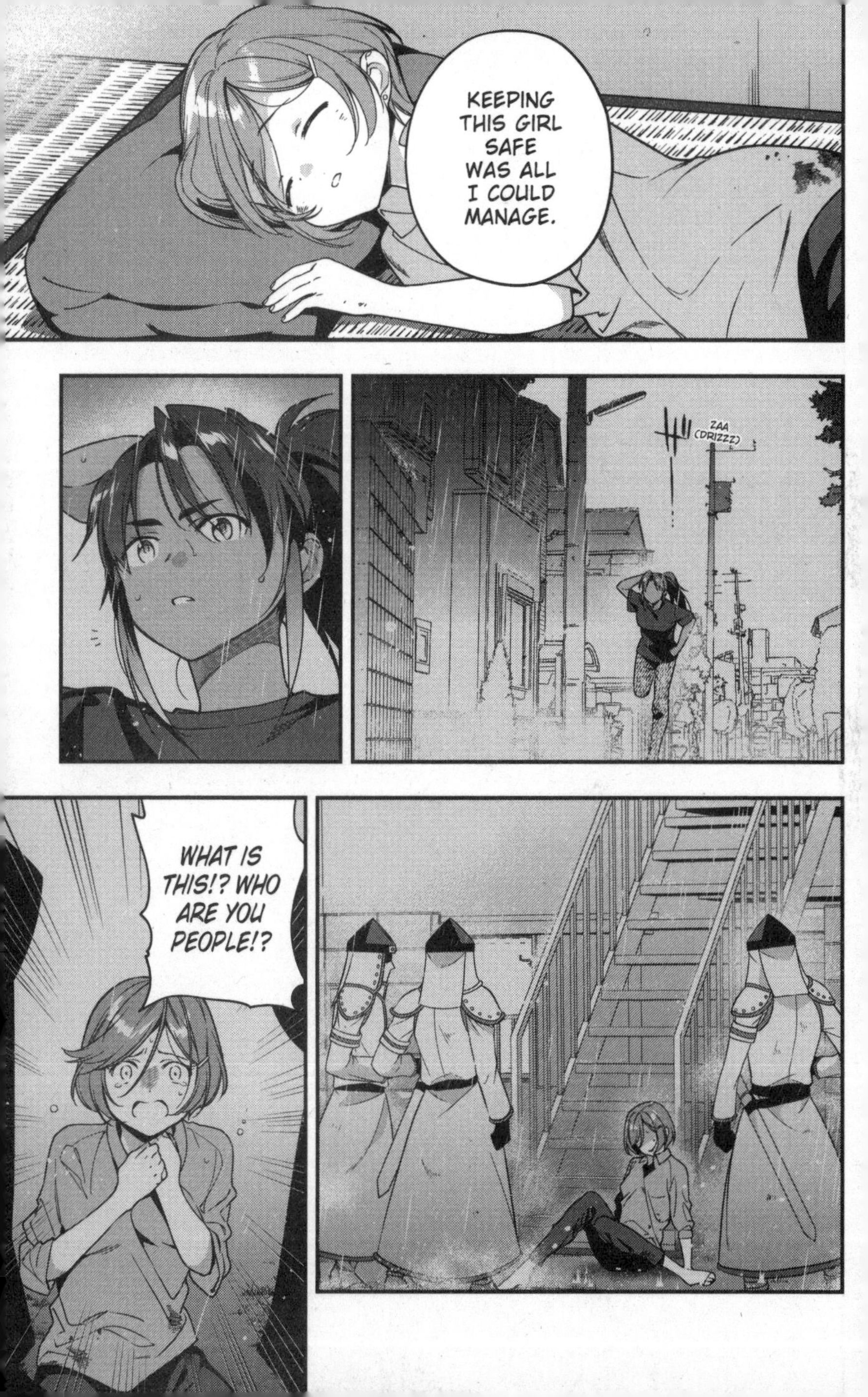
KEEPING THIS GIRL SAFE WAS ALL I COULD MANAGE.
ZAA (DRIZZZ)
WHAT IS THIS!? WHO ARE YOU PEOPLE!?

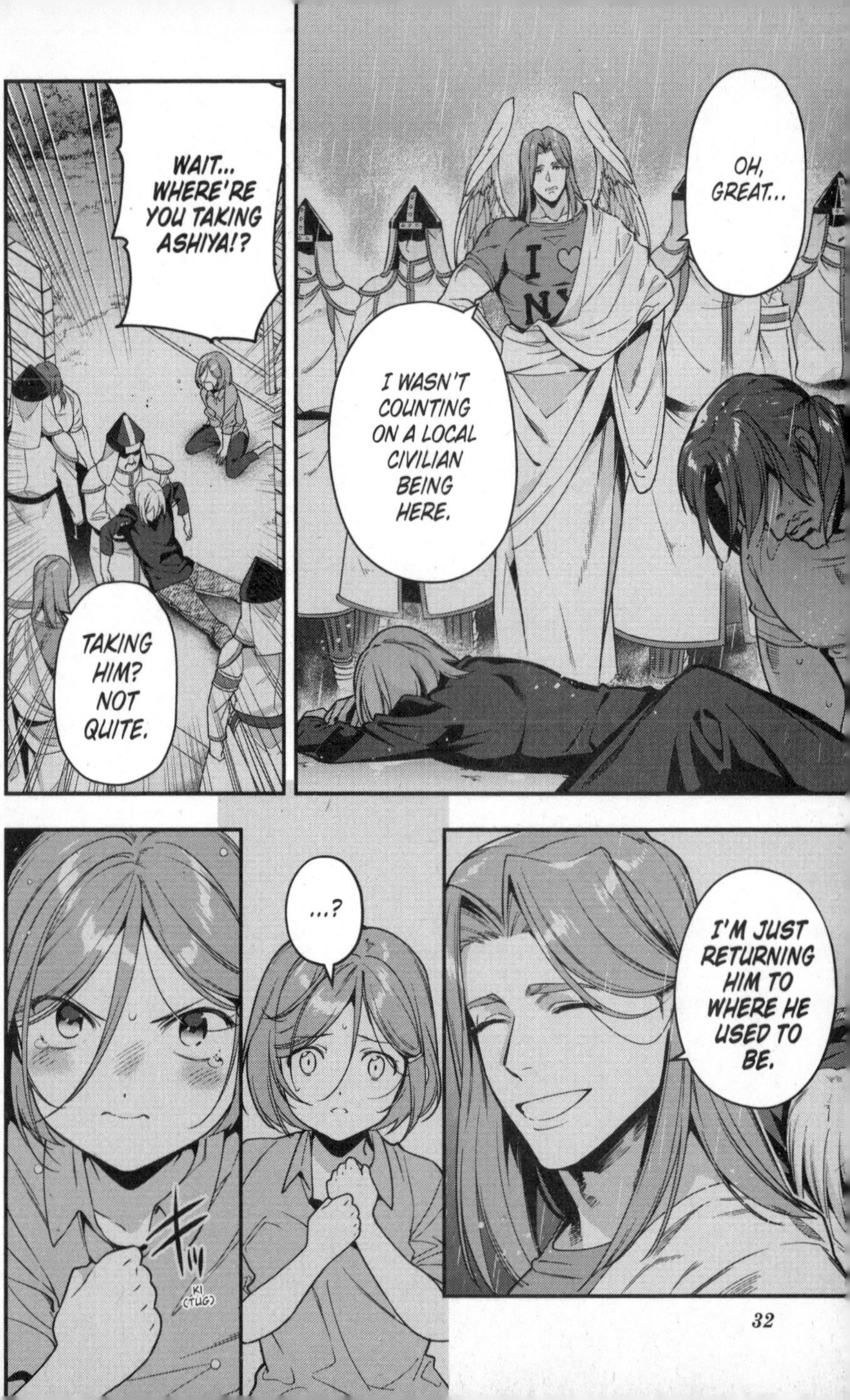
OH, GREAT...
I WASN'T COUNTING ON A LOCAL CIVILIAN BEING HERE.
WAIT... WHERE'RE YOU TAKING ASHIYA!?
TAKING HIM? NOT QUITE.
I'M JUST RETURNING HIM TO WHERE HE USED TO BE.
...?
KI (TUG)

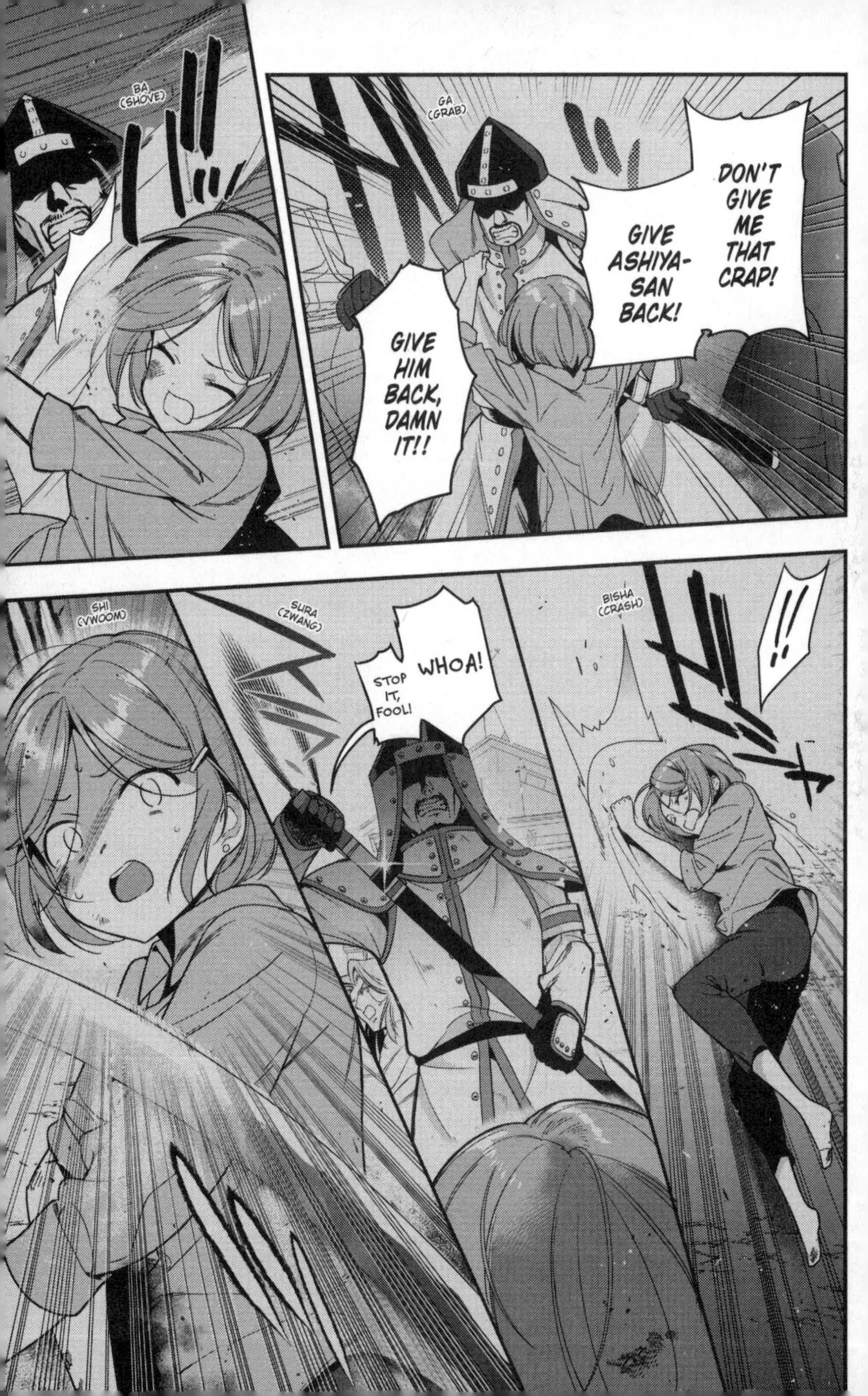

DON'T GIVE ME THAT CRAP!
GIVE ASHIYA-SAN BACK!
GA (GRAB)
GIVE HIM BACK, DAMN IT!!
BA (SHOVE)
!!
BISHA (CRASH)
WHOA!
STOP IT, FOOL!
SURA (ZWANG)
SHI (VWOOM)

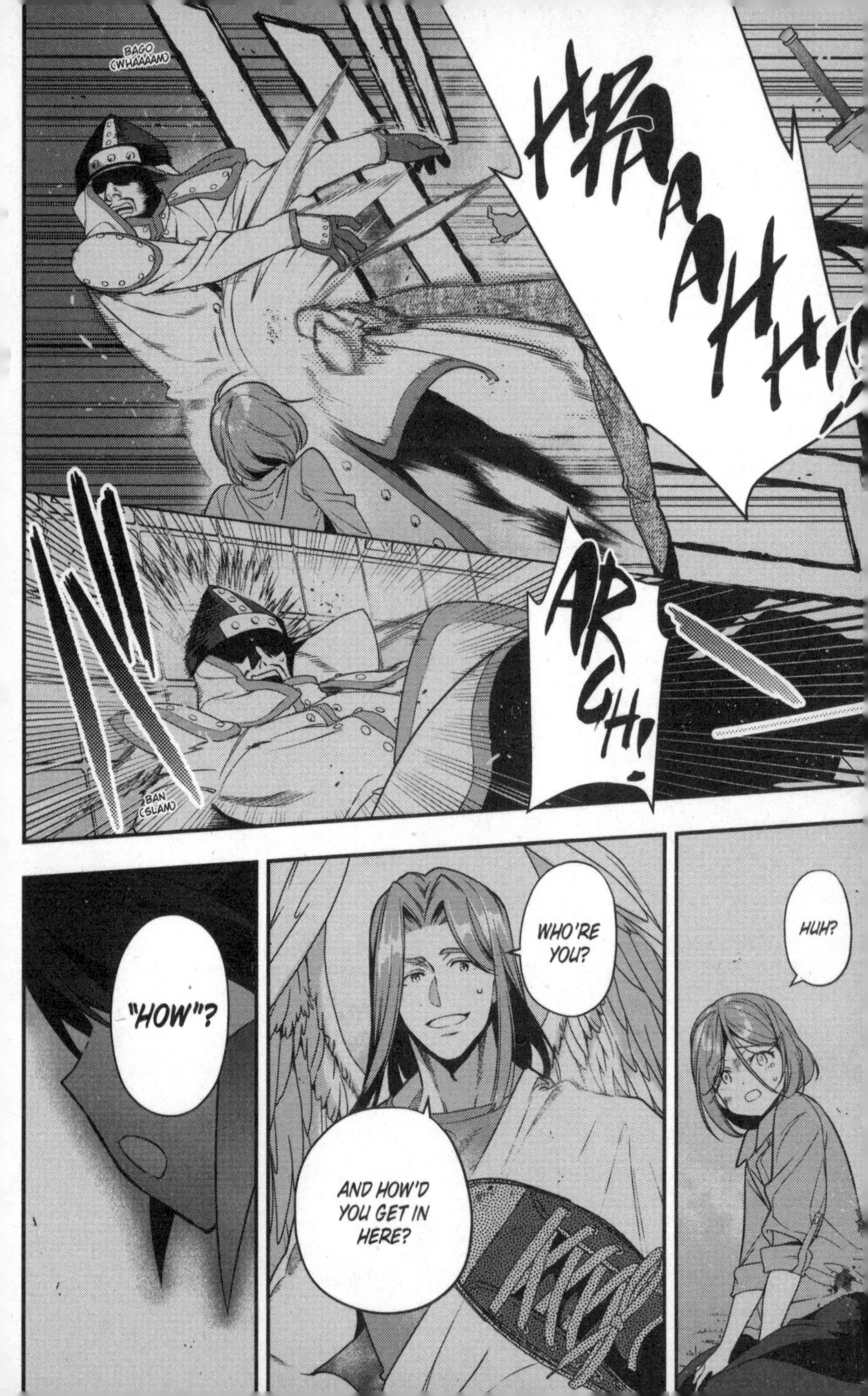
HRAAAHH!!
BAGO (WHAAAAM)
ARGH!
BAN (SLAM)
HUH?
WHO'RE YOU?
AND HOW'D YOU GET IN HERE?
"HOW"?

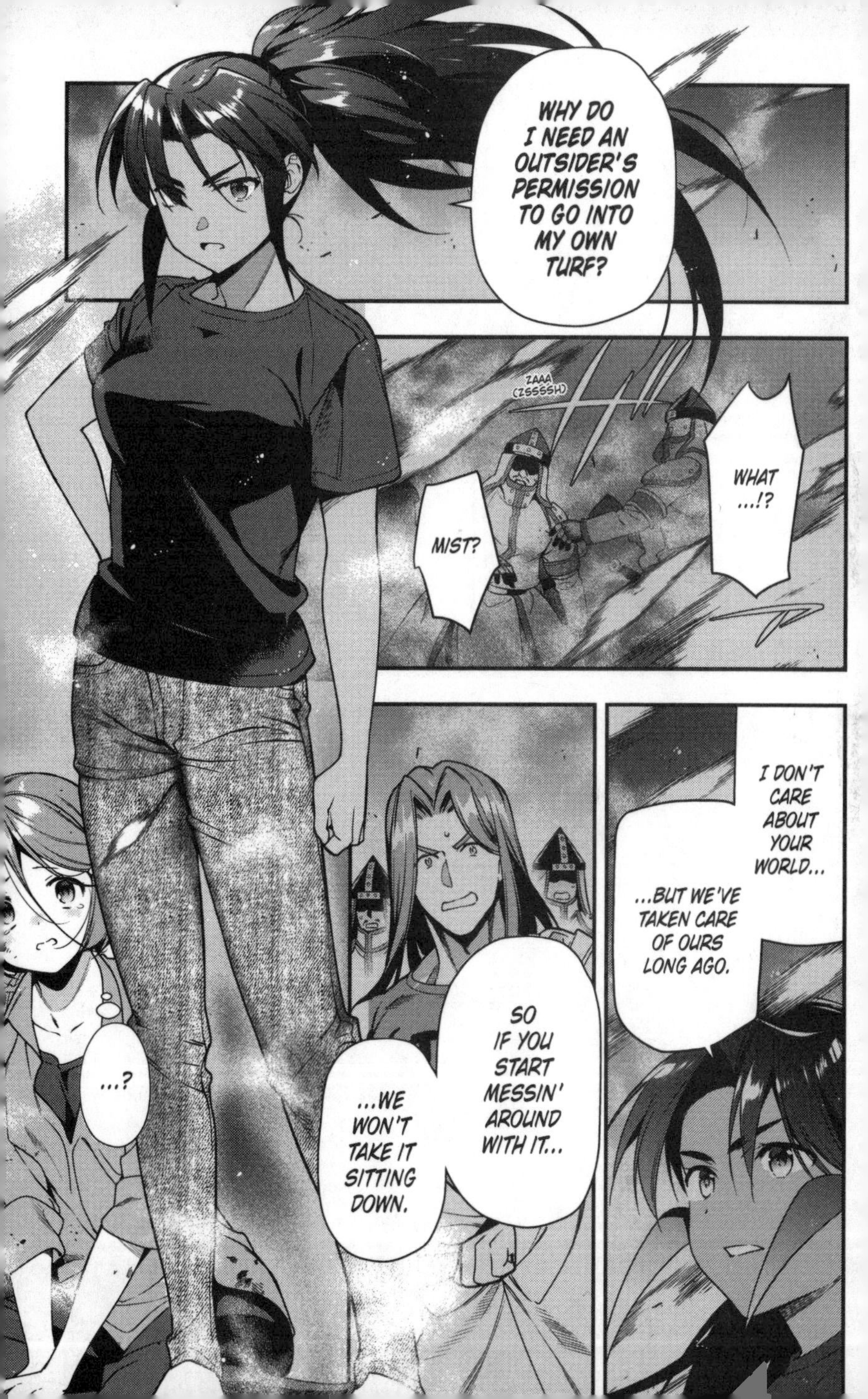
WHY DO I NEED AN OUTSIDER'S PERMISSION TO GO INTO MY OWN TURF?
WHAT ...!?
ZAAA (ZSSSSH)
MIST?
I DON'T CARE ABOUT YOUR WORLD...
...BUT WE'VE TAKEN CARE OF OURS LONG AGO.
SO IF YOU START MESSIN' AROUND WITH IT...
...WE WON'T TAKE IT SITTING DOWN.
...?

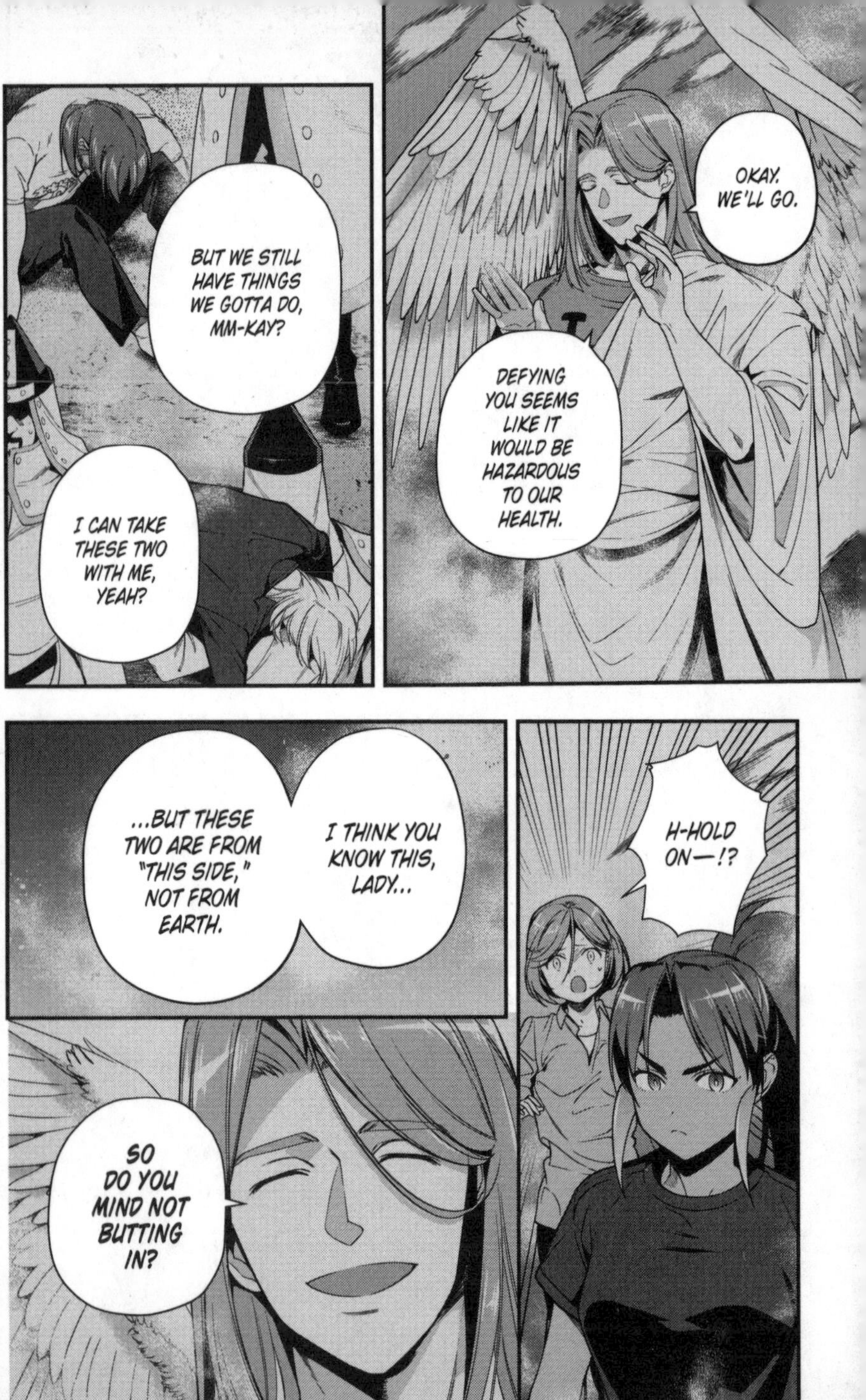
OKAY. WE'LL GO.
DEFYING YOU SEEMS LIKE IT WOULD BE HAZARDOUS TO OUR HEALTH.
BUT WE STILL HAVE THINGS WE GOTTA DO, MM-KAY?
I CAN TAKE THESE TWO WITH ME, YEAH?
H-HOLD ON—!?
I THINK YOU KNOW THIS, LADY...
...BUT THESE TWO ARE FROM "THIS SIDE," NOT FROM EARTH.
SO DO YOU MIND NOT BUTTING IN?

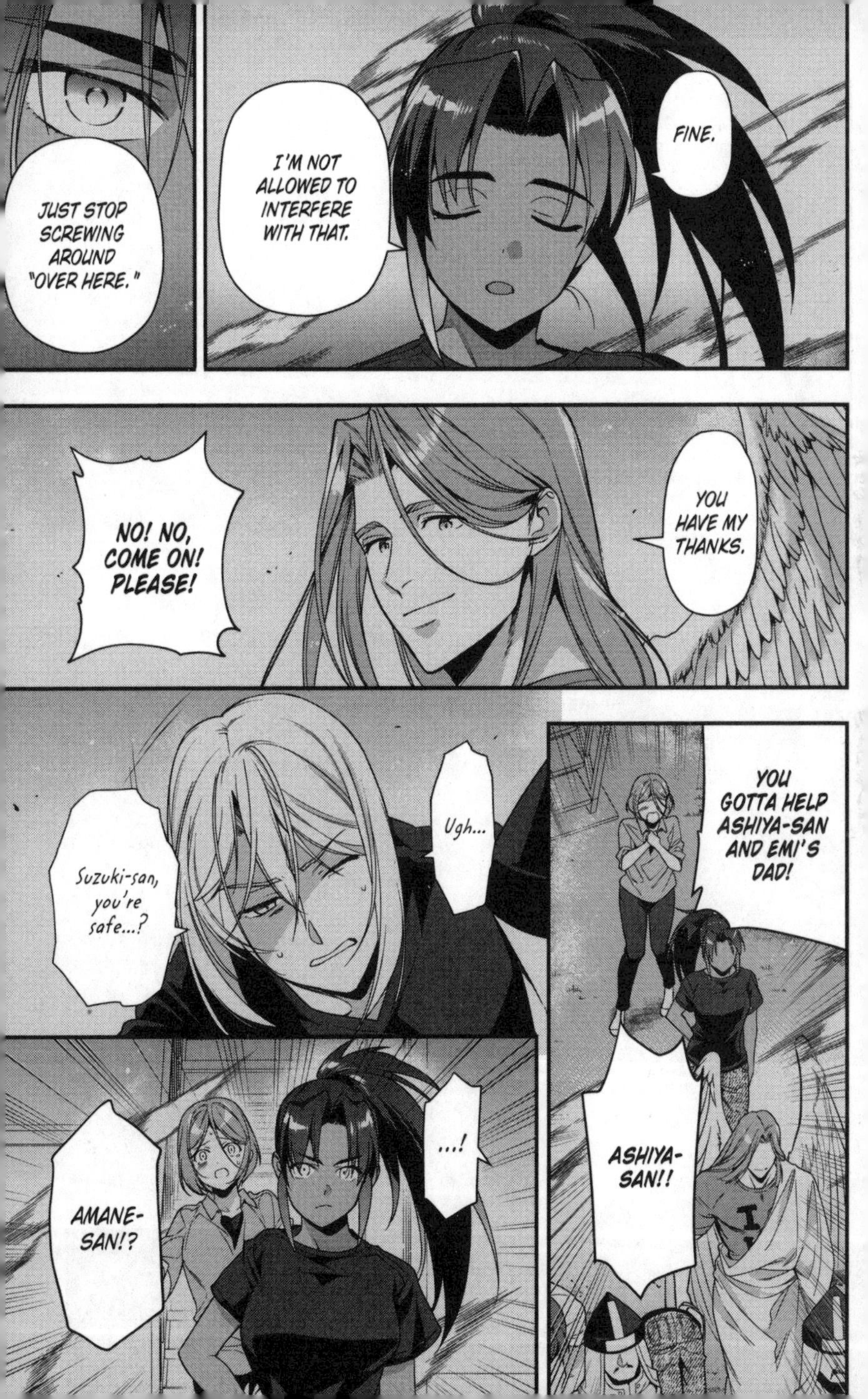
FINE.
I'M NOT ALLOWED TO INTERFERE WITH THAT.
JUST STOP SCREWING AROUND "OVER HERE."
YOU HAVE MY THANKS.
NO! NO, COME ON! PLEASE!
YOU GOTTA HELP ASHIYA-SAN AND EMI'S DAD!
ASHIYA-SAN!!
Ugh...
Suzuki-san, you're safe...?
...!
AMANE-SAN!?

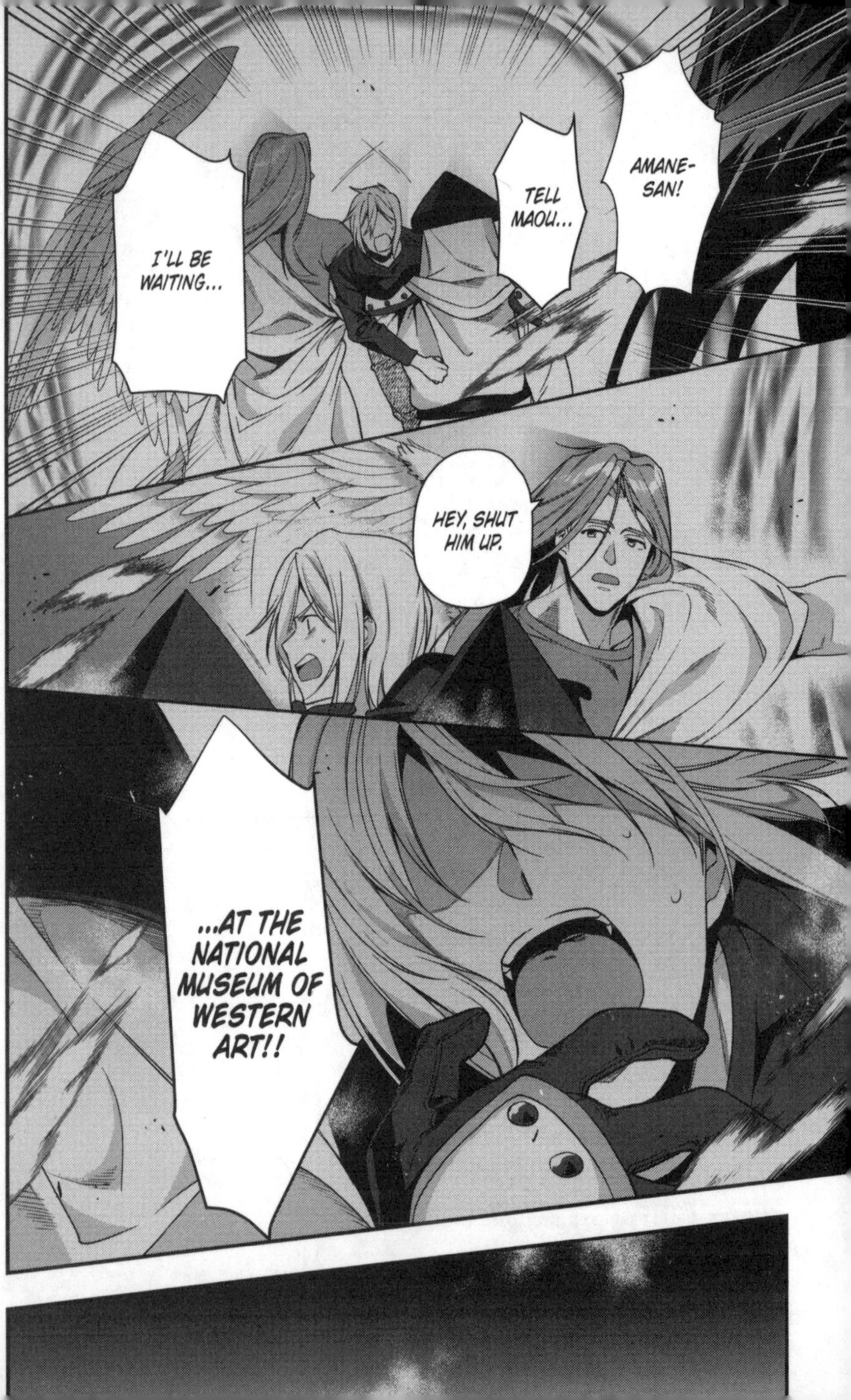
AMANE-SAN!
TELL MAOU...
I'LL BE WAITING...
HEY, SHUT HIM UP.
...AT THE NATIONAL MUSEUM OF WESTERN ART!!

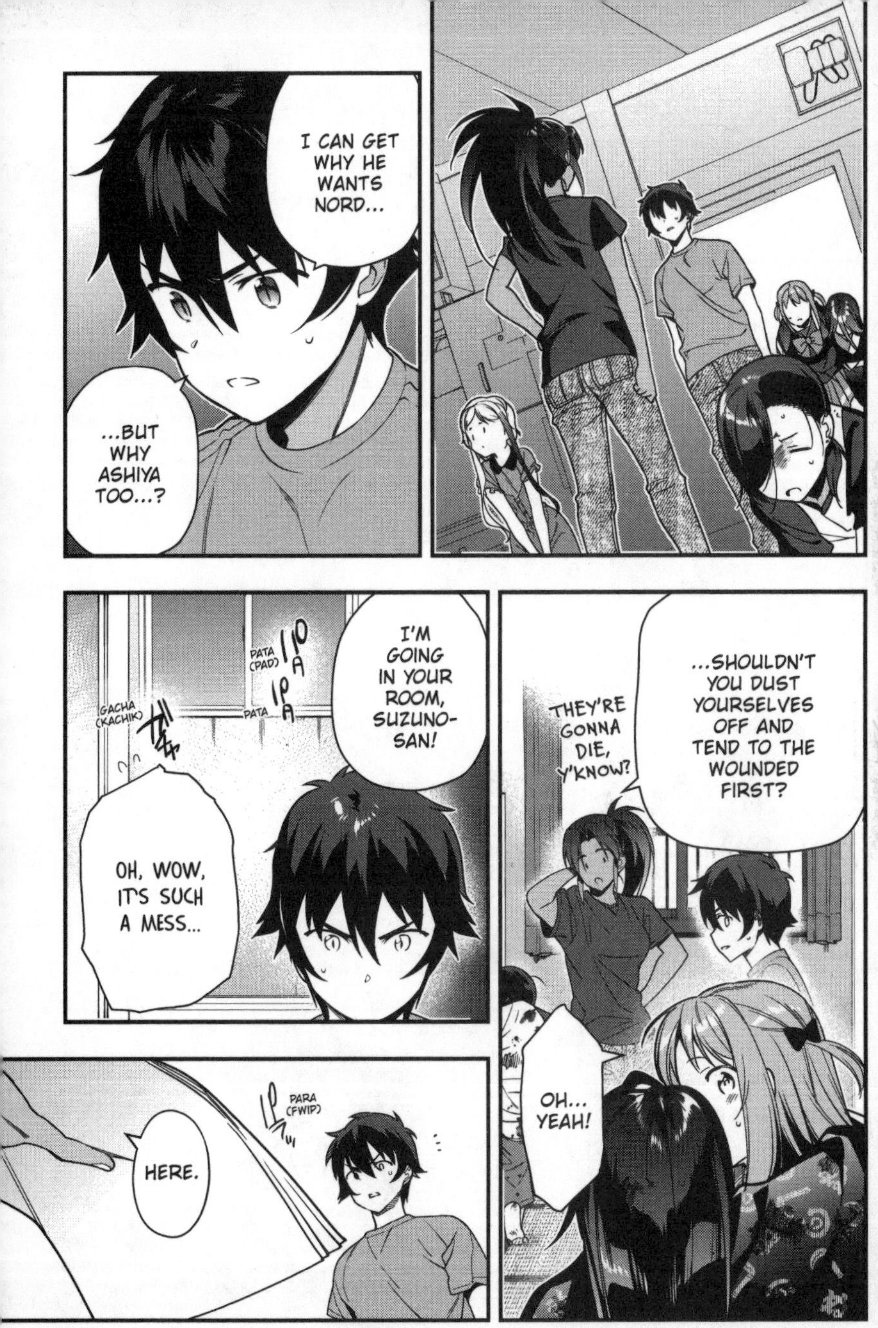
I CAN GET WHY HE WANTS NORD...
...BUT WHY ASHIYA TOO...?
...SHOULDN'T YOU DUST YOURSELVES OFF AND TEND TO THE WOUNDED FIRST?
THEY'RE GONNA DIE, Y'KNOW?
OH... YEAH!
I'M GOING IN YOUR ROOM, SUZUNO-SAN!
PATA (PAD)
PATA
GACHA (KACHIK)
OH, WOW, IT'S SUCH A MESS...
PARA (FWIP)
HERE.

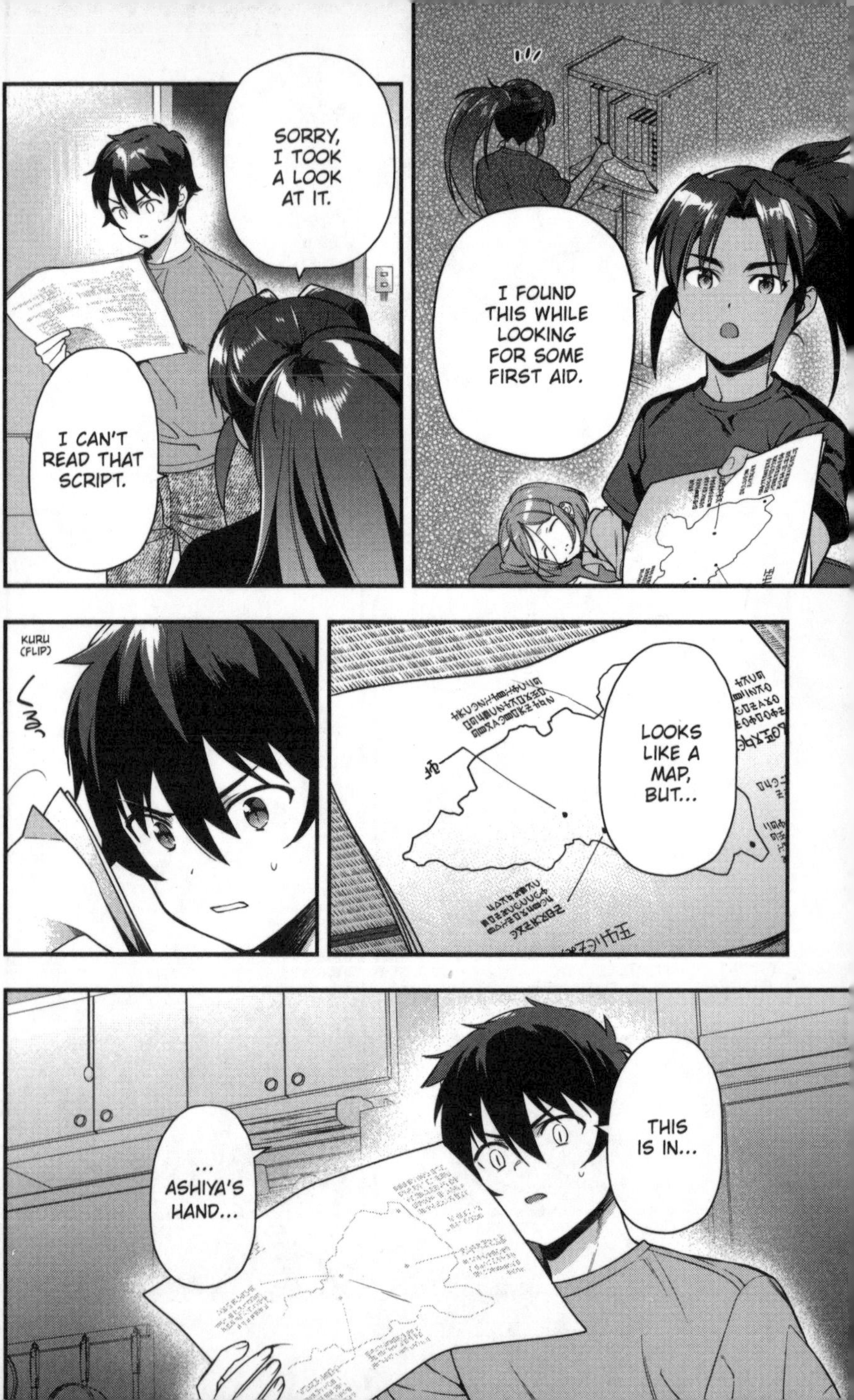
I FOUND THIS WHILE LOOKING FOR SOME FIRST AID.
SORRY, I TOOK A LOOK AT IT.
I CAN'T READ THAT SCRIPT.
LOOKS LIKE A MAP, BUT...
KURU (FLIP)
THIS IS IN...
... ASHIYA'S HAND...

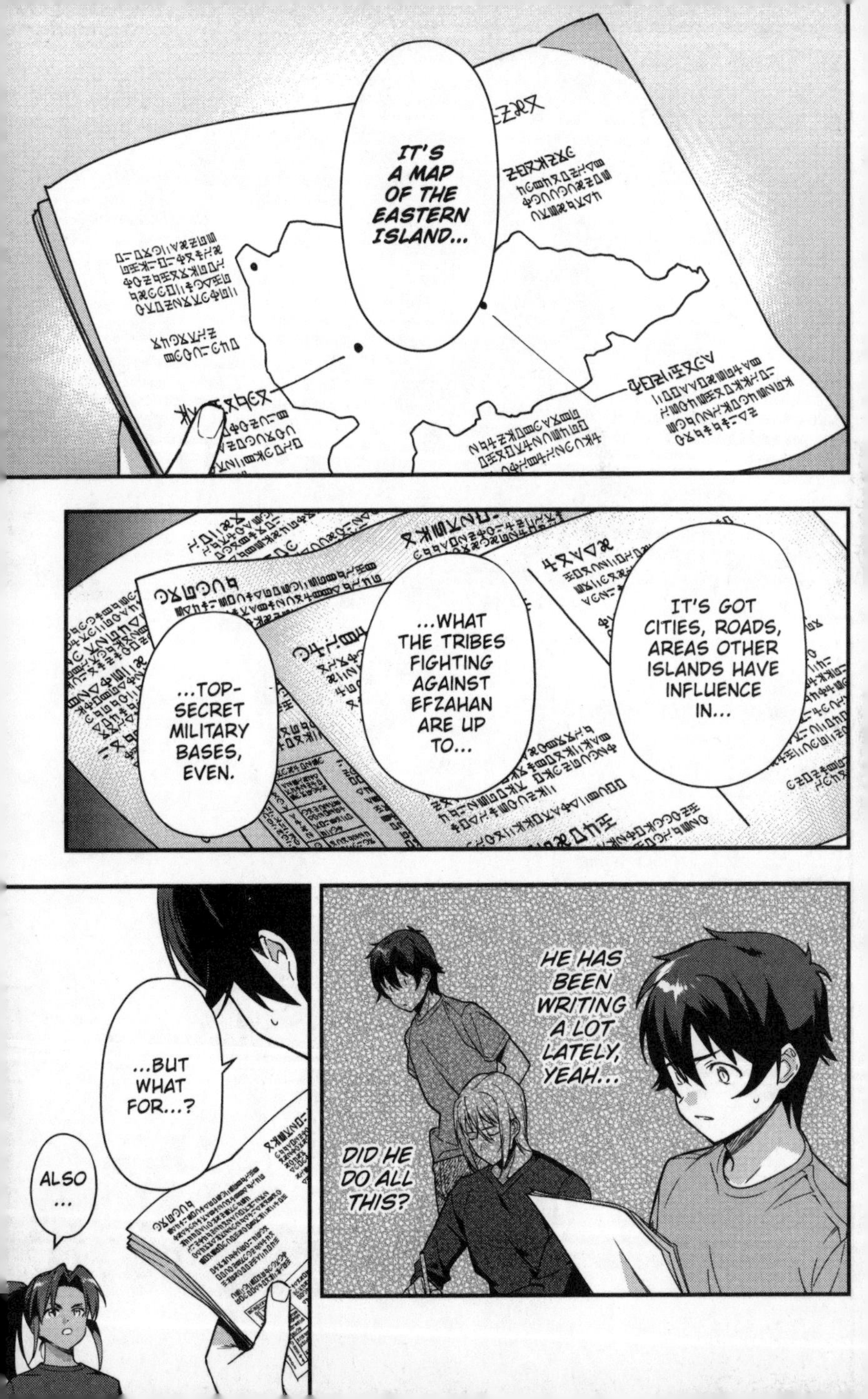
IT'S A MAP OF THE EASTERN ISLAND...
IT'S GOT CITIES, ROADS, AREAS OTHER ISLANDS HAVE INFLUENCE IN...
...WHAT THE TRIBES FIGHTING AGAINST EFZAHAN ARE UP TO...
...TOP-SECRET MILITARY BASES, EVEN.
HE HAS BEEN WRITING A LOT LATELY, YEAH...
DID HE DO ALL THIS?
...BUT WHAT FOR...?
ALSO ...

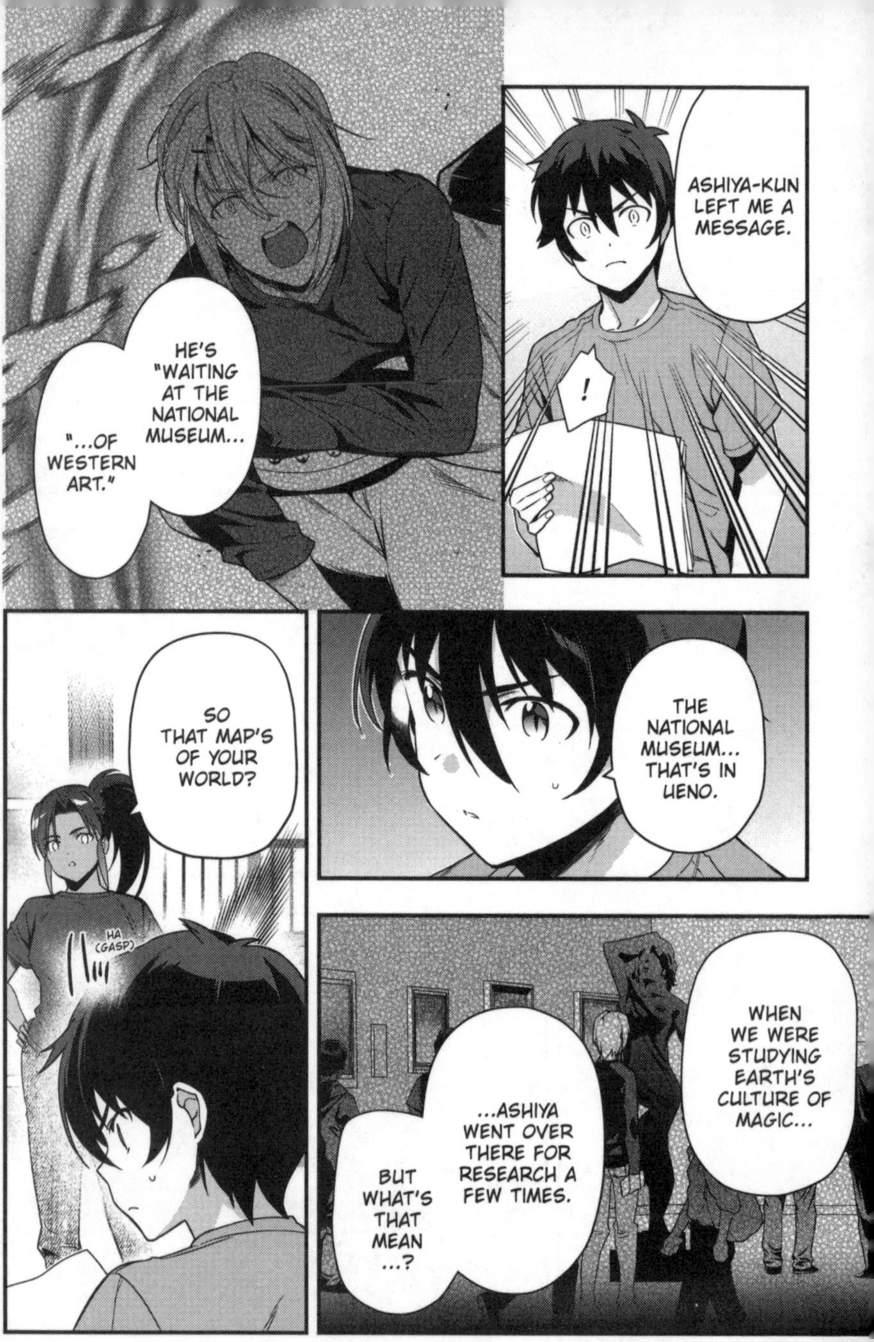
ASHIYA-KUN LEFT ME A MESSAGE.
!
HE'S "WAITING AT THE NATIONAL MUSEUM...
"...OF WESTERN ART."
THE NATIONAL MUSEUM... THAT'S IN UENO.
WHEN WE WERE STUDYING EARTH'S CULTURE OF MAGIC...
...ASHIYA WENT OVER THERE FOR RESEARCH A FEW TIMES.
BUT WHAT'S THAT MEAN ...?
SO THAT MAP'S OF YOUR WORLD?
HA (GASP)

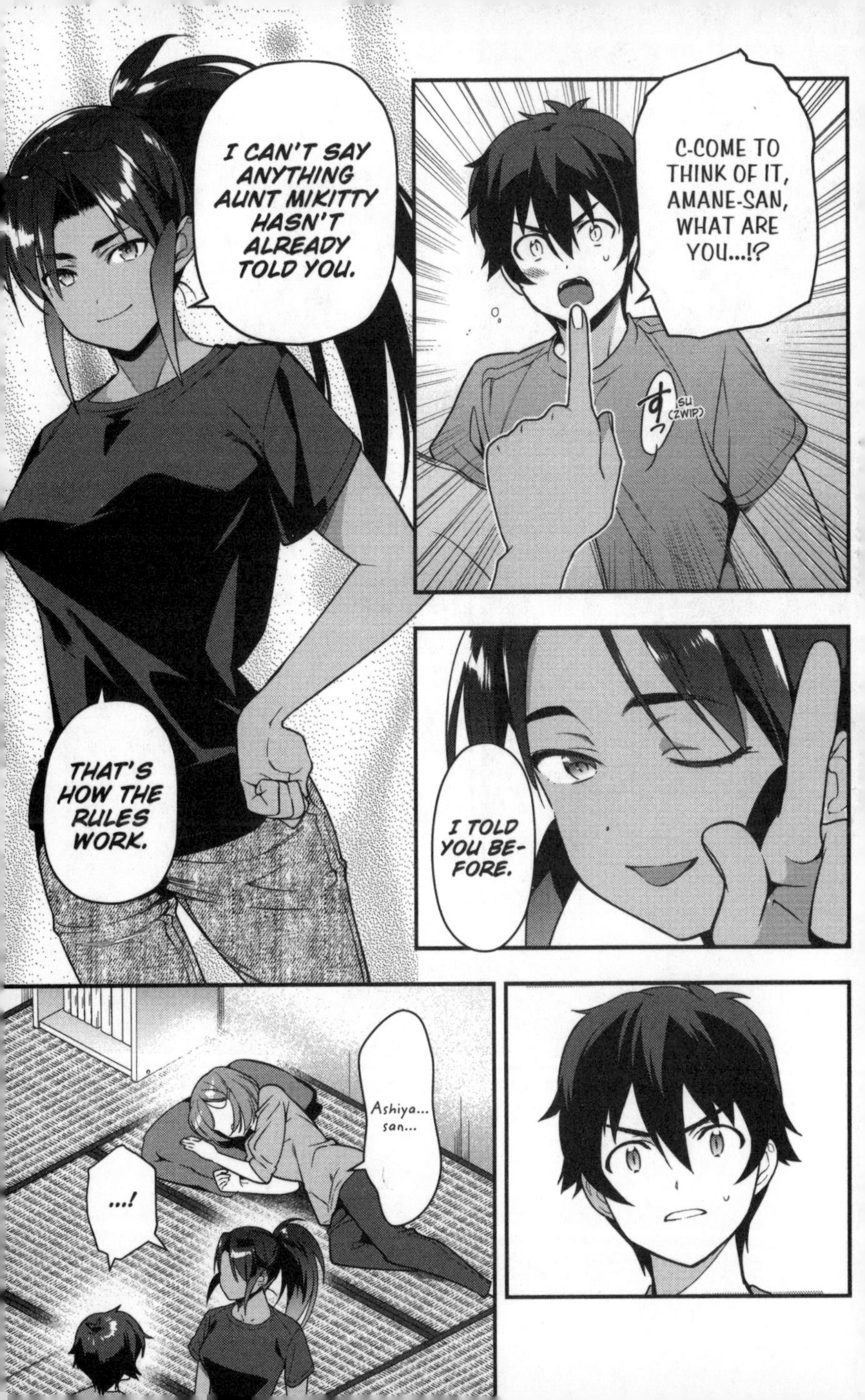
C-COME TO THINK OF IT, AMANE-SAN, WHAT ARE YOU...!?
すっ
SU (ZWIP)
I TOLD YOU BE-FORE.
I CAN'T SAY ANYTHING AUNT MIKITTY HASN'T ALREADY TOLD YOU.
THAT'S HOW THE RULES WORK.
Ashiya... san...
...!

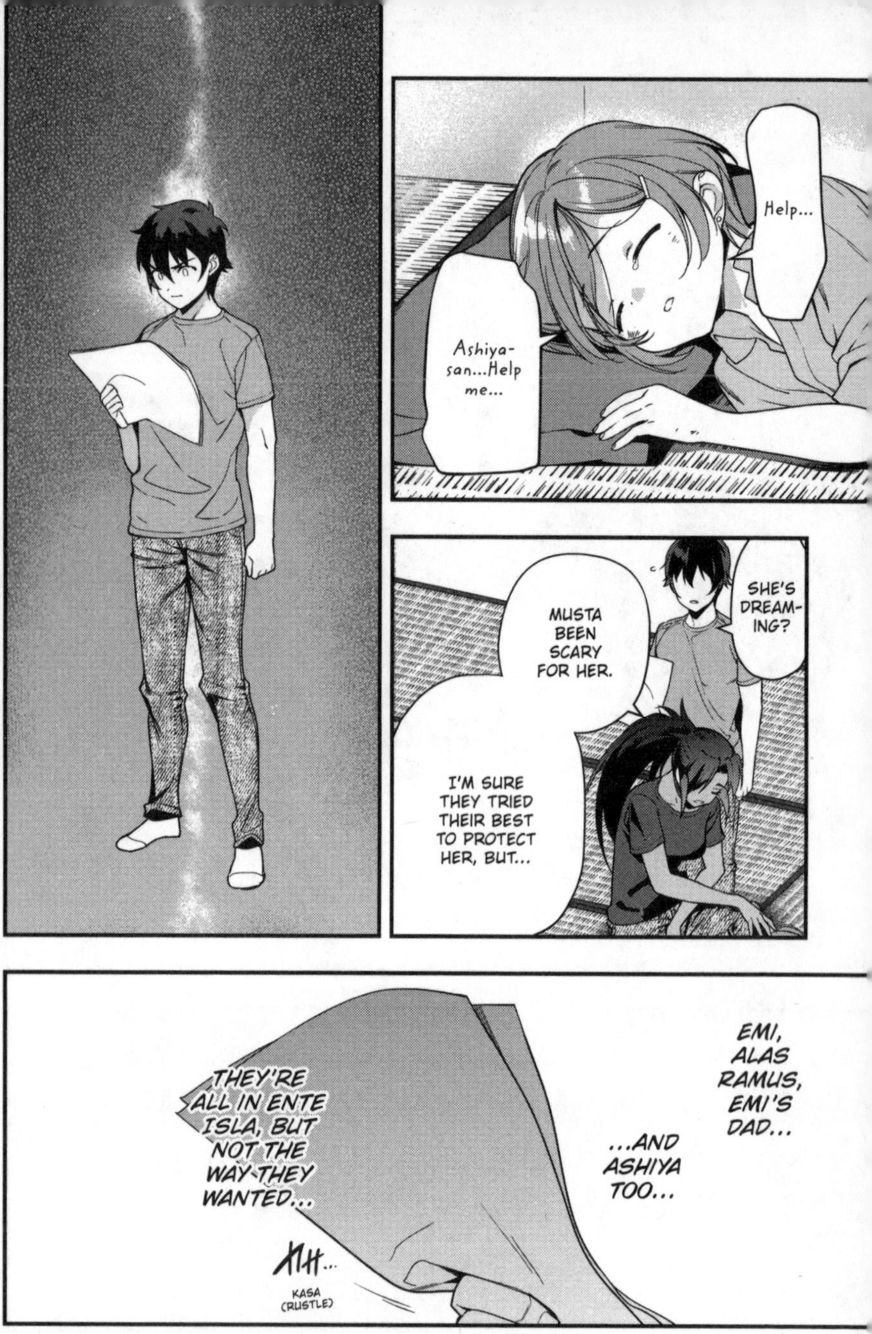
Help...
Ashiya-san...Help me...
SHE'S DREAMING?
MUSTA BEEN SCARY FOR HER.
I'M SURE THEY TRIED THEIR BEST TO PROTECT HER, BUT...
EMI, ALAS RAMUS, EMI'S DAD...
...AND ASHIYA TOO...
THEY'RE ALL IN ENTE ISLA, BUT NOT THE WAY THEY WANTED...
KASA (RUSTLE)

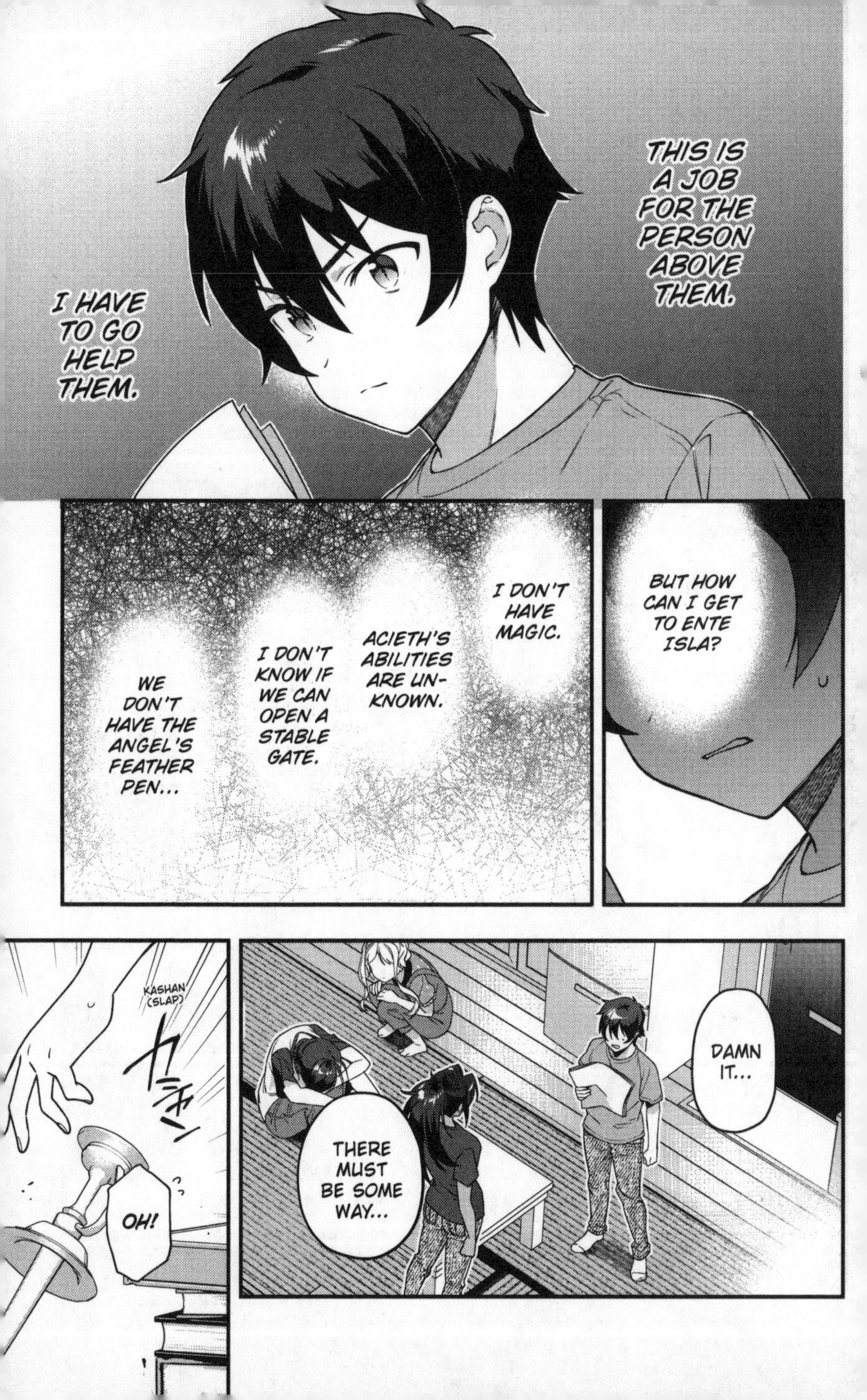
THIS IS A JOB FOR THE PERSON ABOVE THEM.
I HAVE TO GO HELP THEM.
BUT HOW CAN I GET TO ENTE ISLA?
I DON'T HAVE MAGIC.
ACIETH'S ABILITIES ARE UN-KNOWN.
I DON'T KNOW IF WE CAN OPEN A STABLE GATE.
WE DON'T HAVE THE ANGEL'S FEATHER PEN...
DAMN IT...
THERE MUST BE SOME WAY...
KASHAN (SLAP)
OH!

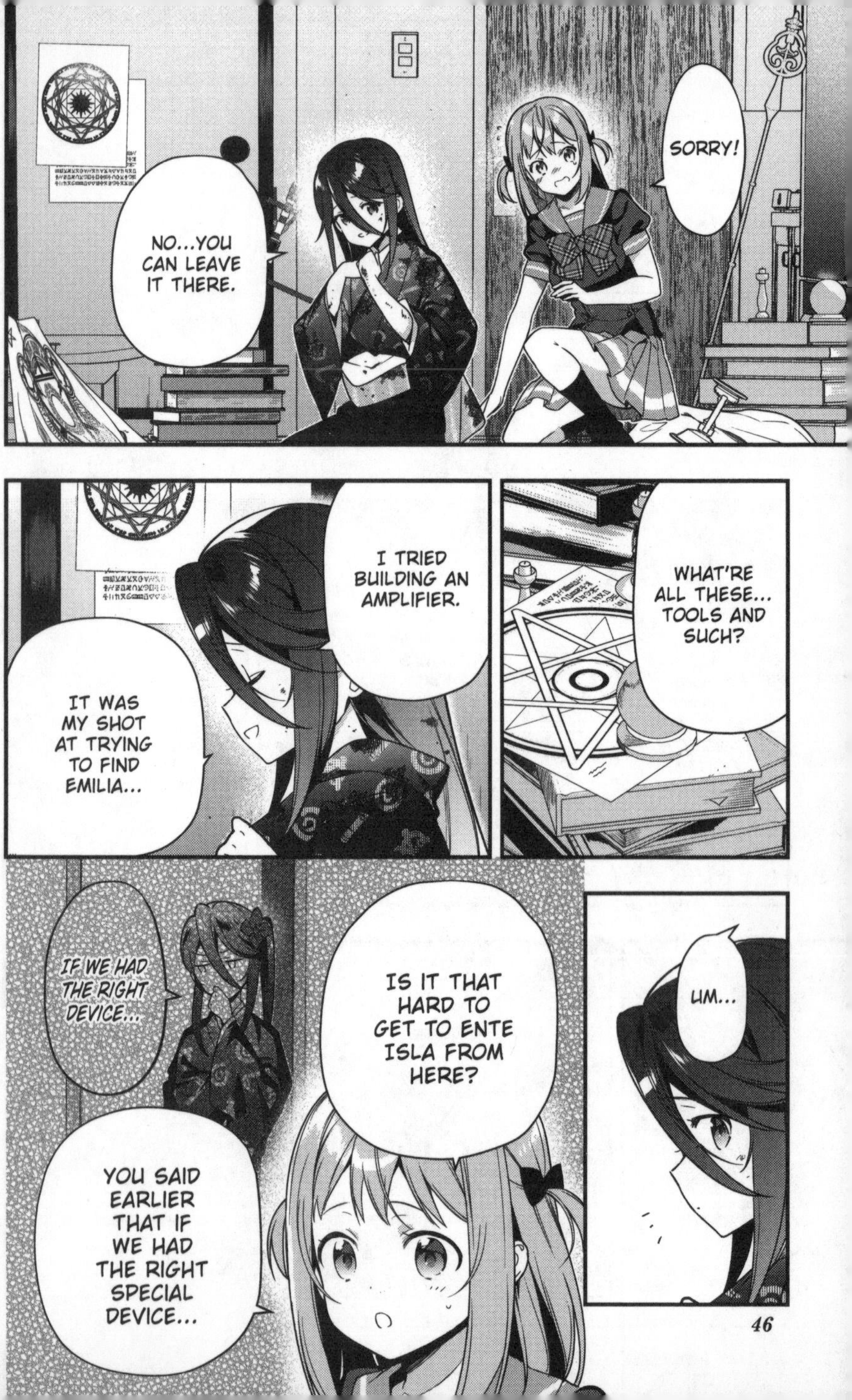
SORRY!
NO...YOU CAN LEAVE IT THERE.
WHAT'RE ALL THESE... TOOLS AND SUCH?
I TRIED BUILDING AN AMPLIFIER.
IT WAS MY SHOT AT TRYING TO FIND EMILIA...
UM...
IS IT THAT HARD TO GET TO ENTE ISLA FROM HERE?
IF WE HAD THE RIGHT DEVICE...
YOU SAID EARLIER THAT IF WE HAD THE RIGHT SPECIAL DEVICE...

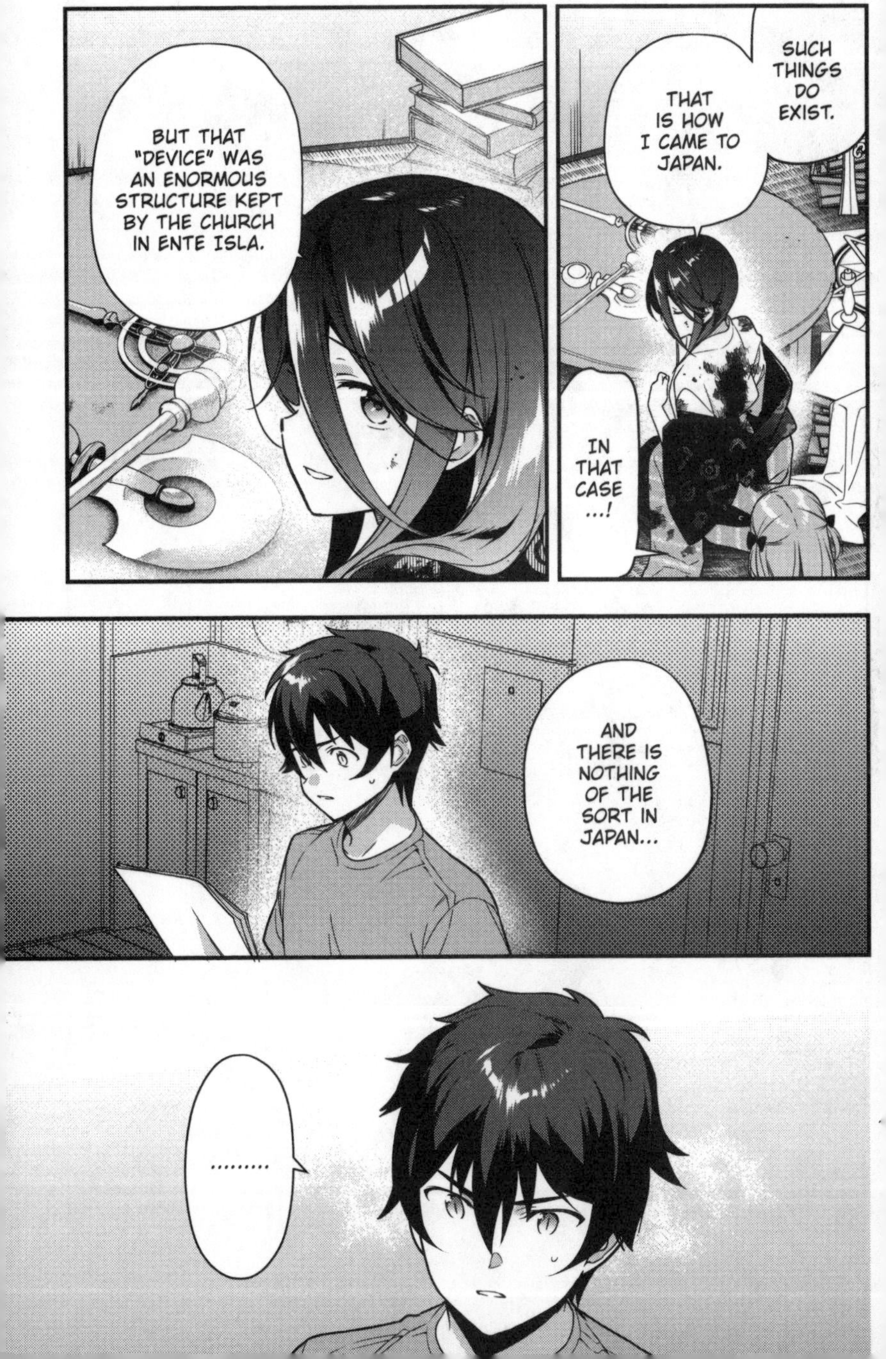
SUCH THINGS DO EXIST.
THAT IS HOW I CAME TO JAPAN.
IN THAT CASE ...!
BUT THAT "DEVICE" WAS AN ENORMOUS STRUCTURE KEPT BY THE CHURCH IN ENTE ISLA.
AND THERE IS NOTHING OF THE SORT IN JAPAN...
....

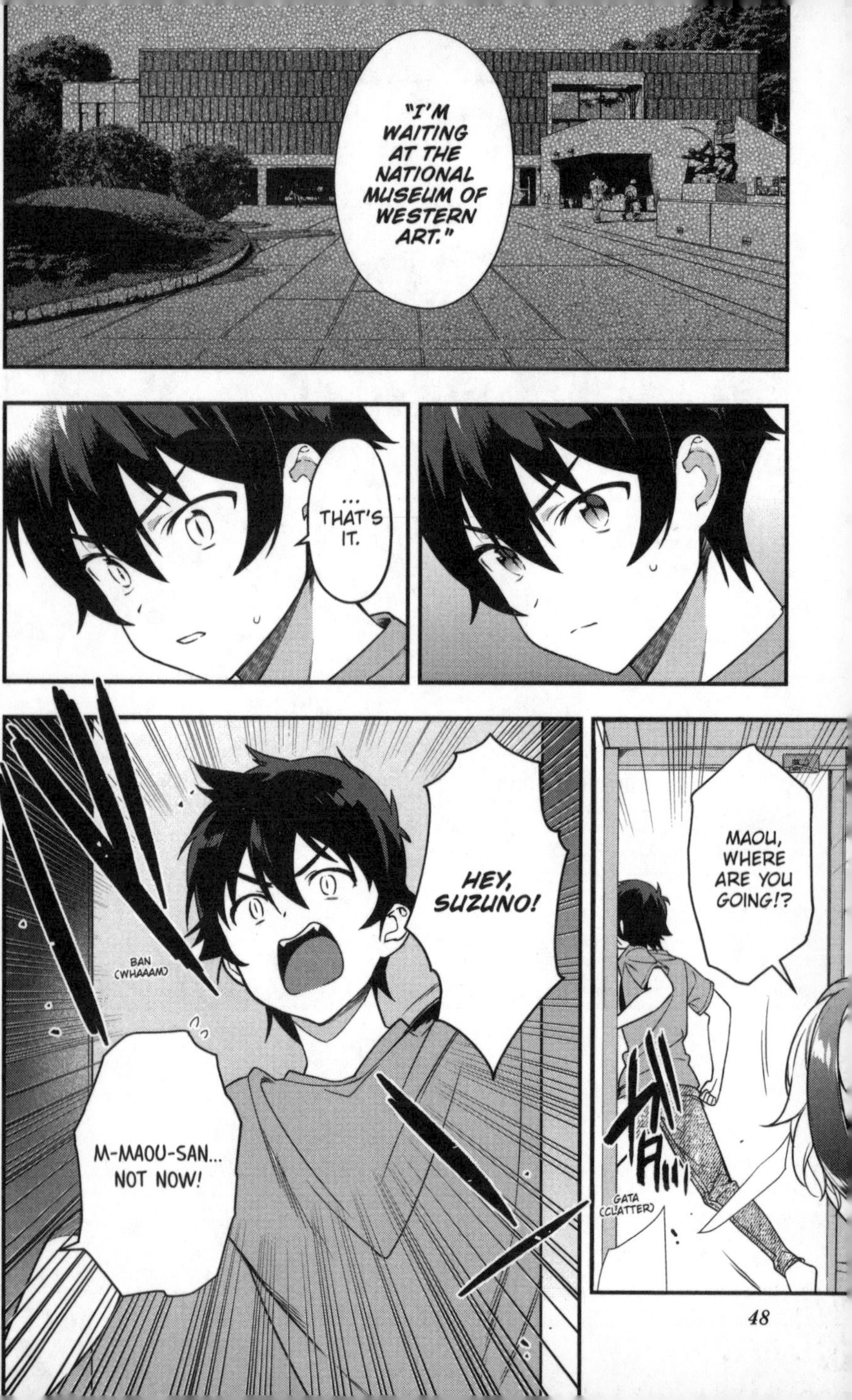
"I'M WAITING AT THE NATIONAL MUSEUM OF WESTERN ART."
...THAT'S IT.
MAOU, WHERE ARE YOU GOING!?
GATA (CLATTER)
HEY, SUZUNO!
BAN (WHAAAM)
M-MAOU-SAN... NOT NOW!

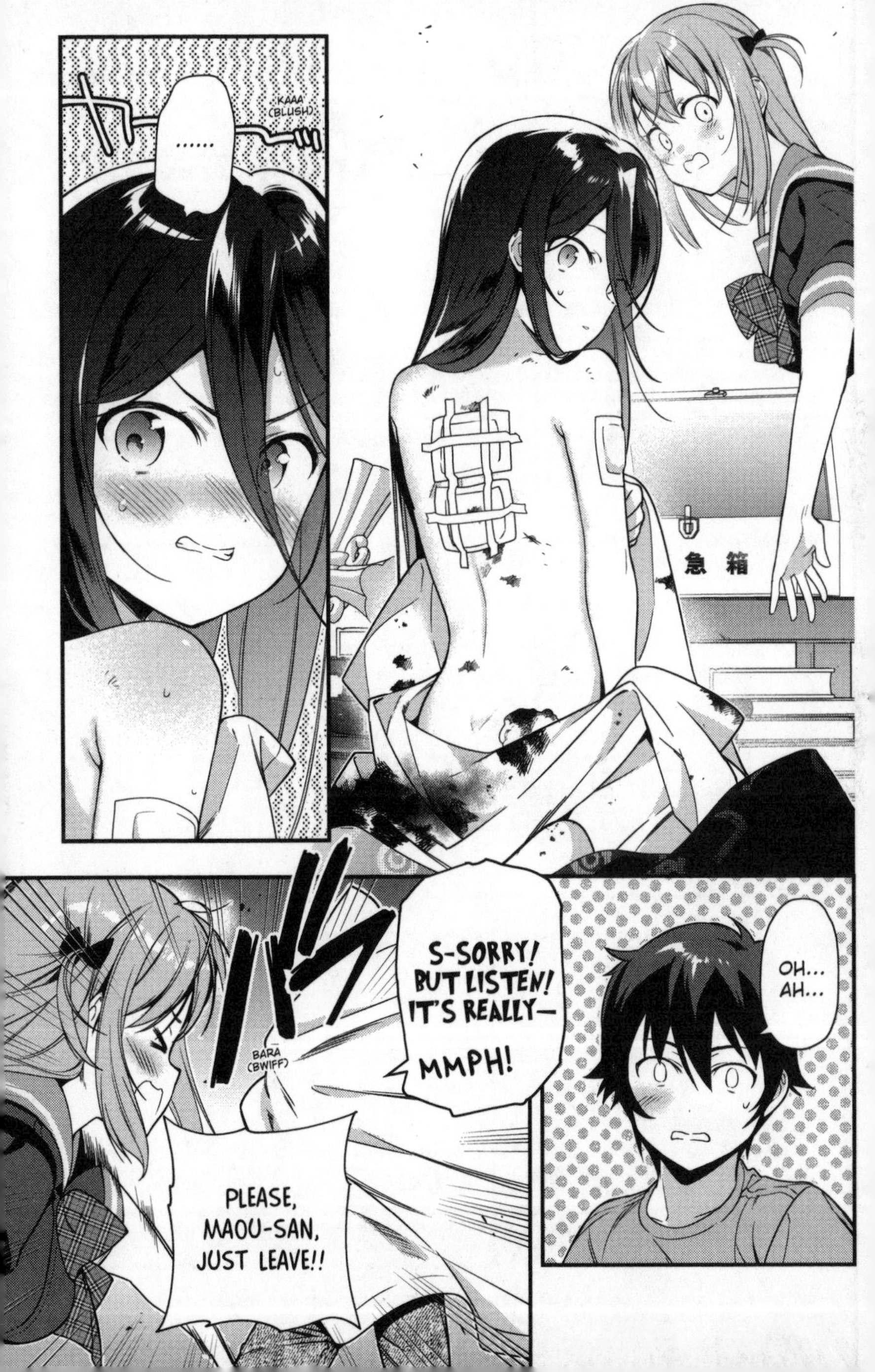
急箱
......
KAAA (BLUSH)
OH... AH...
S-SORRY! BUT LISTEN! IT'S REALLY—
MMPH!
BARA (BWIFF)
PLEASE, MAOU-SAN, JUST LEAVE!!

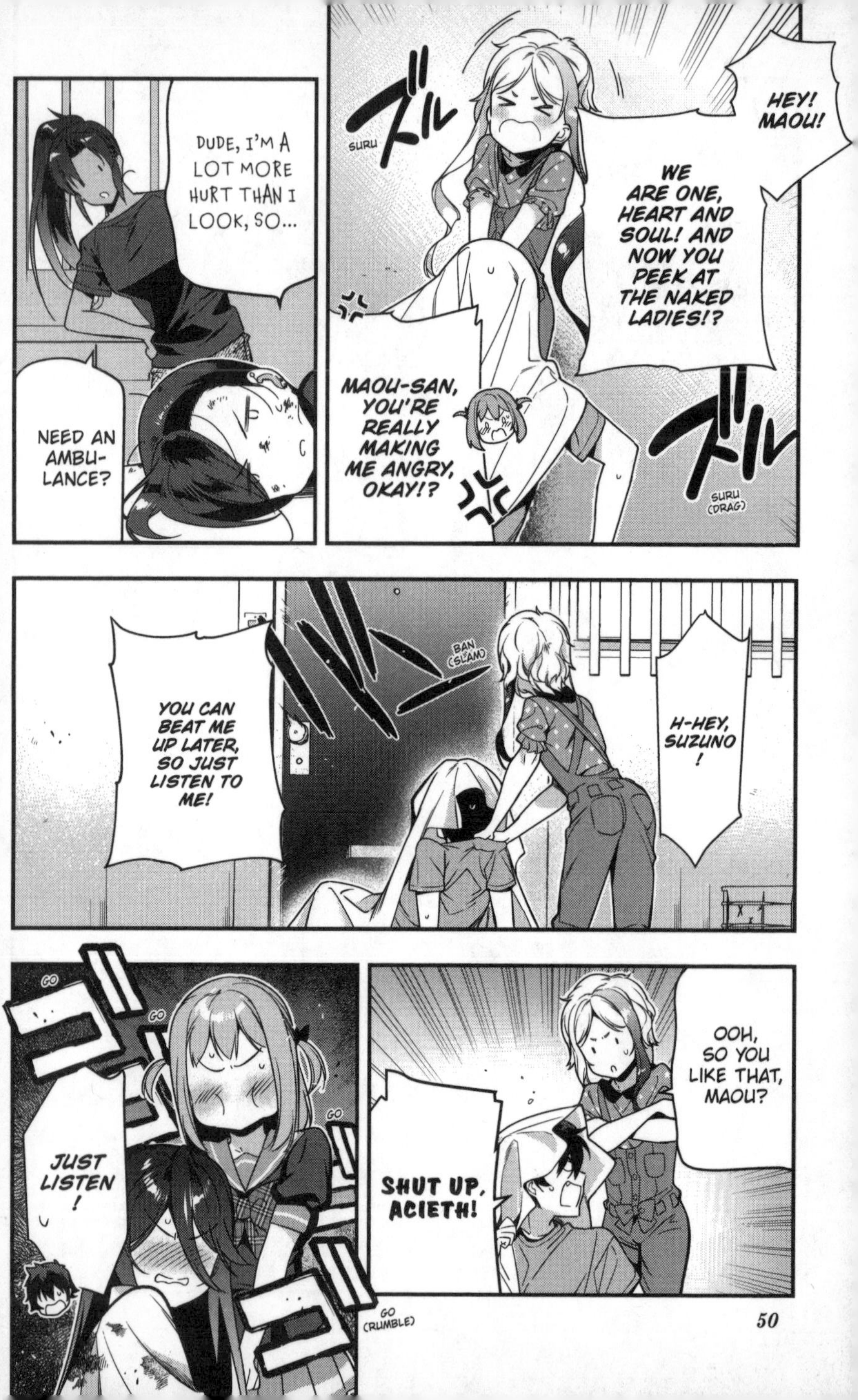
HEY! MAOU!
WE ARE ONE, HEART AND SOUL! AND NOW YOU PEEK AT THE NAKED LADIES!?
SURU
MAOU-SAN, YOU'RE REALLY MAKING ME ANGRY, OKAY!?
SURU (DRAG)
DUDE, I'M A LOT MORE HURT THAN I LOOK, SO...
NEED AN AMBULANCE?
H-HEY, SUZUNO!
BAN (SLAM)
YOU CAN BEAT ME UP LATER, SO JUST LISTEN TO ME!
OOH, SO YOU LIKE THAT, MAOU?
SHUT UP, ACIETH!
GO
GO
GO
JUST LISTEN!
GO (RUMBLE)

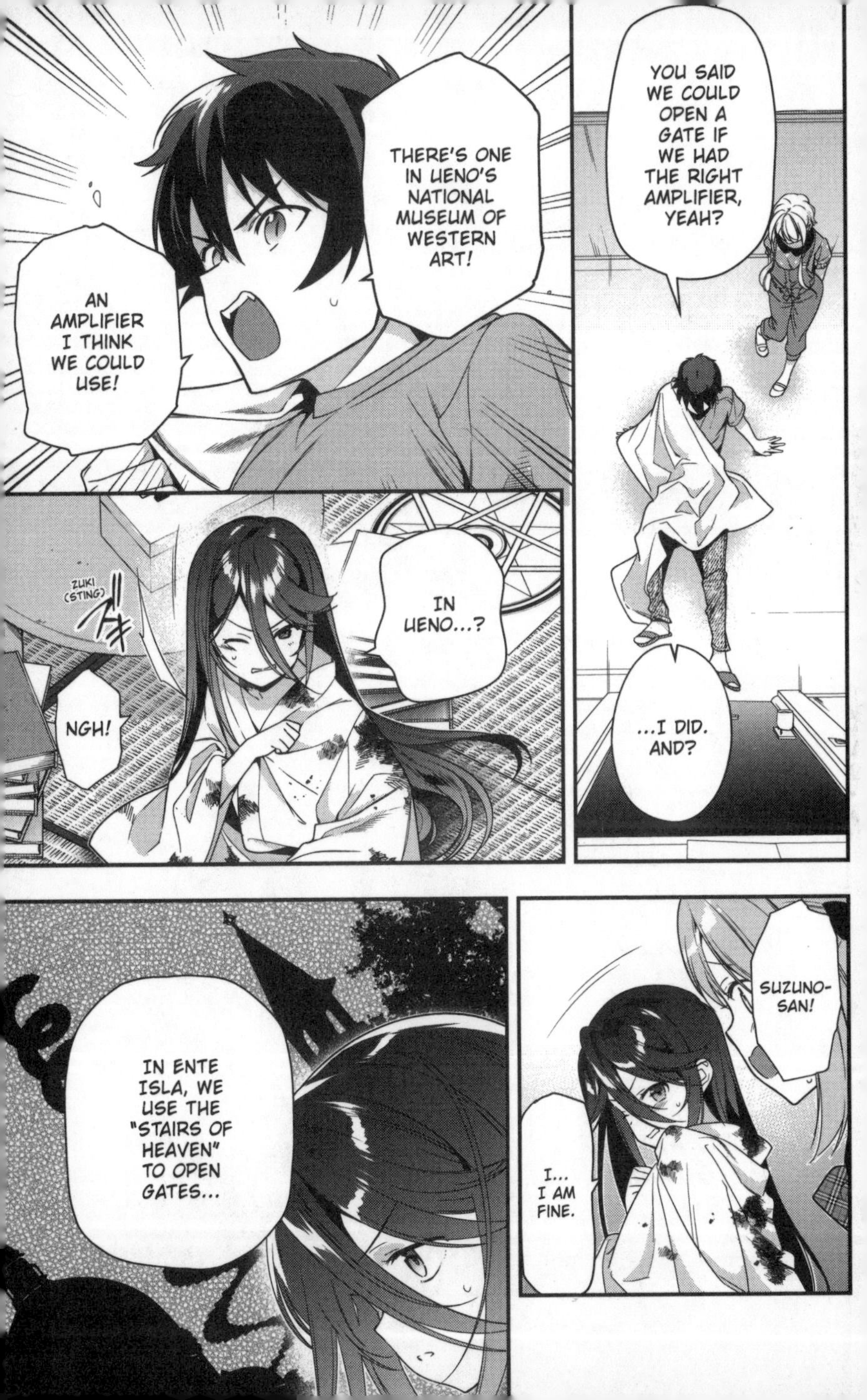
YOU SAID WE COULD OPEN A GATE IF WE HAD THE RIGHT AMPLIFIER, YEAH?
...I DID. AND?
THERE'S ONE IN UENO'S NATIONAL MUSEUM OF WESTERN ART!
AN AMPLIFIER I THINK WE COULD USE!
IN UENO...?
ZUKI (STING)
NGH!
SUZUNO-SAN!
I... I AM FINE.
IN ENTE ISLA, WE USE THE "STAIRS OF HEAVEN" TO OPEN GATES...

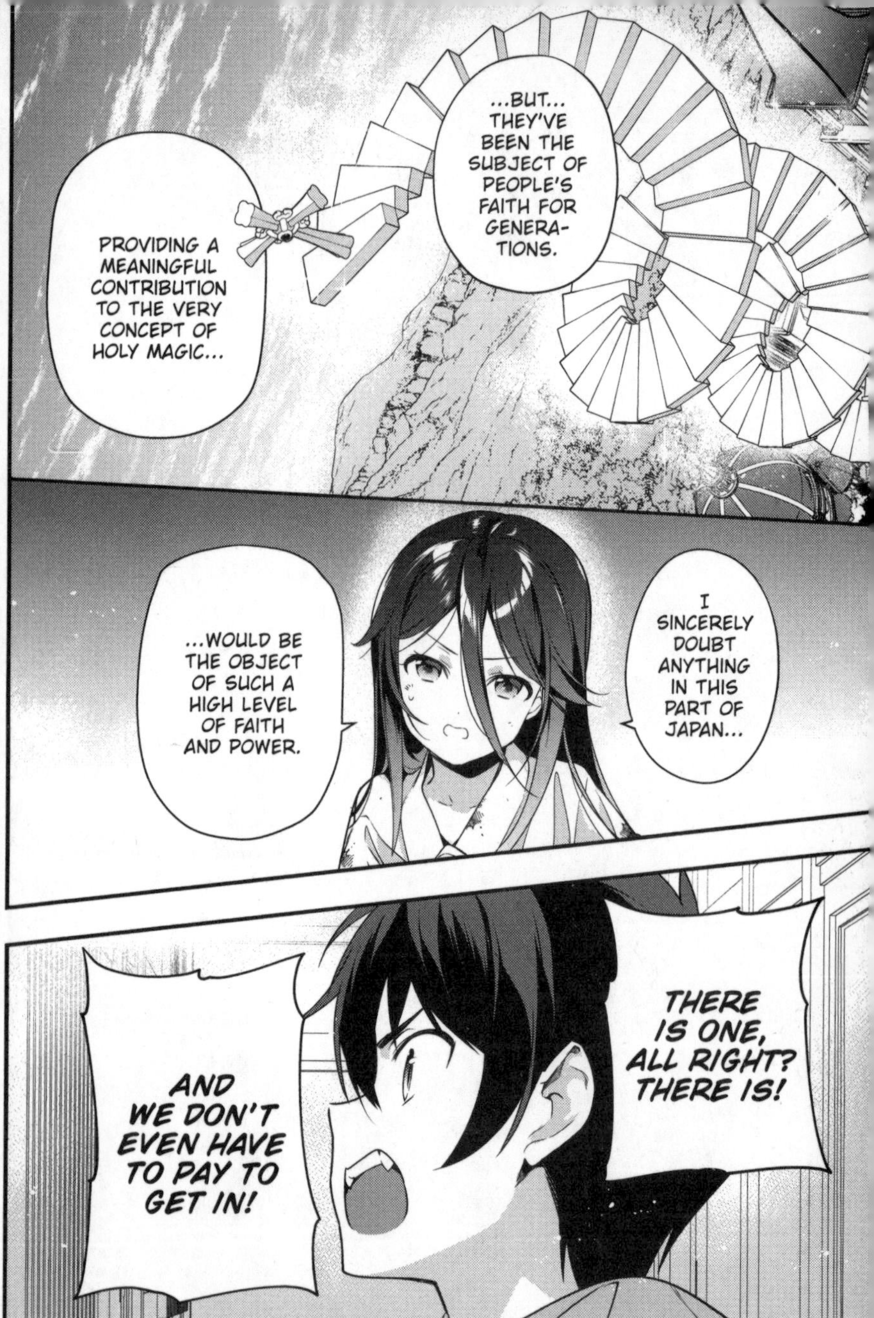
...BUT... THEY'VE BEEN THE SUBJECT OF PEOPLE'S FAITH FOR GENERA-TIONS.
PROVIDING A MEANINGFUL CONTRIBUTION TO THE VERY CONCEPT OF HOLY MAGIC...
I SINCERELY DOUBT ANYTHING IN THIS PART OF JAPAN...
...WOULD BE THE OBJECT OF SUCH A HIGH LEVEL OF FAITH AND POWER.
THERE IS ONE, ALL RIGHT? THERE IS!
AND WE DON'T EVEN HAVE TO PAY TO GET IN!

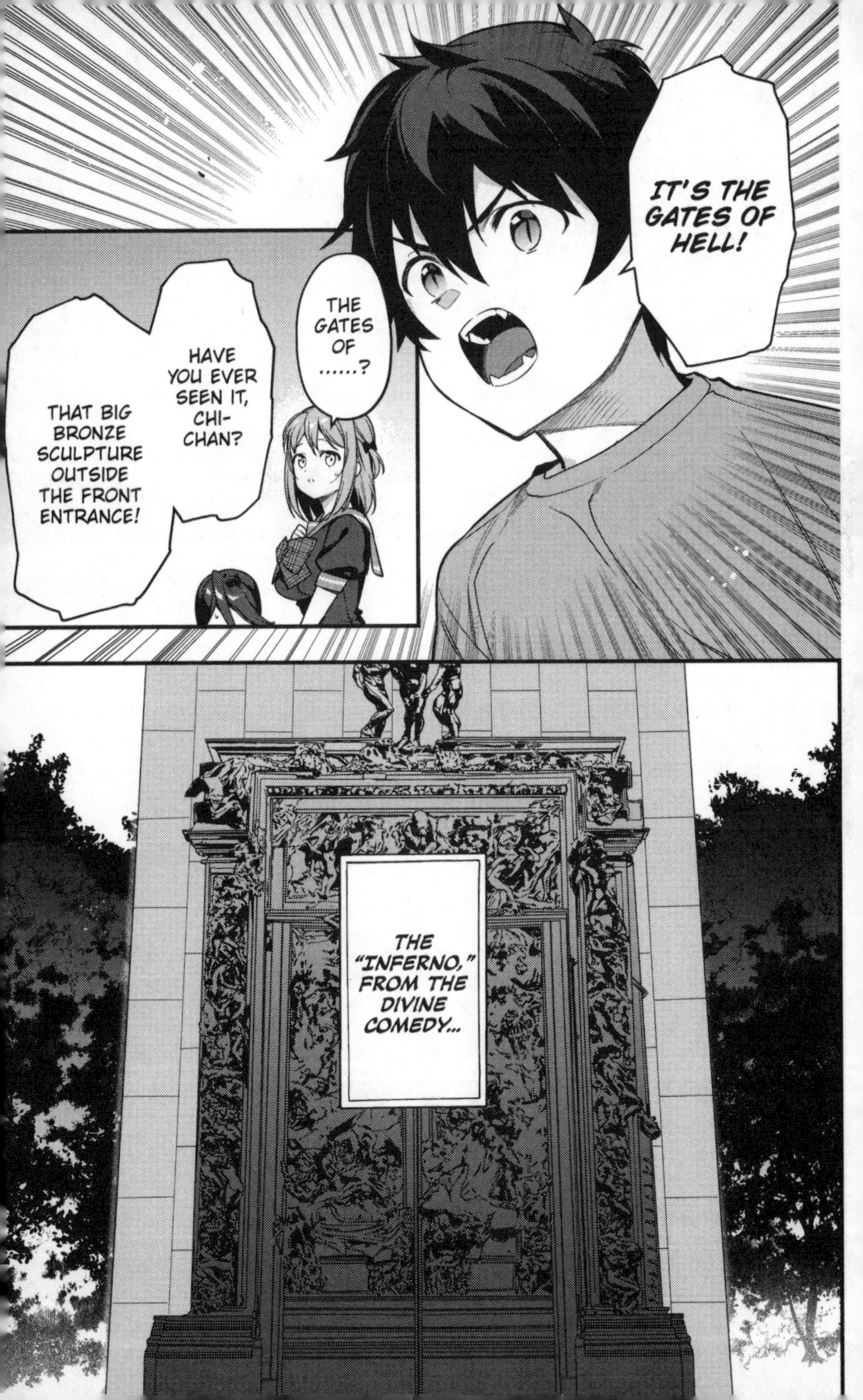
IT'S THE GATES OF HELL!
THE GATES OF ......?
HAVE YOU EVER SEEN IT, CHI-CHAN?
THAT BIG BRONZE SCULPTURE OUTSIDE THE FRONT ENTRANCE!
THE "INFERNO," FROM THE DIVINE COMEDY...

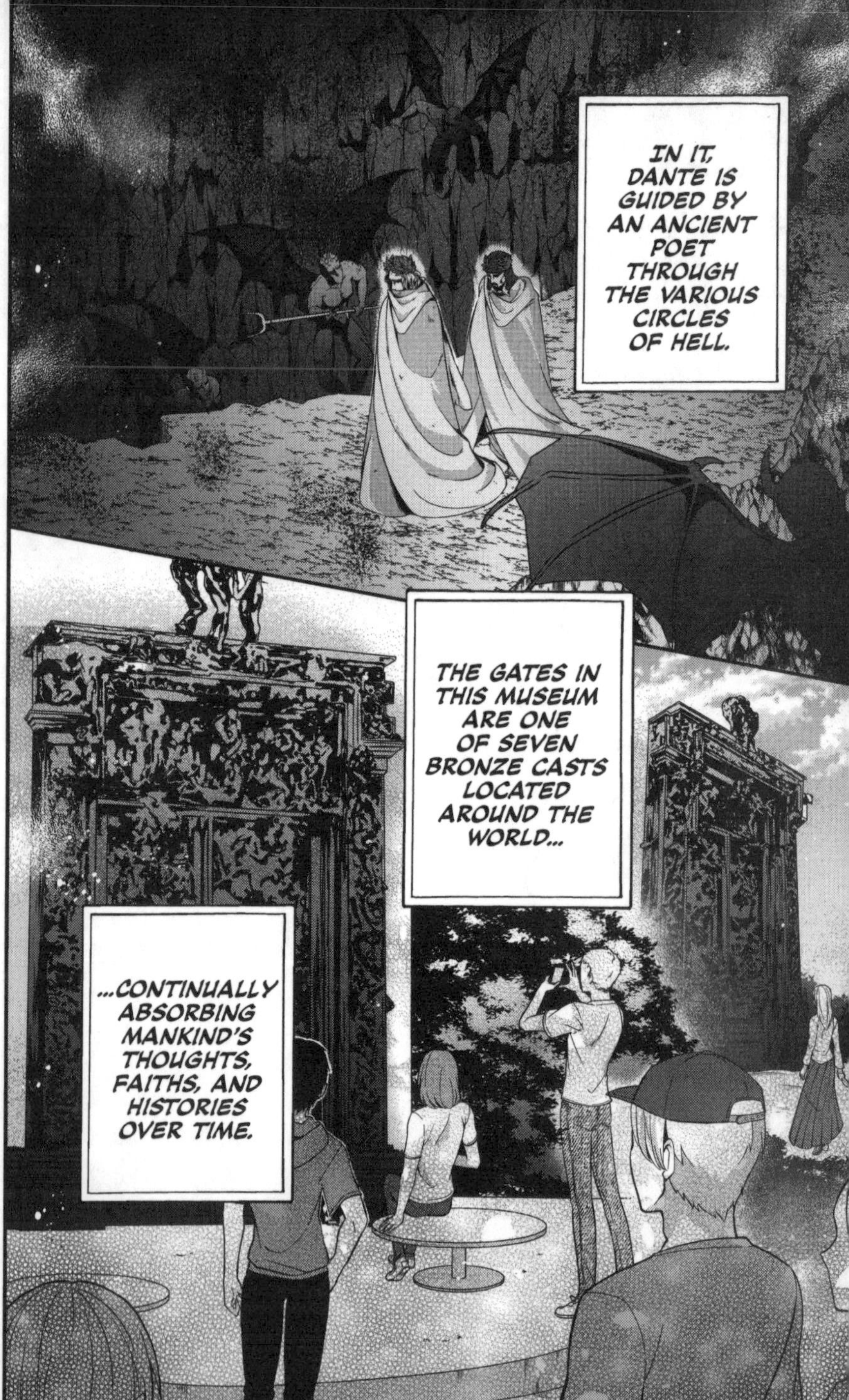
IN IT, DANTE IS GUIDED BY AN ANCIENT POET THROUGH THE VARIOUS CIRCLES OF HELL.
THE GATES IN THIS MUSEUM ARE ONE OF SEVEN BRONZE CASTS LOCATED AROUND THE WORLD...
...CONTINUALLY ABSORBING MANKIND'S THOUGHTS, FAITHS, AND HISTORIES OVER TIME.

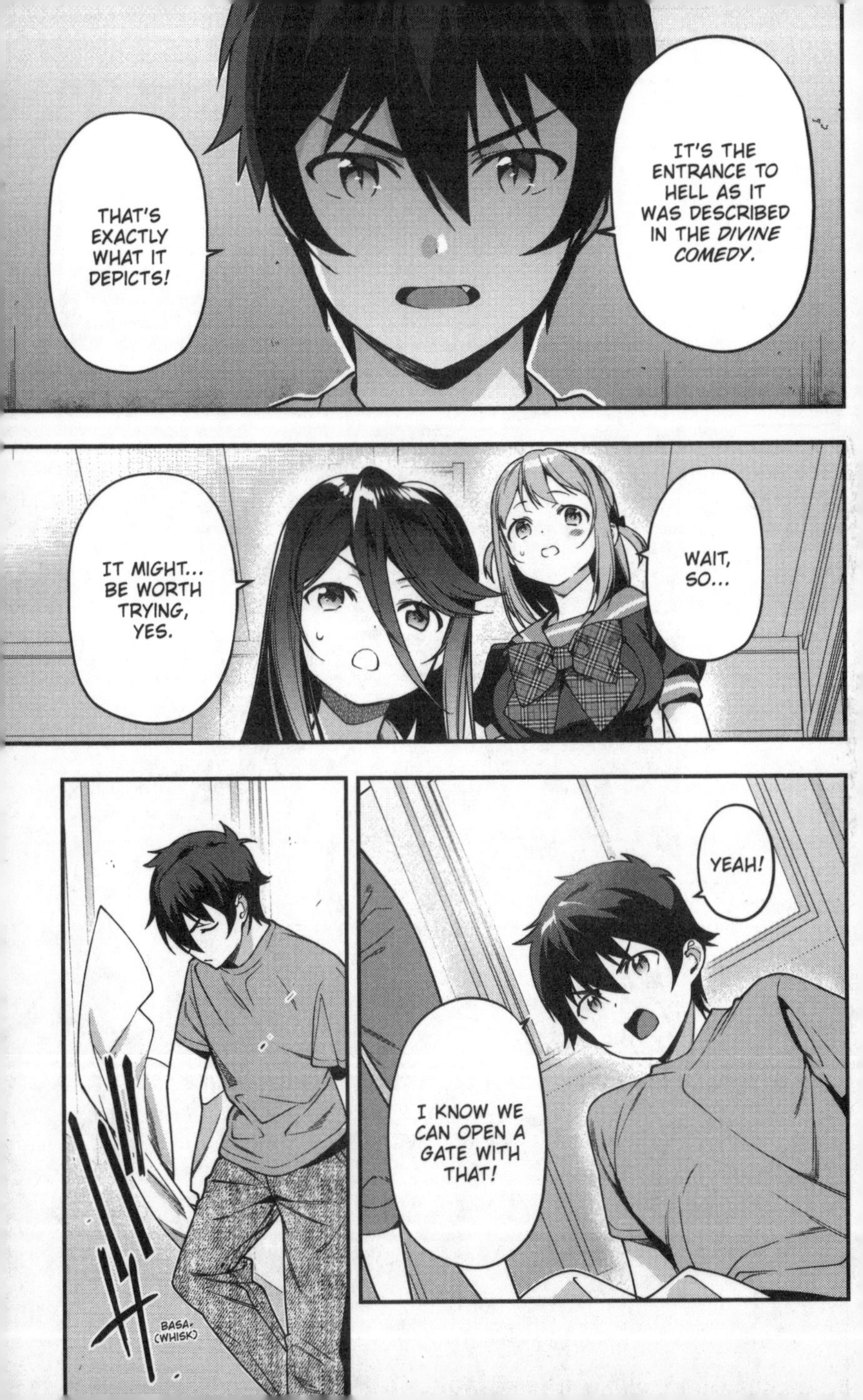
IT'S THE ENTRANCE TO HELL AS IT WAS DESCRIBED IN THE *DIVINE COMEDY*.
THAT'S EXACTLY WHAT IT DEPICTS!
WAIT, SO...
IT MIGHT... BE WORTH TRYING, YES.
YEAH!
I KNOW WE CAN OPEN A GATE WITH THAT!
BASA (WHISK)

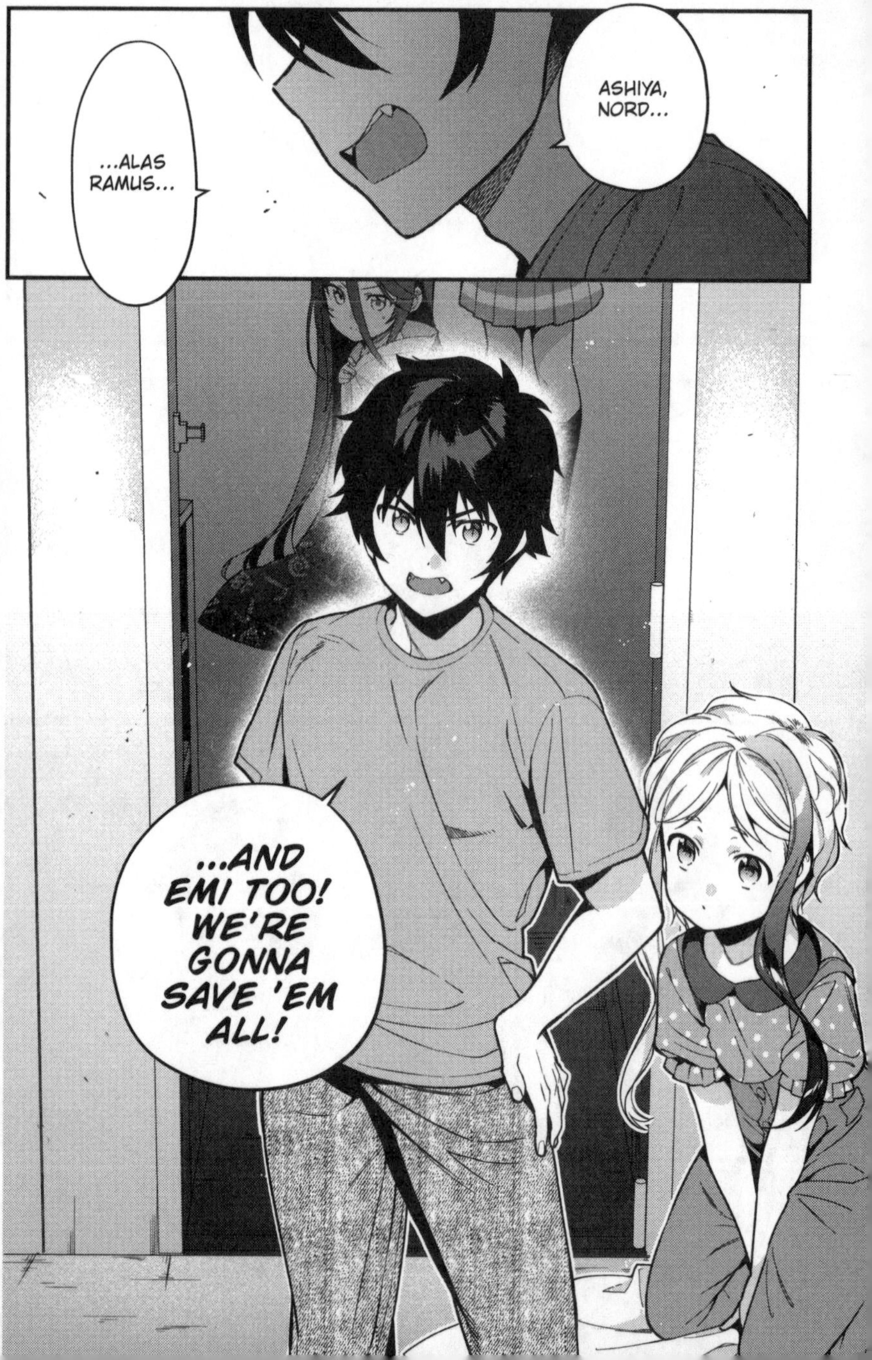
ASHIYA, NORD...
...ALAS RAMUS...
...AND EMI TOO! WE'RE GONNA SAVE 'EM ALL!

Shirou
Ashiya

THE DEVIL IS A PART-TIMER!

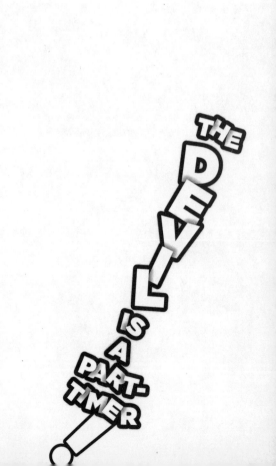

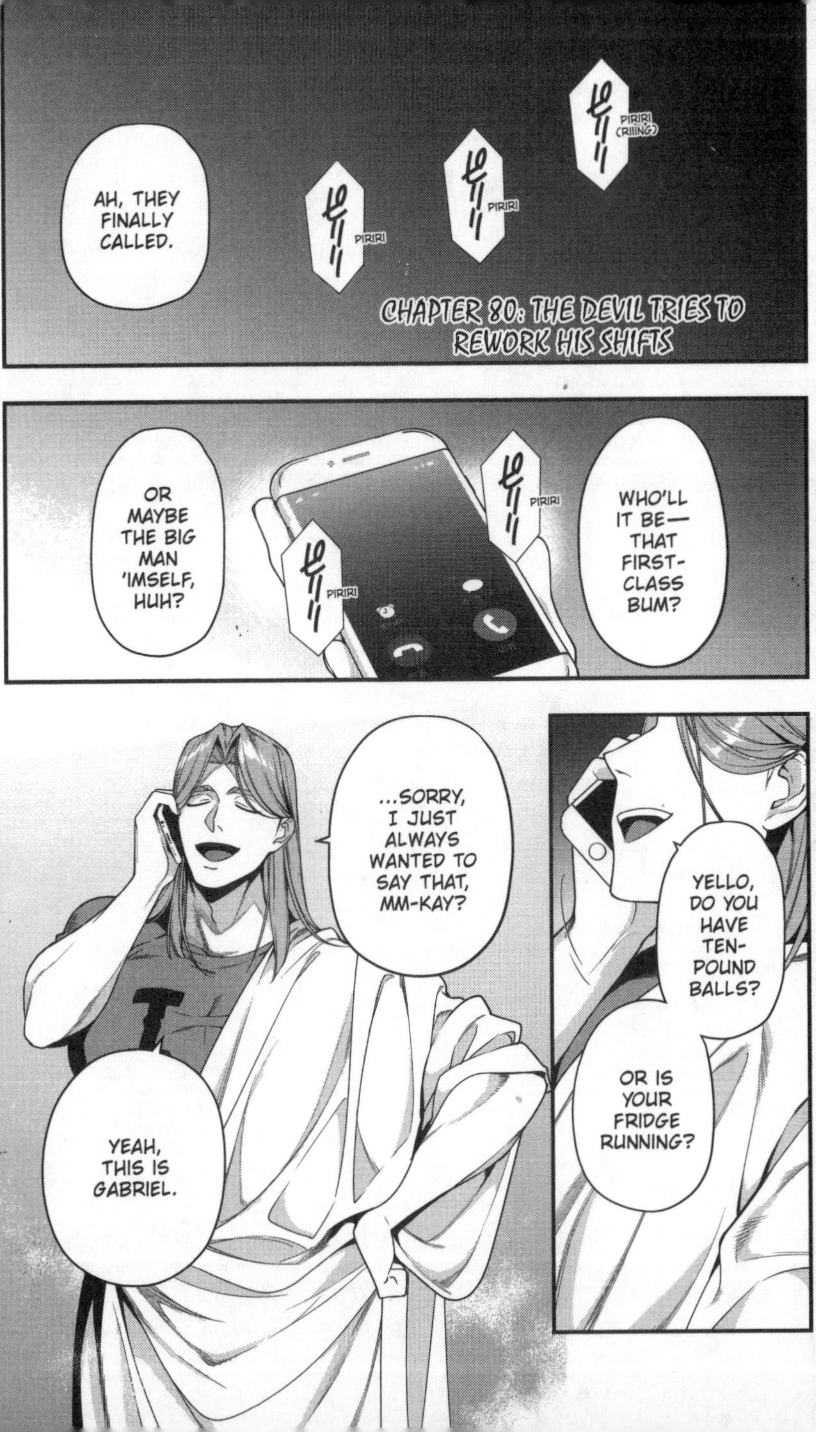
PIRIRI (RIIING)
PIRIRI
PIRIRI
AH, THEY FINALLY CALLED.
CHAPTER 80: THE DEVIL TRIES TO REWORK HIS SHIFTS
WHO'LL IT BE— THAT FIRST-CLASS BUM?
PIRIRI
PIRIRI
OR MAYBE THE BIG MAN 'IMSELF, HUH?
YELLO, DO YOU HAVE TEN-POUND BALLS?
OR IS YOUR FRIDGE RUNNING?
...SORRY, I JUST ALWAYS WANTED TO SAY THAT, MM-KAY?
YEAH, THIS IS GABRIEL.

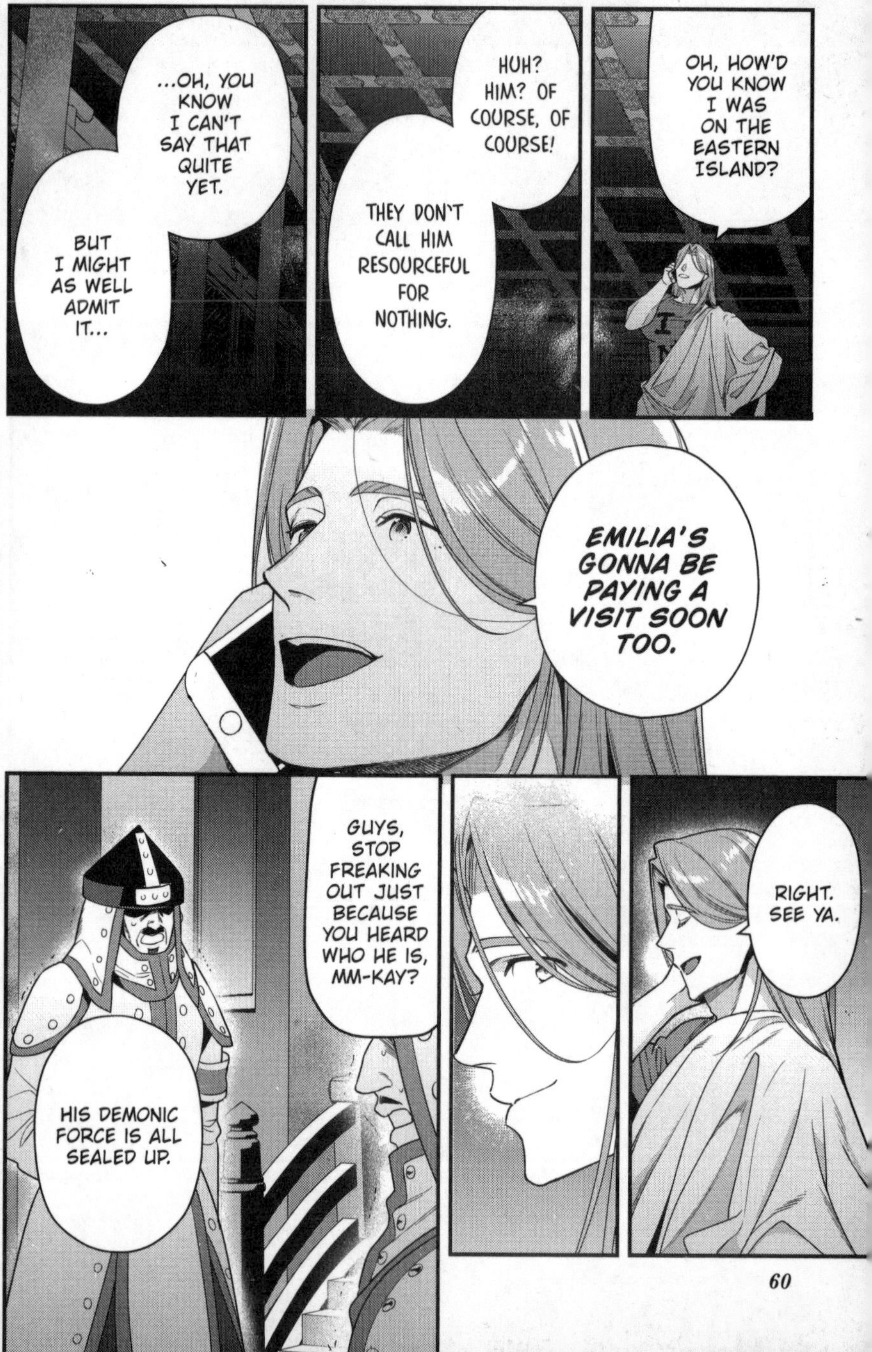
OH, HOW'D YOU KNOW I WAS ON THE EASTERN ISLAND?
HUH? HIM? OF COURSE, OF COURSE!
THEY DON'T CALL HIM RESOURCEFUL FOR NOTHING.
...OH, YOU KNOW I CAN'T SAY THAT QUITE YET.
BUT I MIGHT AS WELL ADMIT IT...
EMILIA'S GONNA BE PAYING A VISIT SOON TOO.
RIGHT. SEE YA.
GUYS, STOP FREAKING OUT JUST BECAUSE YOU HEARD WHO HE IS, MM-KAY?
HIS DEMONIC FORCE IS ALL SEALED UP.

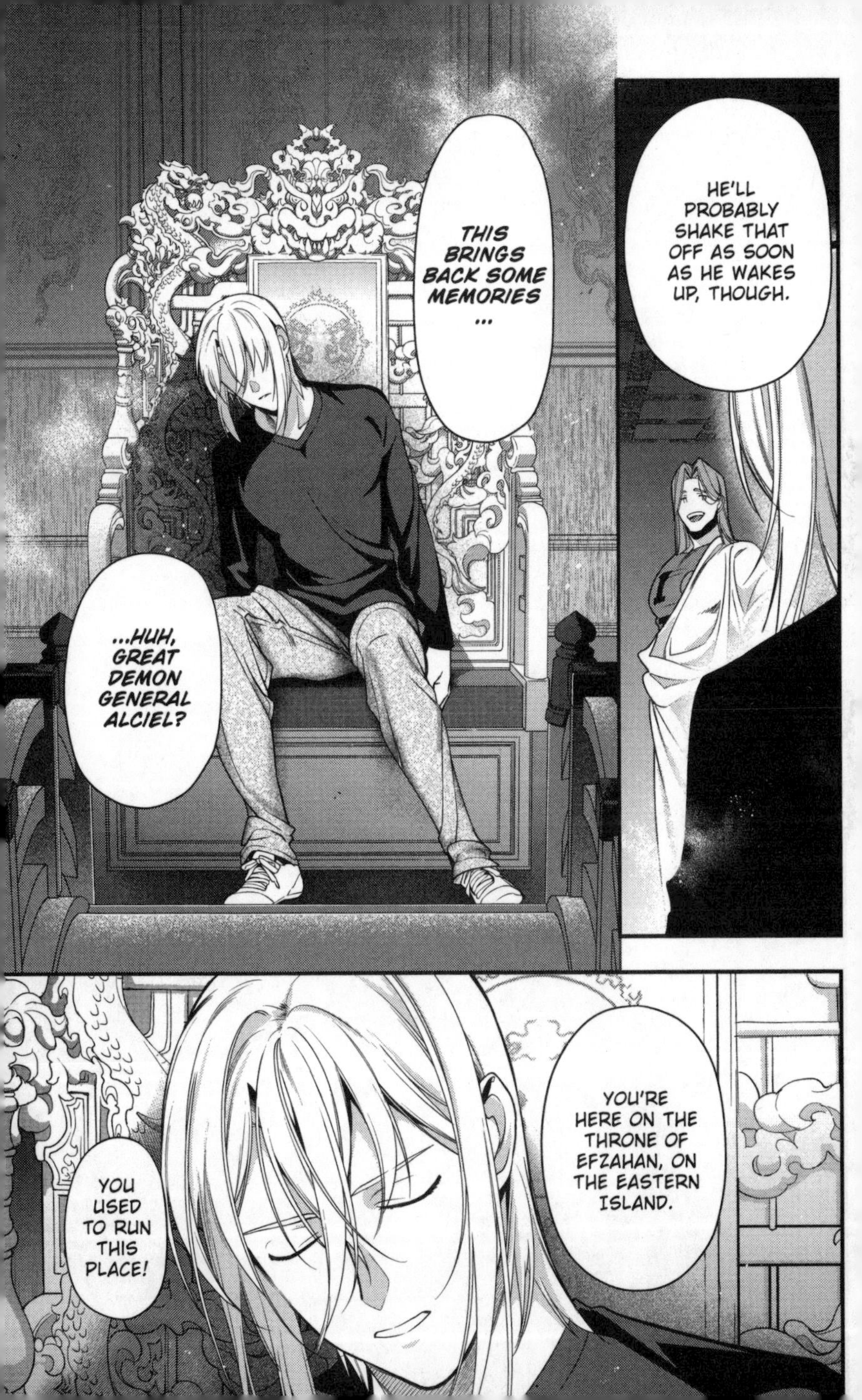
HE'LL PROBABLY SHAKE THAT OFF AS SOON AS HE WAKES UP, THOUGH.
THIS BRINGS BACK SOME MEMORIES ...
...HUH, GREAT DEMON GENERAL ALCIEL?
YOU'RE HERE ON THE THRONE OF EFZAHAN, ON THE EASTERN ISLAND.
YOU USED TO RUN THIS PLACE!

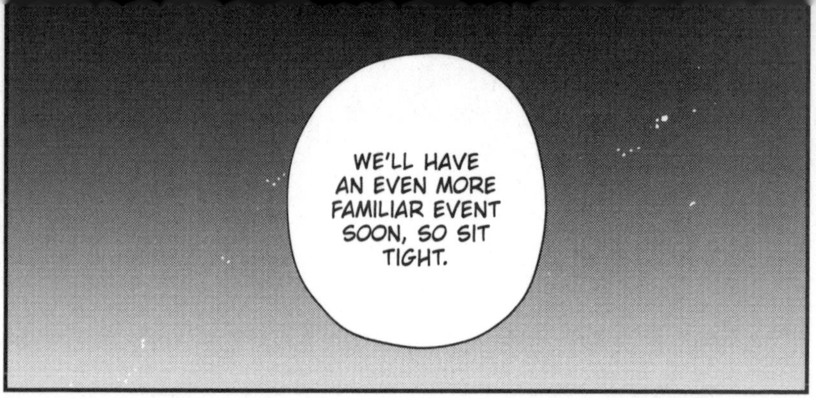
WE'LL HAVE AN EVEN MORE FAMILIAR EVENT SOON, SO SIT TIGHT.

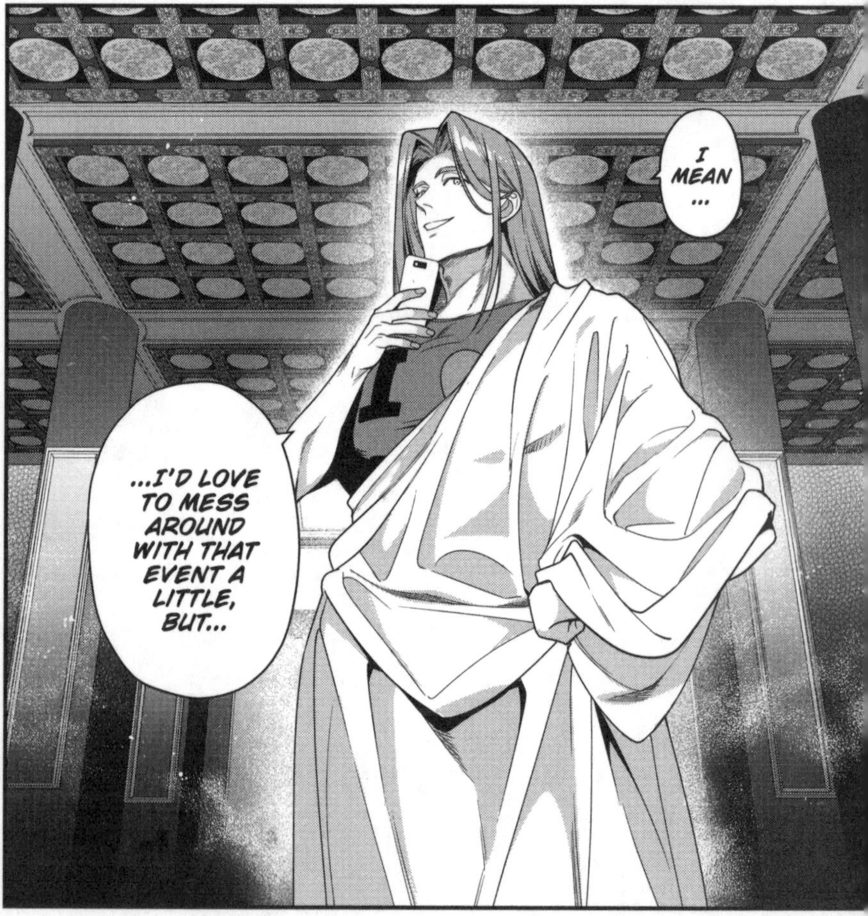
I MEAN...
...I'D LOVE TO MESS AROUND WITH THAT EVENT A LITTLE, BUT...

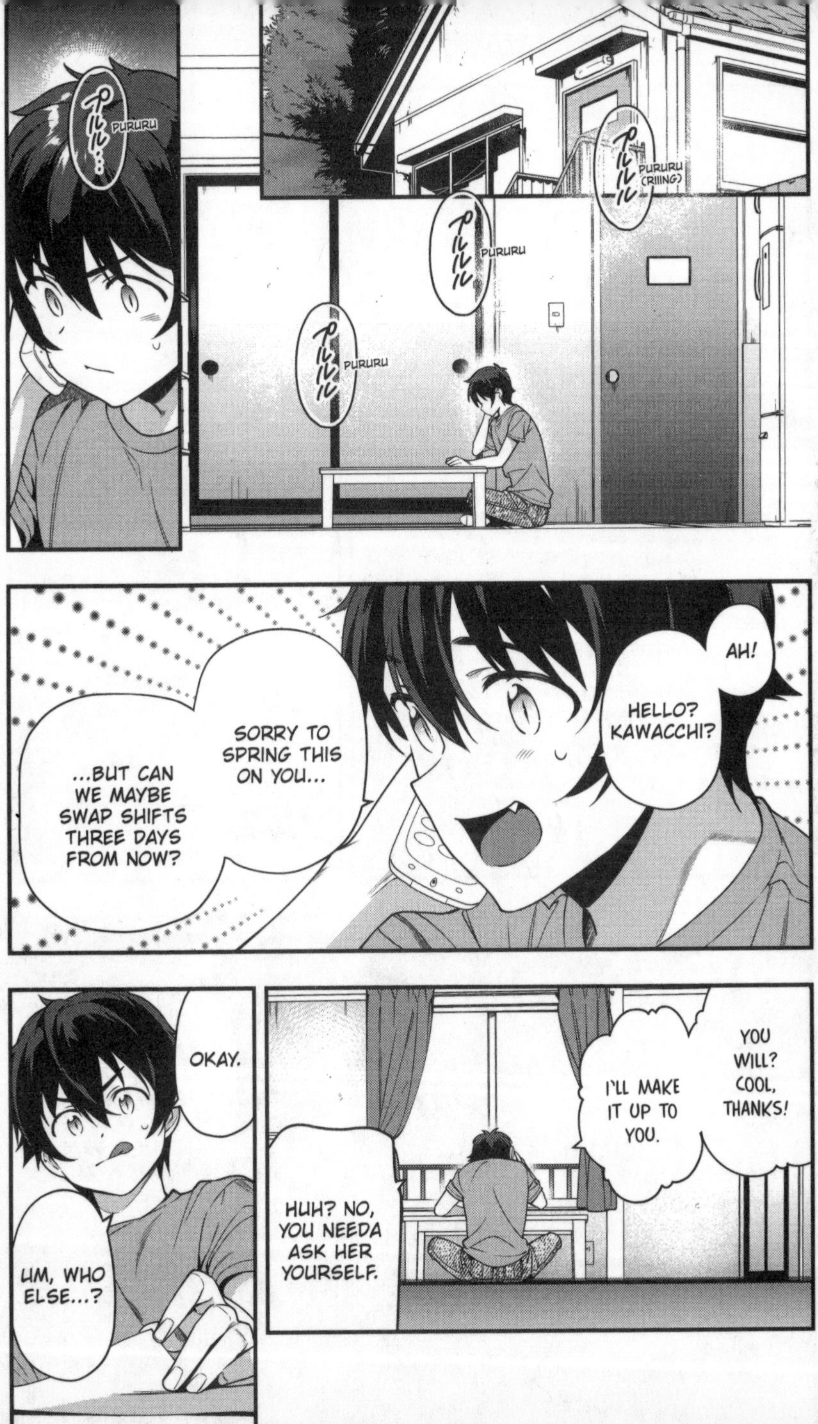
プルルル
PURURU (RIIING)
プルルル
PURURU
プルルル
PURURU
プルル…
PURURU
AH!
HELLO? KAWACCHI?
SORRY TO SPRING THIS ON YOU...
...BUT CAN WE MAYBE SWAP SHIFTS THREE DAYS FROM NOW?
YOU WILL? COOL, THANKS!
I'LL MAKE IT UP TO YOU.
HUH? NO, YOU NEEDA ASK HER YOURSELF.
OKAY.
UM, WHO ELSE...?

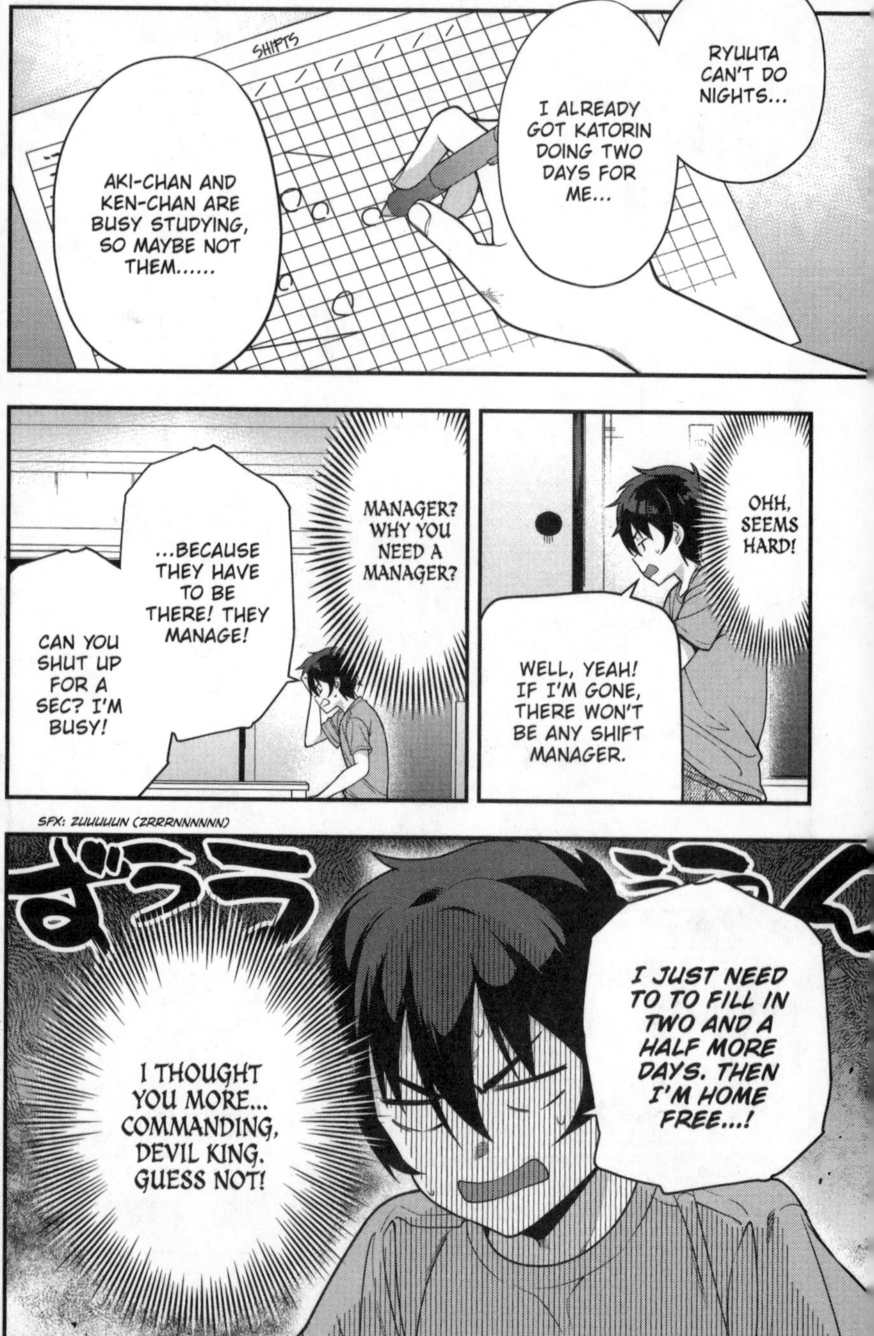
SHIFTS
RYUUTA CAN'T DO NIGHTS...
I ALREADY GOT KATORIN DOING TWO DAYS FOR ME...
AKI-CHAN AND KEN-CHAN ARE BUSY STUDYING, SO MAYBE NOT THEM......
OHH, SEEMS HARD!
WELL, YEAH! IF I'M GONE, THERE WON'T BE ANY SHIFT MANAGER.
MANAGER? WHY YOU NEED A MANAGER?
...BECAUSE THEY HAVE TO BE THERE! THEY MANAGE!
CAN YOU SHUT UP FOR A SEC? I'M BUSY!
SFX: ZUUUUUN (ZRRRNNNNNN)
I JUST NEED TO TO FILL IN TWO AND A HALF MORE DAYS. THEN I'M HOME FREE...!
I THOUGHT YOU MORE... COMMANDING, DEVIL KING. GUESS NOT!

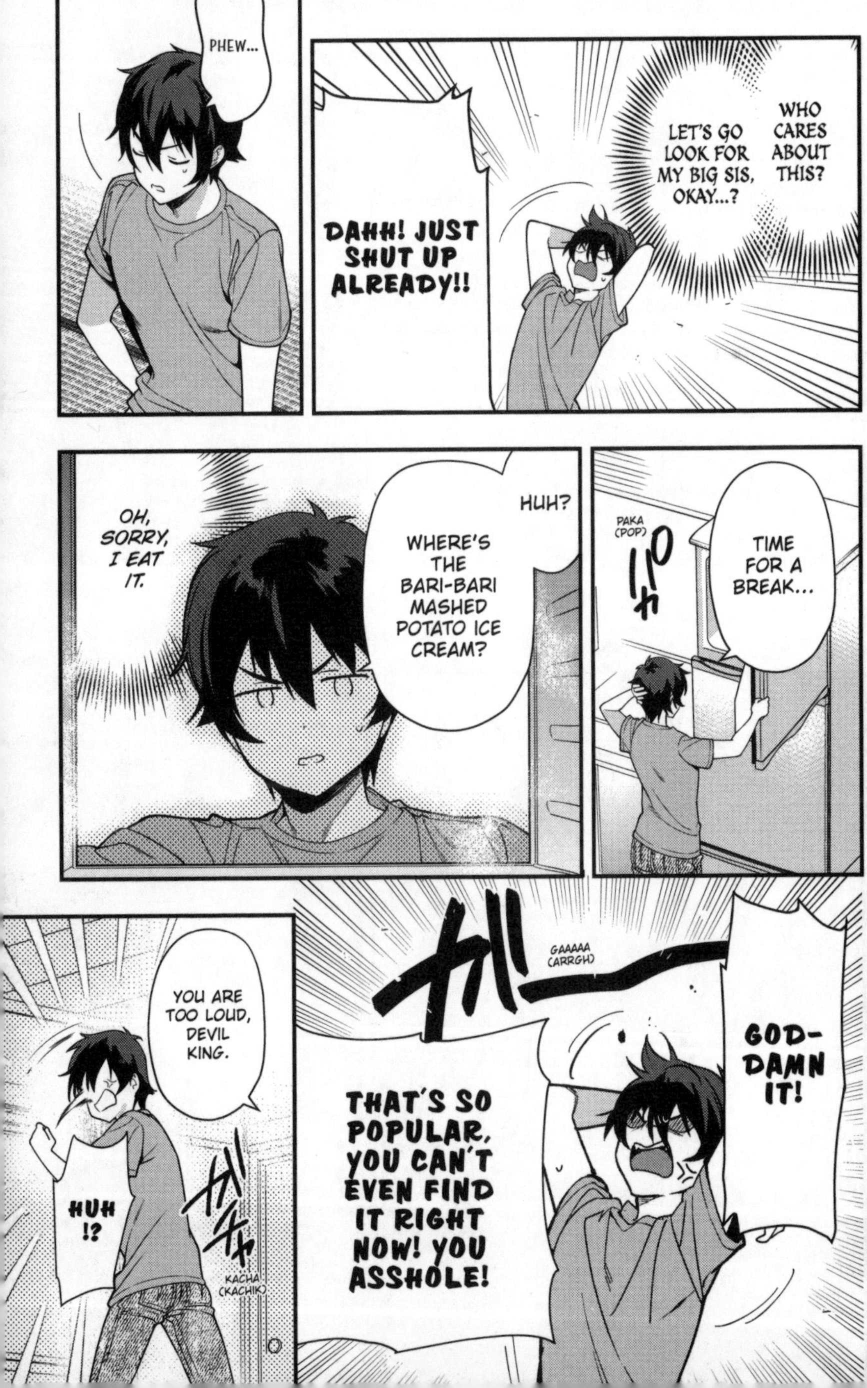
WHO CARES ABOUT THIS?
LET'S GO LOOK FOR MY BIG SIS, OKAY...?
DAHH! JUST SHUT UP ALREADY!!
PHEW...
PAKA (POP)
TIME FOR A BREAK...
HUH?
WHERE'S THE BARI-BARI MASHED POTATO ICE CREAM?
OH, SORRY, I EAT IT.
GAAAAA (ARRGH)
GOD-DAMN IT!
THAT'S SO POPULAR, YOU CAN'T EVEN FIND IT RIGHT NOW! YOU ASSHOLE!
YOU ARE TOO LOUD, DEVIL KING.
KACHA (KACHIK)
HUH !?

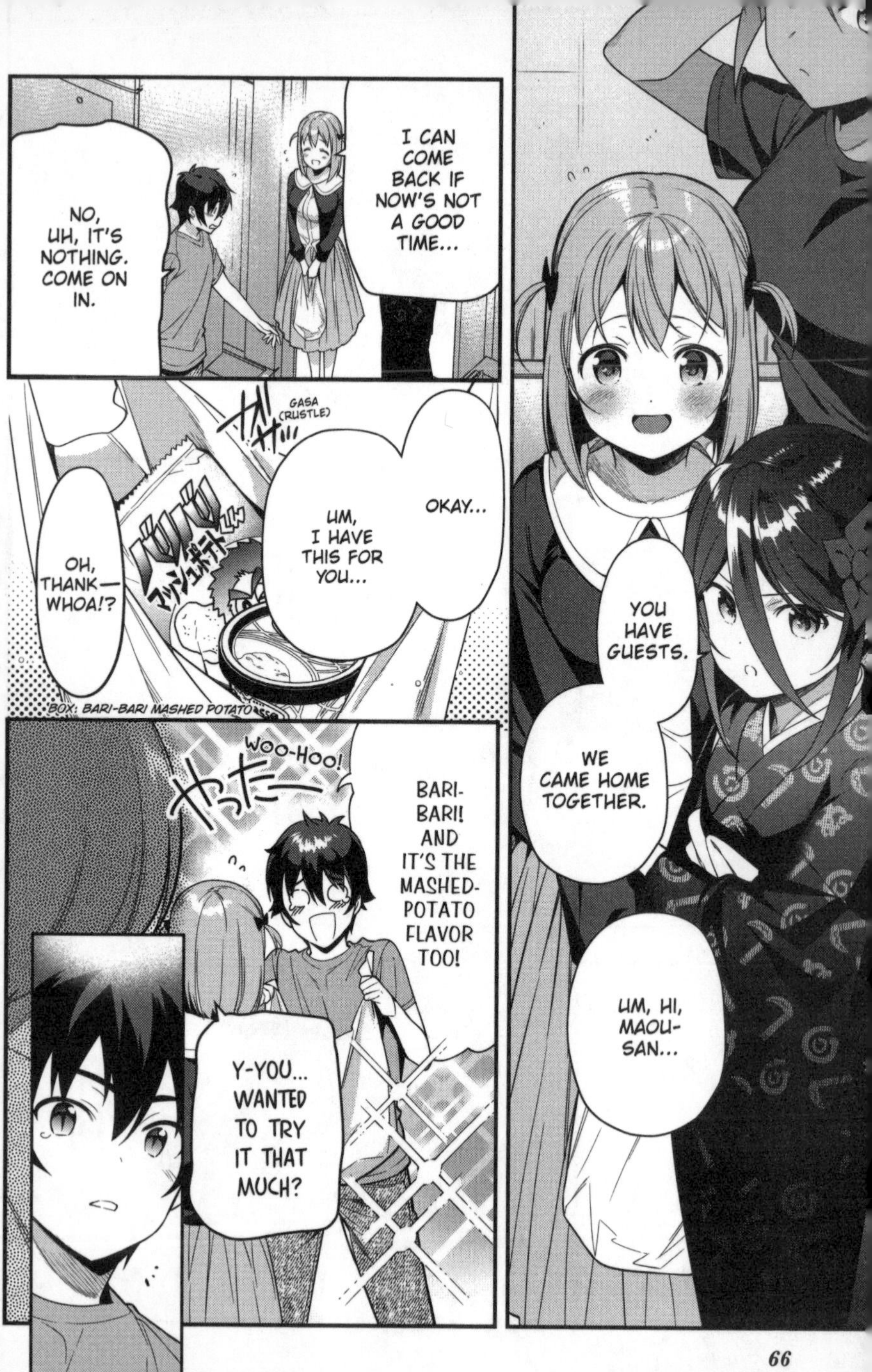
YOU HAVE GUESTS.
WE CAME HOME TOGETHER.
UM, HI, MAOU-SAN...
I CAN COME BACK IF NOW'S NOT A GOOD TIME...
NO, UH, IT'S NOTHING. COME ON IN.
OKAY...
GASA (RUSTLE)
UM, I HAVE THIS FOR YOU...
OH, THANK— WHOA!?
BOX: BARI-BARI MASHED POTATO
WOO-HOO!
BARI-BARI! AND IT'S THE MASHED-POTATO FLAVOR TOO!
Y-YOU... WANTED TO TRY IT THAT MUCH?

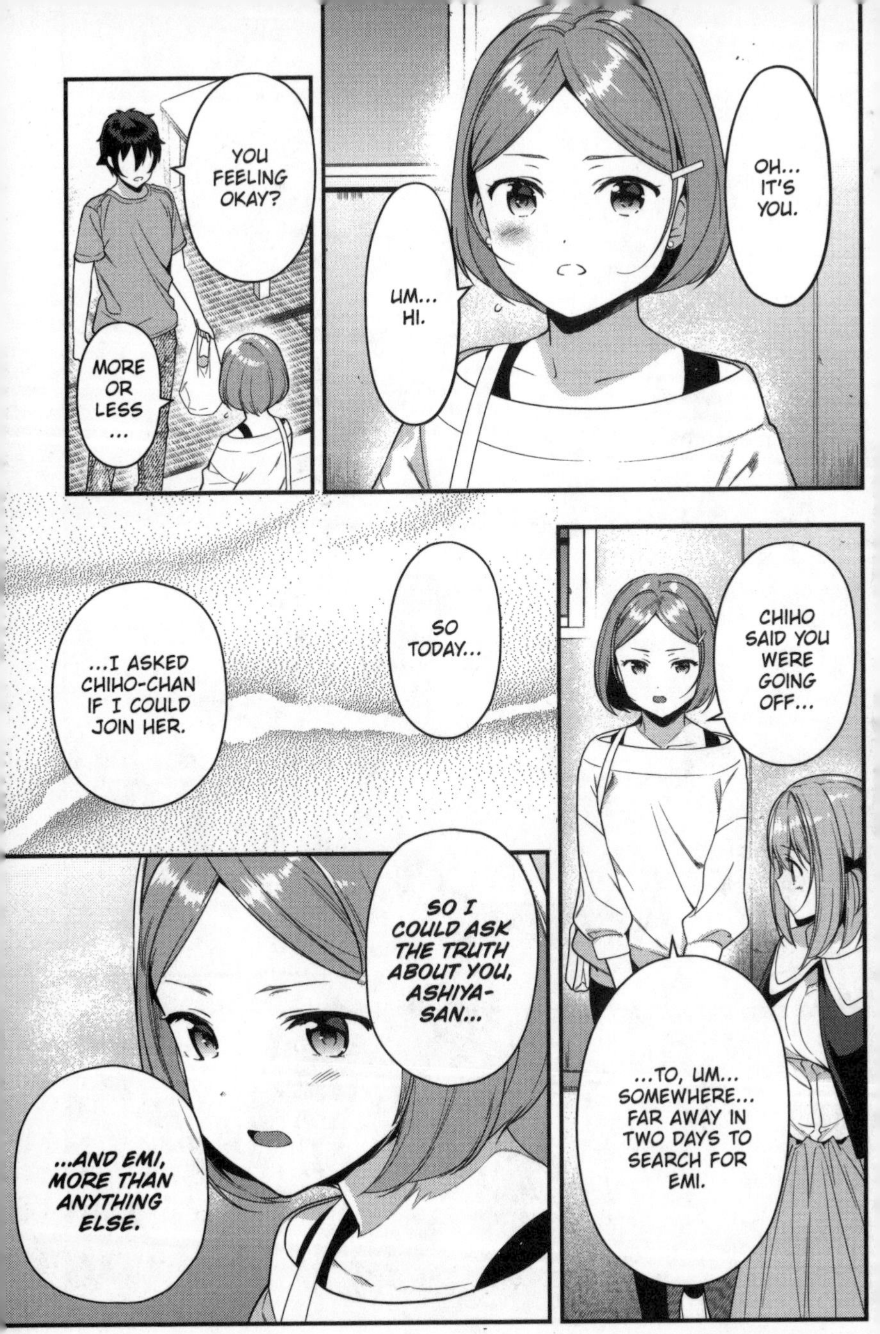
OH... IT'S YOU.
UM... HI.
YOU FEELING OKAY?
MORE OR LESS ...
CHIHO SAID YOU WERE GOING OFF...
...TO, UM... SOMEWHERE... FAR AWAY IN TWO DAYS TO SEARCH FOR EMI.
SO TODAY...
...I ASKED CHIHO-CHAN IF I COULD JOIN HER.
SO I COULD ASK THE TRUTH ABOUT YOU, ASHIYA-SAN...
...AND EMI, MORE THAN ANYTHING ELSE.

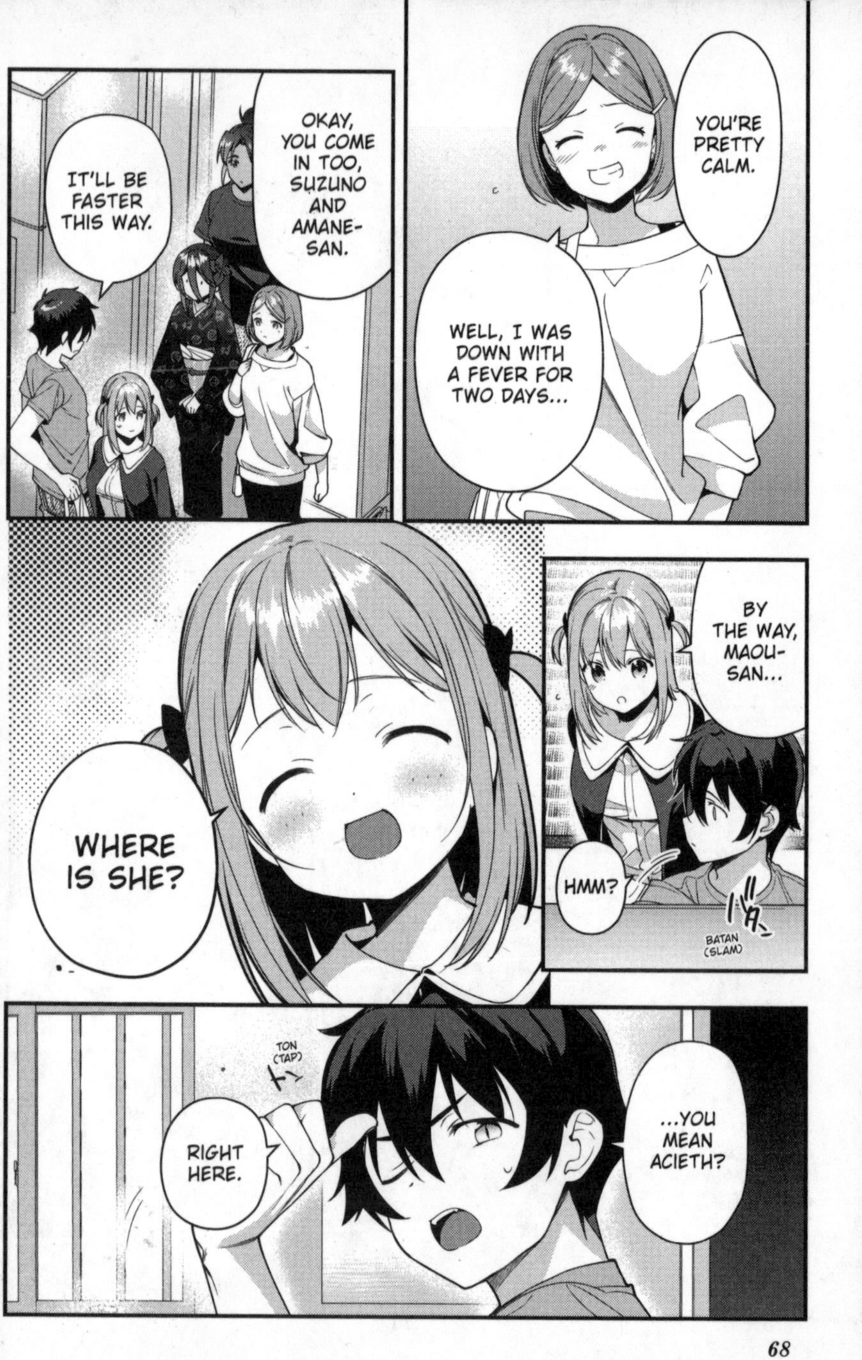
YOU'RE PRETTY CALM.
WELL, I WAS DOWN WITH A FEVER FOR TWO DAYS...
OKAY, YOU COME IN TOO, SUZUNO AND AMANE-SAN.
IT'LL BE FASTER THIS WAY.
BY THE WAY, MAOU-SAN...
HMM?
BATAN (SLAM)
WHERE IS SHE?
...YOU MEAN ACIETH?
TON (TAP)
RIGHT HERE.

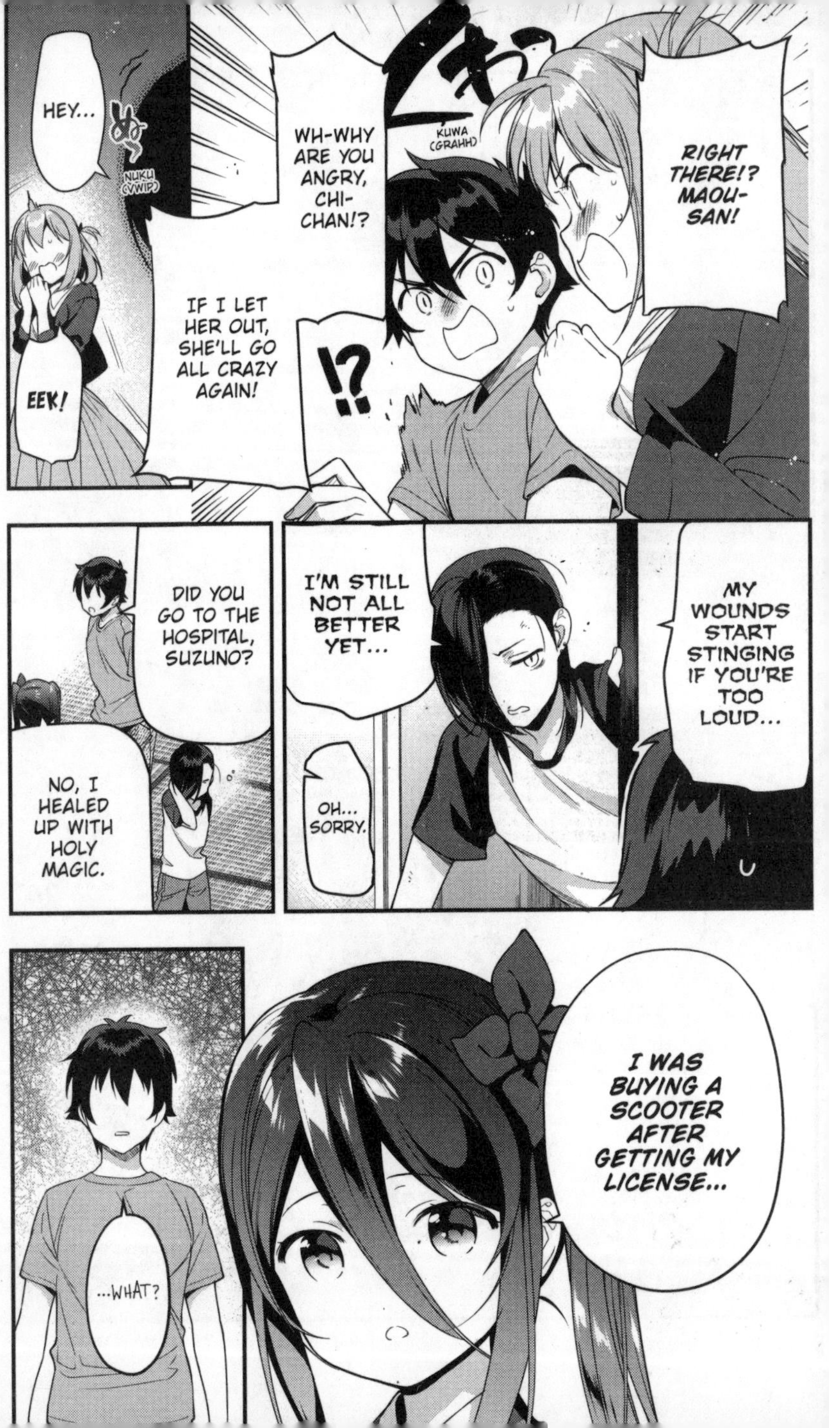
RIGHT THERE!? MAOU-SAN!
KUWA (GRAHH)
WH-WHY ARE YOU ANGRY, CHI-CHAN!?
!?
IF I LET HER OUT, SHE'LL GO ALL CRAZY AGAIN!
HEY...
NUKU (YWIP)
EEK!
MY WOUNDS START STINGING IF YOU'RE TOO LOUD...
I'M STILL NOT ALL BETTER YET...
OH... SORRY.
DID YOU GO TO THE HOSPITAL, SUZUNO?
NO, I HEALED UP WITH HOLY MAGIC.
I WAS BUYING A SCOOTER AFTER GETTING MY LICENSE...
...WHAT?

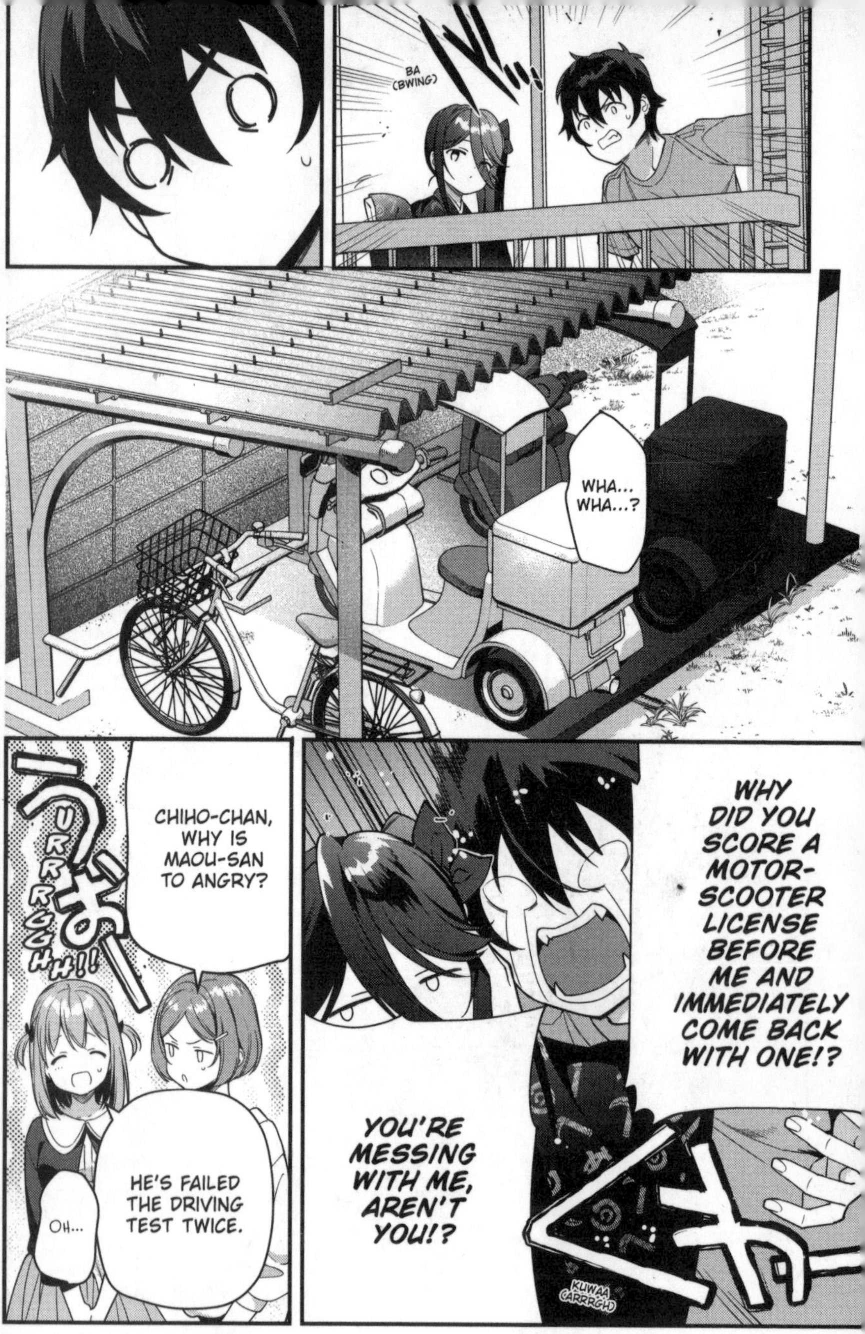
BA (BWING)
WHA... WHA...?
WHY DID YOU SCORE A MOTOR-SCOOTER LICENSE BEFORE ME AND IMMEDIATELY COME BACK WITH ONE!?
YOU'RE MESSING WITH ME, AREN'T YOU!?
KUWAA (ARRRGH)
URRRGGHH!!
CHIHO-CHAN, WHY IS MAOU-SAN TO ANGRY?
HE'S FAILED THE DRIVING TEST TWICE.
OH...

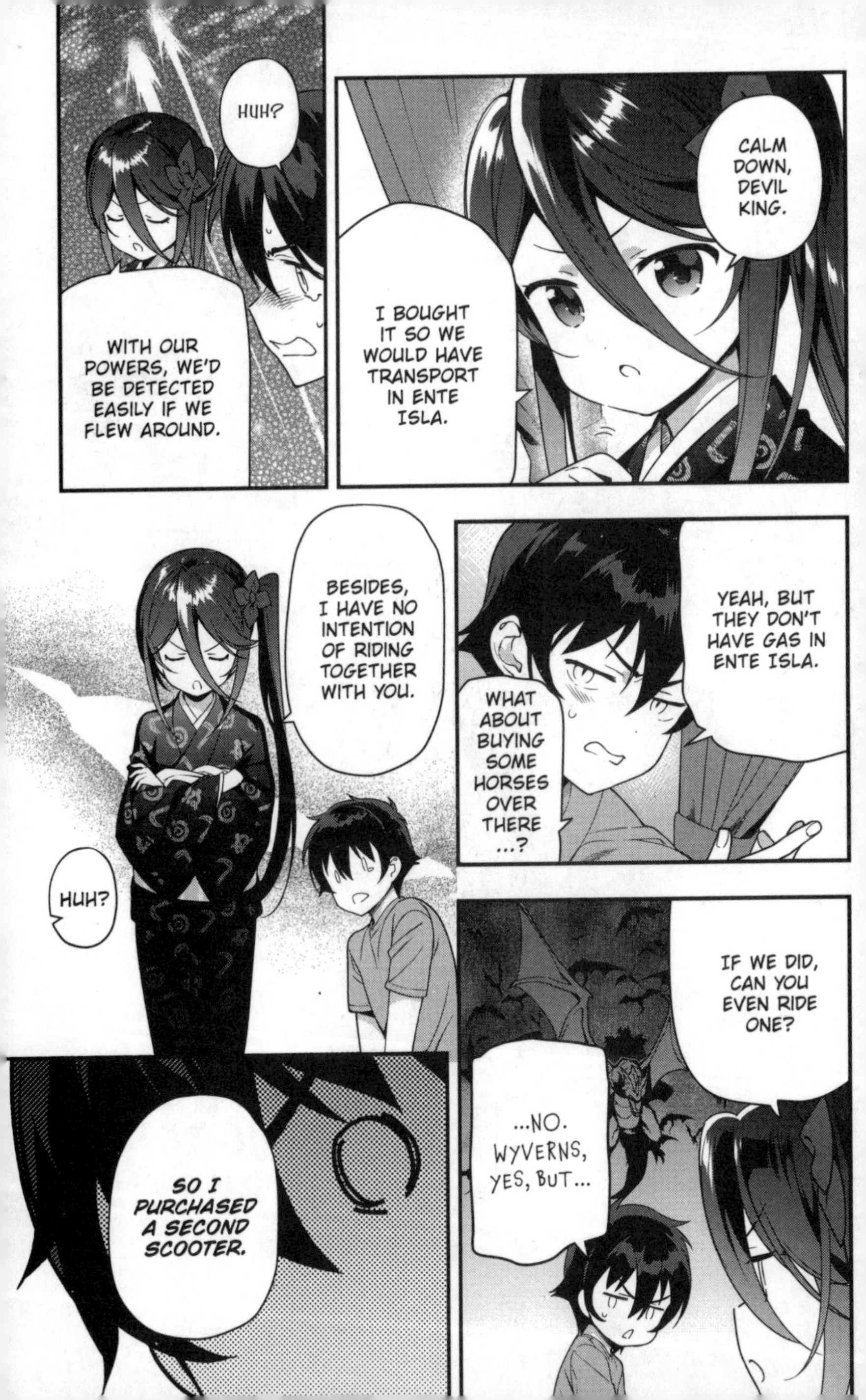
CALM DOWN, DEVIL KING.
I BOUGHT IT SO WE WOULD HAVE TRANSPORT IN ENTE ISLA.
HUH?
WITH OUR POWERS, WE'D BE DETECTED EASILY IF WE FLEW AROUND.
YEAH, BUT THEY DON'T HAVE GAS IN ENTE ISLA.
WHAT ABOUT BUYING SOME HORSES OVER THERE ...?
IF WE DID, CAN YOU EVEN RIDE ONE?
...NO. WYVERNS, YES, BUT...
BESIDES, I HAVE NO INTENTION OF RIDING TOGETHER WITH YOU.
HUH?
SO I PURCHASED A SECOND SCOOTER.

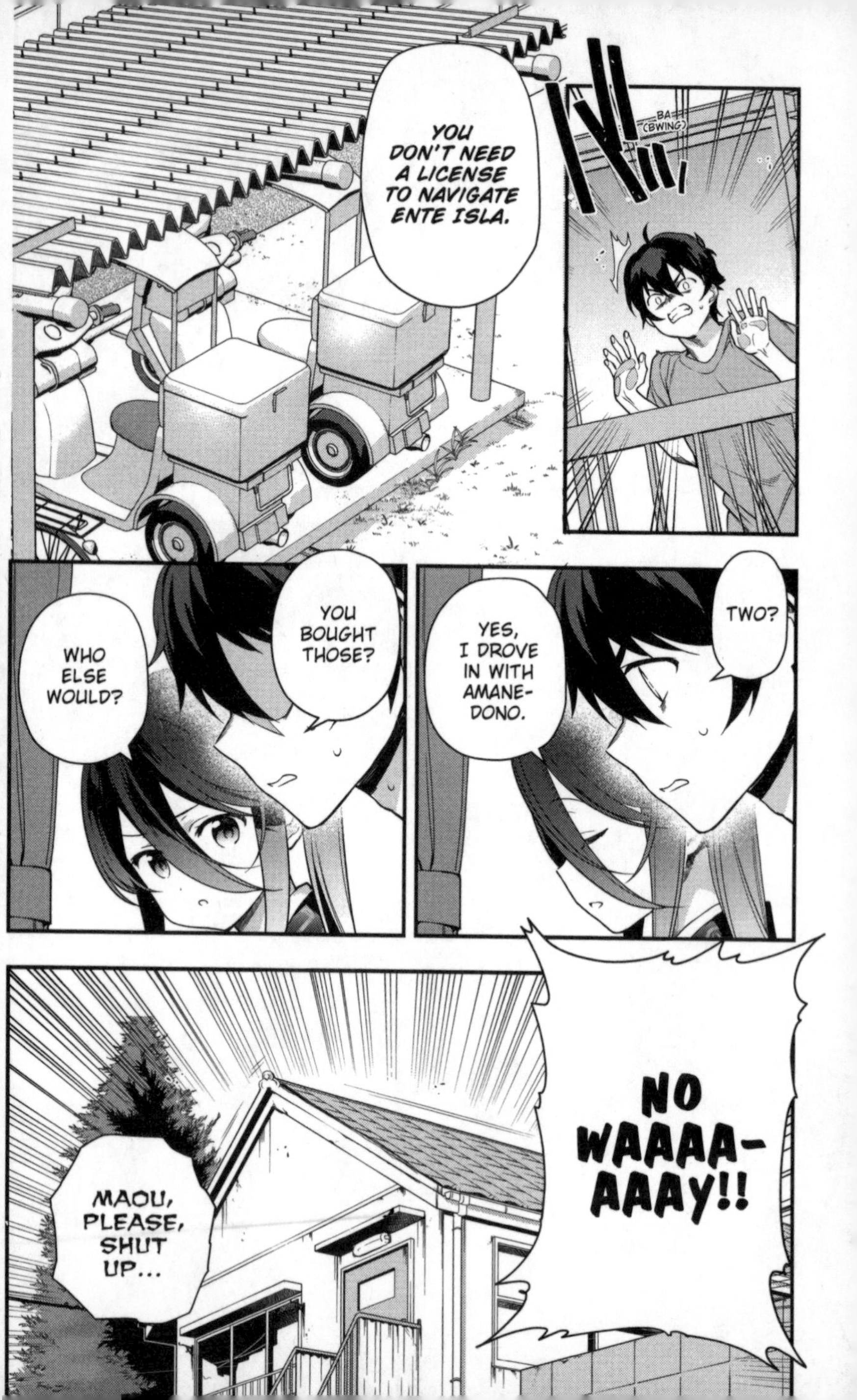
BA (BWING)
YOU DON'T NEED A LICENSE TO NAVIGATE ENTE ISLA.
TWO?
YES, I DROVE IN WITH AMANE-DONO.
YOU BOUGHT THOSE?
WHO ELSE WOULD?
NO WAAAA-AAAY!!
MAOU, PLEASE, SHUT UP...

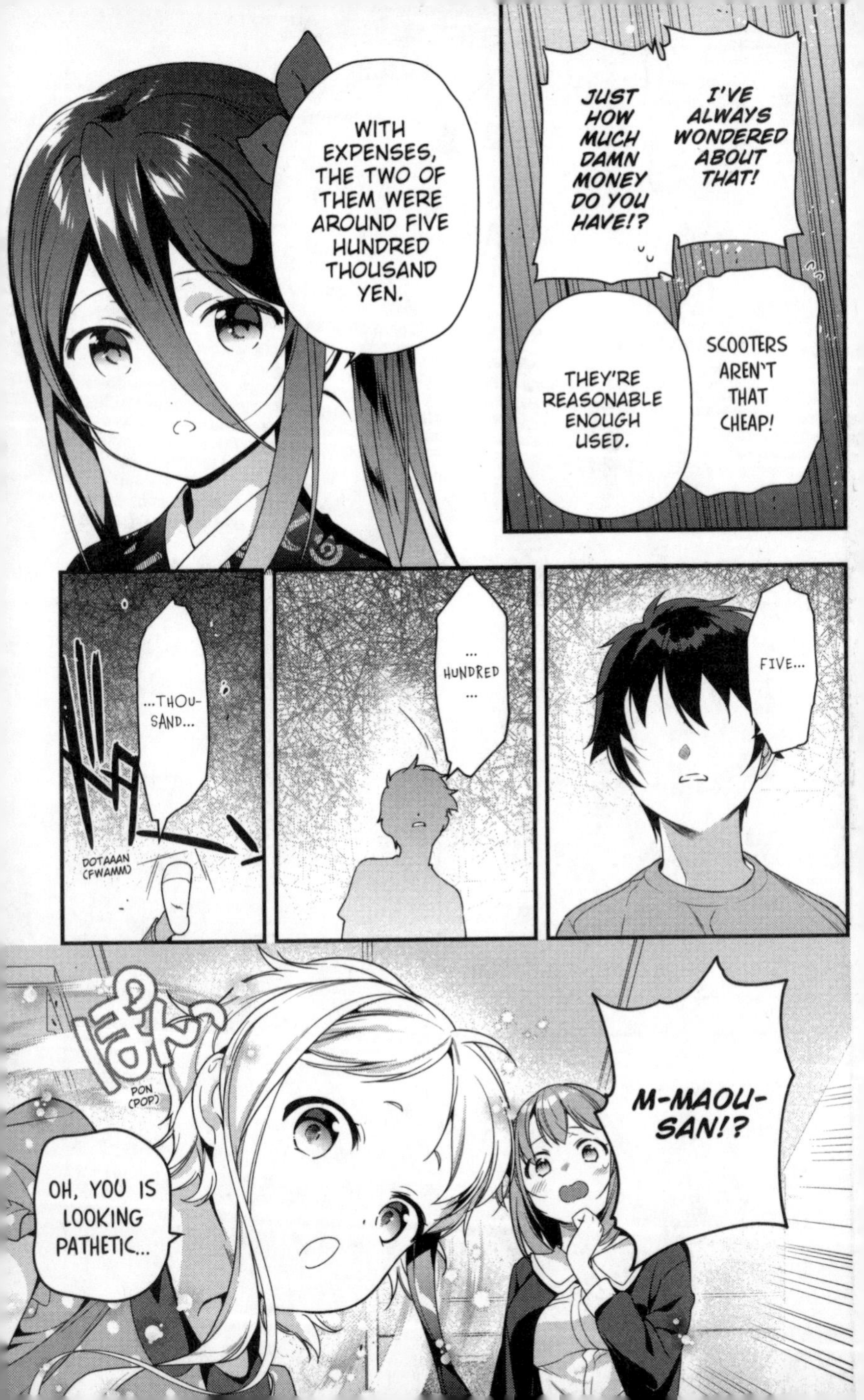
I'VE ALWAYS WONDERED ABOUT THAT!
JUST HOW MUCH DAMN MONEY DO YOU HAVE!?
SCOOTERS AREN'T THAT CHEAP!
THEY'RE REASONABLE ENOUGH USED.
WITH EXPENSES, THE TWO OF THEM WERE AROUND FIVE HUNDRED THOUSAND YEN.
FIVE...
...HUNDRED...
...THOUSAND...
DOTAAAN (FWAMM)
M-MAOU-SAN!?
ぽんっ
PON (POP)
OH, YOU IS LOOKING PATHETIC...

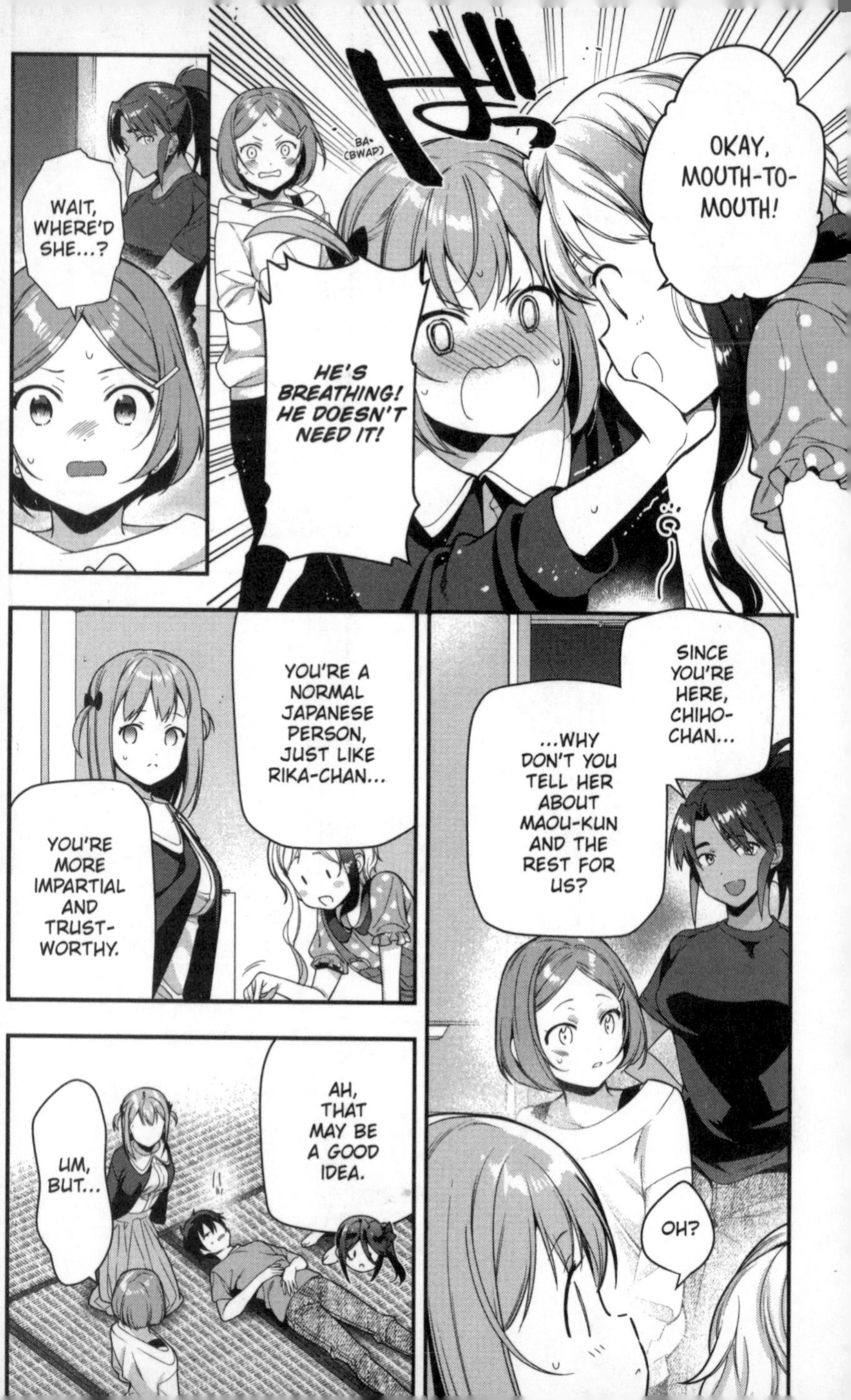
OKAY, MOUTH-TO-MOUTH!
BA- (BWAP)
HE'S BREATHING! HE DOESN'T NEED IT!
WAIT, WHERE'D SHE...?
SINCE YOU'RE HERE, CHIHO-CHAN...
...WHY DON'T YOU TELL HER ABOUT MAOU-KUN AND THE REST FOR US?
OH?
YOU'RE A NORMAL JAPANESE PERSON, JUST LIKE RIKA-CHAN...
YOU'RE MORE IMPARTIAL AND TRUST-WORTHY.
AH, THAT MAY BE A GOOD IDEA.
UM, BUT...

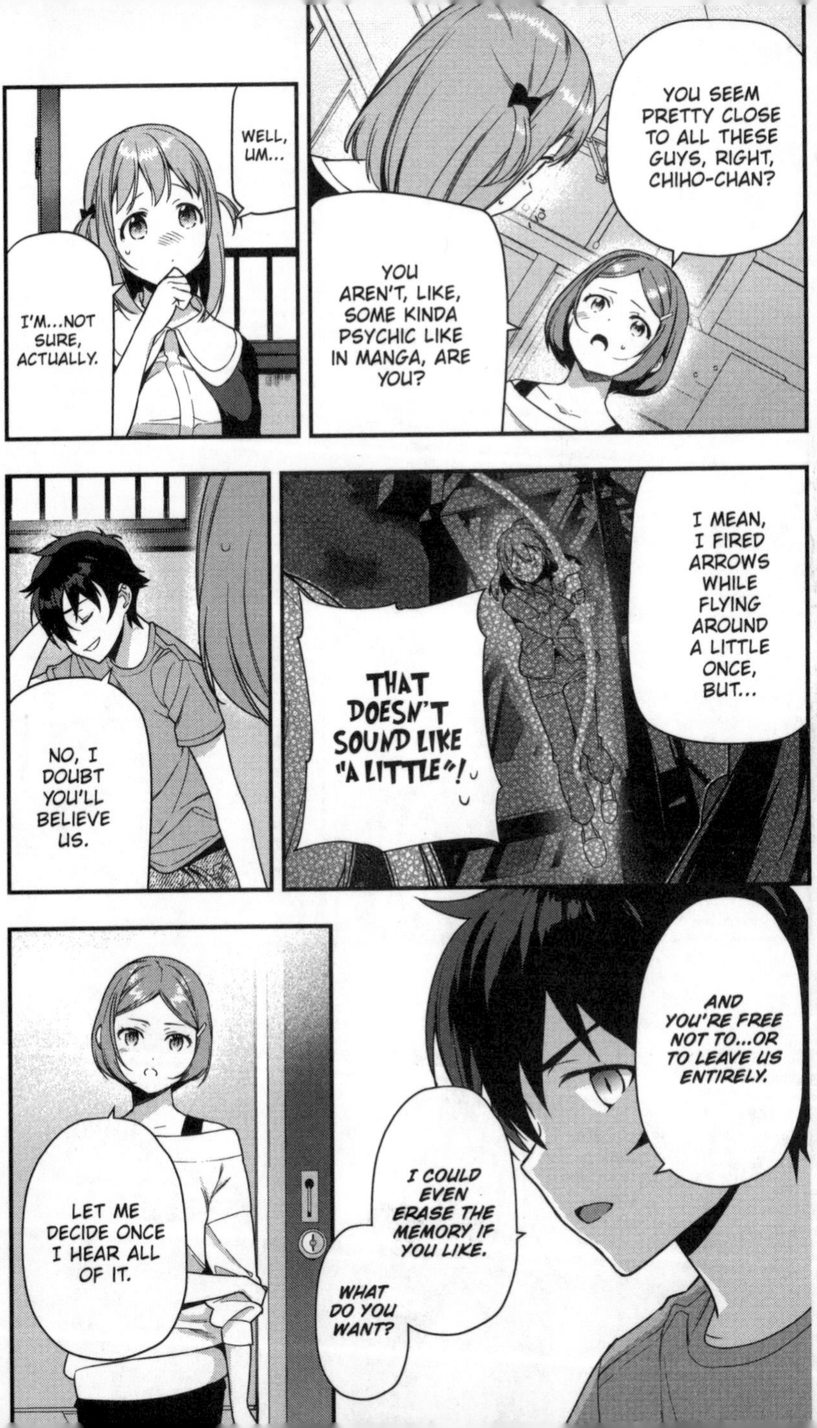
YOU SEEM PRETTY CLOSE TO ALL THESE GUYS, RIGHT, CHIHO-CHAN?
YOU AREN'T, LIKE, SOME KINDA PSYCHIC LIKE IN MANGA, ARE YOU?
WELL, UM...
I'M...NOT SURE, ACTUALLY.
I MEAN, I FIRED ARROWS WHILE FLYING AROUND A LITTLE ONCE, BUT...
THAT DOESN'T SOUND LIKE "A LITTLE"!
NO, I DOUBT YOU'LL BELIEVE US.
AND YOU'RE FREE NOT TO...OR TO LEAVE US ENTIRELY.
I COULD EVEN ERASE THE MEMORY IF YOU LIKE.
WHAT DO YOU WANT?
LET ME DECIDE ONCE I HEAR ALL OF IT.

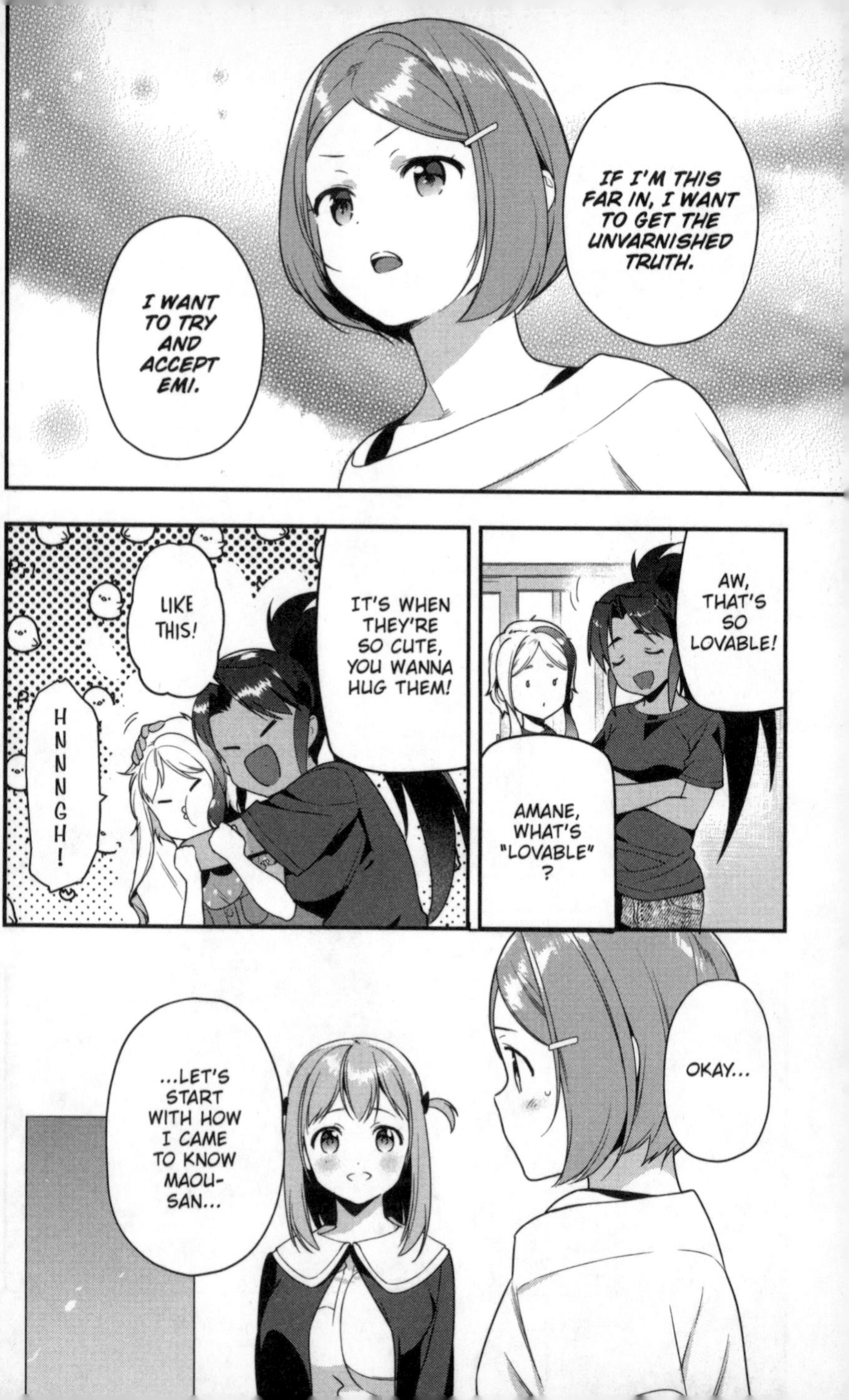
IF I'M THIS FAR IN, I WANT TO GET THE UNVARNISHED TRUTH.
I WANT TO TRY AND ACCEPT EMI.
AW, THAT'S SO LOVABLE!
AMANE, WHAT'S "LOVABLE"?
IT'S WHEN THEY'RE SO CUTE, YOU WANNA HUG THEM!
LIKE THIS!
HNNNGH!
OKAY...
...LET'S START WITH HOW I CAME TO KNOW MAOU-SAN...

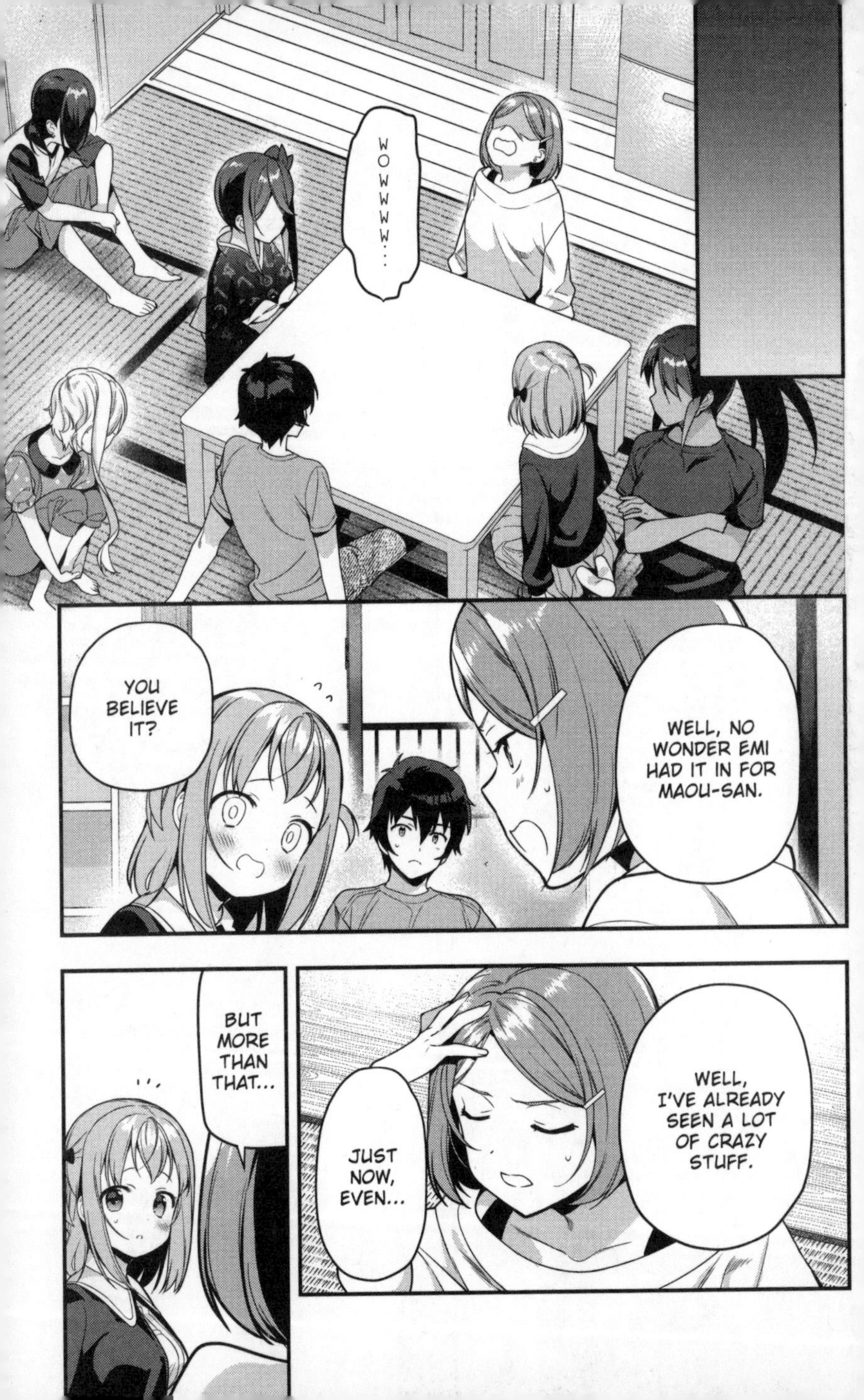
WOWWWW...
WELL, NO WONDER EMI HAD IT IN FOR MAOU-SAN.
YOU BELIEVE IT?
WELL, I'VE ALREADY SEEN A LOT OF CRAZY STUFF.
JUST NOW, EVEN...
BUT MORE THAN THAT...

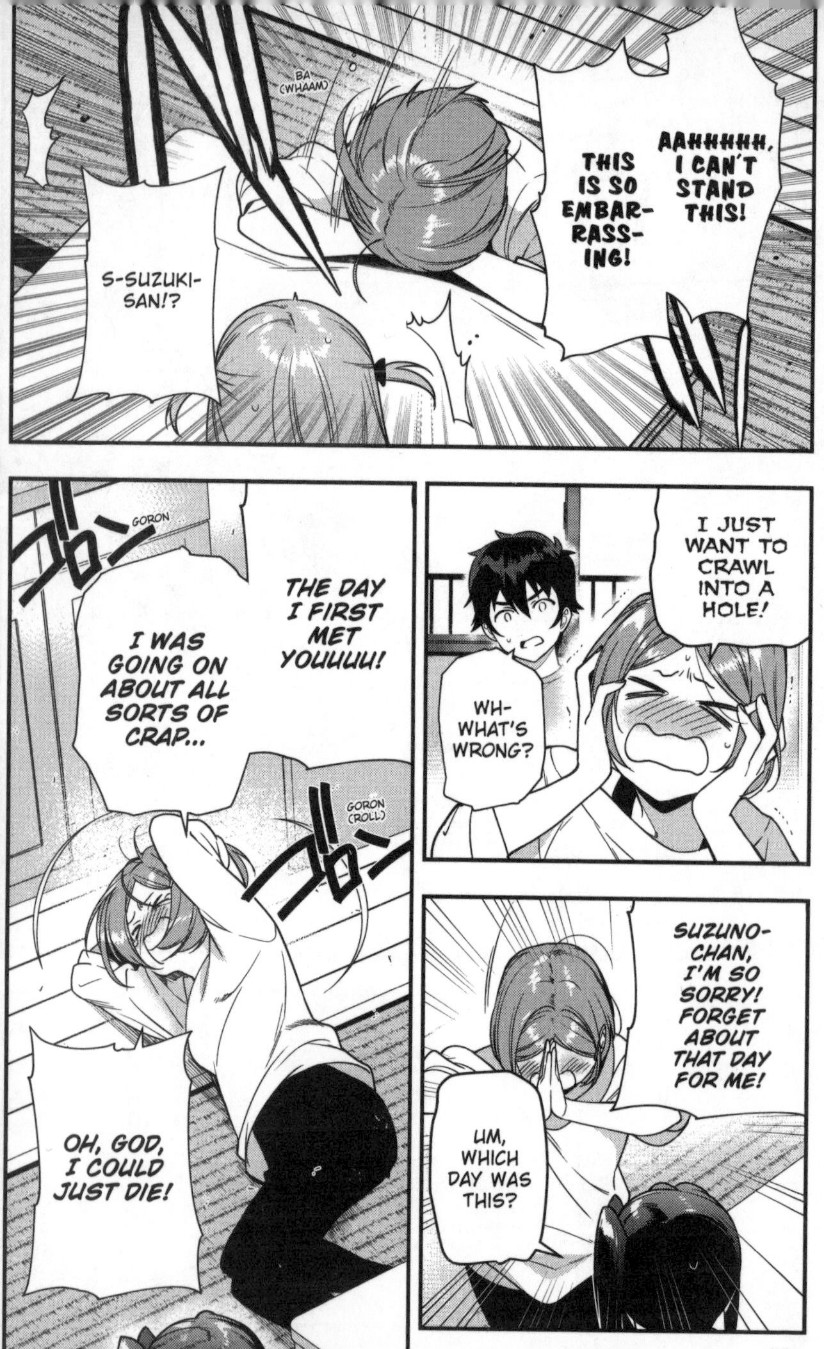
AAHHHHH, I CAN'T STAND THIS!
THIS IS SO EMBARRASSING!
BA (WHAAM)
S-SUZUKI-SAN!?
I JUST WANT TO CRAWL INTO A HOLE!
WH-WHAT'S WRONG?
SUZUNO-CHAN, I'M SO SORRY! FORGET ABOUT THAT DAY FOR ME!
UM, WHICH DAY WAS THIS?
GORON
THE DAY I FIRST MET YOUUUUU!
I WAS GOING ON ABOUT ALL SORTS OF CRAP...
GORON (ROLL)
OH, GOD, I COULD JUST DIE!

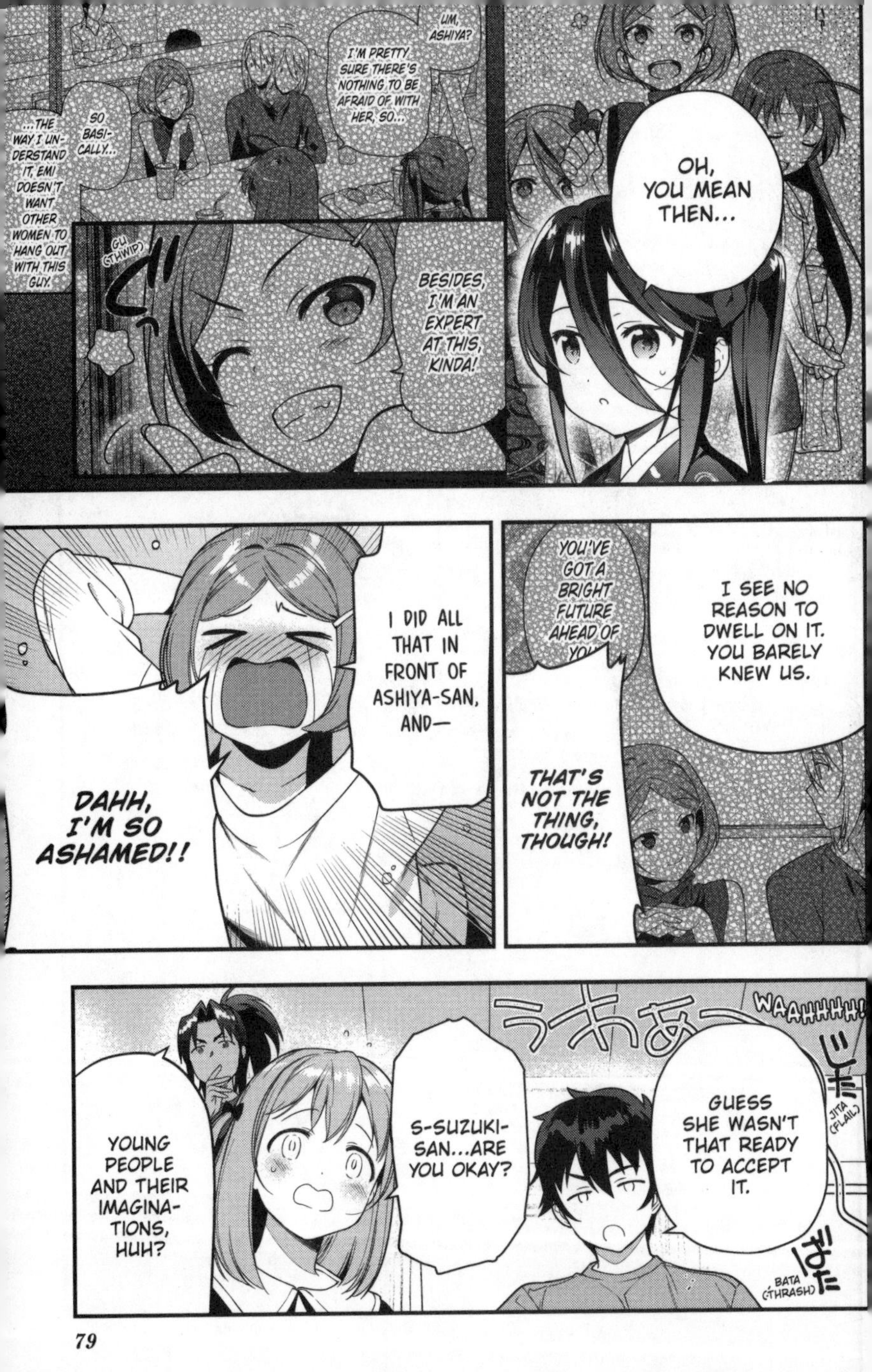
OH, YOU MEAN THEN...
UM, ASHIYA?
I'M PRETTY SURE THERE'S NOTHING TO BE AFRAID OF WITH HER, SO...
SO BASICALLY...
...THE WAY I UNDERSTAND IT, EMI DOESN'T WANT OTHER WOMEN TO HANG OUT WITH THIS GUY.
GU (THWIP)
BESIDES, I'M AN EXPERT AT THIS, KINDA!
I SEE NO REASON TO DWELL ON IT. YOU BARELY KNEW US.
YOU'VE GOT A BRIGHT FUTURE AHEAD OF YOU
THAT'S NOT THE THING, THOUGH!
I DID ALL THAT IN FRONT OF ASHIYA-SAN, AND—
DAHH, I'M SO ASHAMED!!
うわあっ
WAAHHHH!
じた
JITA (FLAIL)
ばた
BATA (THRASH)
GUESS SHE WASN'T THAT READY TO ACCEPT IT.
S-SUZUKI-SAN...ARE YOU OKAY?
YOUNG PEOPLE AND THEIR IMAGINATIONS, HUH?

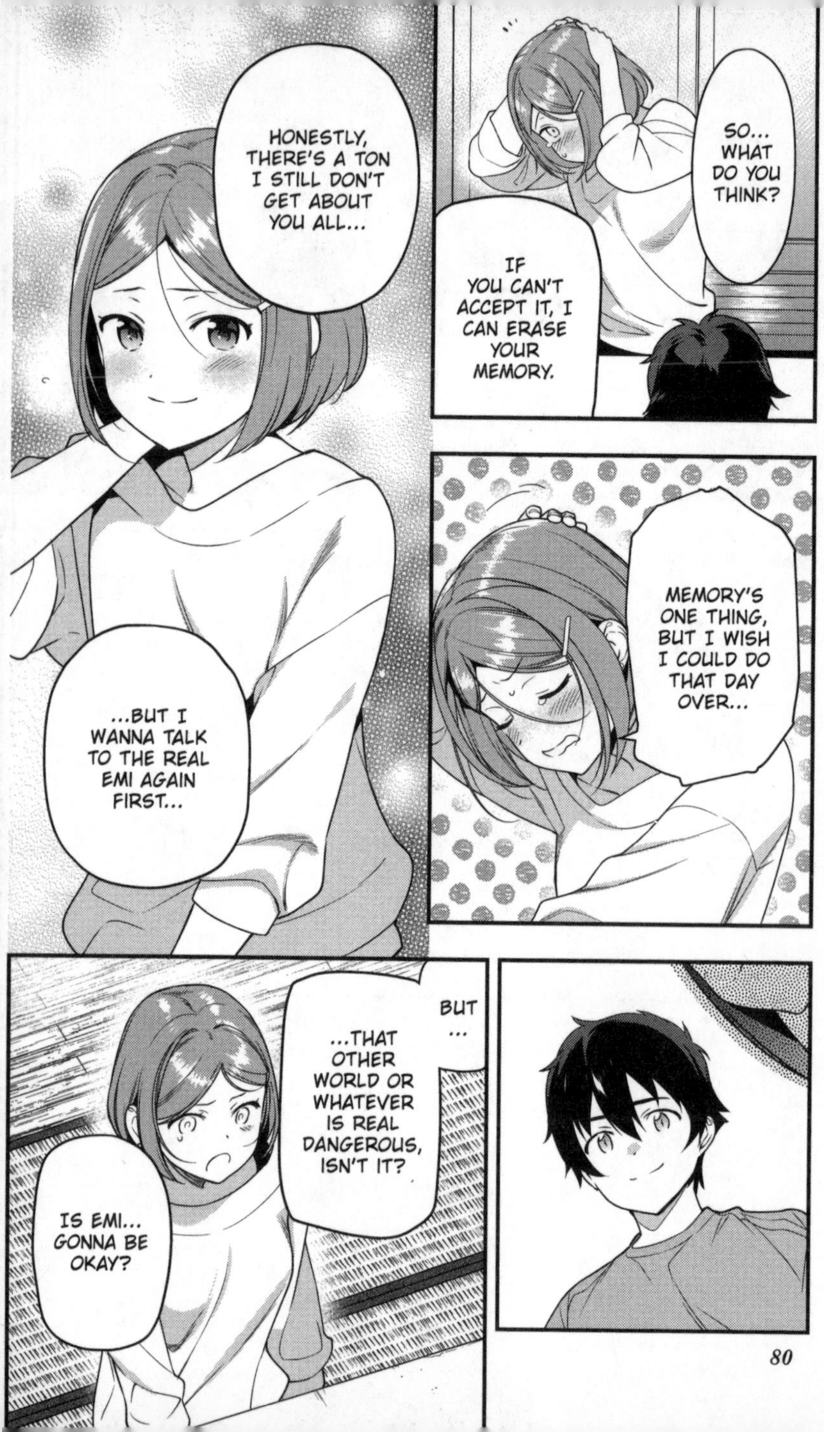
SO... WHAT DO YOU THINK?
IF YOU CAN'T ACCEPT IT, I CAN ERASE YOUR MEMORY.
MEMORY'S ONE THING, BUT I WISH I COULD DO THAT DAY OVER...
HONESTLY, THERE'S A TON I STILL DON'T GET ABOUT YOU ALL...
...BUT I WANNA TALK TO THE REAL EMI AGAIN FIRST...
BUT...
...THAT OTHER WORLD OR WHATEVER IS REAL DANGEROUS, ISN'T IT?
IS EMI... GONNA BE OKAY?

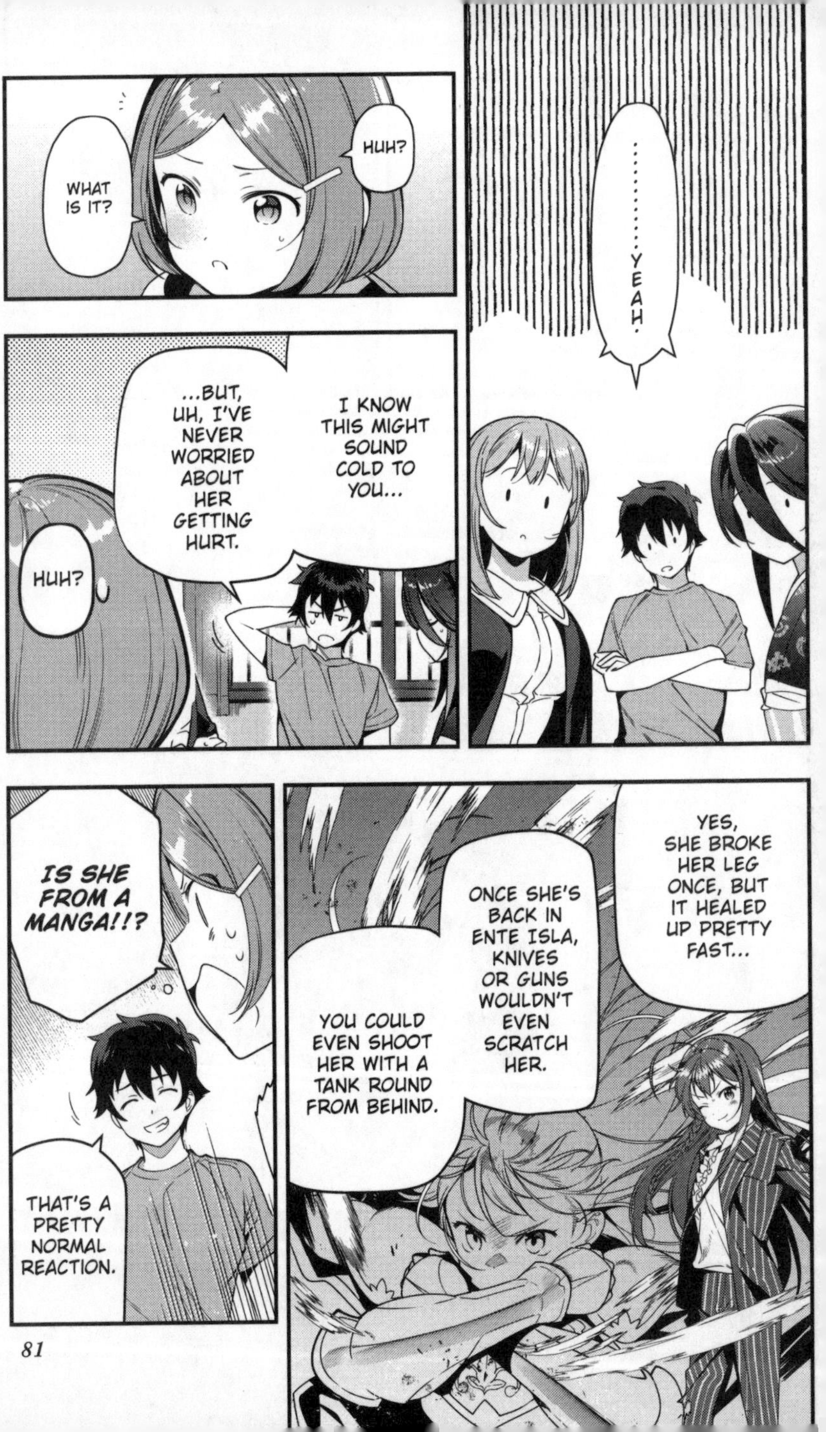
......YEAH.
HUH?
WHAT IS IT?
I KNOW THIS MIGHT SOUND COLD TO YOU...
...BUT, UH, I'VE NEVER WORRIED ABOUT HER GETTING HURT.
HUH?
YES, SHE BROKE HER LEG ONCE, BUT IT HEALED UP PRETTY FAST...
ONCE SHE'S BACK IN ENTE ISLA, KNIVES OR GUNS WOULDN'T EVEN SCRATCH HER.
YOU COULD EVEN SHOOT HER WITH A TANK ROUND FROM BEHIND.
IS SHE FROM A MANGA!!?
THAT'S A PRETTY NORMAL REACTION.

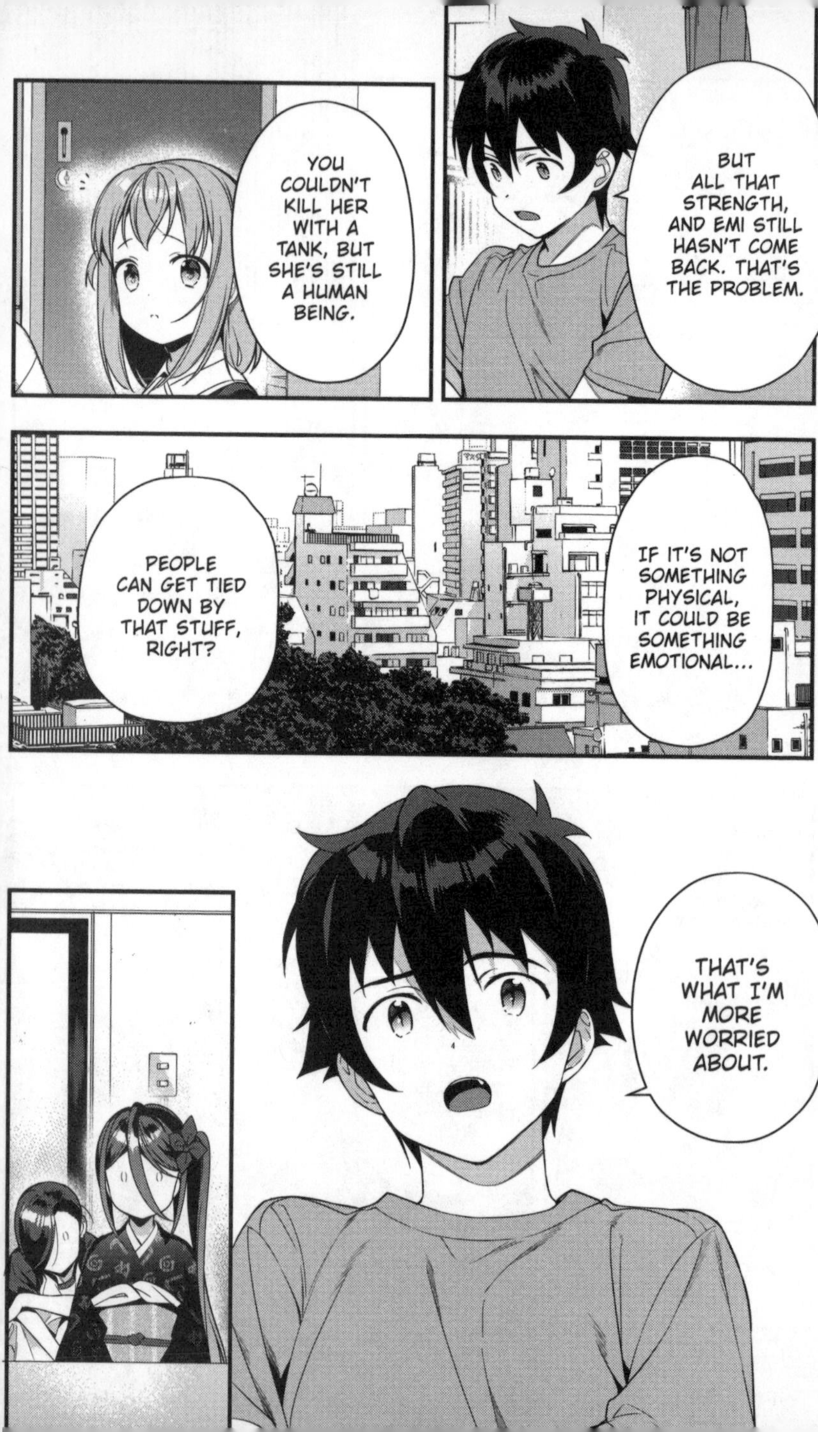
BUT ALL THAT STRENGTH, AND EMI STILL HASN'T COME BACK. THAT'S THE PROBLEM.
YOU COULDN'T KILL HER WITH A TANK, BUT SHE'S STILL A HUMAN BEING.
IF IT'S NOT SOMETHING PHYSICAL, IT COULD BE SOMETHING EMOTIONAL...
PEOPLE CAN GET TIED DOWN BY THAT STUFF, RIGHT?
THAT'S WHAT I'M MORE WORRIED ABOUT.

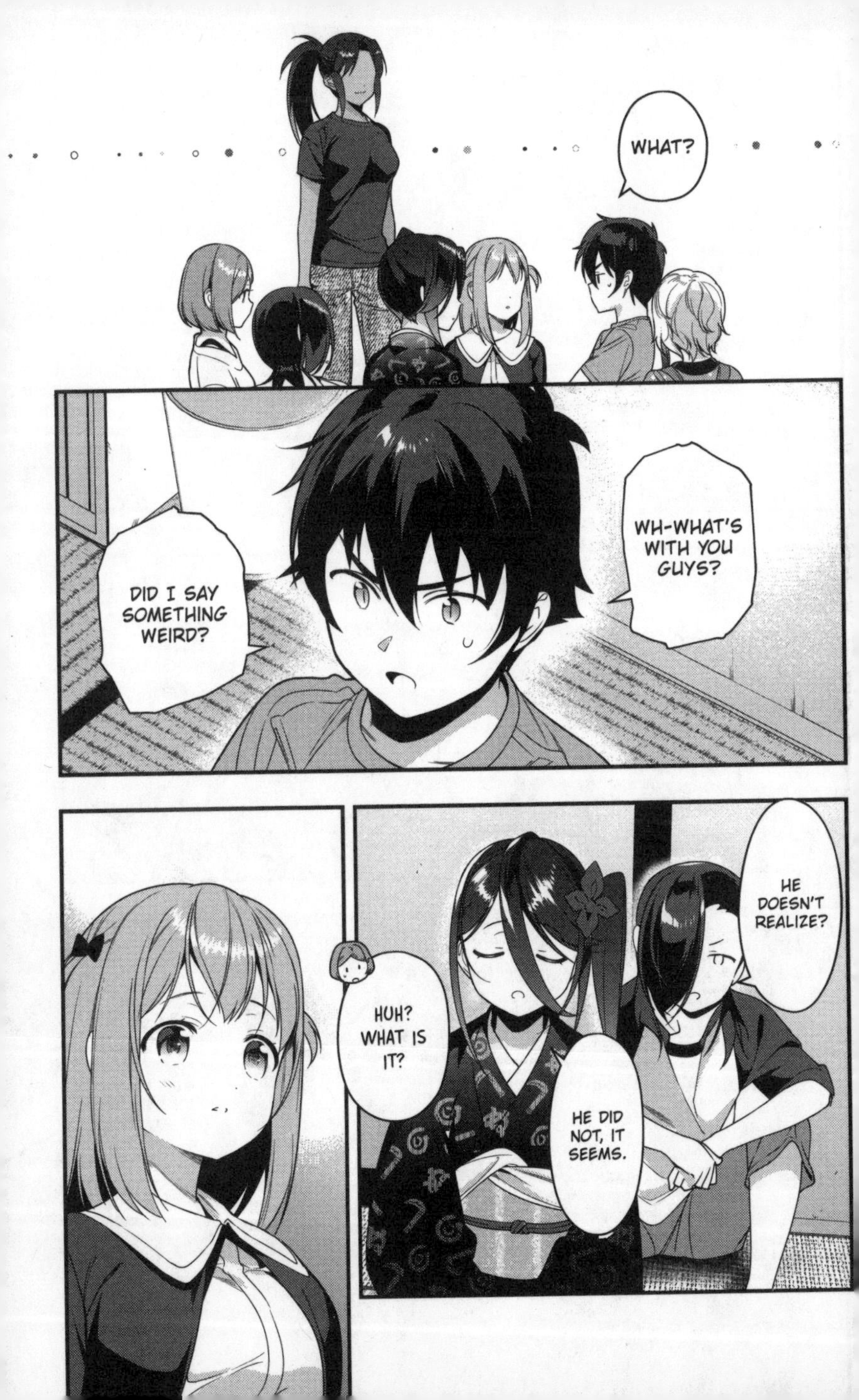
WHAT?
WH-WHAT'S WITH YOU GUYS?
DID I SAY SOMETHING WEIRD?
HE DOESN'T REALIZE?
HE DID NOT, IT SEEMS.
HUH? WHAT IS IT?

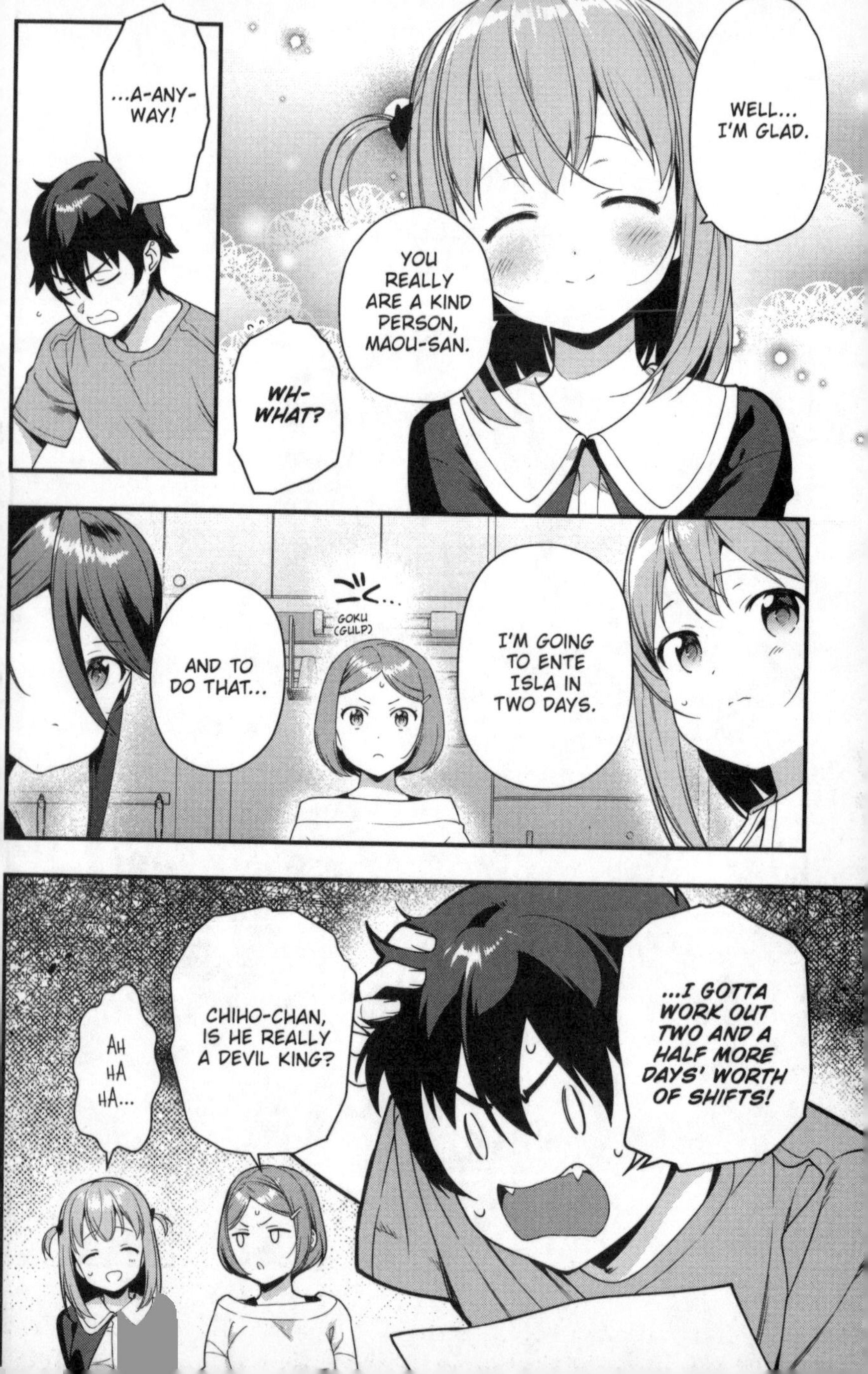
WELL... I'M GLAD.
YOU REALLY ARE A KIND PERSON, MAOU-SAN.
WH-WHAT?
...A-ANY-WAY!
I'M GOING TO ENTE ISLA IN TWO DAYS.
GOKU (GULP)
AND TO DO THAT...
...I GOTTA WORK OUT TWO AND A HALF MORE DAYS' WORTH OF SHIFTS!
CHIHO-CHAN, IS HE REALLY A DEVIL KING?
AH HA HA...

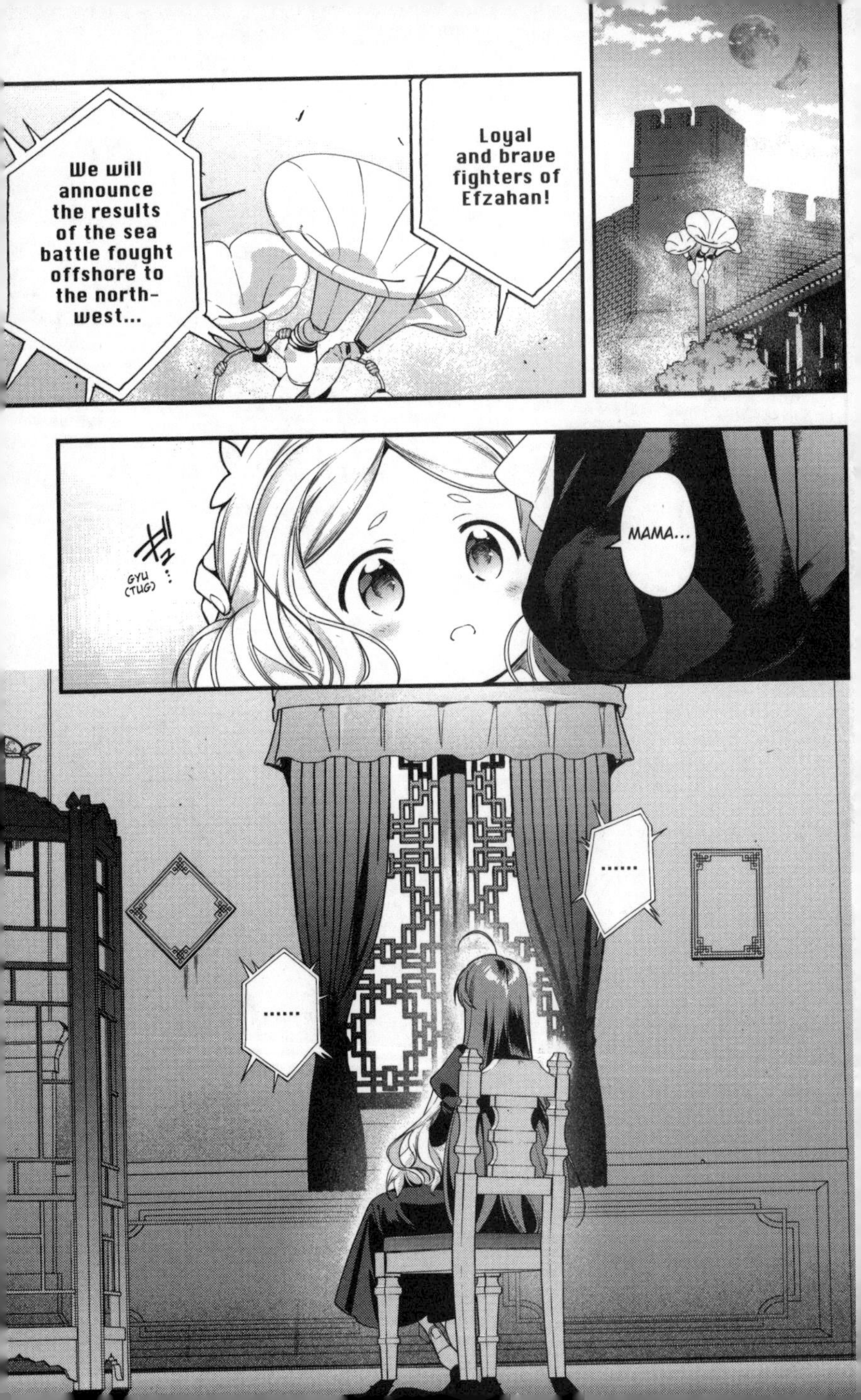
Loyal and brave fighters of Efzahan!
We will announce the results of the sea battle fought offshore to the north-west...
MAMA...
GYU (TUG)
......
......

THE DEVIL IS A PART-TIMER!

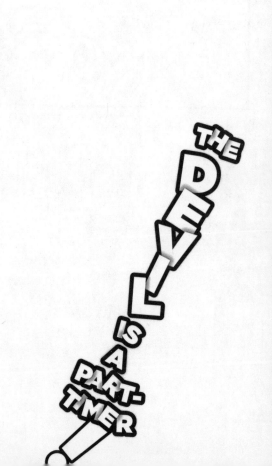

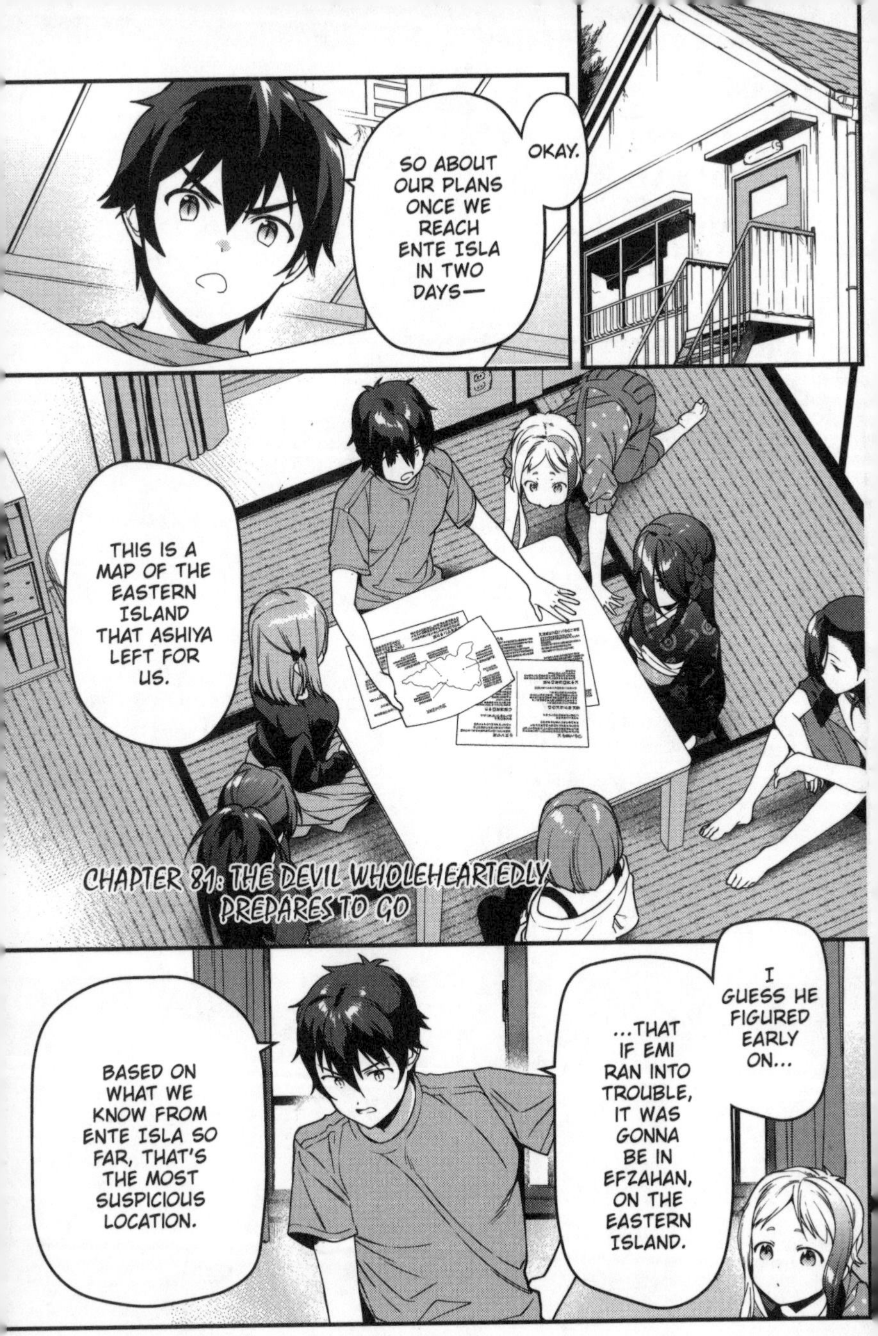
OKAY.
SO ABOUT OUR PLANS ONCE WE REACH ENTE ISLA IN TWO DAYS—
THIS IS A MAP OF THE EASTERN ISLAND THAT ASHIYA LEFT FOR US.
CHAPTER 81: THE DEVIL WHOLEHEARTEDLY PREPARES TO GO
I GUESS HE FIGURED EARLY ON...
...THAT IF EMI RAN INTO TROUBLE, IT WAS GONNA BE IN EFZAHAN, ON THE EASTERN ISLAND.
BASED ON WHAT WE KNOW FROM ENTE ISLA SO FAR, THAT'S THE MOST SUSPICIOUS LOCATION.

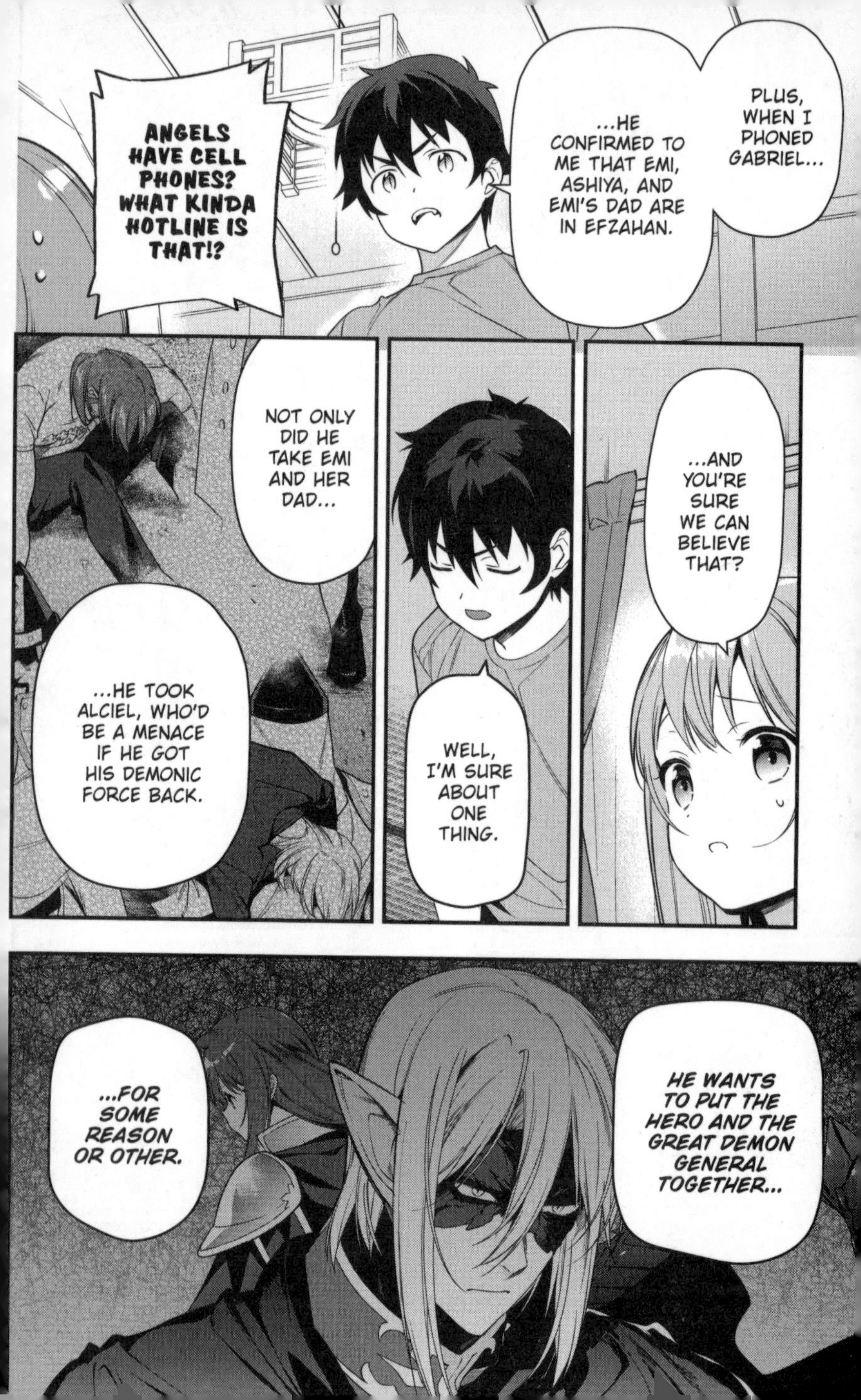
PLUS, WHEN I PHONED GABRIEL...
...HE CONFIRMED TO ME THAT EMI, ASHIYA, AND EMI'S DAD ARE IN EFZAHAN.
ANGELS HAVE CELL PHONES? WHAT KINDA HOTLINE IS THAT!?
...AND YOU'RE SURE WE CAN BELIEVE THAT?
WELL, I'M SURE ABOUT ONE THING.
NOT ONLY DID HE TAKE EMI AND HER DAD...
...HE TOOK ALCIEL, WHO'D BE A MENACE IF HE GOT HIS DEMONIC FORCE BACK.
HE WANTS TO PUT THE HERO AND THE GREAT DEMON GENERAL TOGETHER...
...FOR SOME REASON OR OTHER.

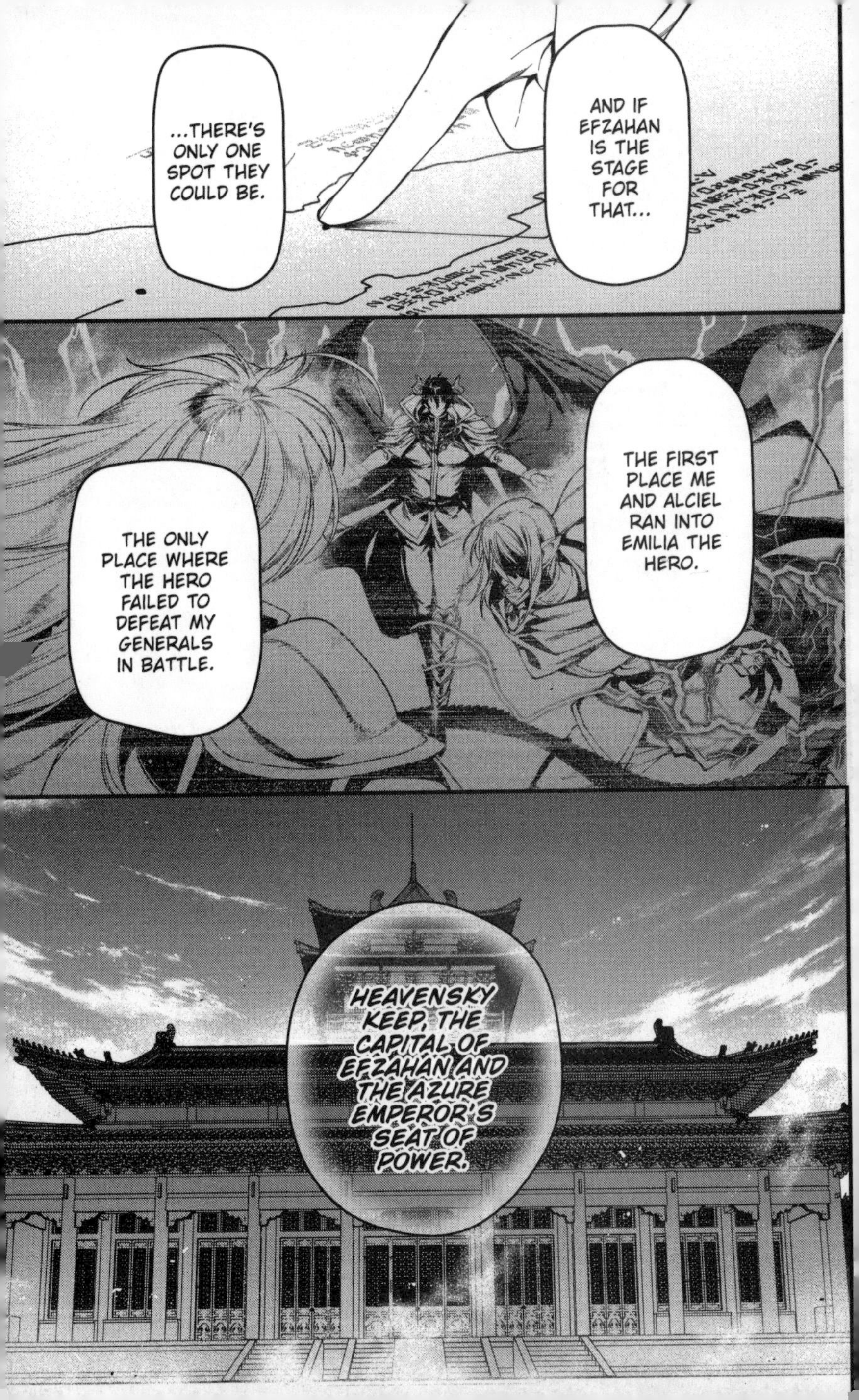
AND IF EFZAHAN IS THE STAGE FOR THAT...
...THERE'S ONLY ONE SPOT THEY COULD BE.
THE FIRST PLACE ME AND ALCIEL RAN INTO EMILIA THE HERO.
THE ONLY PLACE WHERE THE HERO FAILED TO DEFEAT MY GENERALS IN BATTLE.
HEAVENSKY KEEP, THE CAPITAL OF EFZAHAN AND THE AZURE EMPEROR'S SEAT OF POWER.

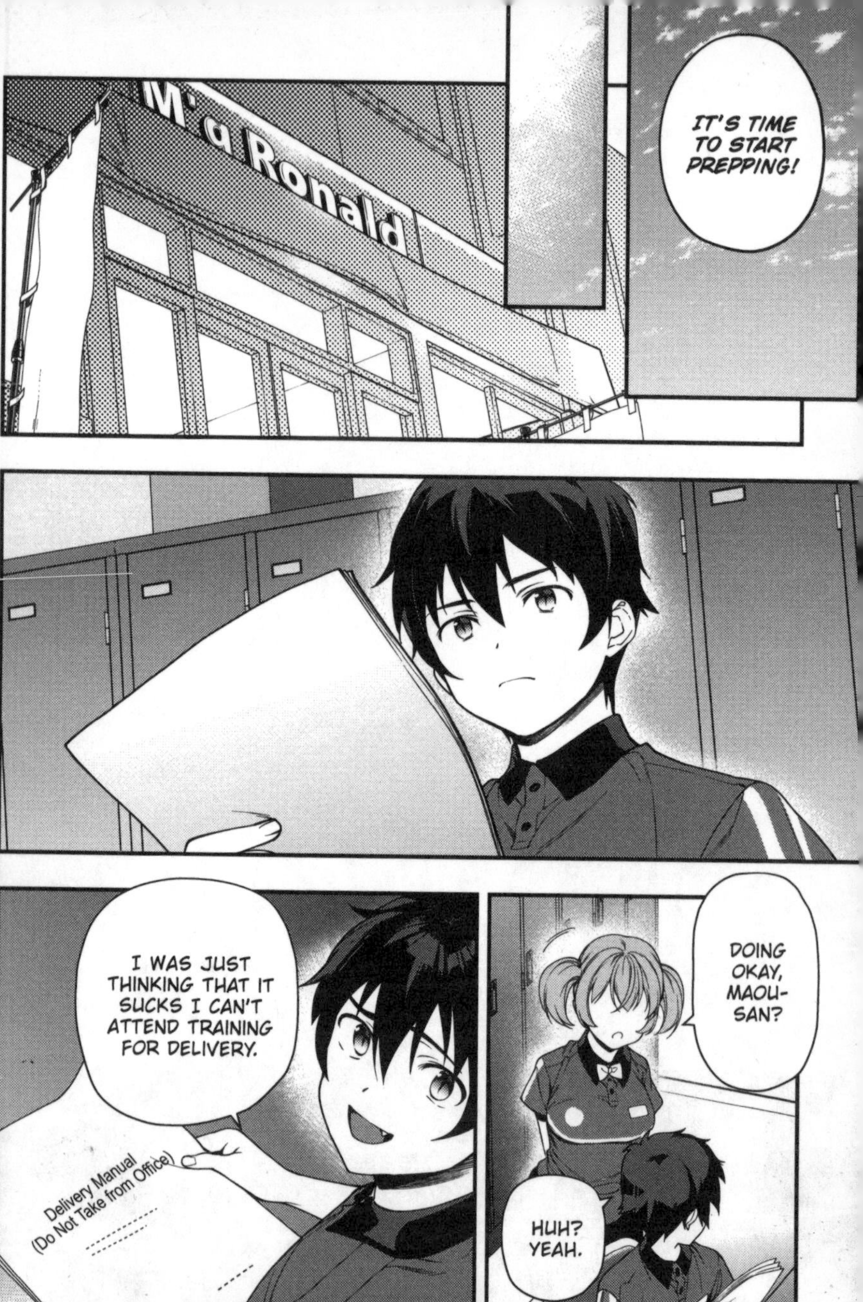
IT'S TIME TO START PREPPING!
DOING OKAY, MAOU-SAN?
HUH? YEAH.
I WAS JUST THINKING THAT IT SUCKS I CAN'T ATTEND TRAINING FOR DELIVERY.
Delivery Manual
(Do Not Take from Office)

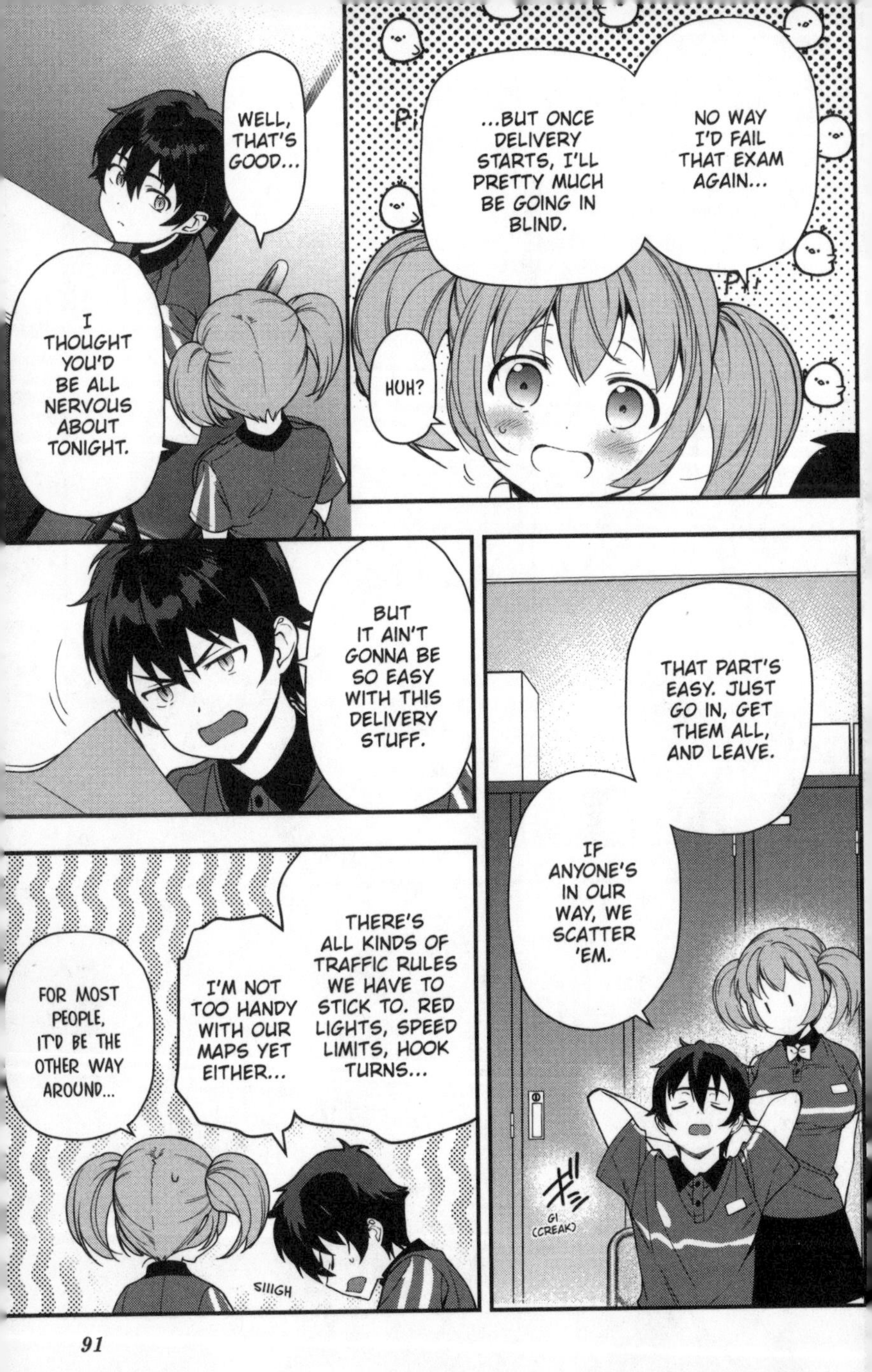
P!
NO WAY I'D FAIL THAT EXAM AGAIN...
...BUT ONCE DELIVERY STARTS, I'LL PRETTY MUCH BE GOING IN BLIND.
P!
HUH?
WELL, THAT'S GOOD...
I THOUGHT YOU'D BE ALL NERVOUS ABOUT TONIGHT.
THAT PART'S EASY. JUST GO IN, GET THEM ALL, AND LEAVE.
IF ANYONE'S IN OUR WAY, WE SCATTER 'EM.
GI (CREAK)
BUT IT AIN'T GONNA BE SO EASY WITH THIS DELIVERY STUFF.
THERE'S ALL KINDS OF TRAFFIC RULES WE HAVE TO STICK TO. RED LIGHTS, SPEED LIMITS, HOOK TURNS...
I'M NOT TOO HANDY WITH OUR MAPS YET EITHER...
FOR MOST PEOPLE, IT'D BE THE OTHER WAY AROUND...
SIIIGH

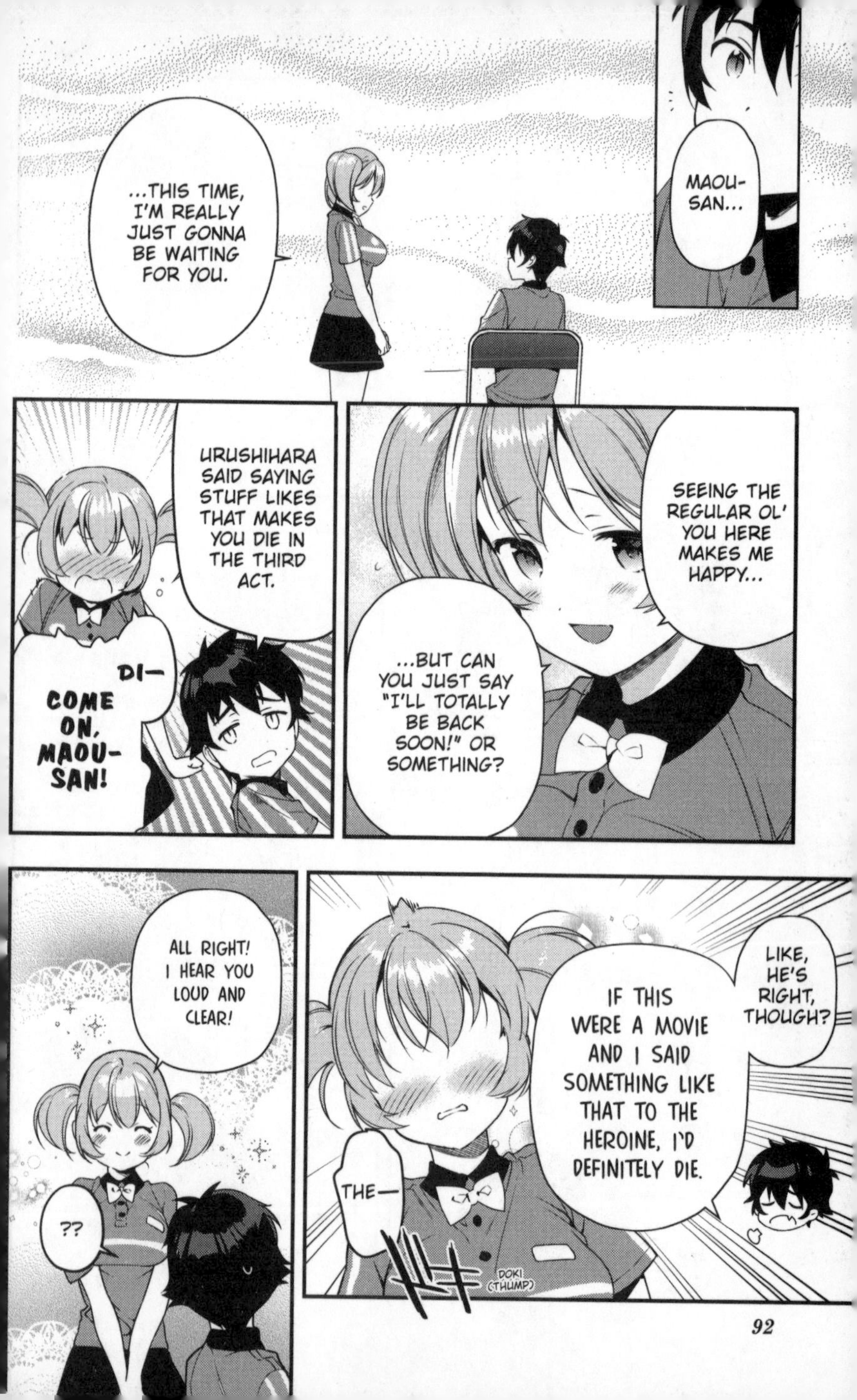
MAOU-SAN...
...THIS TIME, I'M REALLY JUST GONNA BE WAITING FOR YOU.
SEEING THE REGULAR OL' YOU HERE MAKES ME HAPPY...
...BUT CAN YOU JUST SAY "I'LL TOTALLY BE BACK SOON!" OR SOMETHING?
URUSHIHARA SAID SAYING STUFF LIKES THAT MAKES YOU DIE IN THE THIRD ACT.
DI—
COME ON, MAOU-SAN!
LIKE, HE'S RIGHT, THOUGH?
IF THIS WERE A MOVIE AND I SAID SOMETHING LIKE THAT TO THE HEROINE, I'D DEFINITELY DIE.
THE—
DOKI (THUMP)
ALL RIGHT! I HEAR YOU LOUD AND CLEAR!
??

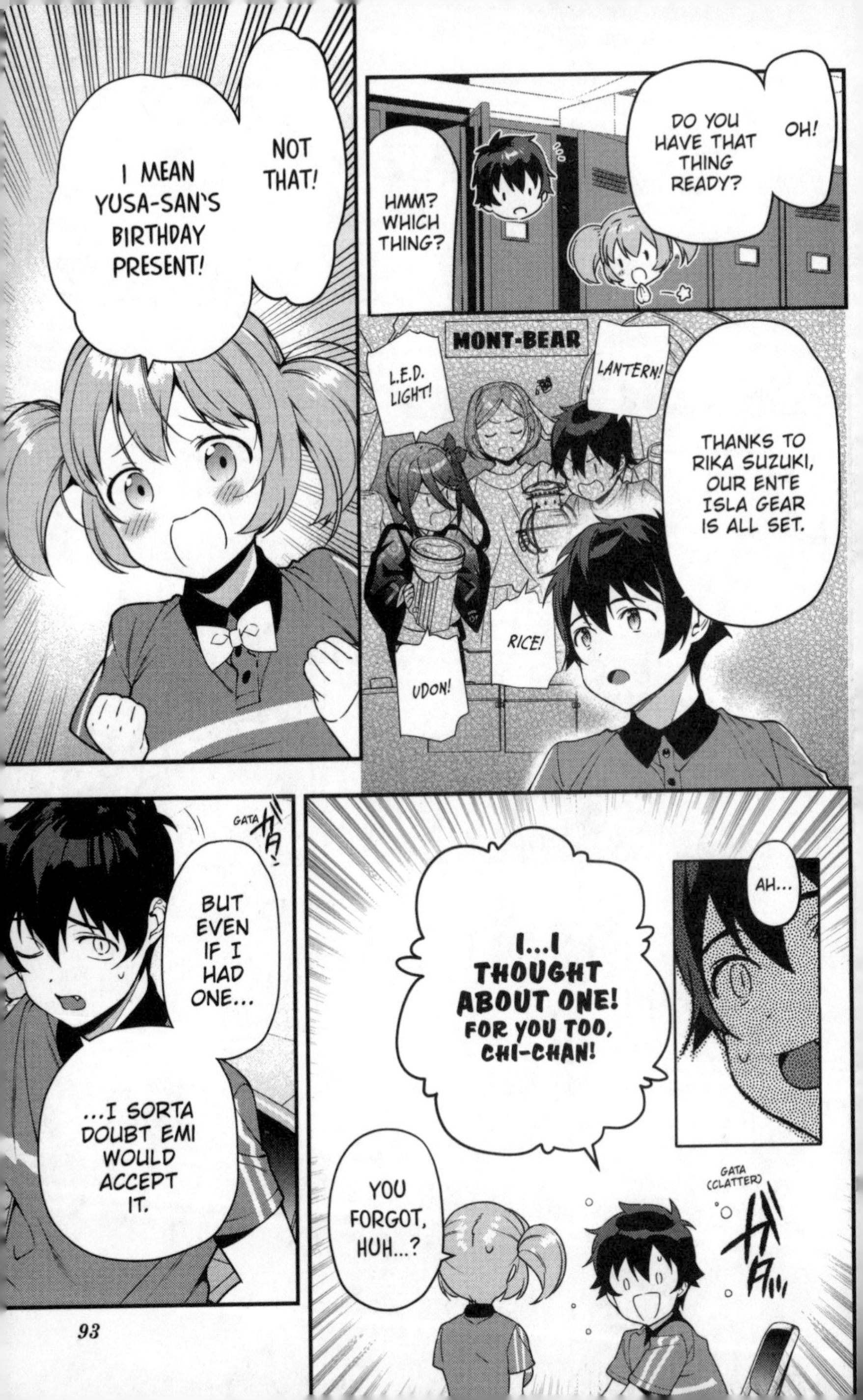
OH!
DO YOU HAVE THAT THING READY?
HMM? WHICH THING?
MONT-BEAR
THANKS TO RIKA SUZUKI, OUR ENTE ISLA GEAR IS ALL SET.
LANTERN!
L.E.D. LIGHT!
RICE!
UDON!
NOT THAT!
I MEAN YUSA-SAN'S BIRTHDAY PRESENT!
AH...
I...I THOUGHT ABOUT ONE! FOR YOU TOO, CHI-CHAN!
GATA (CLATTER)
YOU FORGOT, HUH...?
GATA
BUT EVEN IF I HAD ONE...
...I SORTA DOUBT EMI WOULD ACCEPT IT.

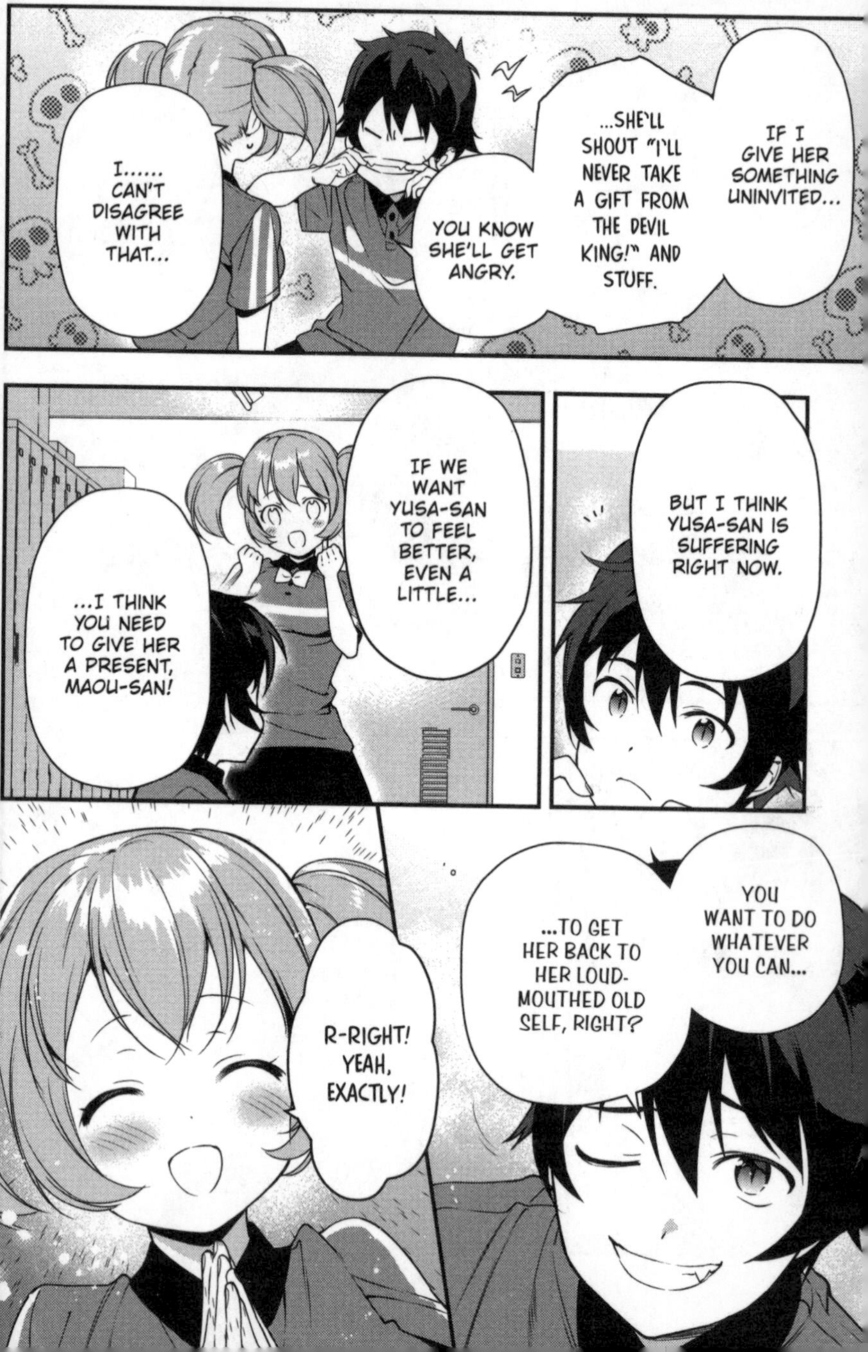
IF I GIVE HER SOMETHING UNINVITED...
...SHE'LL SHOUT "I'LL NEVER TAKE A GIFT FROM THE DEVIL KING!" AND STUFF.
YOU KNOW SHE'LL GET ANGRY.
I...... CAN'T DISAGREE WITH THAT...
BUT I THINK YUSA-SAN IS SUFFERING RIGHT NOW.
IF WE WANT YUSA-SAN TO FEEL BETTER, EVEN A LITTLE...
...I THINK YOU NEED TO GIVE HER A PRESENT, MAOU-SAN!
YOU WANT TO DO WHATEVER YOU CAN...
...TO GET HER BACK TO HER LOUD-MOUTHED OLD SELF, RIGHT?
R-RIGHT! YEAH, EXACTLY!

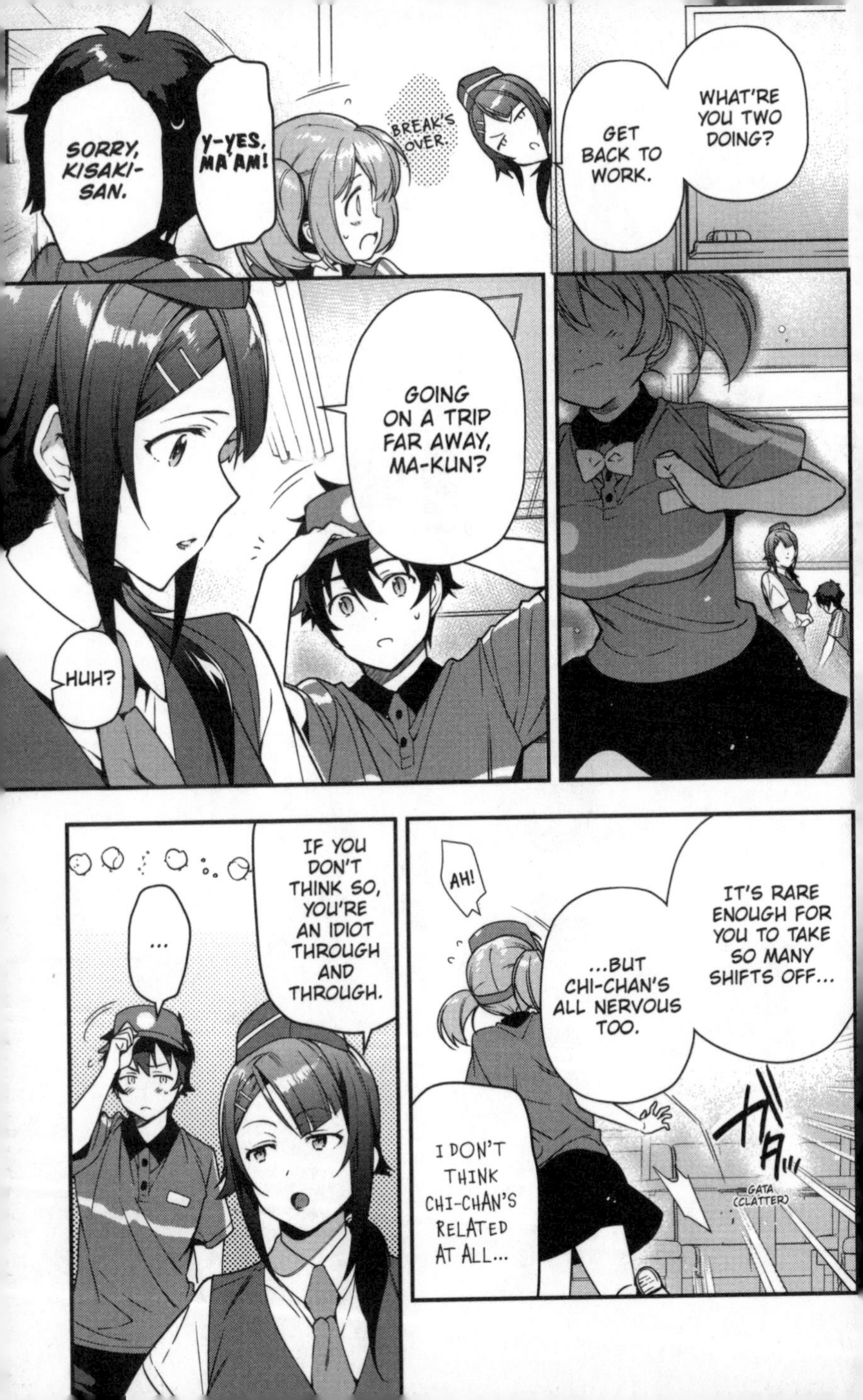
WHAT'RE YOU TWO DOING?
GET BACK TO WORK.
BREAK'S OVER.
Y-YES, MA'AM!
SORRY, KISAKI-SAN.
GOING ON A TRIP FAR AWAY, MA-KUN?
HUH?
AH!
IT'S RARE ENOUGH FOR YOU TO TAKE SO MANY SHIFTS OFF...
...BUT CHI-CHAN'S ALL NERVOUS TOO.
ガタッ
GATA (CLATTER)
I DON'T THINK CHI-CHAN'S RELATED AT ALL...
IF YOU DON'T THINK SO, YOU'RE AN IDIOT THROUGH AND THROUGH.
...

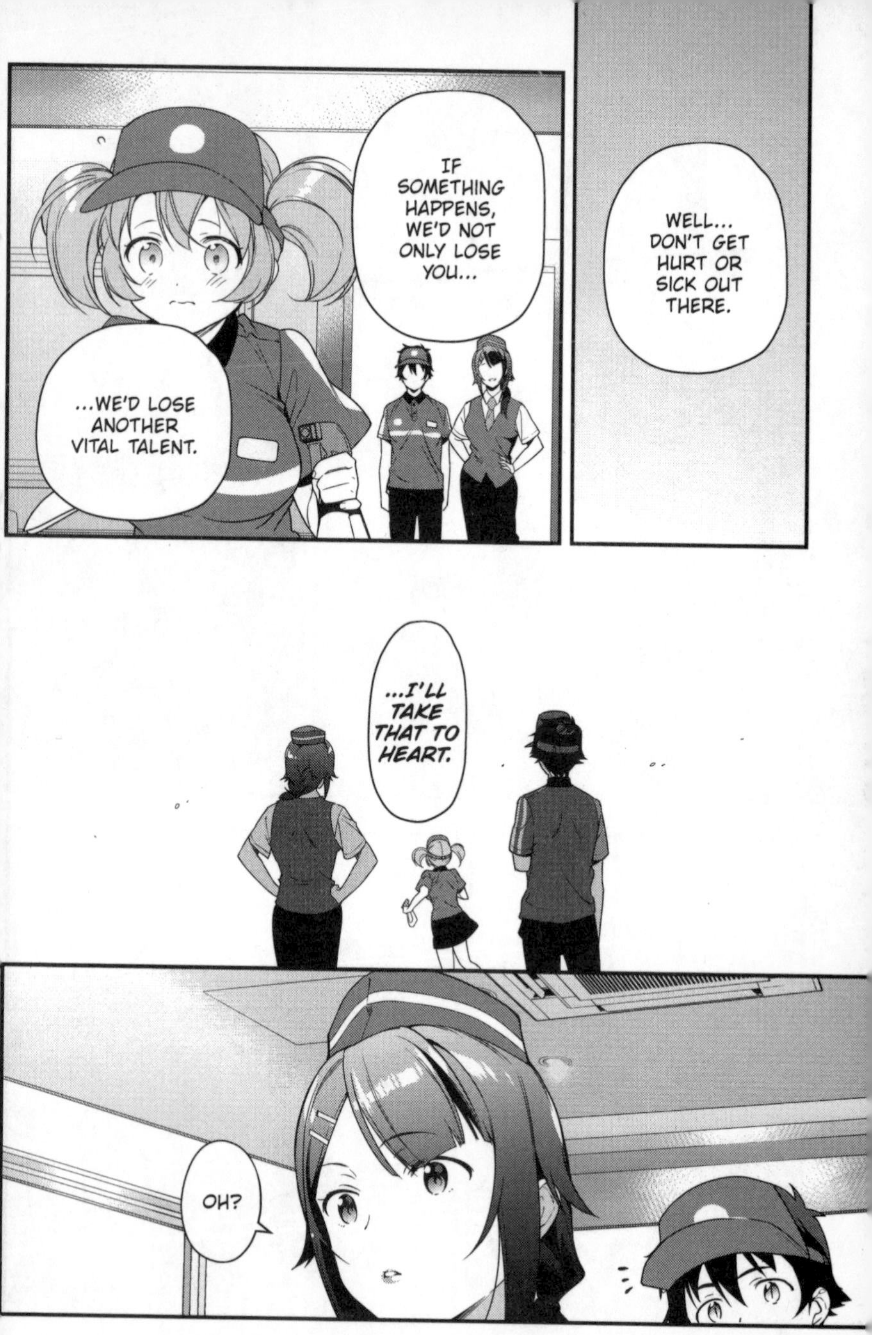
WELL... DON'T GET HURT OR SICK OUT THERE.
IF SOMETHING HAPPENS, WE'D NOT ONLY LOSE YOU...
...WE'D LOSE ANOTHER VITAL TALENT.
...I'LL TAKE THAT TO HEART.
OH?

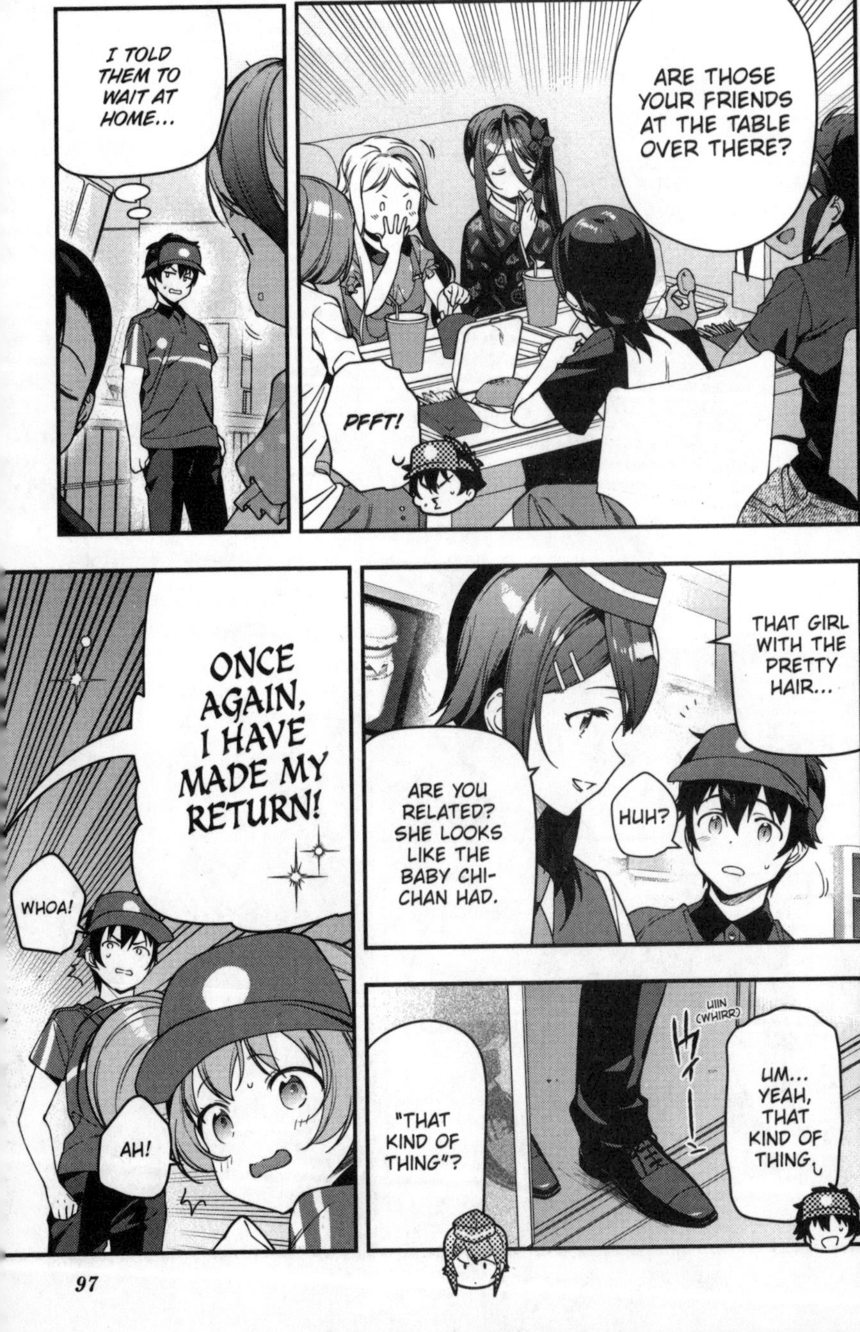
ARE THOSE YOUR FRIENDS AT THE TABLE OVER THERE?
PFFT!
I TOLD THEM TO WAIT AT HOME...
THAT GIRL WITH THE PRETTY HAIR...
ARE YOU RELATED? SHE LOOKS LIKE THE BABY CHI-CHAN HAD.
HUH?
UIIN (WHIRR)
UM... YEAH, THAT KIND OF THING.
"THAT KIND OF THING"?
ONCE AGAIN, I HAVE MADE MY RETURN!
WHOA!
AH!

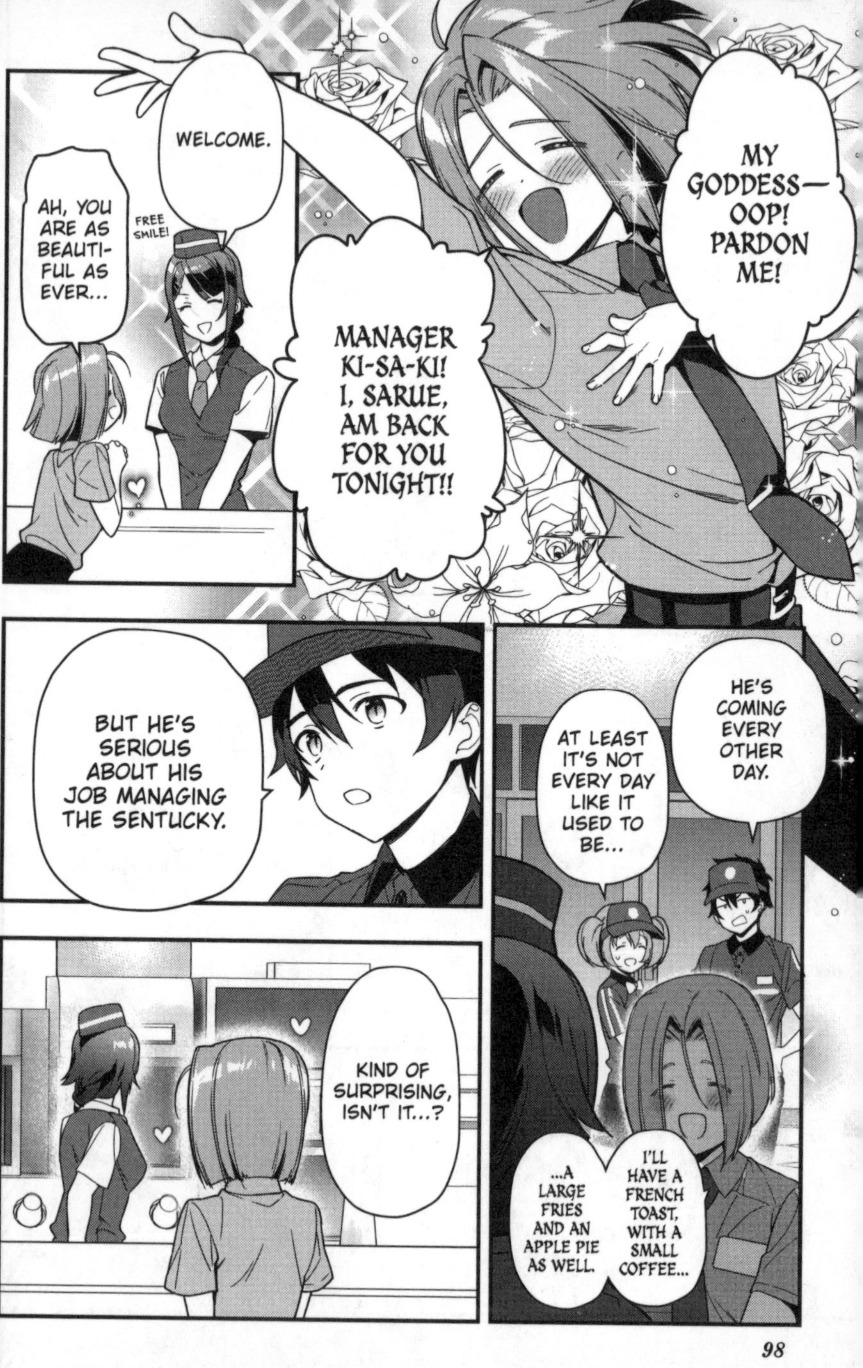
MY GODDESS—OOP! PARDON ME!
MANAGER KI-SA-KI! I, SARUE, AM BACK FOR YOU TONIGHT!!
WELCOME.
FREE SMILE!
AH, YOU ARE AS BEAUTI-FUL AS EVER...
HE'S COMING EVERY OTHER DAY.
AT LEAST IT'S NOT EVERY DAY LIKE IT USED TO BE...
I'LL HAVE A FRENCH TOAST, WITH A SMALL COFFEE...
...A LARGE FRIES AND AN APPLE PIE AS WELL.
BUT HE'S SERIOUS ABOUT HIS JOB MANAGING THE SENTUCKY.
KIND OF SURPRISING, ISN'T IT...?

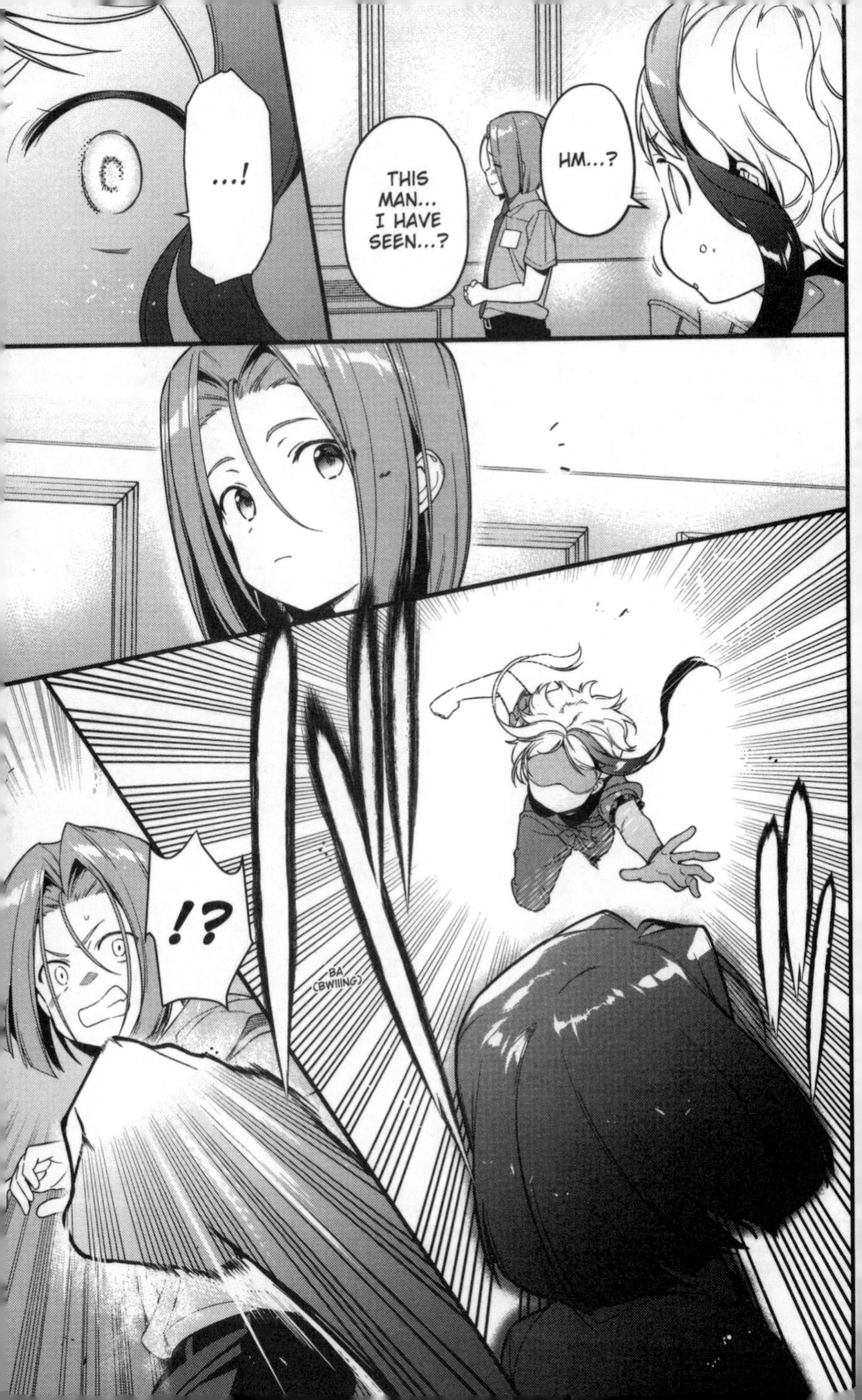
HM...?
THIS MAN... I HAVE SEEN...?
...!
BA (BWIIING)
!?

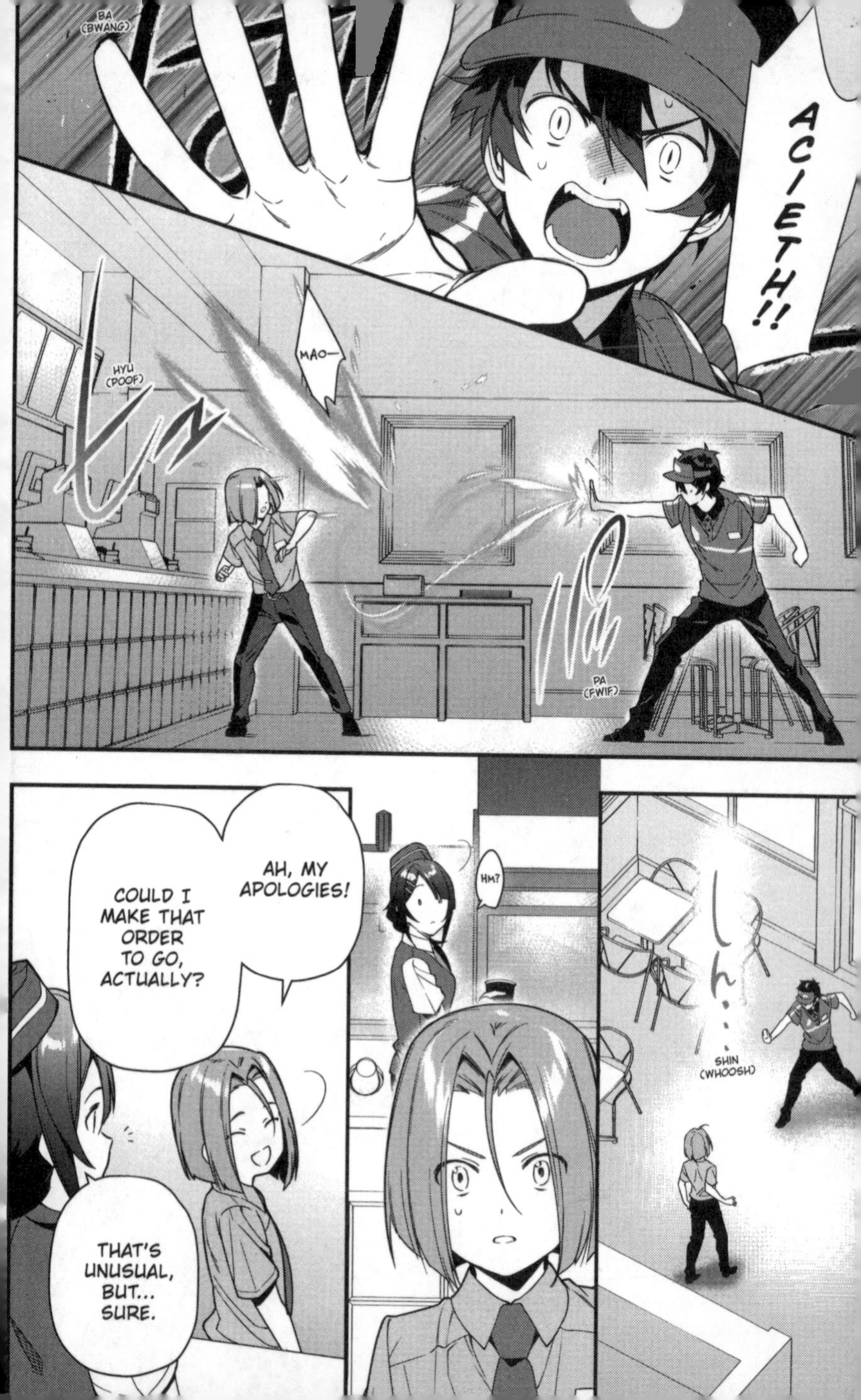
ACIETH!!
BA (BWANG)
MAO—
HYU (POOF)
PA (FWIF)
しん…
SHIN (WHOOSH)
HM?
AH, MY APOLOGIES!
COULD I MAKE THAT ORDER TO GO, ACTUALLY?
THAT'S UNUSUAL, BUT... SURE.

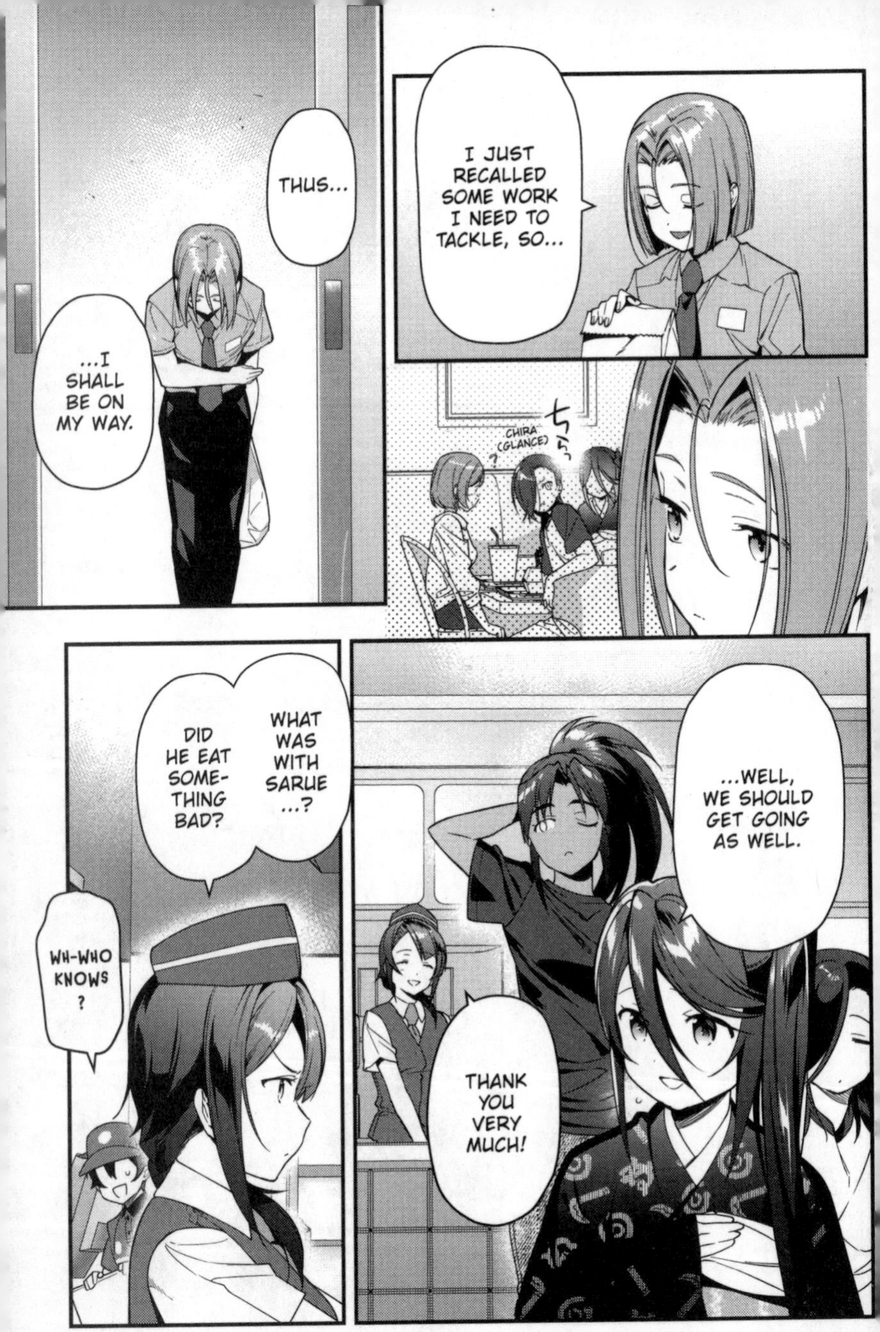
I JUST RECALLED SOME WORK I NEED TO TACKLE, SO...
CHIRA (GLANCE)
THUS...
...I SHALL BE ON MY WAY.
...WELL, WE SHOULD GET GOING AS WELL.
THANK YOU VERY MUCH!
WHAT WAS WITH SARUE ...?
DID HE EAT SOME-THING BAD?
WH-WHO KNOWS ?

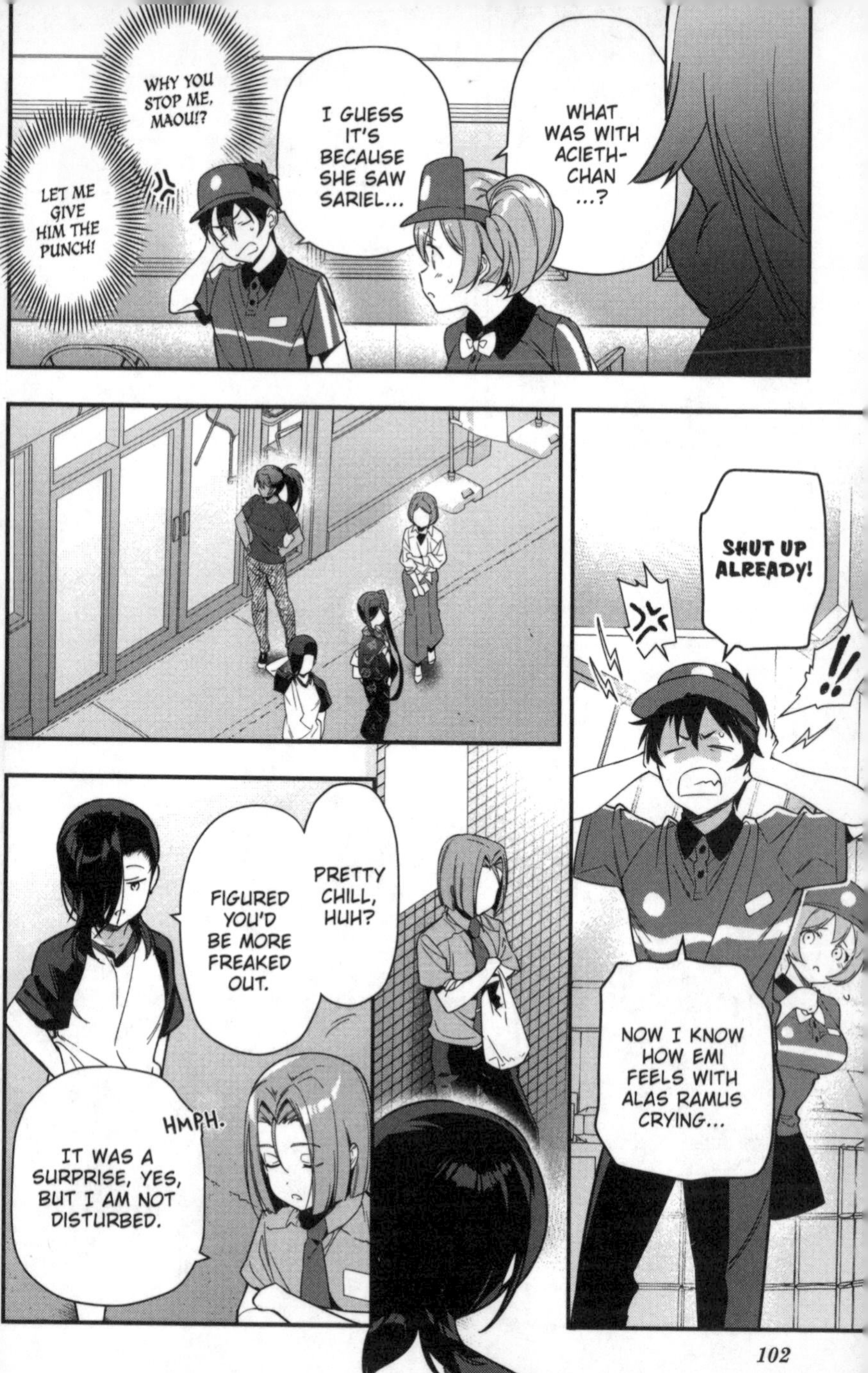
WHAT WAS WITH ACIETH-CHAN ...?
I GUESS IT'S BECAUSE SHE SAW SARIEL...
WHY YOU STOP ME, MAOU!?
LET ME GIVE HIM THE PUNCH!
SHUT UP ALREADY!
!!
NOW I KNOW HOW EMI FEELS WITH ALAS RAMUS CRYING...
PRETTY CHILL, HUH?
FIGURED YOU'D BE MORE FREAKED OUT.
HMPH.
IT WAS A SURPRISE, YES, BUT I AM NOT DISTURBED.

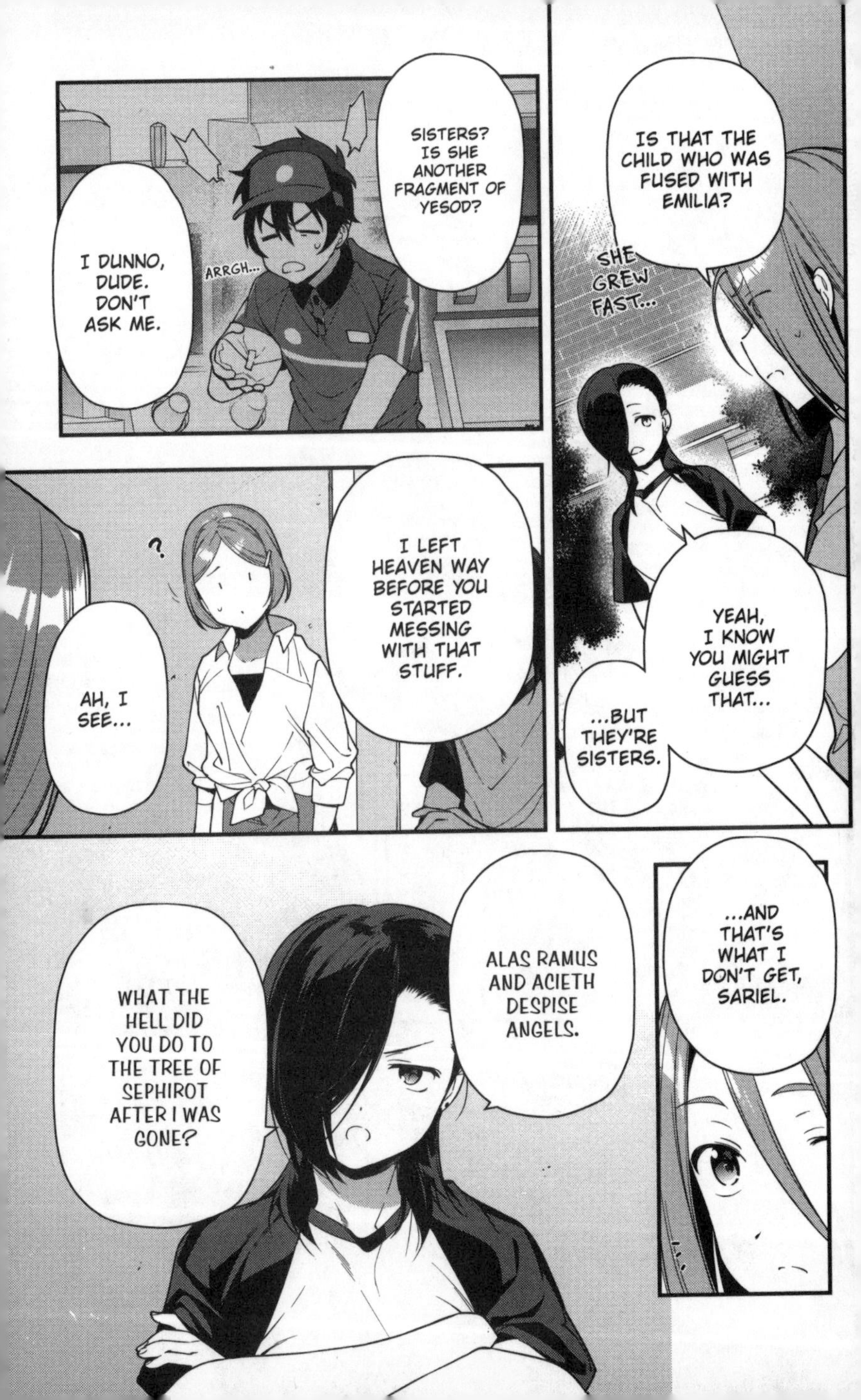
IS THAT THE CHILD WHO WAS FUSED WITH EMILIA?
SHE GREW FAST...
YEAH, I KNOW YOU MIGHT GUESS THAT...
...BUT THEY'RE SISTERS.
SISTERS? IS SHE ANOTHER FRAGMENT OF YESOD?
ARRGH...
I DUNNO, DUDE. DON'T ASK ME.
?
I LEFT HEAVEN WAY BEFORE YOU STARTED MESSING WITH THAT STUFF.
AH, I SEE...
...AND THAT'S WHAT I DON'T GET, SARIEL.
...
ALAS RAMUS AND ACIETH DESPISE ANGELS.
WHAT THE HELL DID YOU DO TO THE TREE OF SEPHIROT AFTER I WAS GONE?

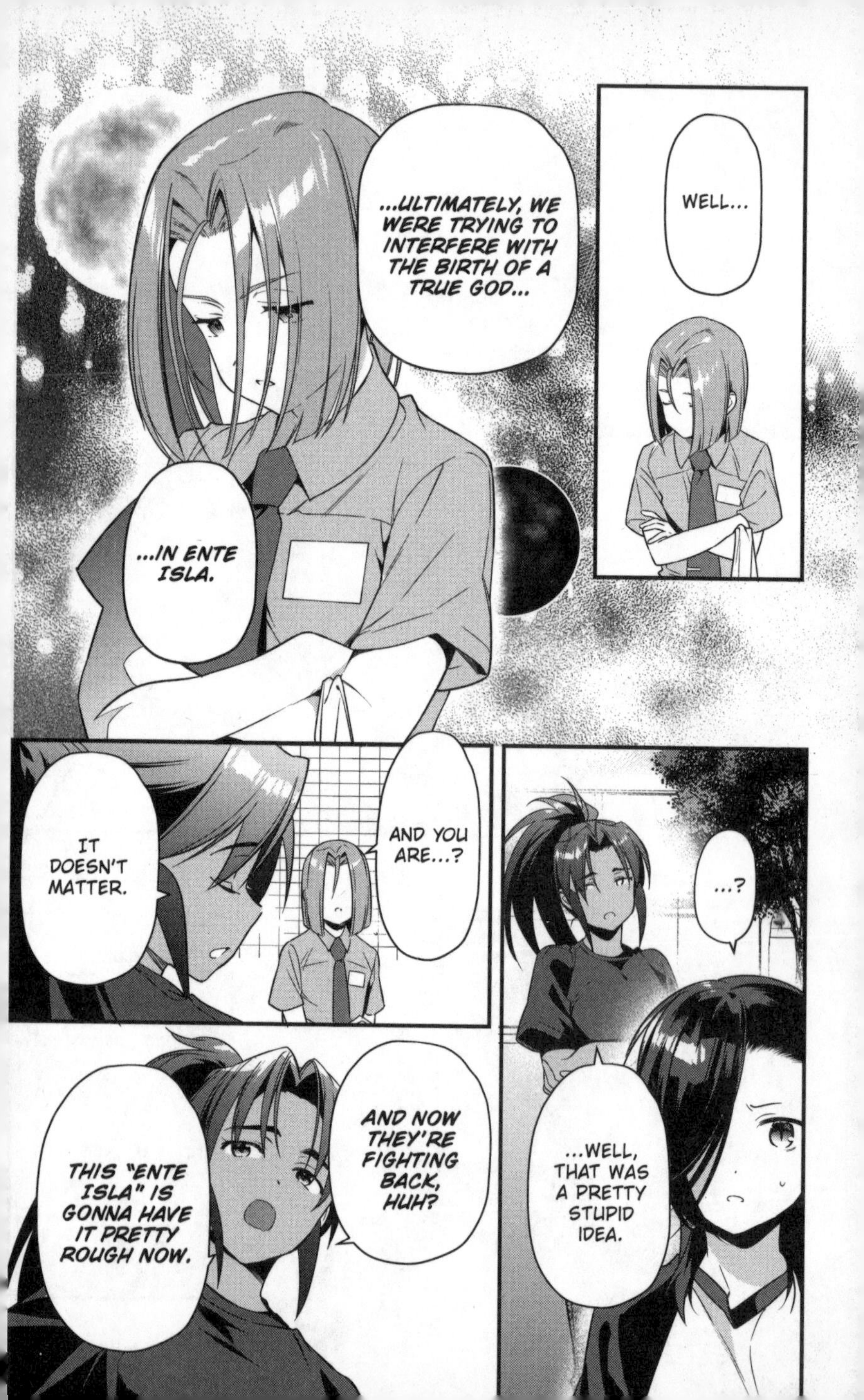
WELL...
...ULTIMATELY, WE WERE TRYING TO INTERFERE WITH THE BIRTH OF A TRUE GOD...
...IN ENTE ISLA.
...?
...WELL, THAT WAS A PRETTY STUPID IDEA.
AND YOU ARE...?
IT DOESN'T MATTER.
AND NOW THEY'RE FIGHTING BACK, HUH?
THIS "ENTE ISLA" IS GONNA HAVE IT PRETTY ROUGH NOW.

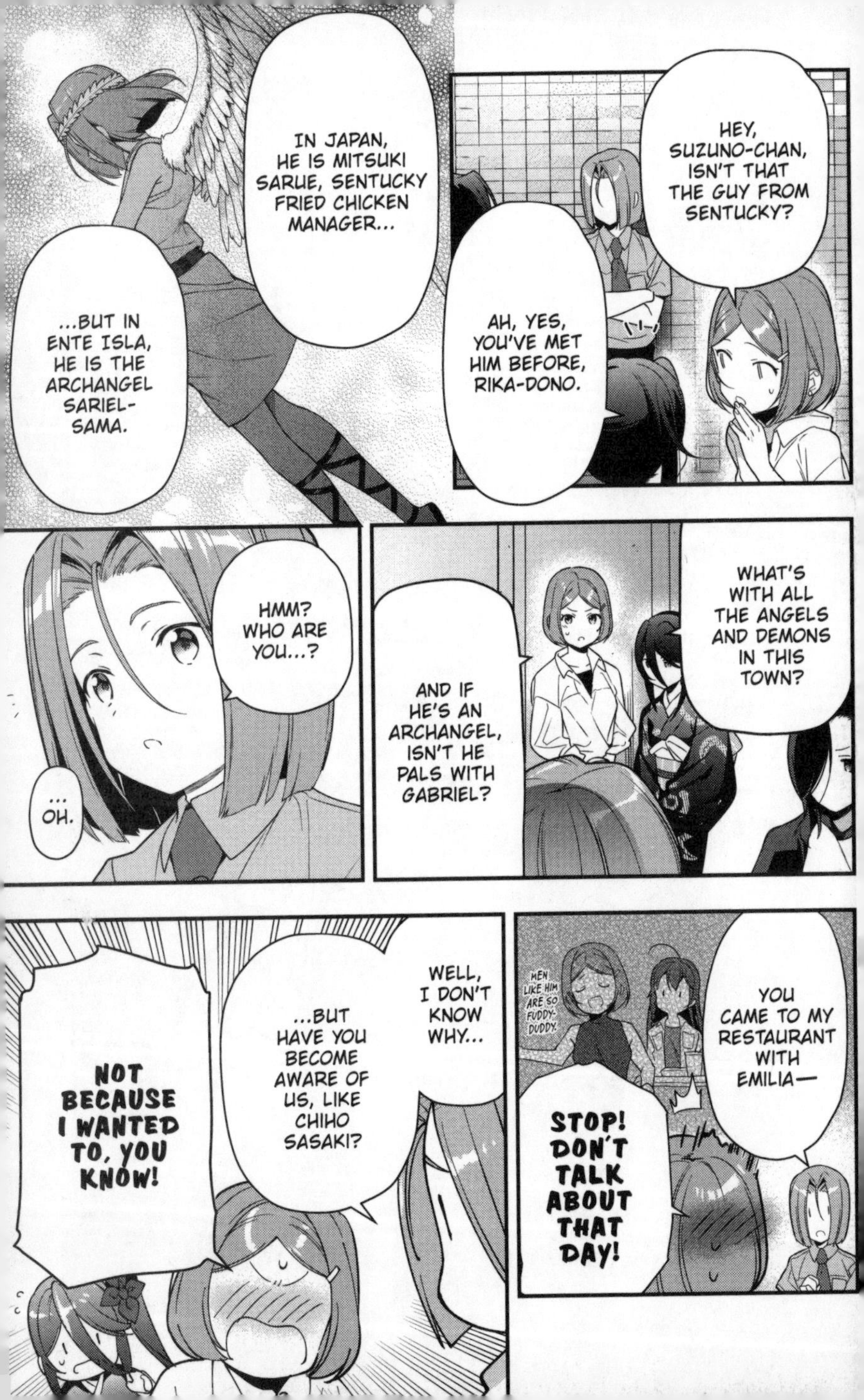
HEY, SUZUNO-CHAN, ISN'T THAT THE GUY FROM SENTUCKY?
AH, YES, YOU'VE MET HIM BEFORE, RIKA-DONO.
IN JAPAN, HE IS MITSUKI SARUE, SENTUCKY FRIED CHICKEN MANAGER...
...BUT IN ENTE ISLA, HE IS THE ARCHANGEL SARIEL-SAMA.
WHAT'S WITH ALL THE ANGELS AND DEMONS IN THIS TOWN?
AND IF HE'S AN ARCHANGEL, ISN'T HE PALS WITH GABRIEL?
HMM? WHO ARE YOU...?
... OH.
YOU CAME TO MY RESTAURANT WITH EMILIA—
MEN LIKE HIM ARE SO FUDDY-DUDDY.
STOP! DON'T TALK ABOUT THAT DAY!
WELL, I DON'T KNOW WHY...
...BUT HAVE YOU BECOME AWARE OF US, LIKE CHIHO SASAKI?
NOT BECAUSE I WANTED TO, YOU KNOW!

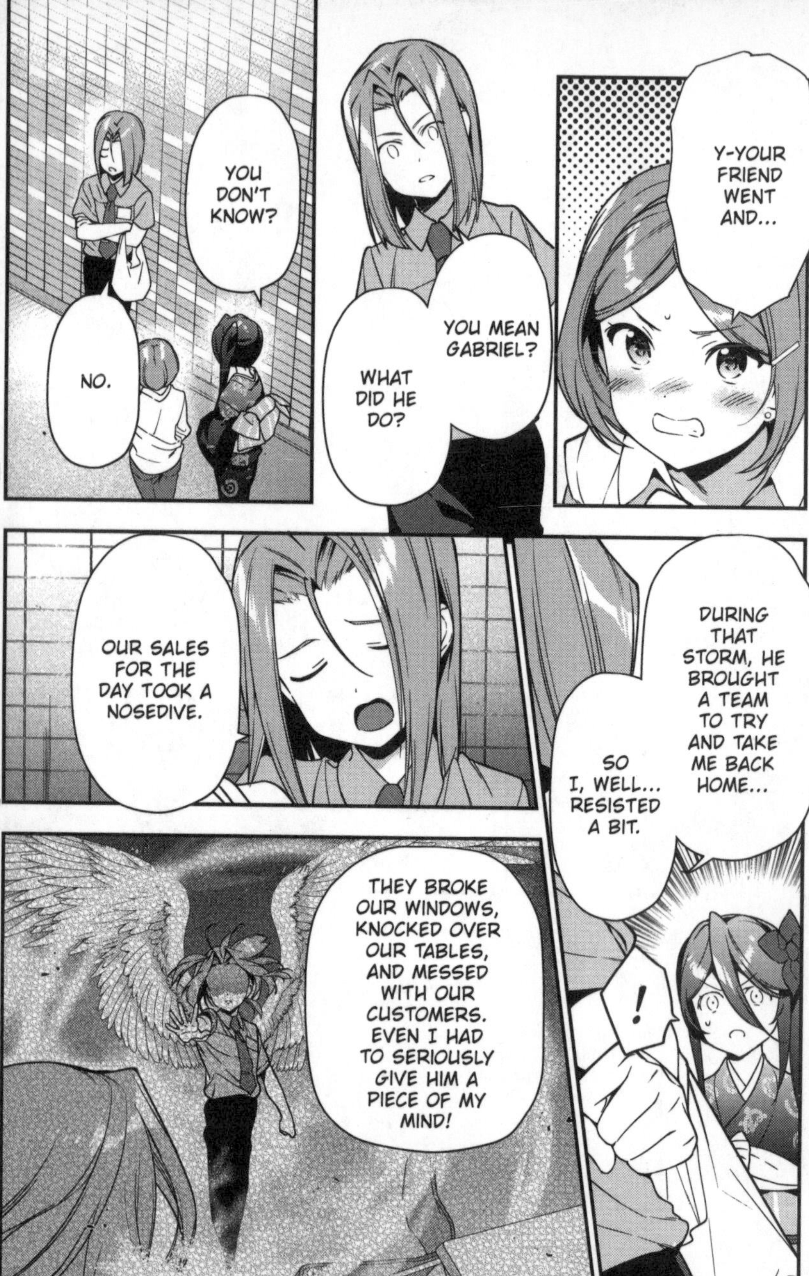
Y-YOUR FRIEND WENT AND...
YOU MEAN GABRIEL?
WHAT DID HE DO?
YOU DON'T KNOW?
NO.
DURING THAT STORM, HE BROUGHT A TEAM TO TRY AND TAKE ME BACK HOME...
SO I, WELL... RESISTED A BIT.
!
OUR SALES FOR THE DAY TOOK A NOSEDIVE.
THEY BROKE OUR WINDOWS, KNOCKED OVER OUR TABLES, AND MESSED WITH OUR CUSTOMERS. EVEN I HAD TO SERIOUSLY GIVE HIM A PIECE OF MY MIND!

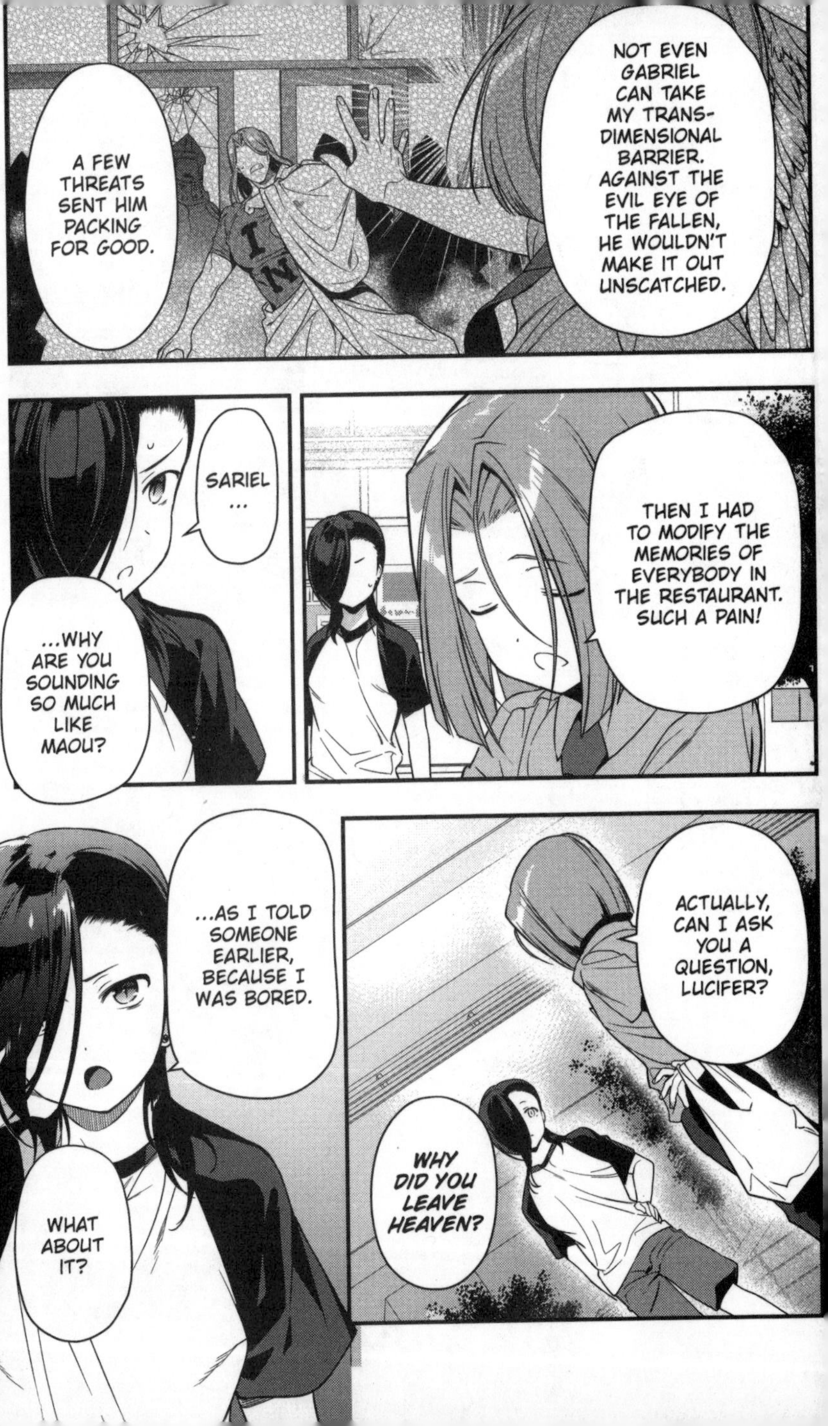
NOT EVEN GABRIEL CAN TAKE MY TRANS-DIMENSIONAL BARRIER. AGAINST THE EVIL EYE OF THE FALLEN, HE WOULDN'T MAKE IT OUT UNSCATCHED.
A FEW THREATS SENT HIM PACKING FOR GOOD.
THEN I HAD TO MODIFY THE MEMORIES OF EVERYBODY IN THE RESTAURANT. SUCH A PAIN!
SARIEL...
...WHY ARE YOU SOUNDING SO MUCH LIKE MAOU?
ACTUALLY, CAN I ASK YOU A QUESTION, LUCIFER?
WHY DID YOU LEAVE HEAVEN?
...AS I TOLD SOMEONE EARLIER, BECAUSE I WAS BORED.
WHAT ABOUT IT?

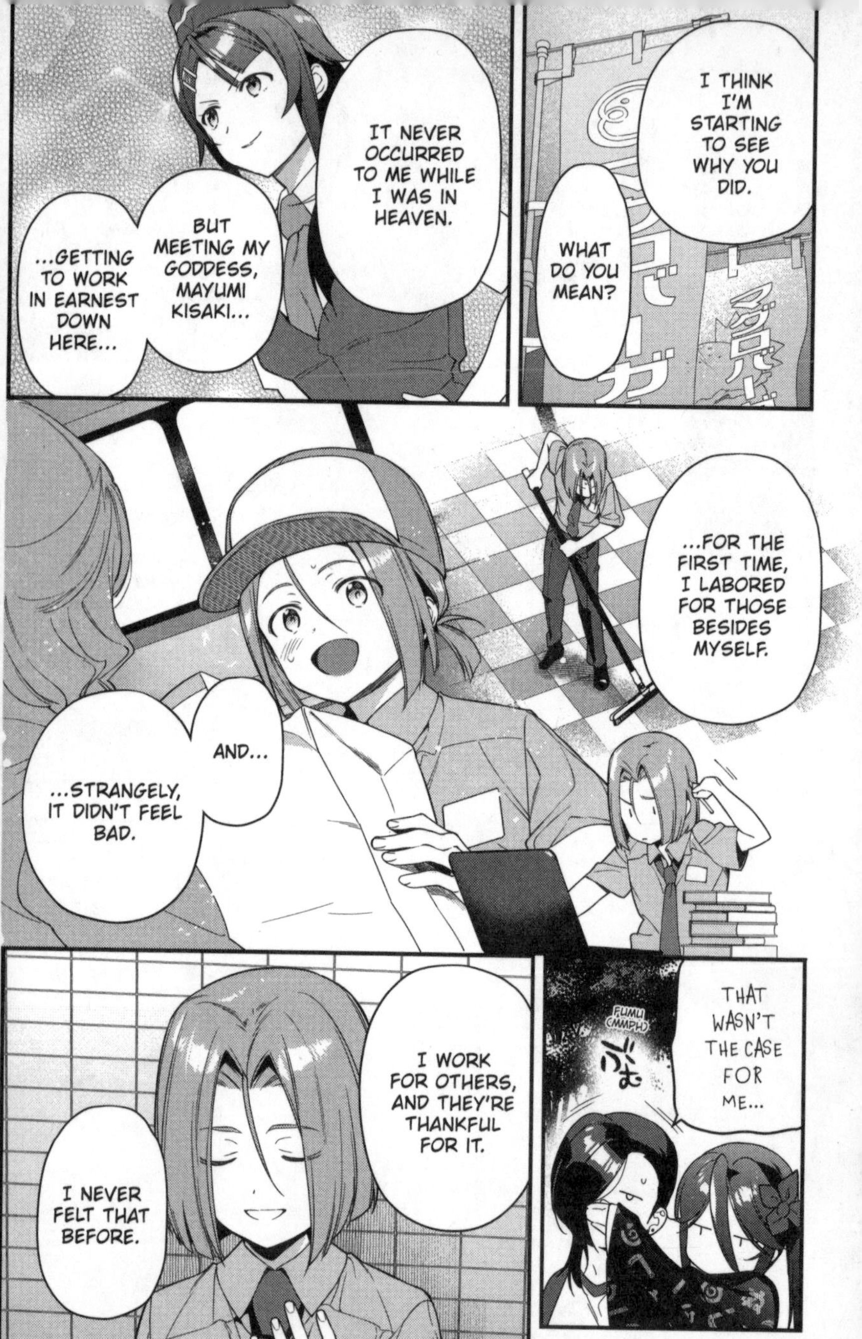
I THINK I'M STARTING TO SEE WHY YOU DID.
WHAT DO YOU MEAN?
IT NEVER OCCURRED TO ME WHILE I WAS IN HEAVEN.
BUT MEETING MY GODDESS, MAYUMI KISAKI...
...GETTING TO WORK IN EARNEST DOWN HERE...
...FOR THE FIRST TIME, I LABORED FOR THOSE BESIDES MYSELF.
AND...
...STRANGELY, IT DIDN'T FEEL BAD.
THAT WASN'T THE CASE FOR ME...
FUMU (MMPH)
ふむ
I WORK FOR OTHERS, AND THEY'RE THANKFUL FOR IT.
I NEVER FELT THAT BEFORE.

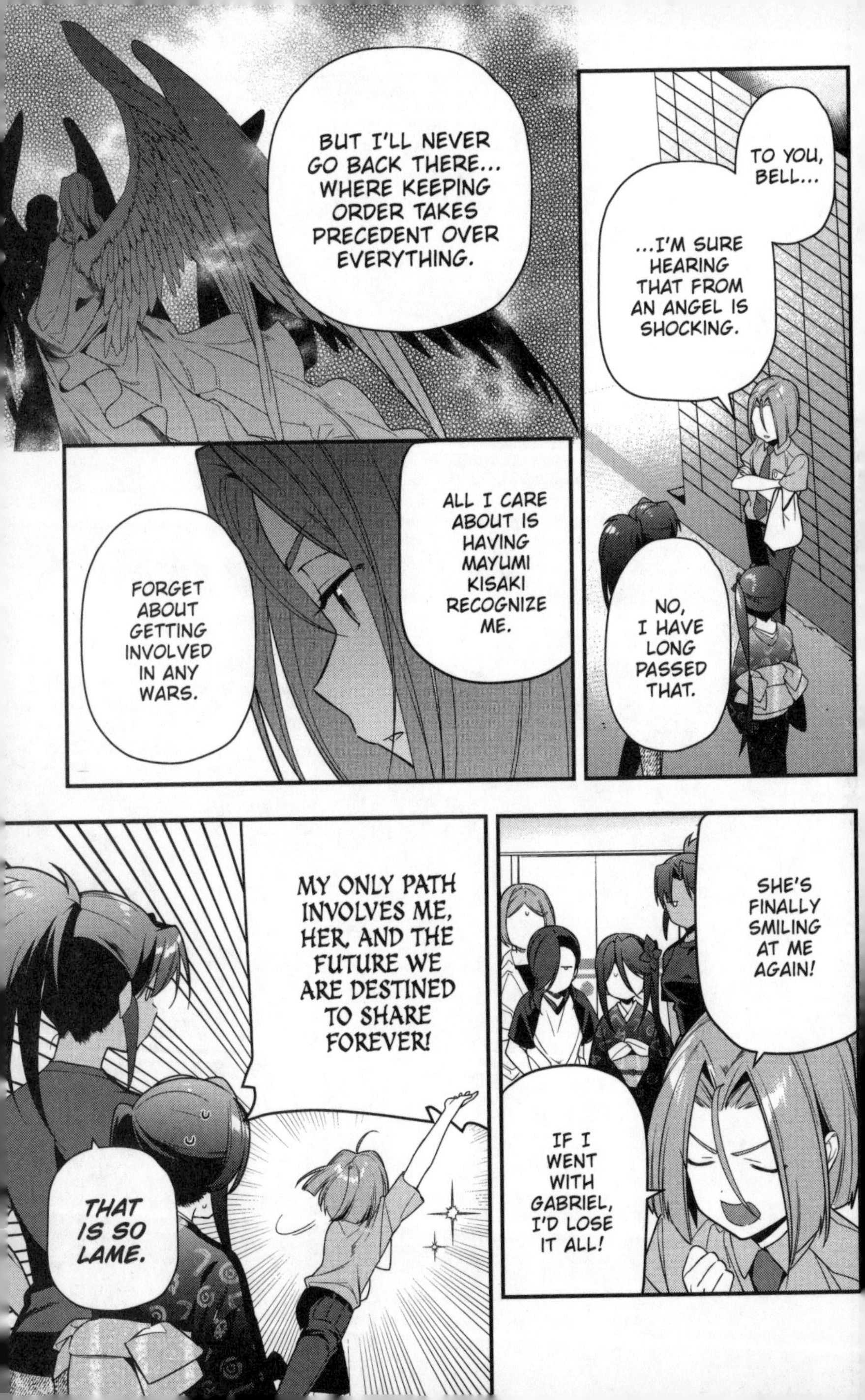
TO YOU, BELL...
...I'M SURE HEARING THAT FROM AN ANGEL IS SHOCKING.
NO, I HAVE LONG PASSED THAT.
BUT I'LL NEVER GO BACK THERE... WHERE KEEPING ORDER TAKES PRECEDENT OVER EVERYTHING.
ALL I CARE ABOUT IS HAVING MAYUMI KISAKI RECOGNIZE ME.
FORGET ABOUT GETTING INVOLVED IN ANY WARS.
SHE'S FINALLY SMILING AT ME AGAIN!
IF I WENT WITH GABRIEL, I'D LOSE IT ALL!
MY ONLY PATH INVOLVES ME, HER, AND THE FUTURE WE ARE DESTINED TO SHARE FOREVER!
THAT IS SO LAME.

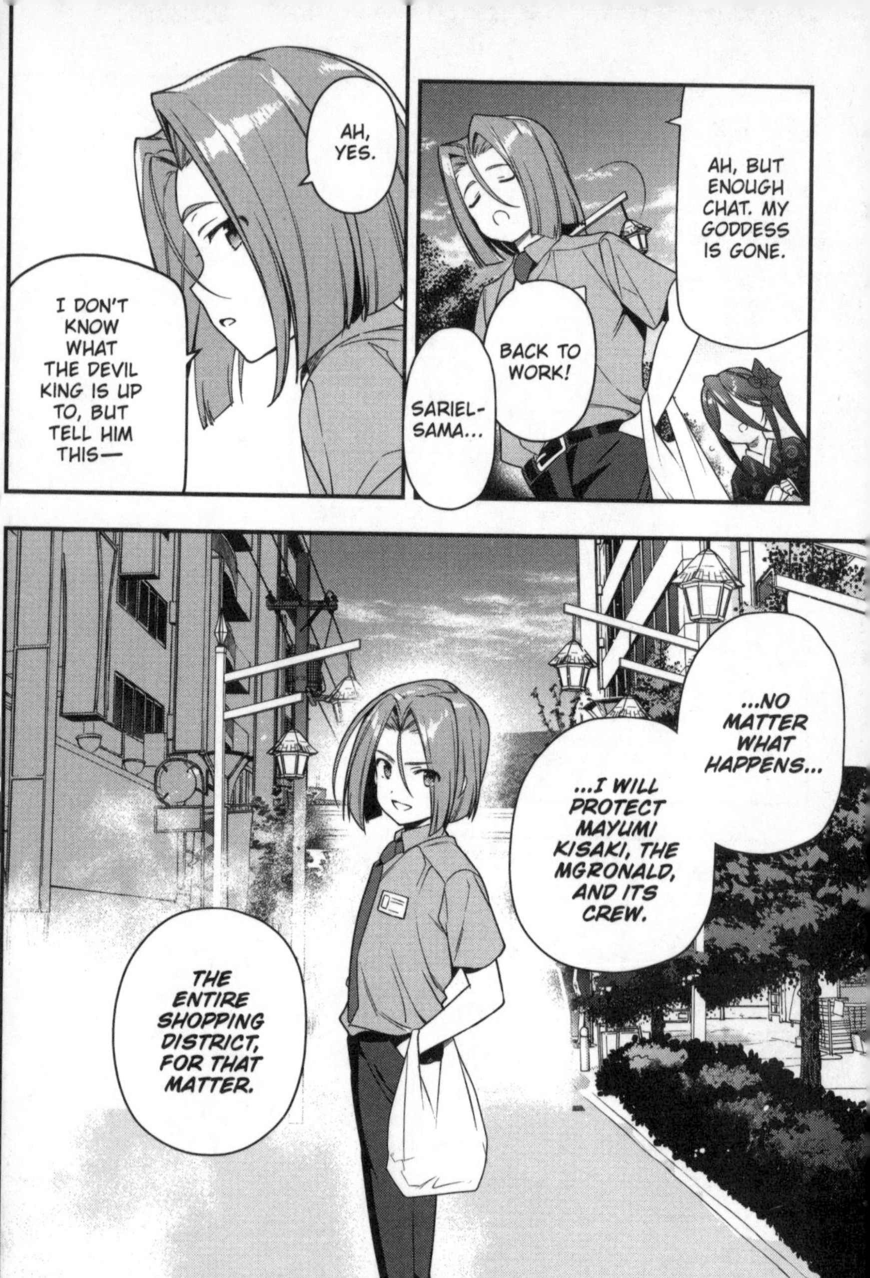
AH, BUT ENOUGH CHAT. MY GODDESS IS GONE.
BACK TO WORK!
SARIEL-SAMA...
AH, YES.
I DON'T KNOW WHAT THE DEVIL KING IS UP TO, BUT TELL HIM THIS—
...NO MATTER WHAT HAPPENS...
...I WILL PROTECT MAYUMI KISAKI, THE MGRONALD, AND ITS CREW.
THE ENTIRE SHOPPING DISTRICT, FOR THAT MATTER.

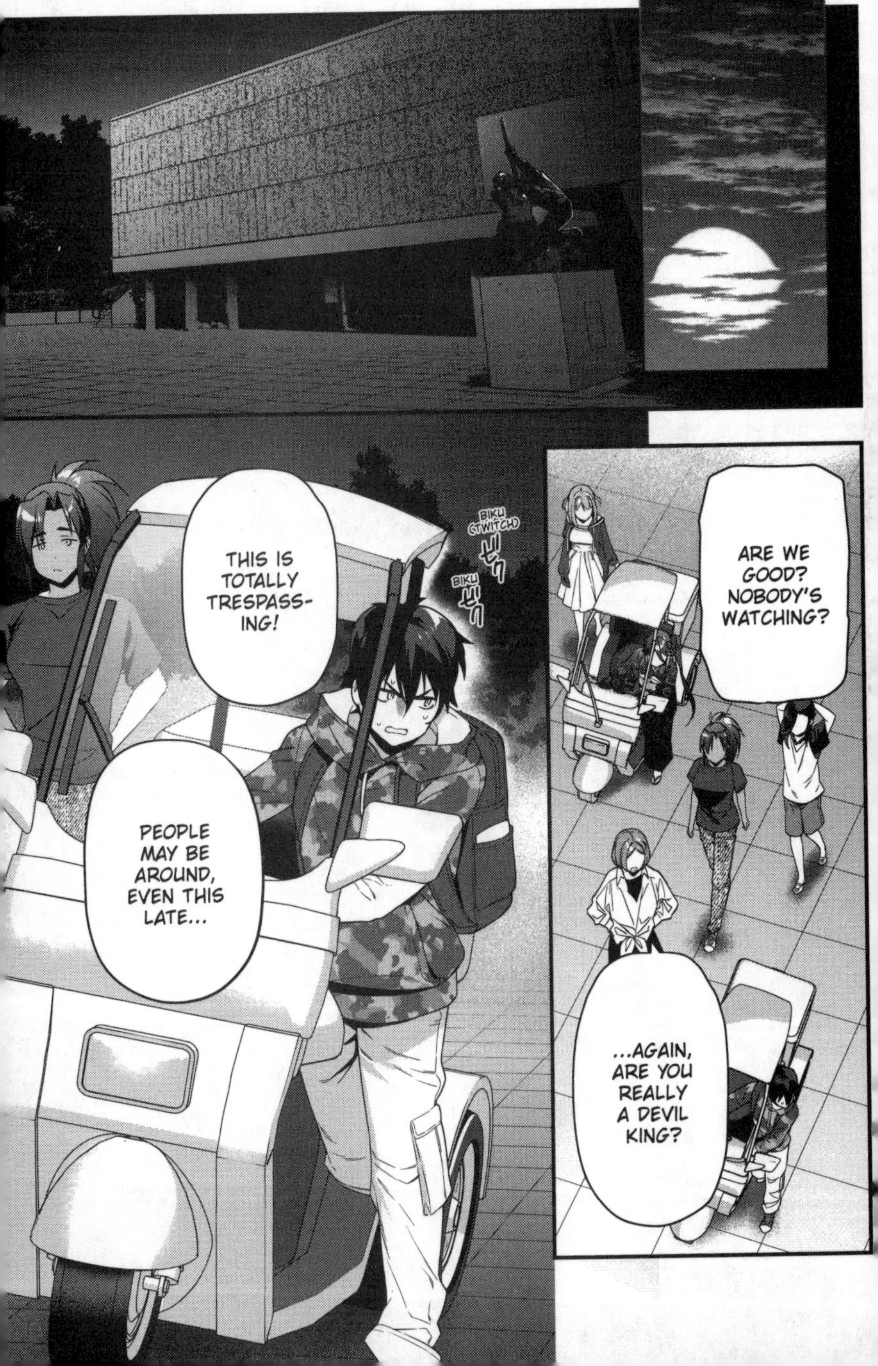
ARE WE GOOD? NOBODY'S WATCHING?
...AGAIN, ARE YOU REALLY A DEVIL KING?
BIKU (TWITCH)
BIKU
THIS IS TOTALLY TRESPASS-ING!
PEOPLE MAY BE AROUND, EVEN THIS LATE...

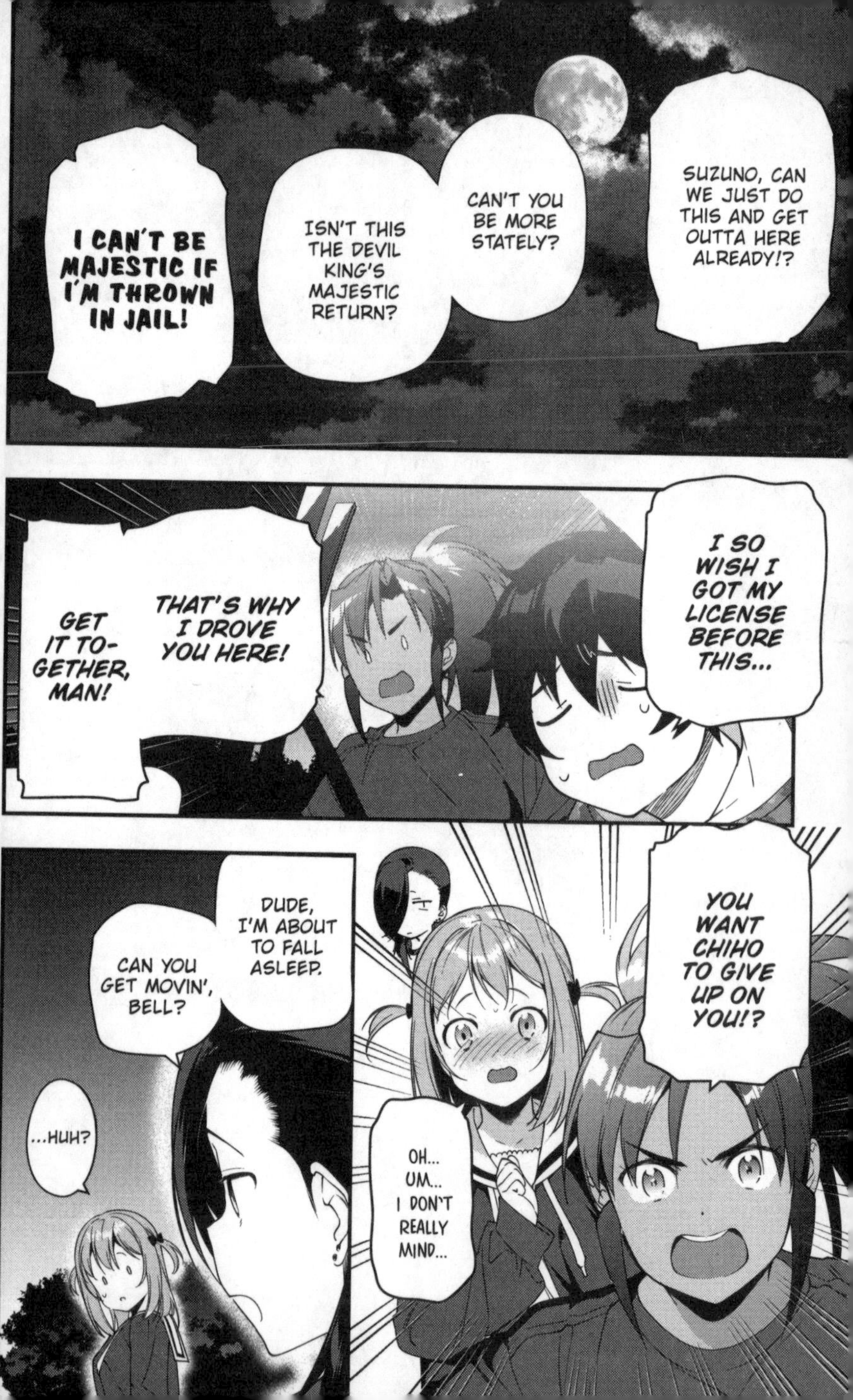
SUZUNO, CAN WE JUST DO THIS AND GET OUTTA HERE ALREADY!?
CAN'T YOU BE MORE STATELY?
ISN'T THIS THE DEVIL KING'S MAJESTIC RETURN?
I CAN'T BE MAJESTIC IF I'M THROWN IN JAIL!
I SO WISH I GOT MY LICENSE BEFORE THIS...
THAT'S WHY I DROVE YOU HERE!
GET IT TO-GETHER, MAN!
YOU WANT CHIHO TO GIVE UP ON YOU!?
DUDE, I'M ABOUT TO FALL ASLEEP.
CAN YOU GET MOVIN', BELL?
OH... UM... I DON'T REALLY MIND...
...HUH?

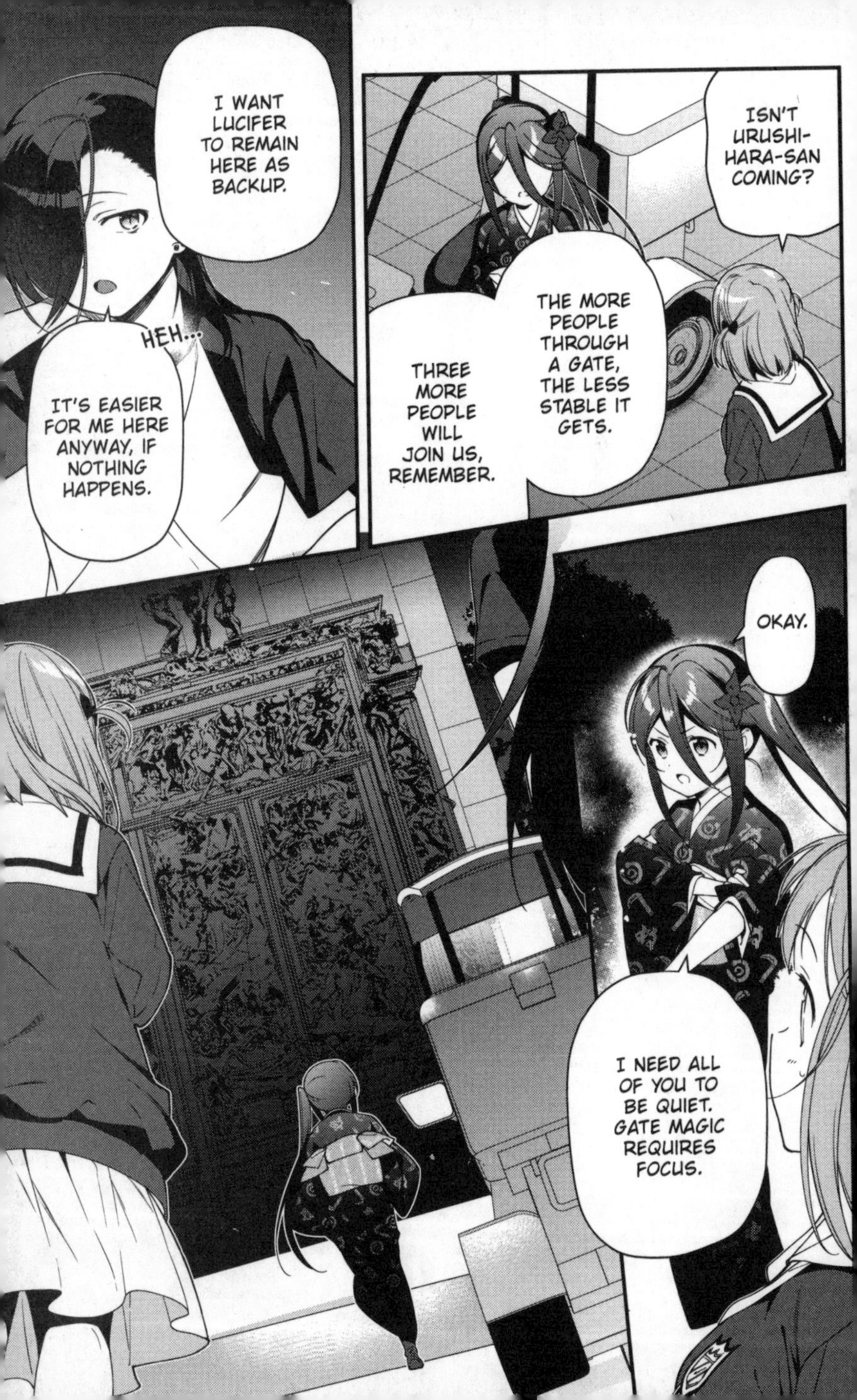
ISN'T URUSHI-HARA-SAN COMING?
THE MORE PEOPLE THROUGH A GATE, THE LESS STABLE IT GETS.
THREE MORE PEOPLE WILL JOIN US, REMEMBER.
I WANT LUCIFER TO REMAIN HERE AS BACKUP.
HEH...
IT'S EASIER FOR ME HERE ANYWAY, IF NOTHING HAPPENS.
OKAY.
I NEED ALL OF YOU TO BE QUIET. GATE MAGIC REQUIRES FOCUS.

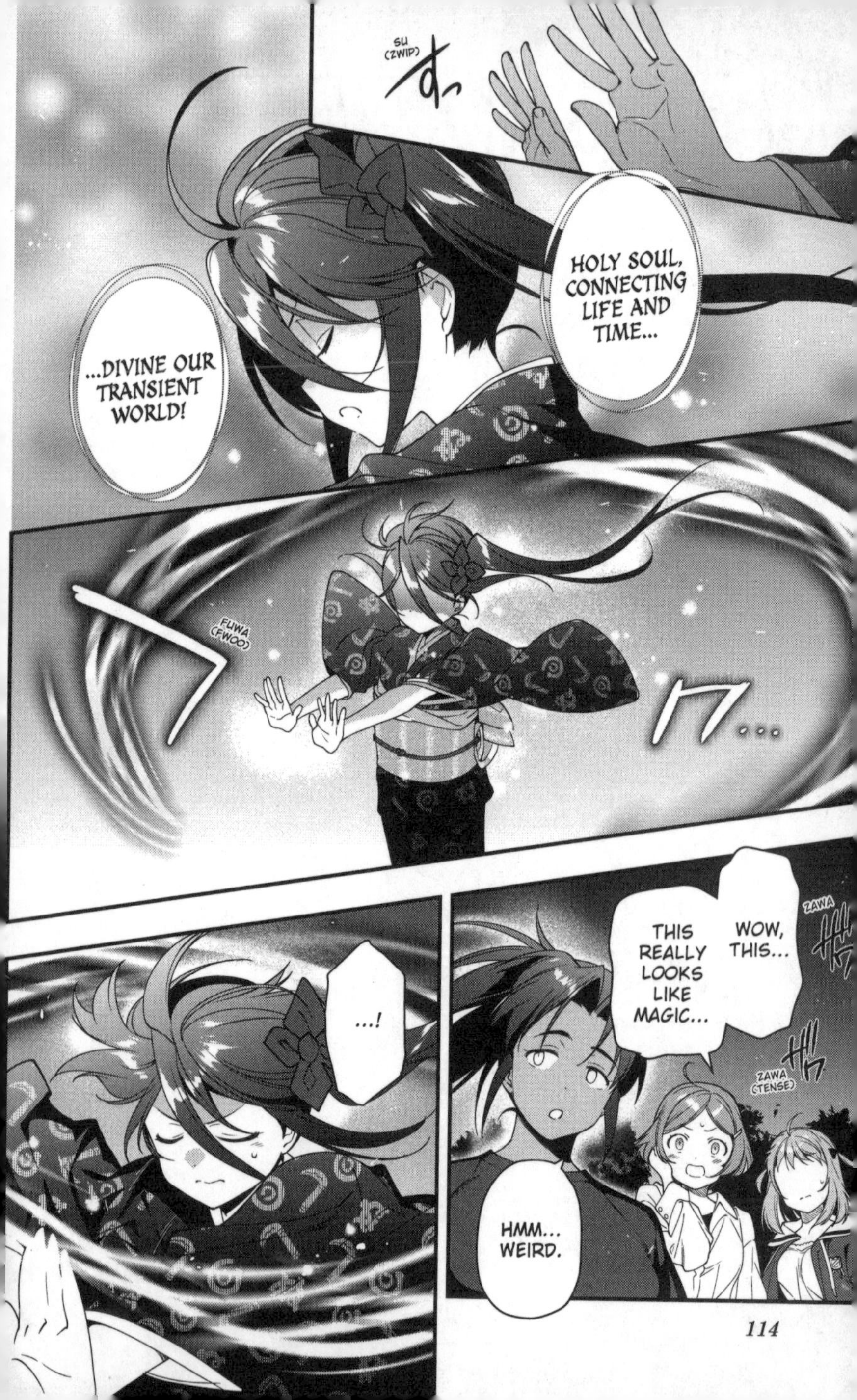
SU (ZWIP)
HOLY SOUL, CONNECTING LIFE AND TIME...
...DIVINE OUR TRANSIENT WORLD!
FUWA (FWOO)
ZAWA
WOW, THIS...
THIS REALLY LOOKS LIKE MAGIC...
ZAWA (TENSE)
HMM... WEIRD.
...!

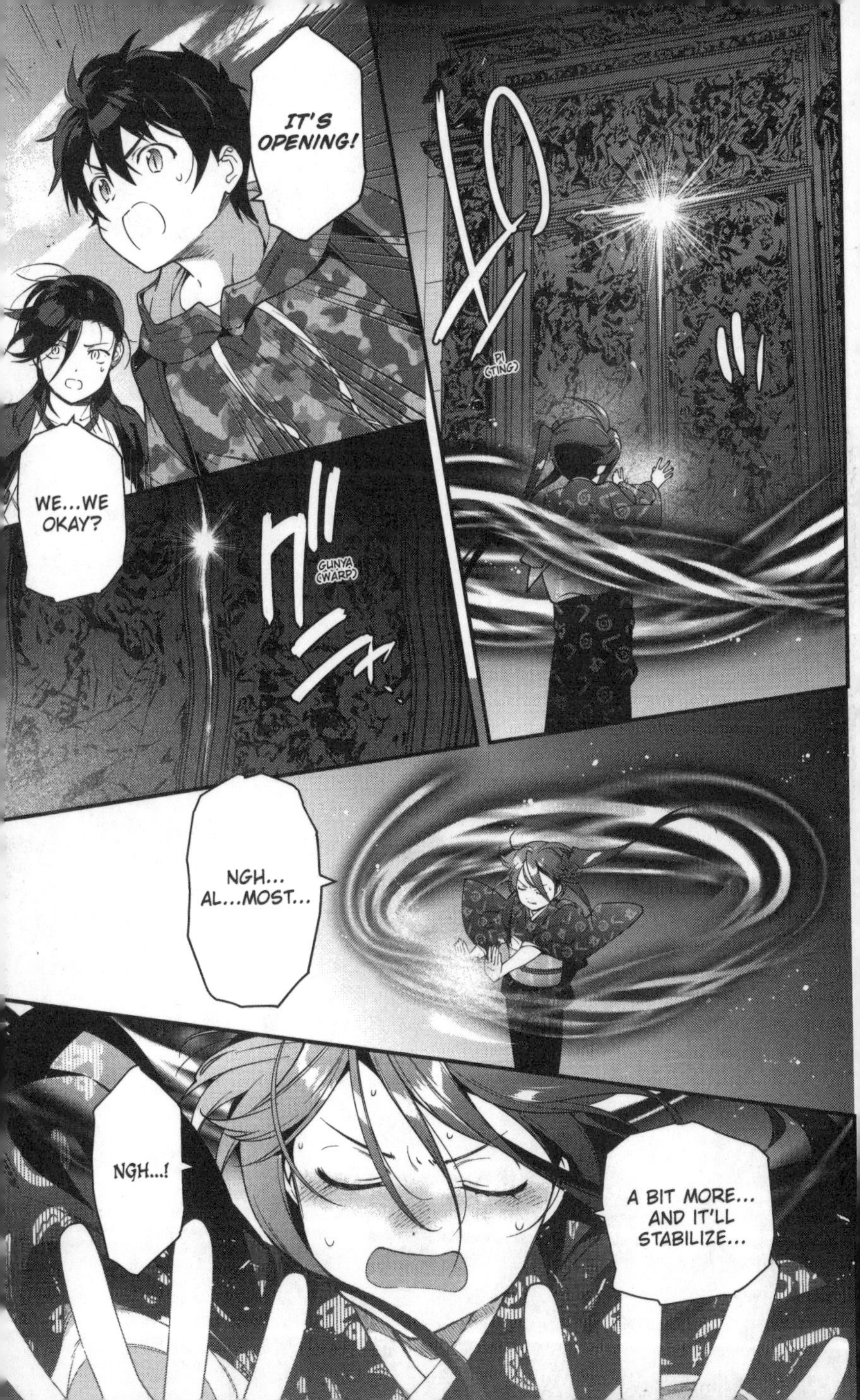
PI (STING)
IT'S OPENING!
WE...WE OKAY?
GUNYA (WARP)
NGH... AL...MOST...
A BIT MORE... AND IT'LL STABILIZE...
NGH...!

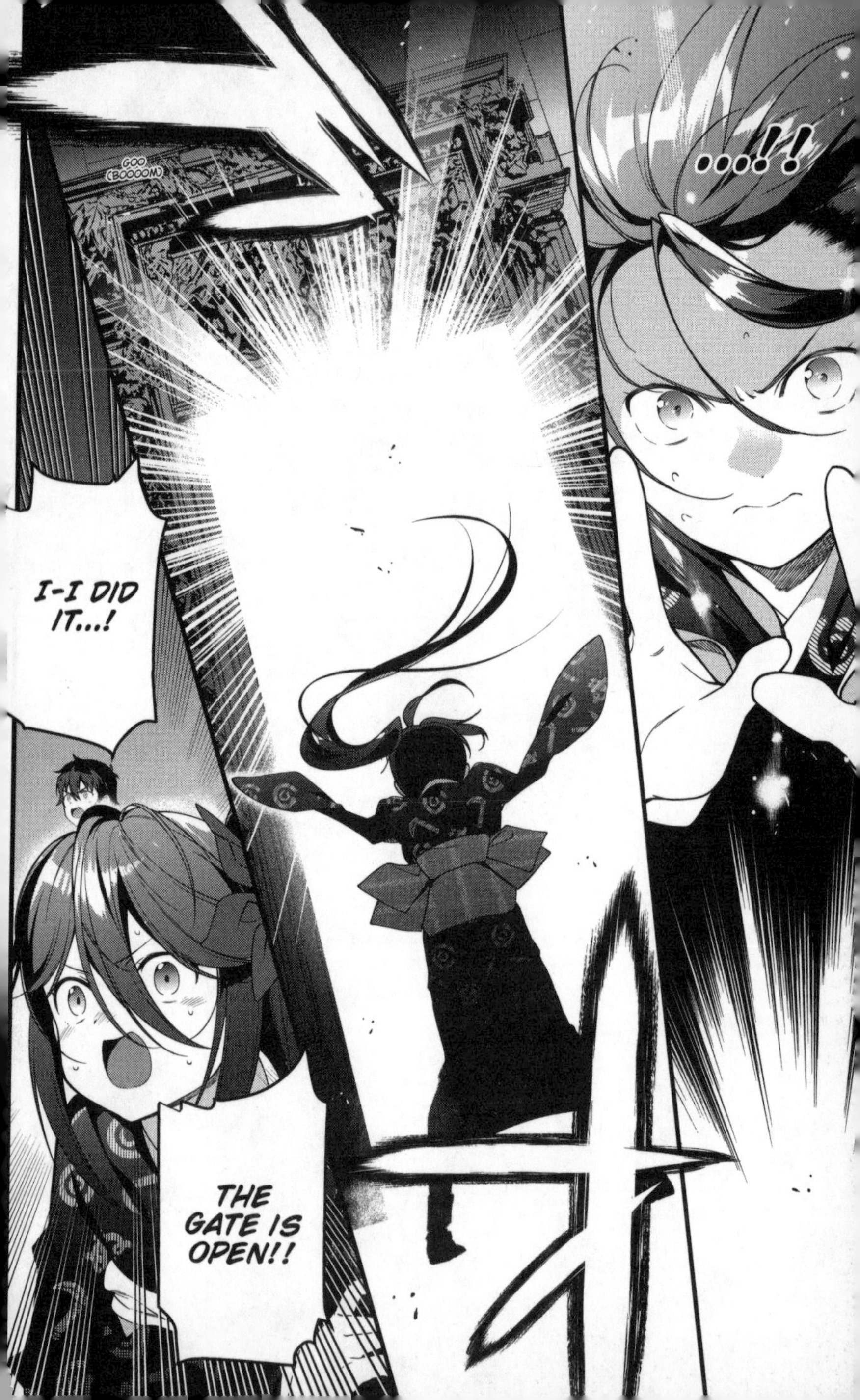
...!!
GOO
(BOOOOM)
I-I DID IT...!
THE GATE IS OPEN!!

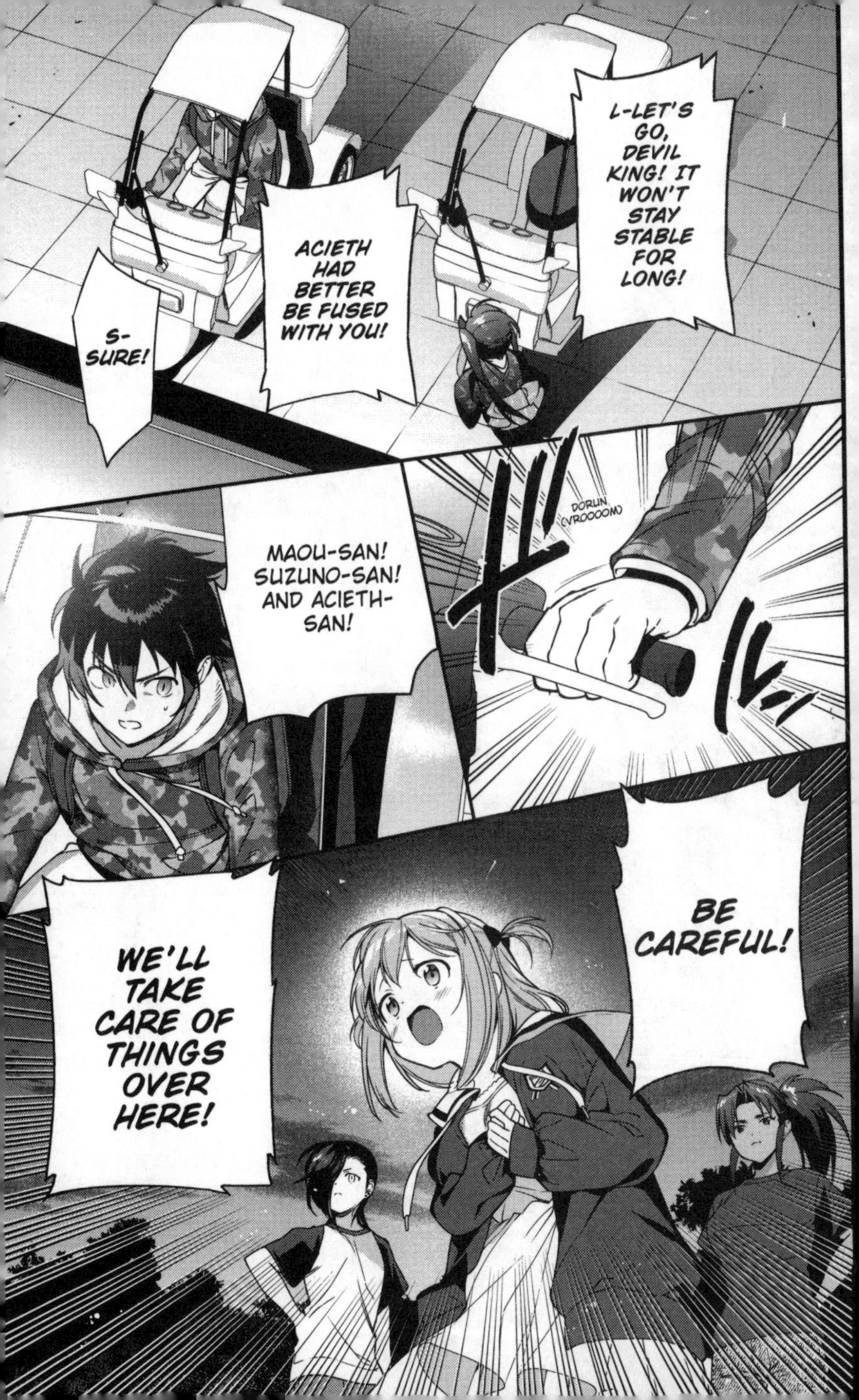
L-LET'S GO, DEVIL KING! IT WON'T STAY STABLE FOR LONG!
ACIETH HAD BETTER BE FUSED WITH YOU!
S-SURE!
DORUN (VROOOOM)
MAOU-SAN! SUZUNO-SAN! AND ACIETH-SAN!
BE CAREFUL!
WE'LL TAKE CARE OF THINGS OVER HERE!

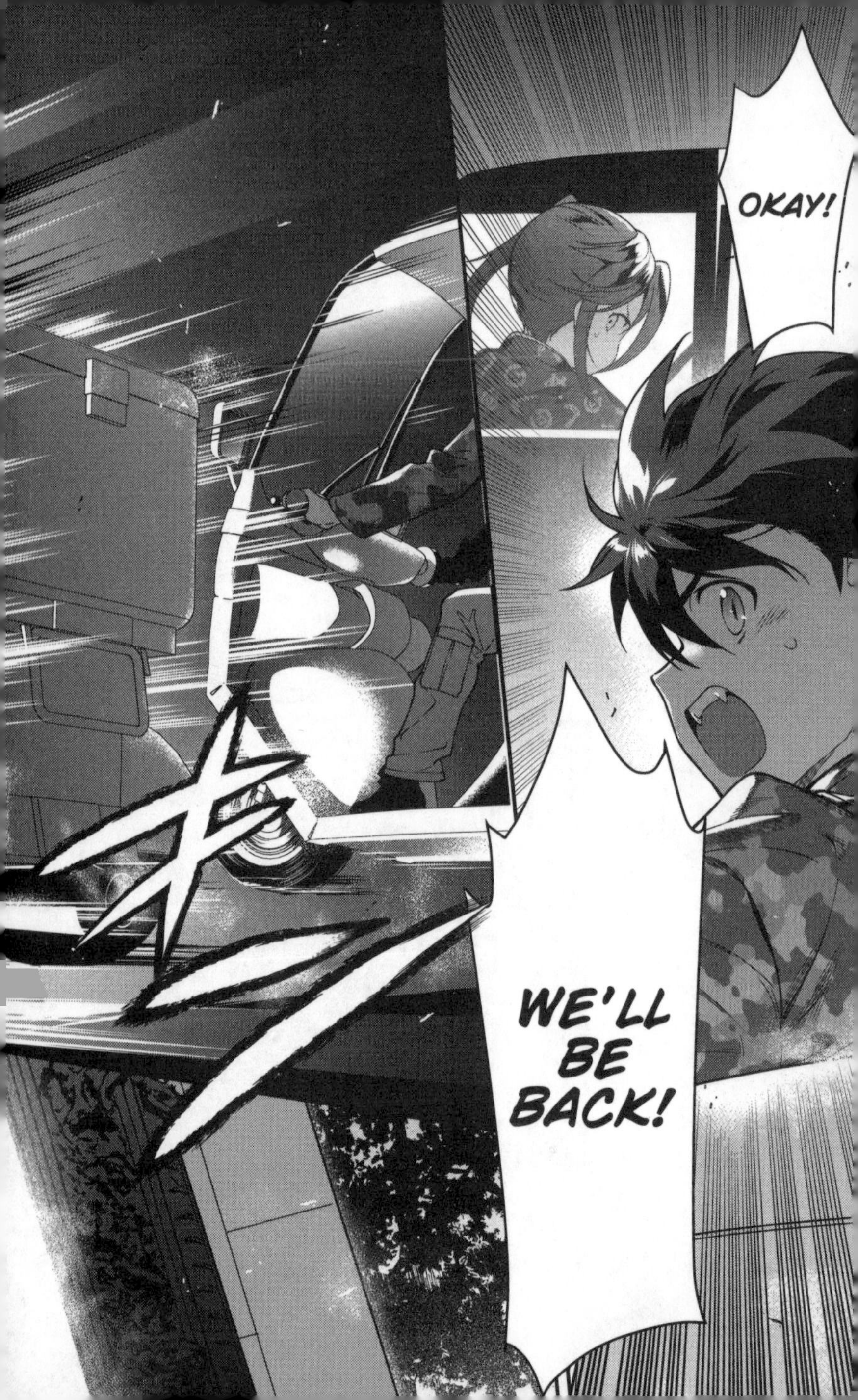
OKAY!
WE'LL BE BACK!

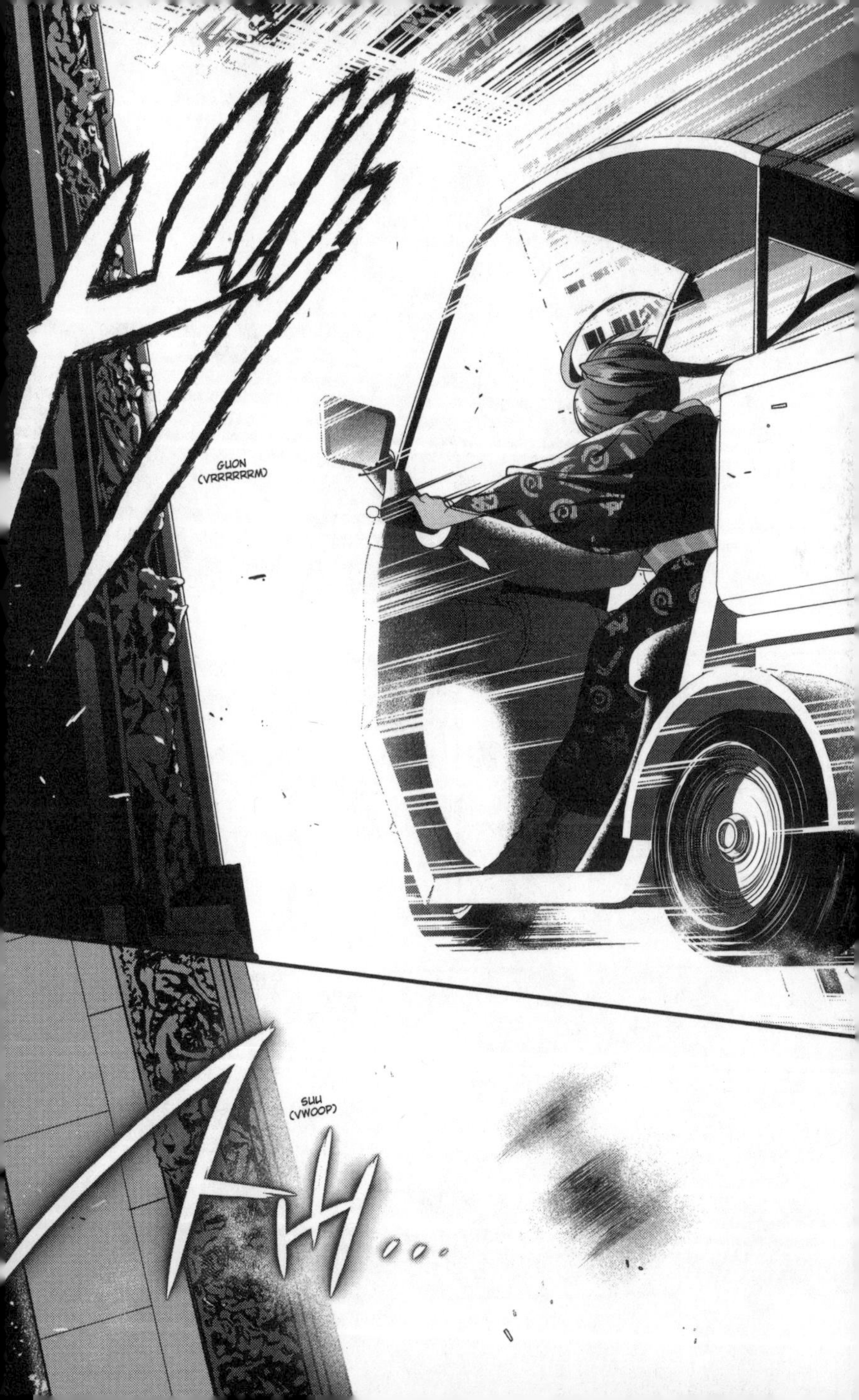
GUON
(VRRRRRRM)
SUU
(VWOOP)

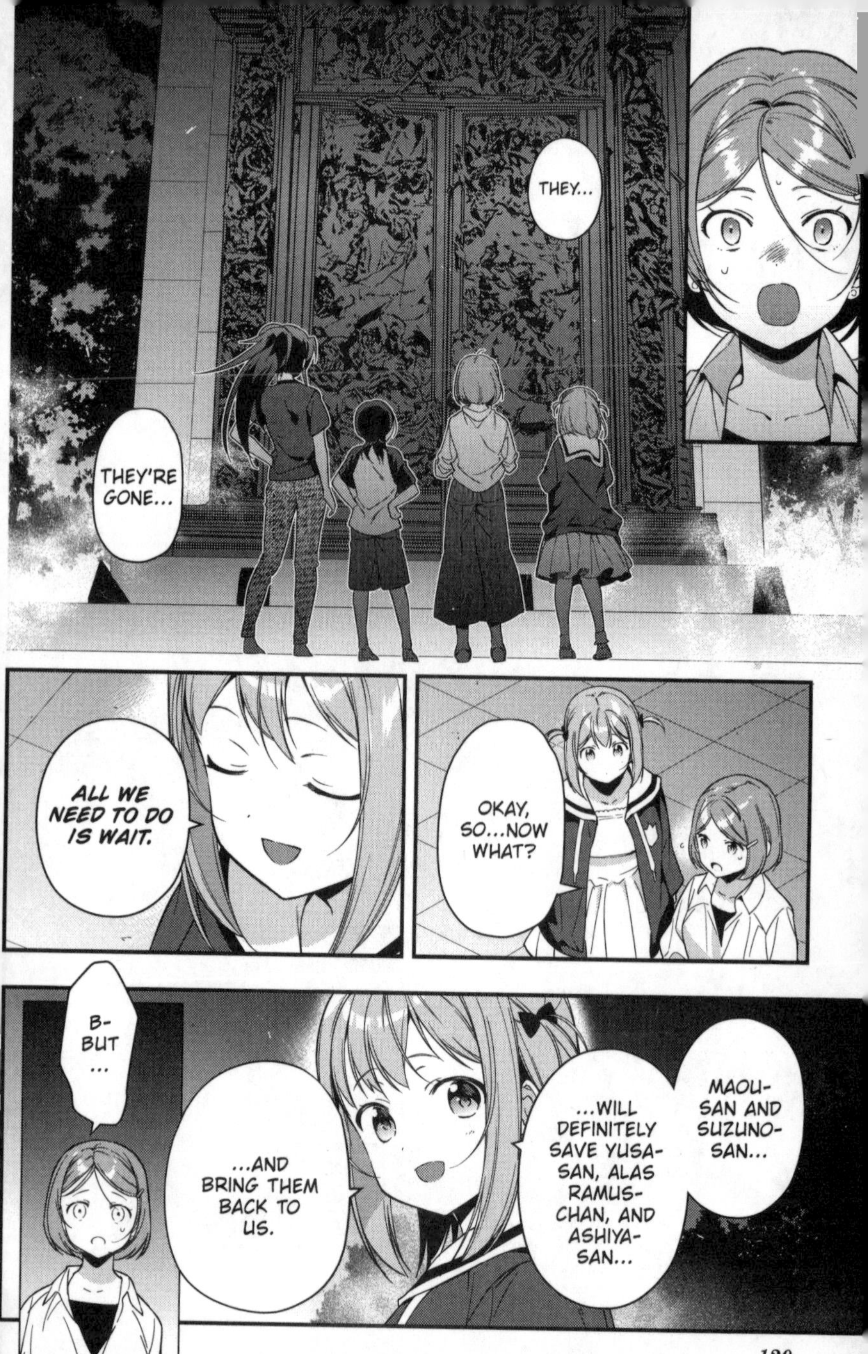
THEY...
THEY'RE GONE...
OKAY, SO...NOW WHAT?
ALL WE NEED TO DO IS WAIT.
MAOU-SAN AND SUZUNO-SAN...
...WILL DEFINITELY SAVE YUSA-SAN, ALAS RAMUS-CHAN, AND ASHIYA-SAN...
...AND BRING THEM BACK TO US.
B-BUT...

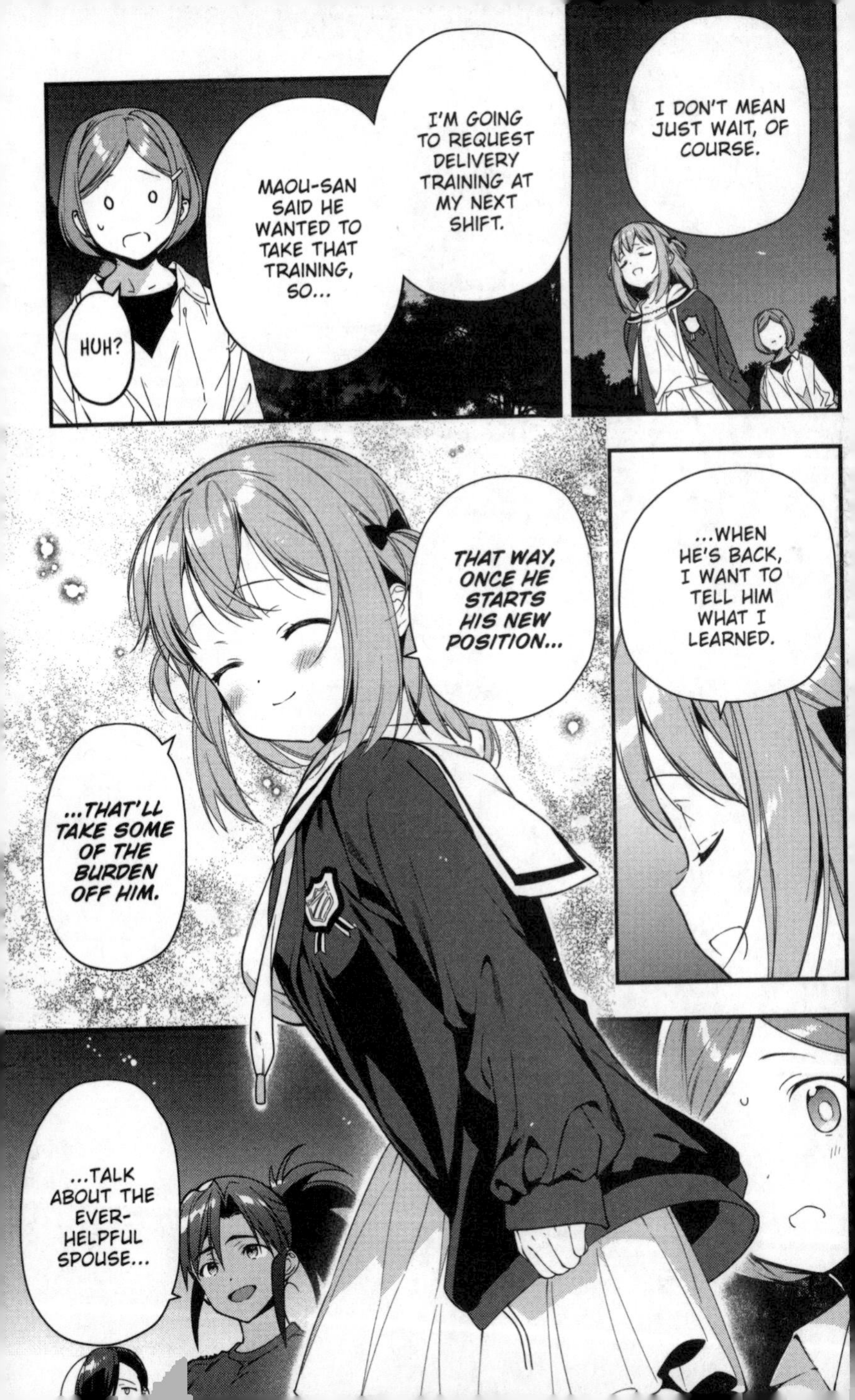
I DON'T MEAN JUST WAIT, OF COURSE.
I'M GOING TO REQUEST DELIVERY TRAINING AT MY NEXT SHIFT.
MAOU-SAN SAID HE WANTED TO TAKE THAT TRAINING, SO...
HUH?
...WHEN HE'S BACK, I WANT TO TELL HIM WHAT I LEARNED.
THAT WAY, ONCE HE STARTS HIS NEW POSITION...
...THAT'LL TAKE SOME OF THE BURDEN OFF HIM.
...TALK ABOUT THE EVER-HELPFUL SPOUSE...

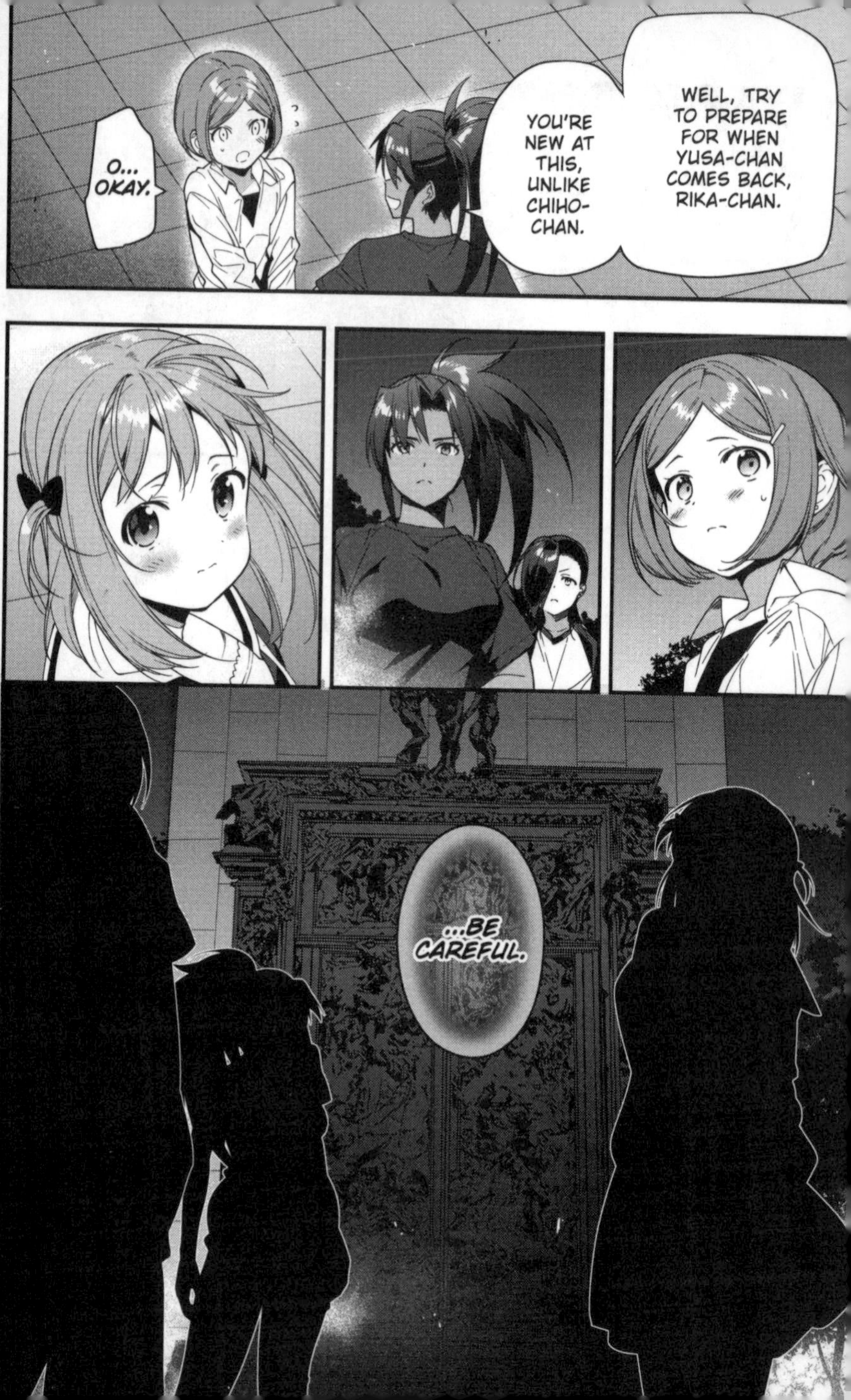
WELL, TRY TO PREPARE FOR WHEN YUSA-CHAN COMES BACK, RIKA-CHAN.
YOU'RE NEW AT THIS, UNLIKE CHIHO-CHAN.
O... OKAY.
...BE CAREFUL.

Chiho
Sasaki

THE DEVIL IS A PART-TIMER!

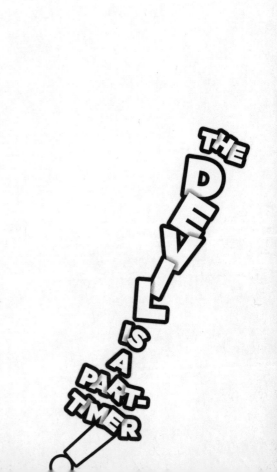

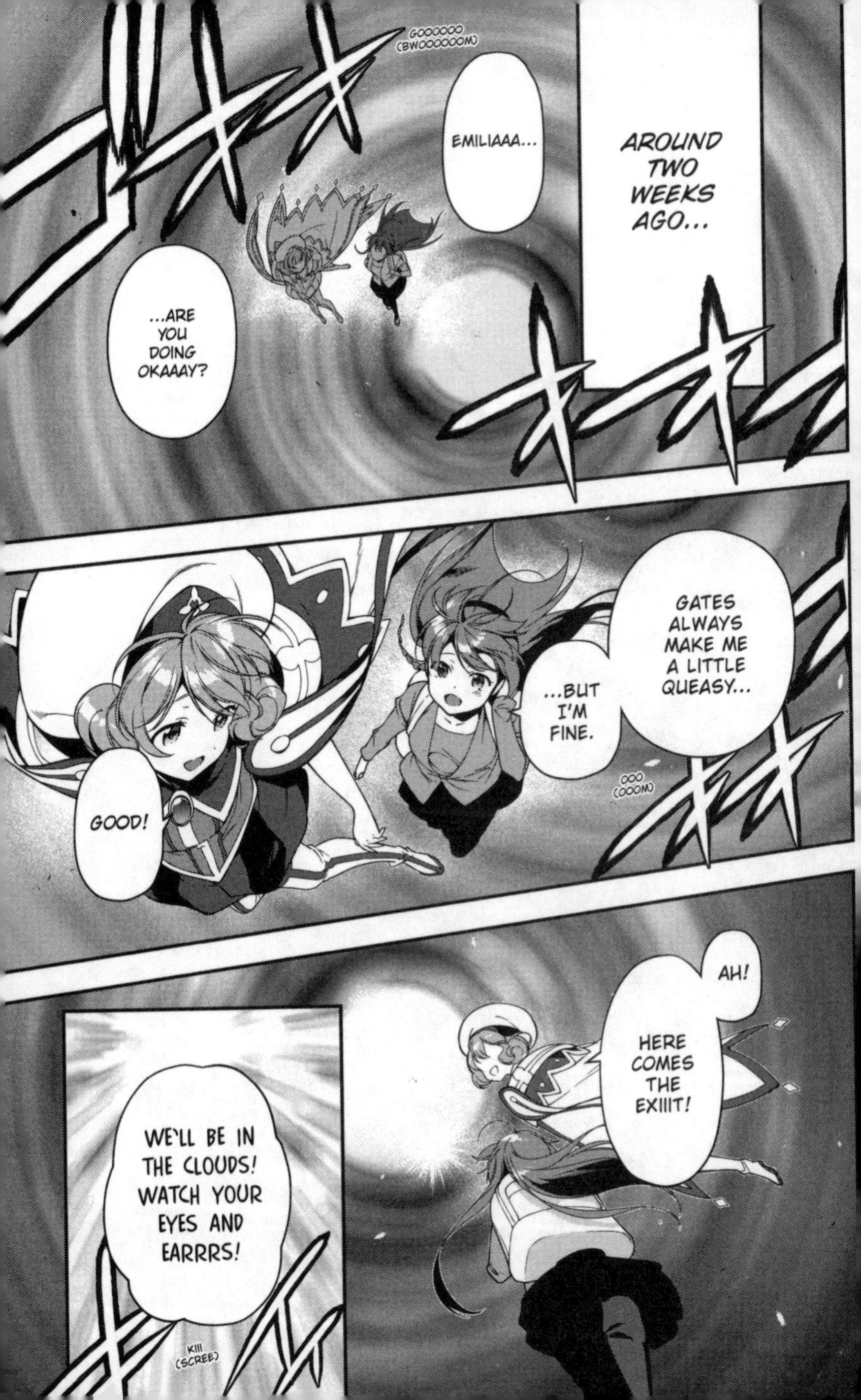
AROUND TWO WEEKS AGO...
GOOOOOO (BWOOOOOOM)
EMILIAAA...
...ARE YOU DOING OKAAAY?
GATES ALWAYS MAKE ME A LITTLE QUEASY...
...BUT I'M FINE.
OOO (OOOM)
GOOD!
AH!
HERE COMES THE EXIIIT!
WE'LL BE IN THE CLOUDS! WATCH YOUR EYES AND EARRRS!
KIII (SCREE)

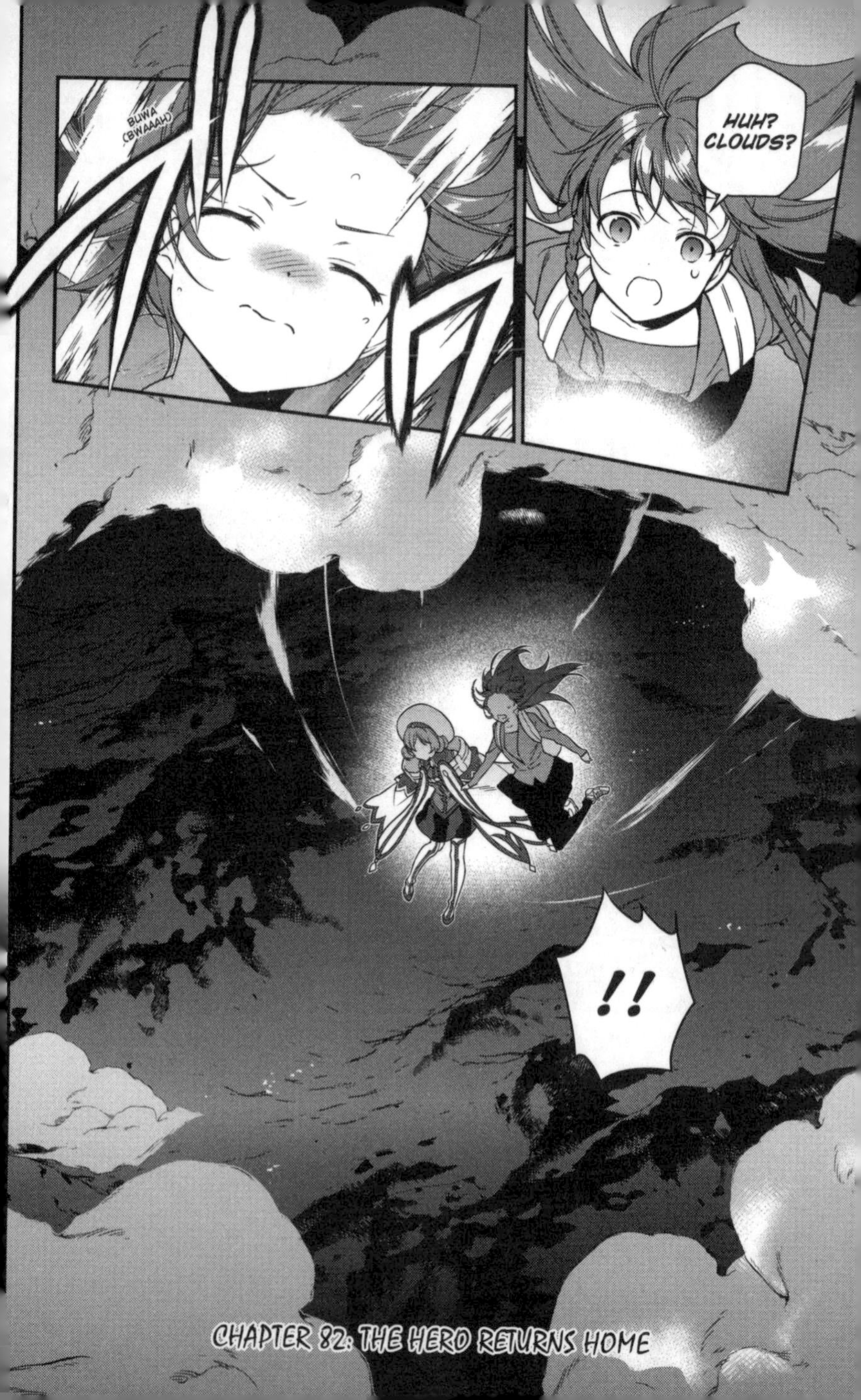
HUH? CLOUDS?
BUWA (BWAAAH)
!!
CHAPTER 82: THE HERO RETURNS HOME

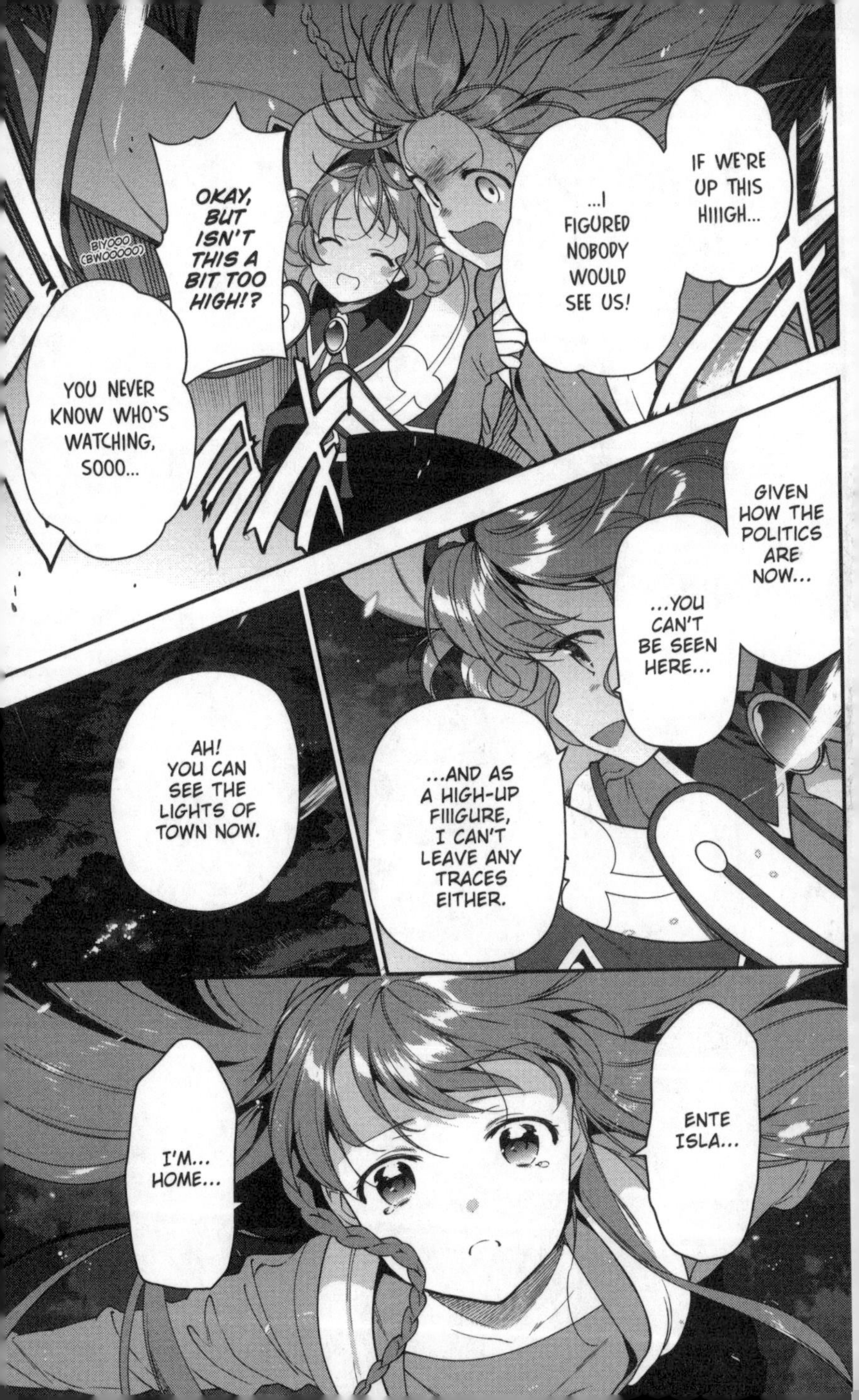
IF WE'RE UP THIS HIIIGH...
...I FIGURED NOBODY WOULD SEE US!
OKAY, BUT ISN'T THIS A BIT TOO HIGH!?
BIYOOO (BWOOOOO)
YOU NEVER KNOW WHO'S WATCHING, SOOO...
GIVEN HOW THE POLITICS ARE NOW...
...YOU CAN'T BE SEEN HERE...
...AND AS A HIGH-UP FIIIGURE, I CAN'T LEAVE ANY TRACES EITHER.
AH! YOU CAN SEE THE LIGHTS OF TOWN NOW.
ENTE ISLA...
I'M... HOME...

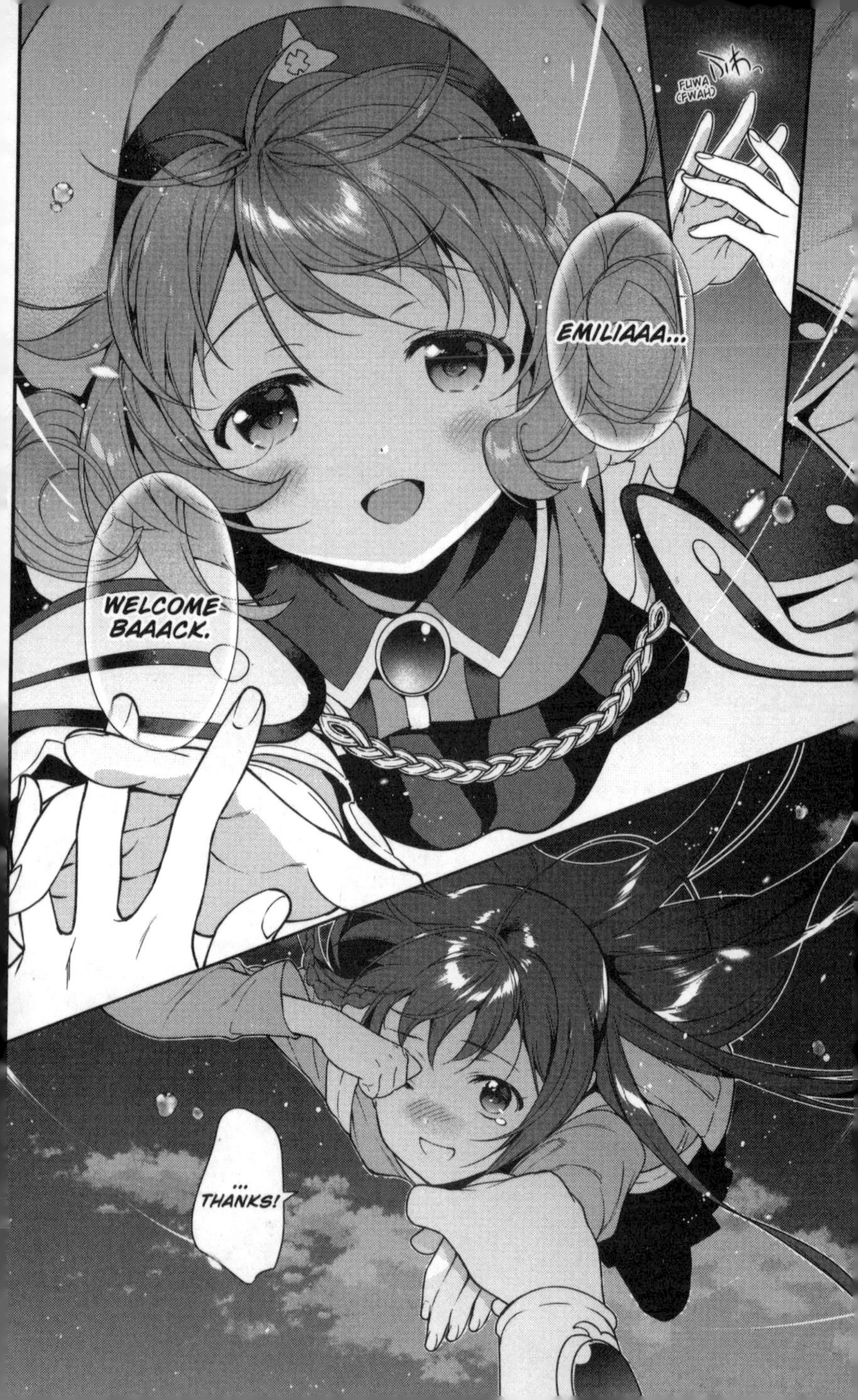
ふわ
FUWA (FWAH)
EMILIAAA...
WELCOME BAAACK.
...THANKS!

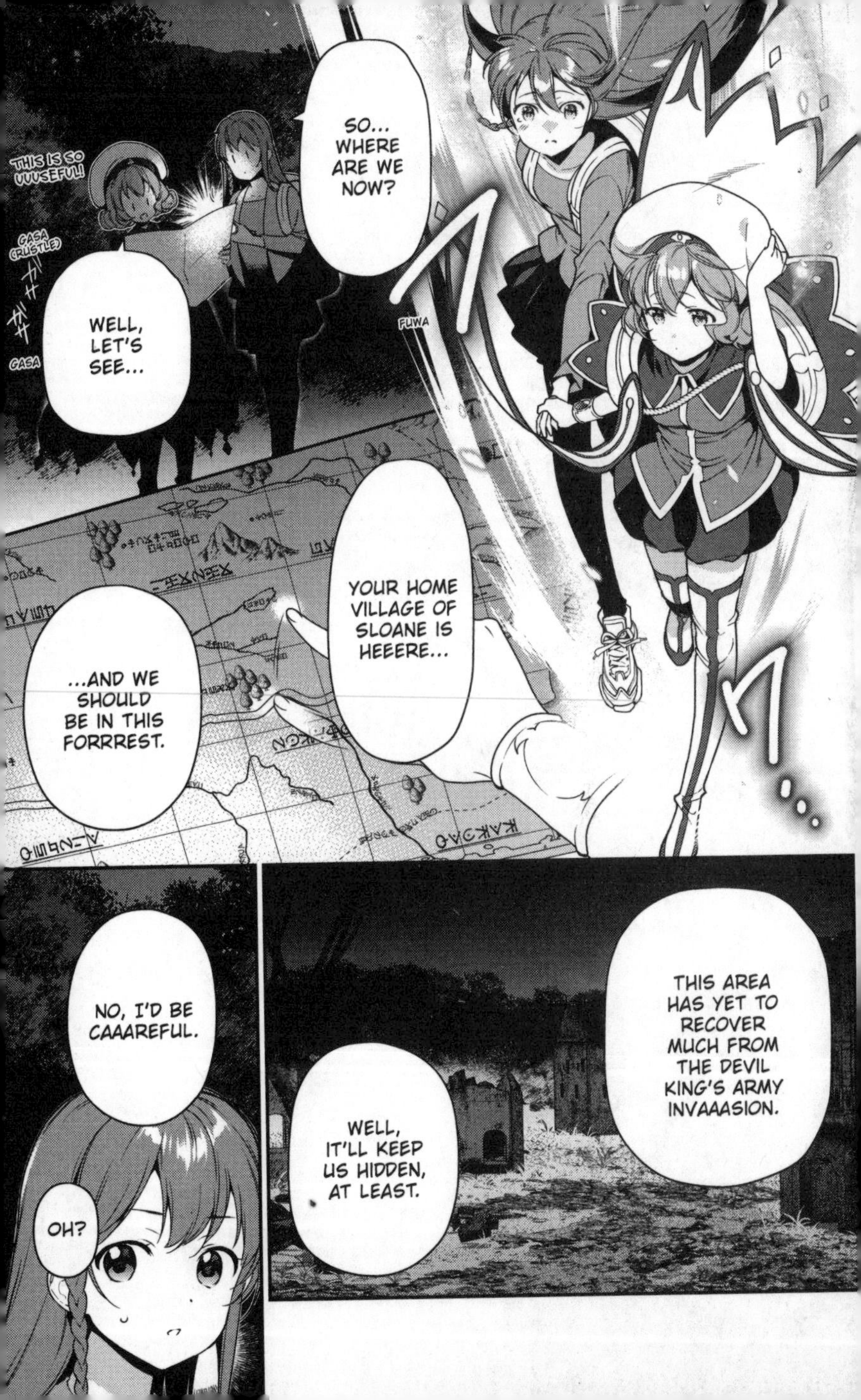
FUWA
...
SO... WHERE ARE WE NOW?
THIS IS SO UUUSEFUL!
GASA (RUSTLE)
WELL, LET'S SEE...
GASA
YOUR HOME VILLAGE OF SLOANE IS HEEERE...
...AND WE SHOULD BE IN THIS FORRREST.
THIS AREA HAS YET TO RECOVER MUCH FROM THE DEVIL KING'S ARMY INVAAASION.
WELL, IT'LL KEEP US HIDDEN, AT LEAST.
NO, I'D BE CAAAREFUL.
OH?

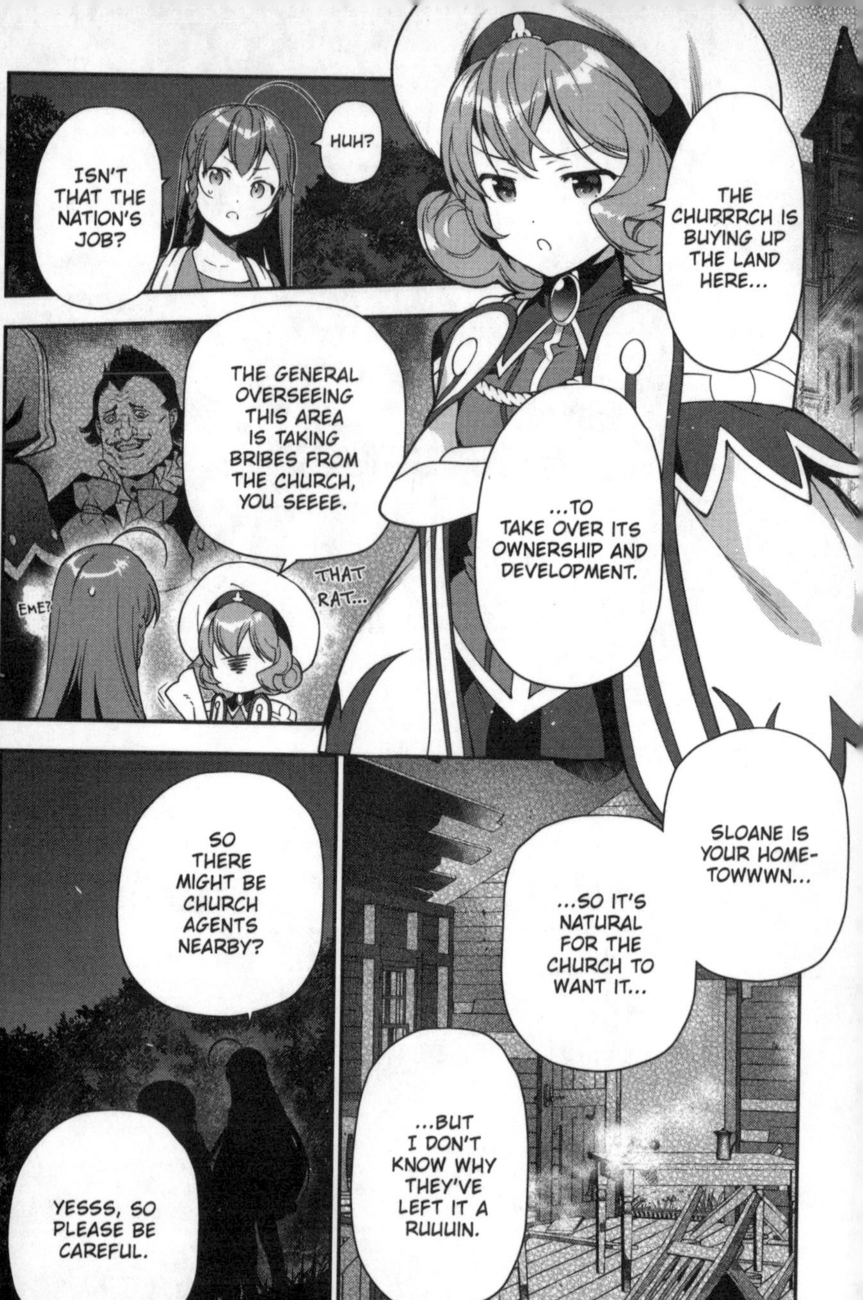
THE CHURRRCH IS BUYING UP THE LAND HERE...
...TO TAKE OVER ITS OWNERSHIP AND DEVELOPMENT.
HUH?
ISN'T THAT THE NATION'S JOB?
THE GENERAL OVERSEEING THIS AREA IS TAKING BRIBES FROM THE CHURCH, YOU SEEEE.
THAT RAT...
EME?
SLOANE IS YOUR HOME-TOWWWN...
...SO IT'S NATURAL FOR THE CHURCH TO WANT IT...
...BUT I DON'T KNOW WHY THEY'VE LEFT IT A RUUUIN.
SO THERE MIGHT BE CHURCH AGENTS NEARBY?
YESSS, SO PLEASE BE CAREFUL.

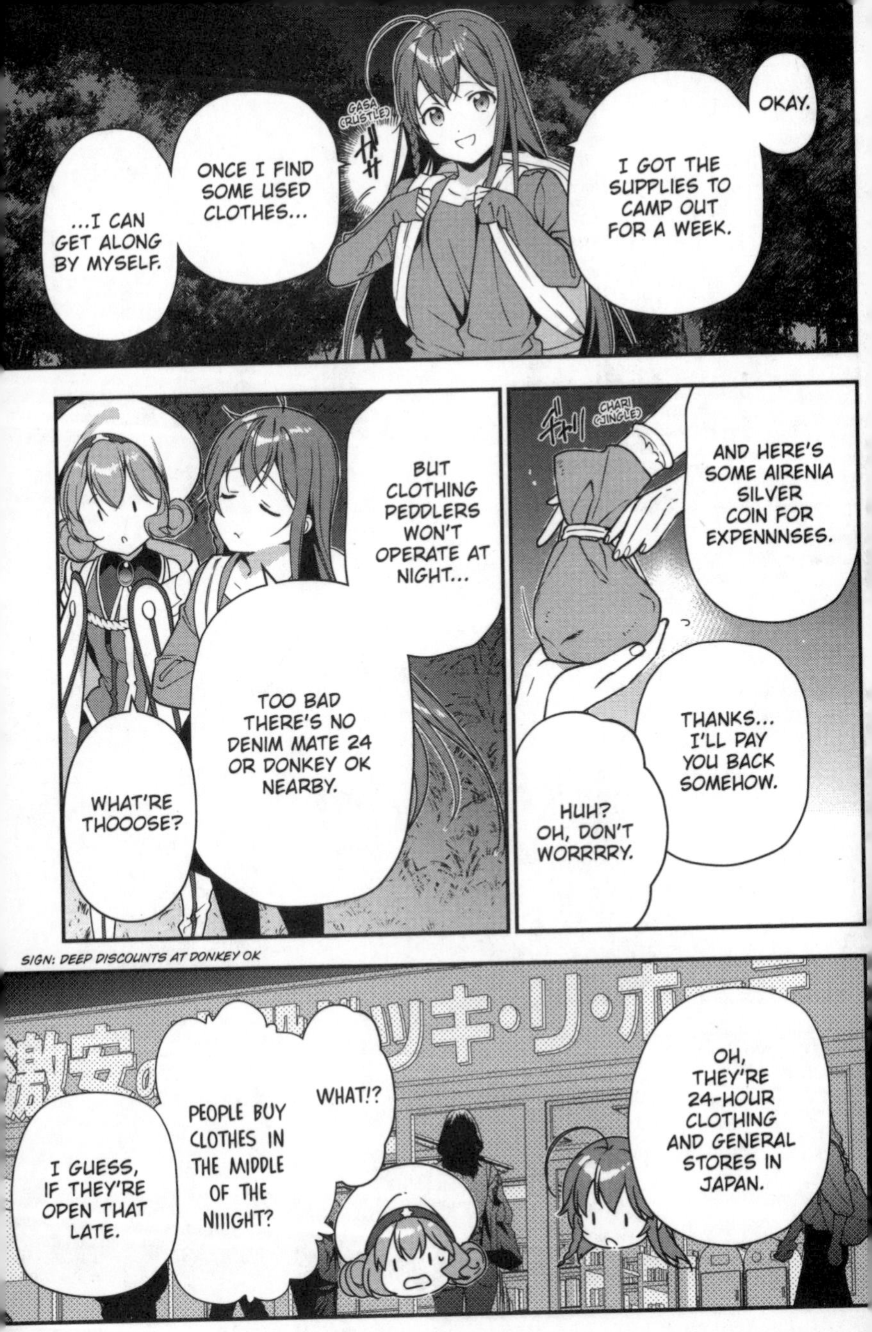
OKAY.
I GOT THE SUPPLIES TO CAMP OUT FOR A WEEK.
GASA (RUSTLE)
ONCE I FIND SOME USED CLOTHES...
...I CAN GET ALONG BY MYSELF.
CHARI (JINGLE)
AND HERE'S SOME AIRENIA SILVER COIN FOR EXPENNNSES.
THANKS... I'LL PAY YOU BACK SOMEHOW.
HUH? OH, DON'T WORRRRY.
BUT CLOTHING PEDDLERS WON'T OPERATE AT NIGHT...
TOO BAD THERE'S NO DENIM MATE 24 OR DONKEY OK NEARBY.
WHAT'RE THOOOSE?
SIGN: DEEP DISCOUNTS AT DONKEY OK
OH, THEY'RE 24-HOUR CLOTHING AND GENERAL STORES IN JAPAN.
WHAT!?
PEOPLE BUY CLOTHES IN THE MIDDLE OF THE NIIIGHT?
I GUESS, IF THEY'RE OPEN THAT LATE.

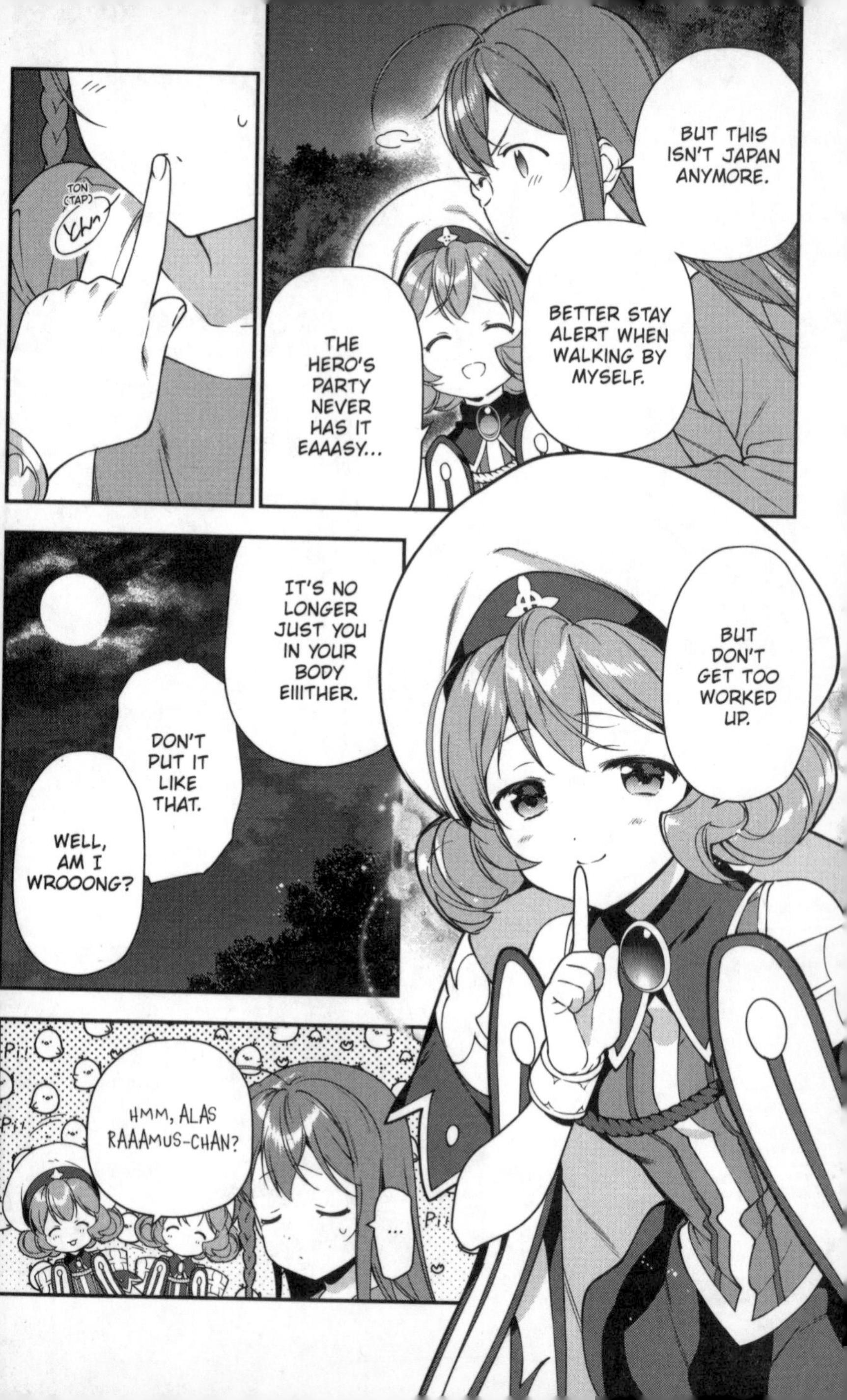
BUT THIS ISN'T JAPAN ANYMORE.
BETTER STAY ALERT WHEN WALKING BY MYSELF.
THE HERO'S PARTY NEVER HAS IT EAAASY...
TON (TAP)
BUT DON'T GET TOO WORKED UP.
IT'S NO LONGER JUST YOU IN YOUR BODY EIIITHER.
DON'T PUT IT LIKE THAT.
WELL, AM I WROOONG?
Pi!
Pi
HMM, ALAS RAAAMUS-CHAN?
...
Pi!

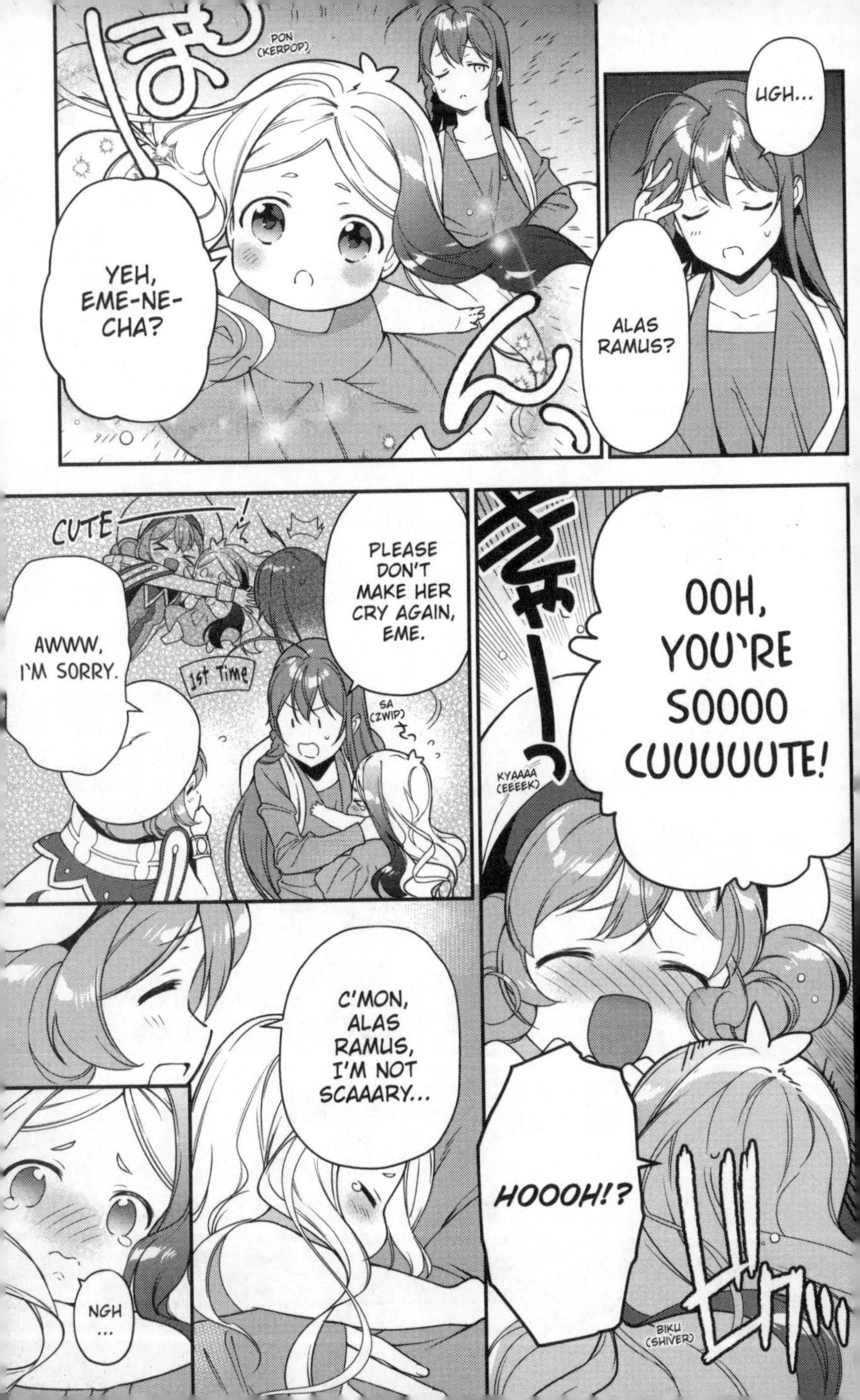
UGH...
ALAS RAMUS?
PON (KERPOP)
YEH, EME-NE-CHA?
KYAAAA (EEEEK)
OOH, YOU'RE SOOOO CUUUUUTE!
PLEASE DON'T MAKE HER CRY AGAIN, EME.
CUTE
1st Time
SA (ZWIP)
AWWW, I'M SORRY.
HOOOH!?
BIKU (SHIVER)
C'MON, ALAS RAMUS, I'M NOT SCAAARY...
NGH ...

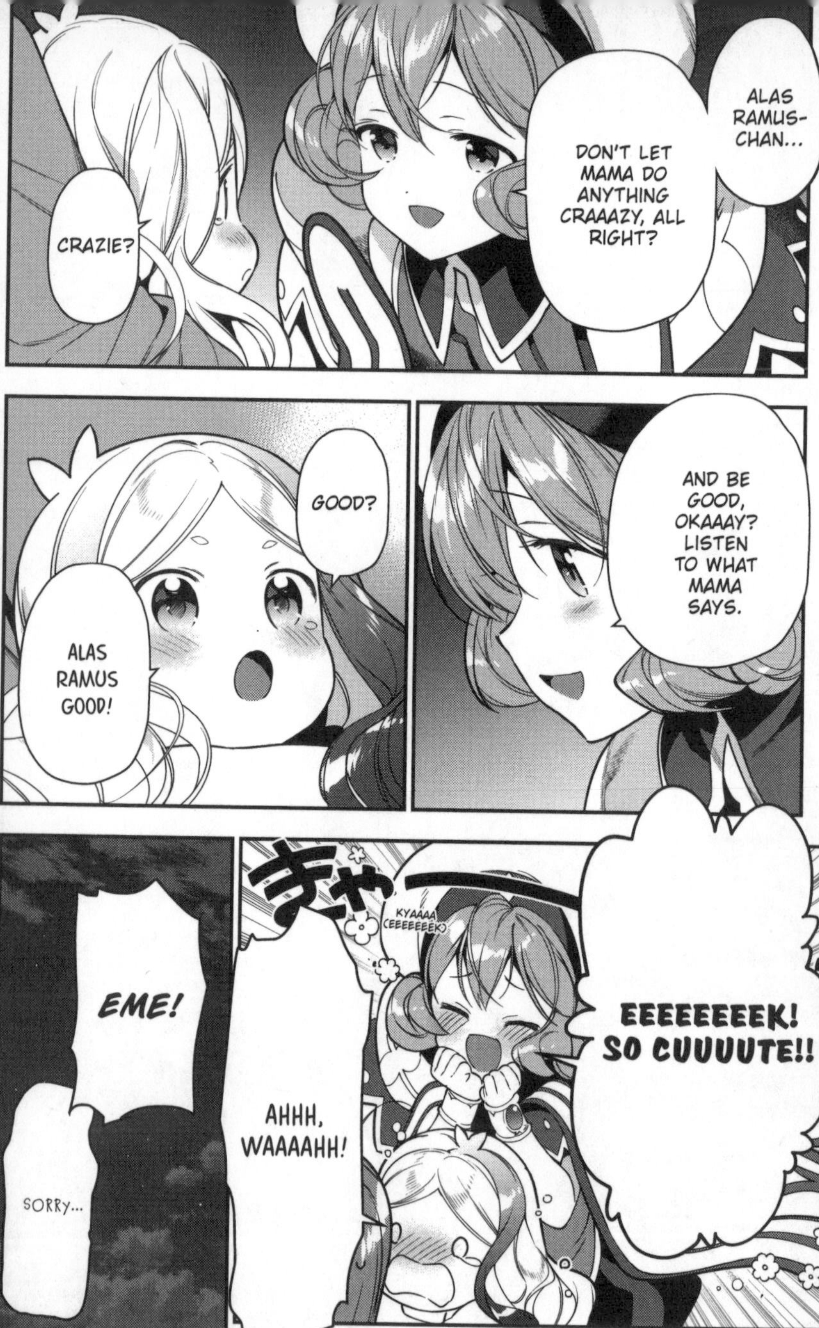
ALAS RAMUS-CHAN...
DON'T LET MAMA DO ANYTHING CRAAAZY, ALL RIGHT?
CRAZIE?
AND BE GOOD, OKAAAY? LISTEN TO WHAT MAMA SAYS.
GOOD?
ALAS RAMUS GOOD!
EEEEEEEEK! SO CUUUUTE!!
きゃー
KYAAAA (EEEEEEEK)
AHHH, WAAAAHH!
EME!
SORRY...

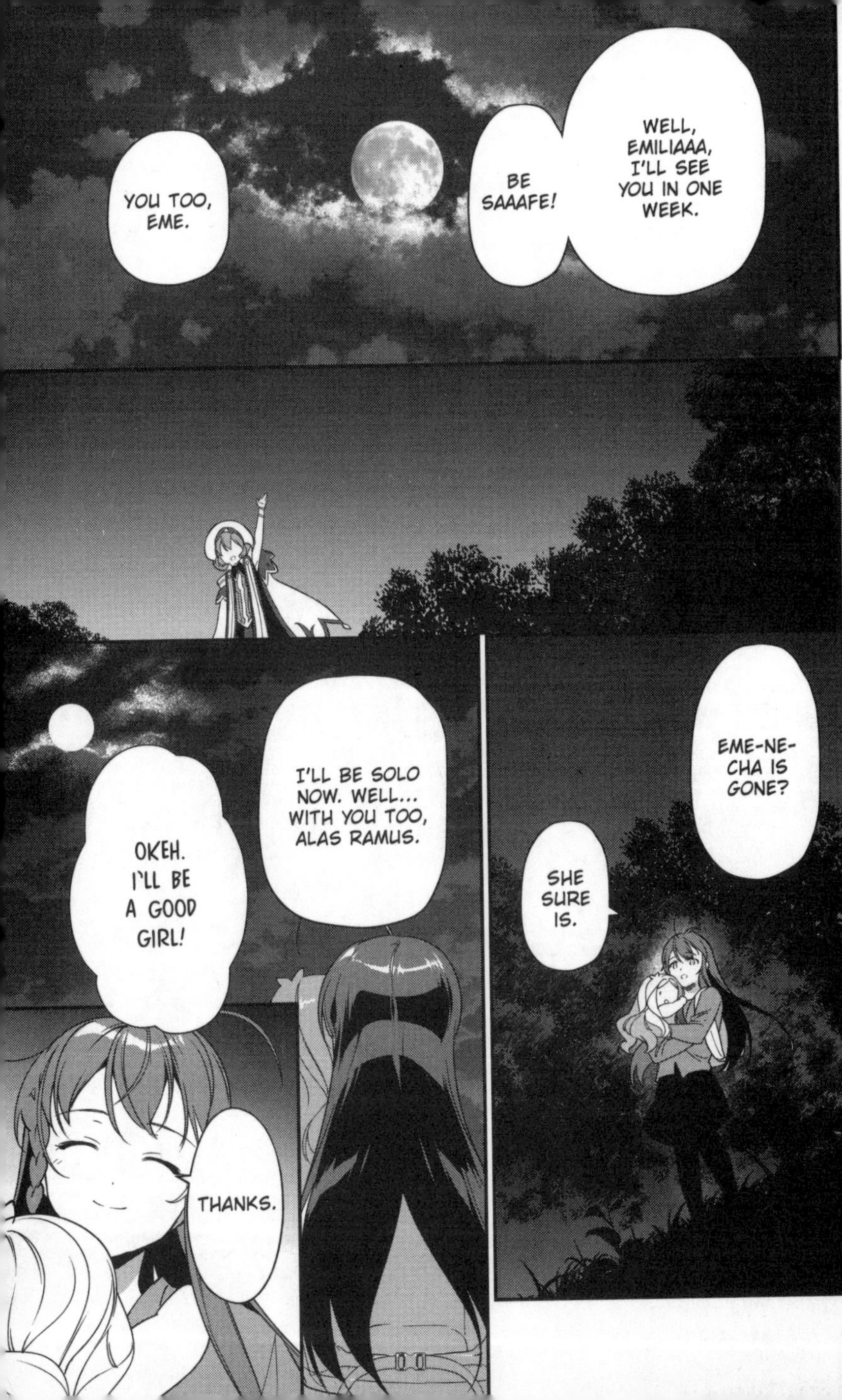
WELL, EMILIAAA, I'LL SEE YOU IN ONE WEEK.
BE SAAAFE!
YOU TOO, EME.
EME-NE-CHA IS GONE?
SHE SURE IS.
I'LL BE SOLO NOW. WELL... WITH YOU TOO, ALAS RAMUS.
OKEH. I'LL BE A GOOD GIRL!
THANKS.

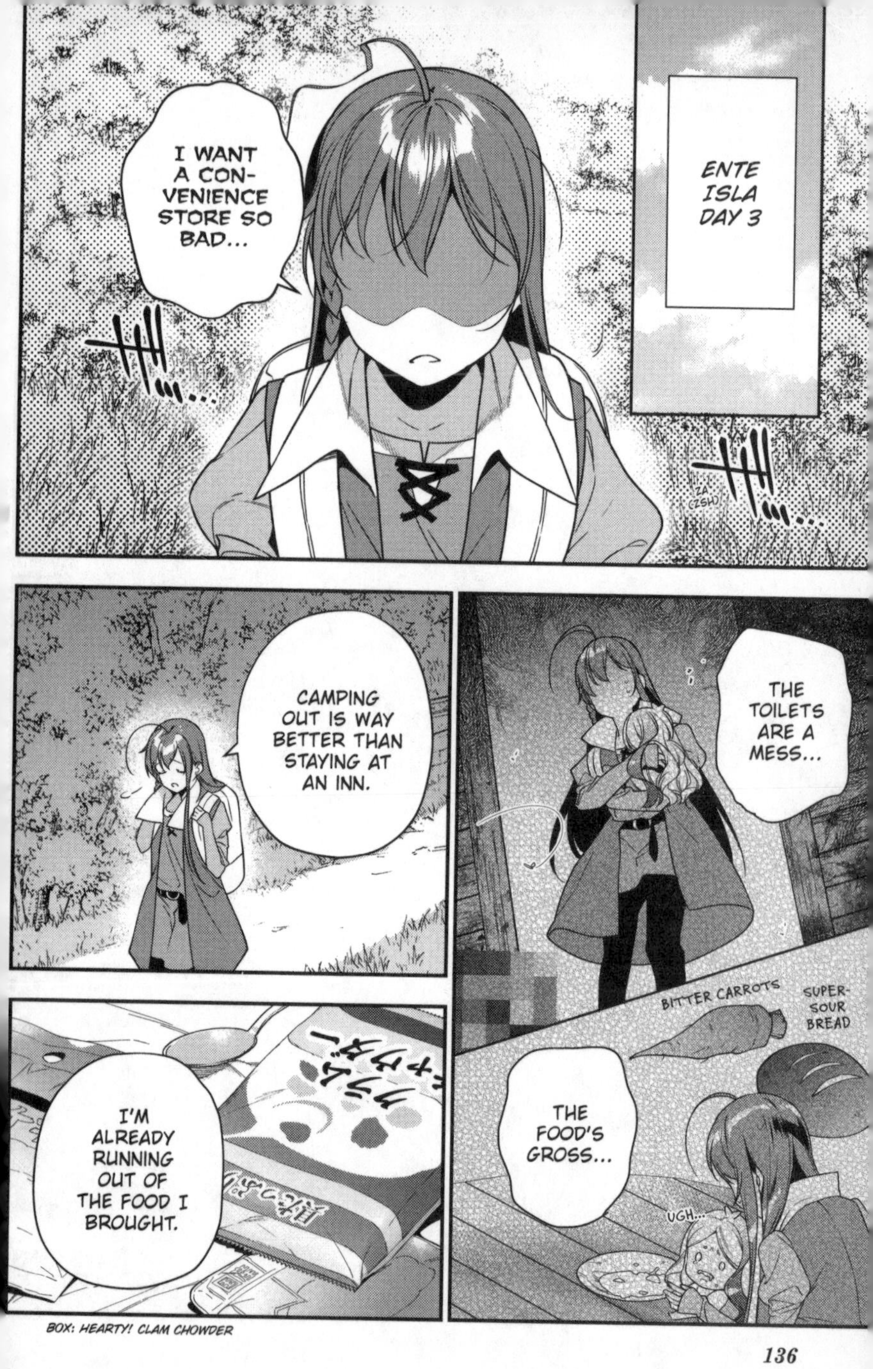
ENTE ISLA DAY 3
I WANT A CON- VENIENCE STORE SO BAD...
ZA
ZA (ZSH)
THE TOILETS ARE A MESS...
CAMPING OUT IS WAY BETTER THAN STAYING AT AN INN.
BITTER CARROTS
SUPER-SOUR BREAD
THE FOOD'S GROSS...
UGH...
I'M ALREADY RUNNING OUT OF THE FOOD I BROUGHT.

BOX: HEARTY! CLAM CHOWDER

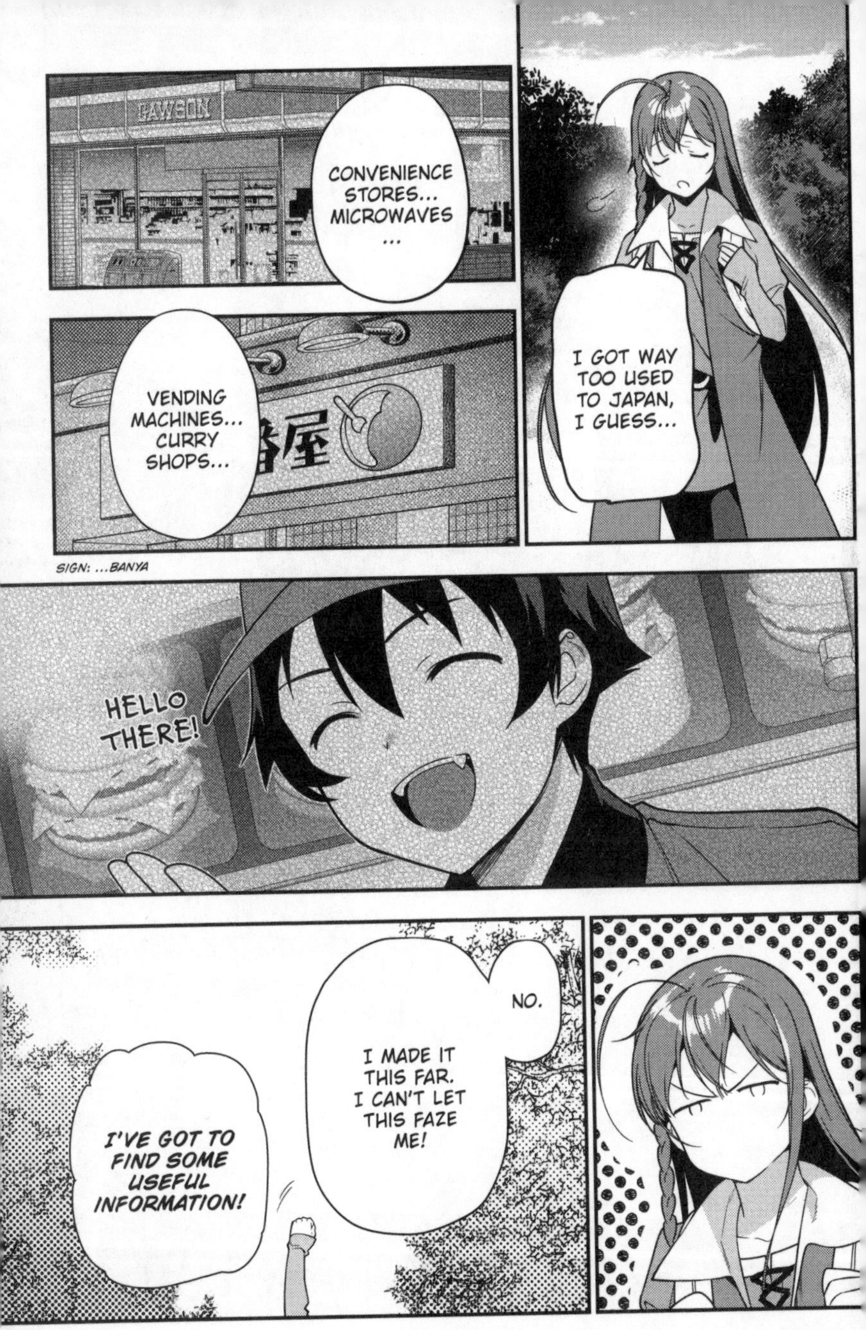
I GOT WAY TOO USED TO JAPAN, I GUESS...
LAWSON
CONVENIENCE STORES... MICROWAVES ...
VENDING MACHINES... CURRY SHOPS...
SIGN: ...BANYA
HELLO THERE!
NO.
I MADE IT THIS FAR. I CAN'T LET THIS FAZE ME!
I'VE GOT TO FIND SOME USEFUL INFORMATION!

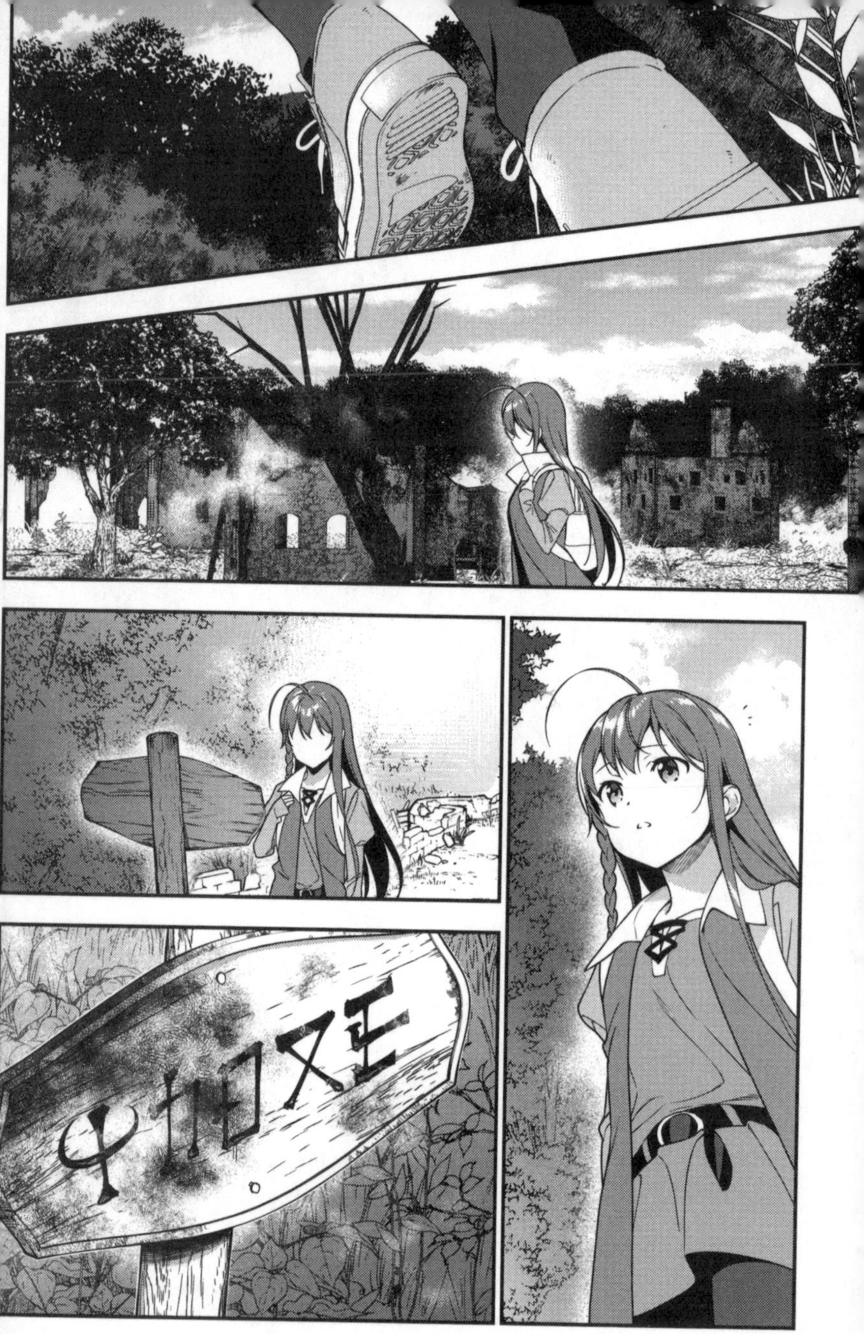

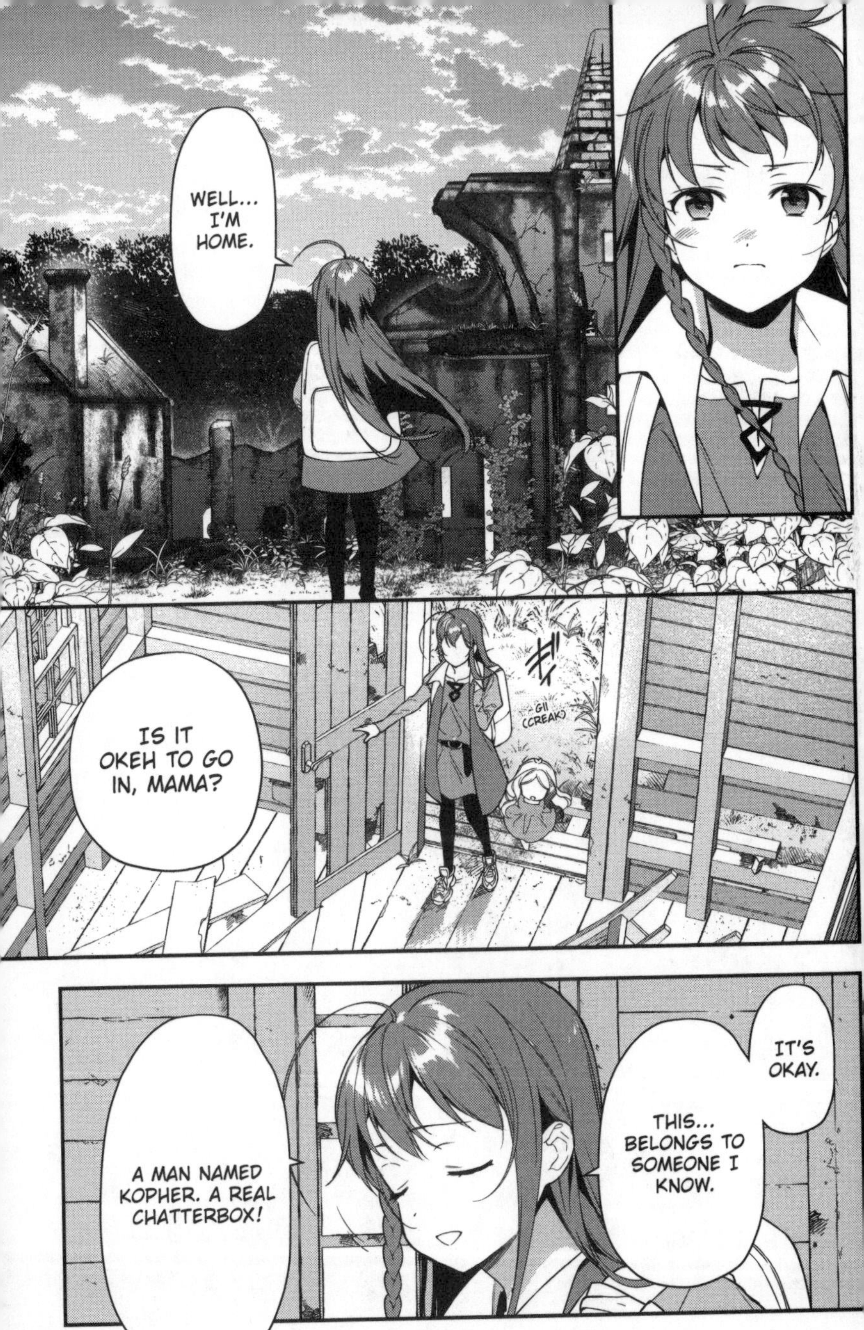
WELL... I'M HOME.
GII (CREAK)
IS IT OKEH TO GO IN, MAMA?
IT'S OKAY.
THIS... BELONGS TO SOMEONE I KNOW.
A MAN NAMED KOPHER. A REAL CHATTERBOX!

BOX: GOTOU RICE

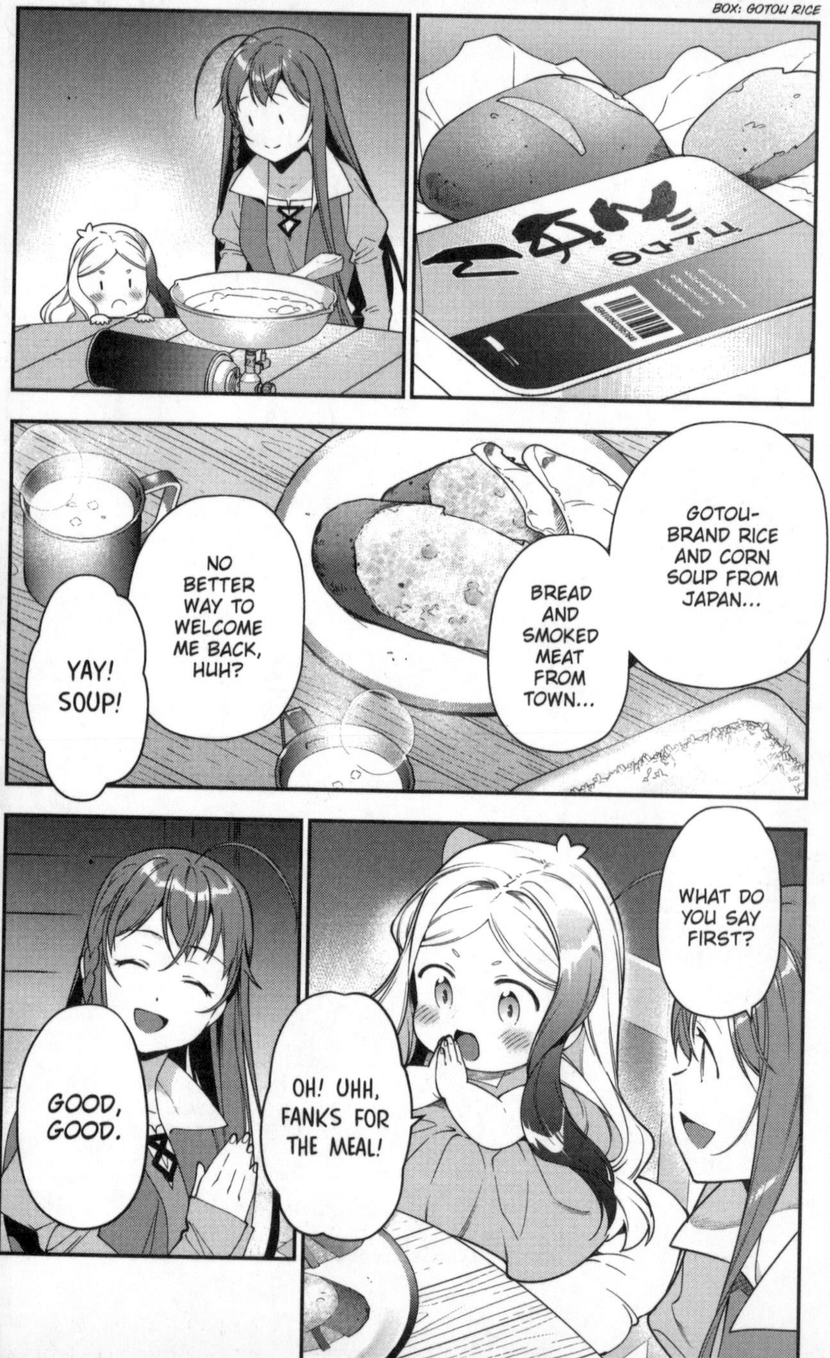
GOTOU-BRAND RICE AND CORN SOUP FROM JAPAN...
BREAD AND SMOKED MEAT FROM TOWN...
NO BETTER WAY TO WELCOME ME BACK, HUH?
YAY! SOUP!
WHAT DO YOU SAY FIRST?
OH! UHH, FANKS FOR THE MEAL!
GOOD, GOOD.

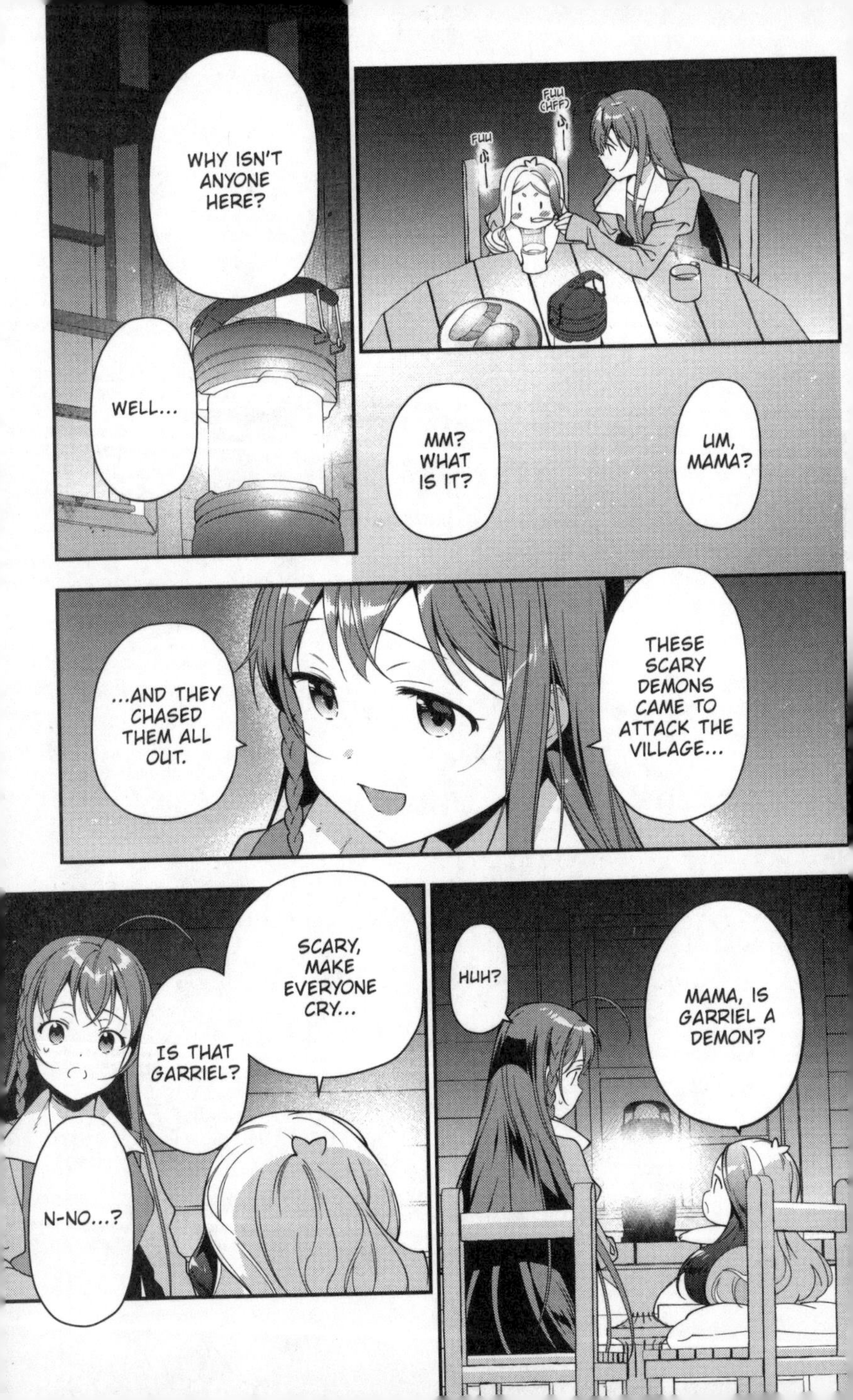
FUU (HFF)
FUU
UM, MAMA?
MM? WHAT IS IT?
WHY ISN'T ANYONE HERE?
WELL...
THESE SCARY DEMONS CAME TO ATTACK THE VILLAGE...
...AND THEY CHASED THEM ALL OUT.
MAMA, IS GARRIEL A DEMON?
HUH?
SCARY, MAKE EVERYONE CRY...
IS THAT GARRIEL?
N-NO...?

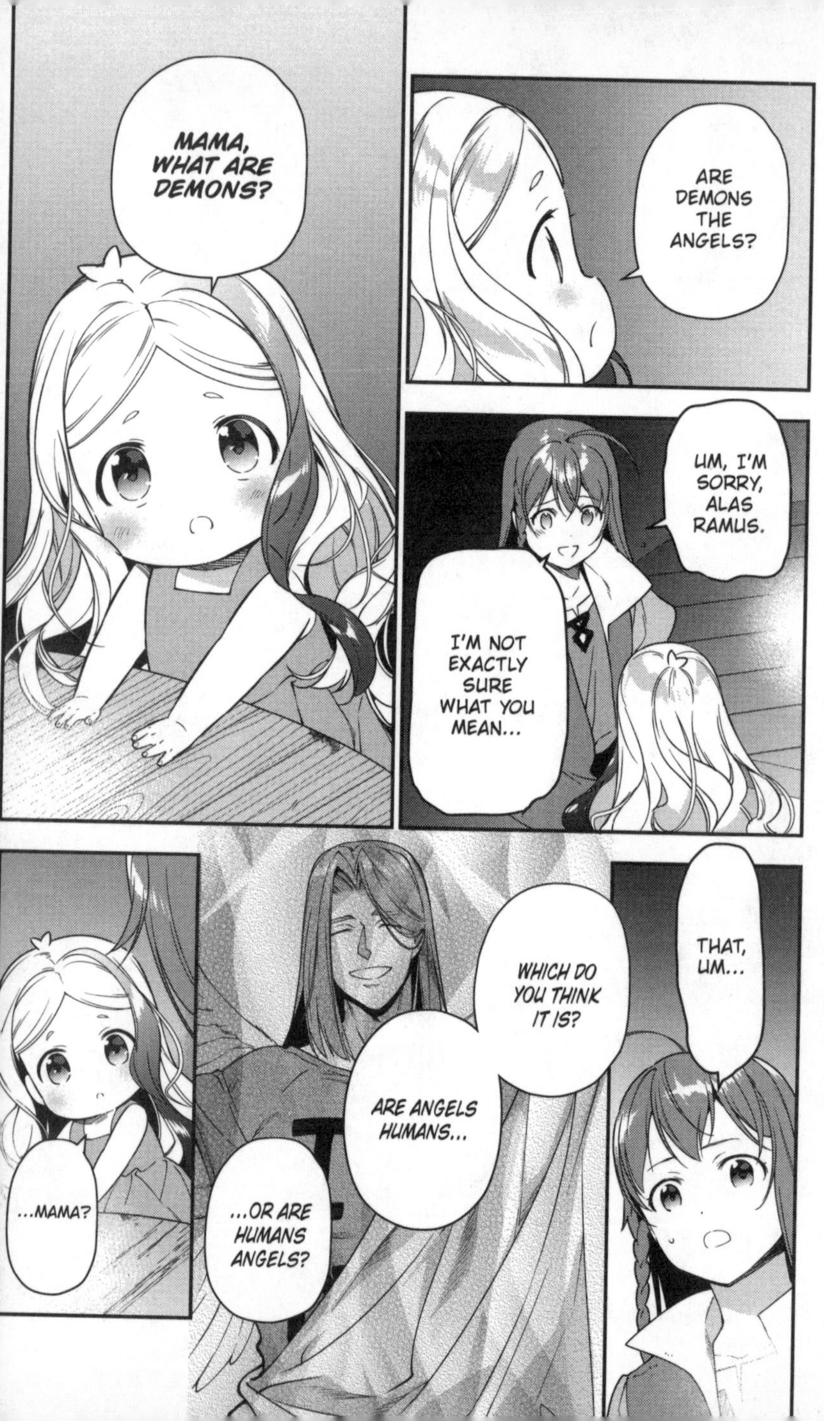
ARE DEMONS THE ANGELS?
UM, I'M SORRY, ALAS RAMUS.
I'M NOT EXACTLY SURE WHAT YOU MEAN...
MAMA, WHAT ARE DEMONS?
THAT, UM...
WHICH DO YOU THINK IT IS?
ARE ANGELS HUMANS...
...OR ARE HUMANS ANGELS?
...MAMA?

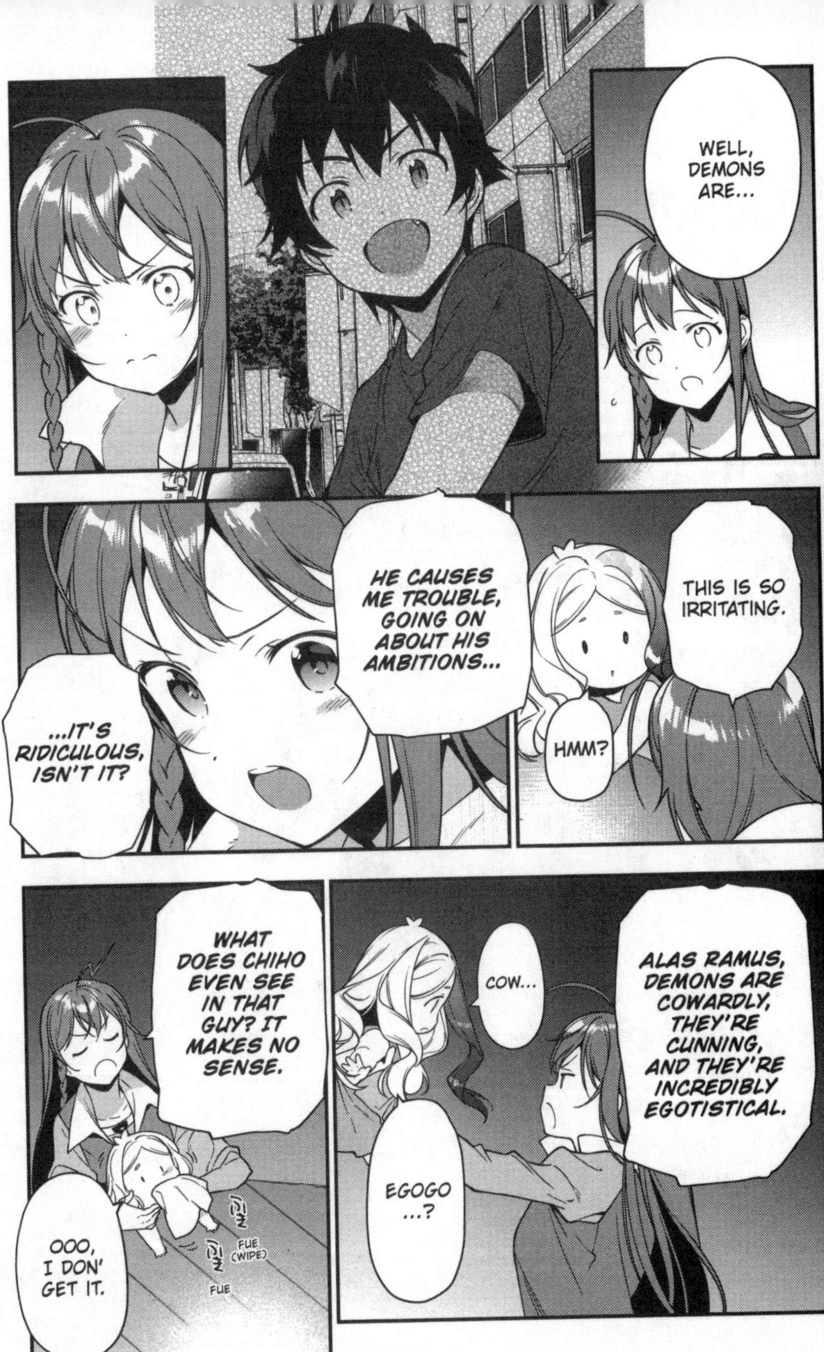
WELL, DEMONS ARE...
THIS IS SO IRRITATING.
HMM?
HE CAUSES ME TROUBLE, GOING ON ABOUT HIS AMBITIONS...
...IT'S RIDICULOUS, ISN'T IT?
ALAS RAMUS, DEMONS ARE COWARDLY, THEY'RE CUNNING, AND THEY'RE INCREDIBLY EGOTISTICAL.
COW...
EGOGO ...?
WHAT DOES CHIHO EVEN SEE IN THAT GUY? IT MAKES NO SENSE.
FUE (WIPE)
FUE
OOO, I DON' GET IT.

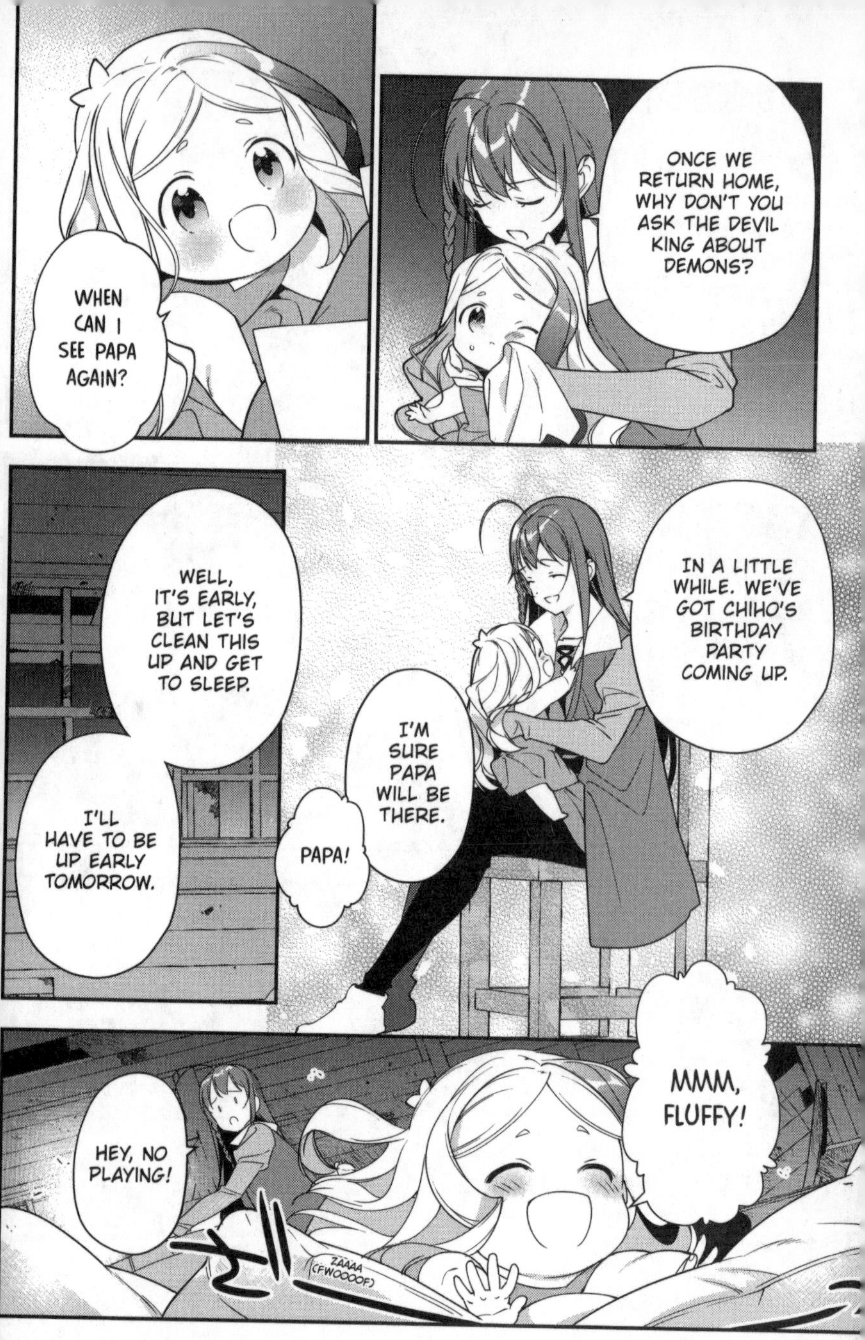

ONCE WE RETURN HOME, WHY DON'T YOU ASK THE DEVIL KING ABOUT DEMONS?
WHEN CAN I SEE PAPA AGAIN?
IN A LITTLE WHILE. WE'VE GOT CHIHO'S BIRTHDAY PARTY COMING UP.
I'M SURE PAPA WILL BE THERE.
PAPA!
WELL, IT'S EARLY, BUT LET'S CLEAN THIS UP AND GET TO SLEEP.
I'LL HAVE TO BE UP EARLY TOMORROW.
MMM, FLUFFY!
ZAAAA (FWOOOOF)
HEY, NO PLAYING!

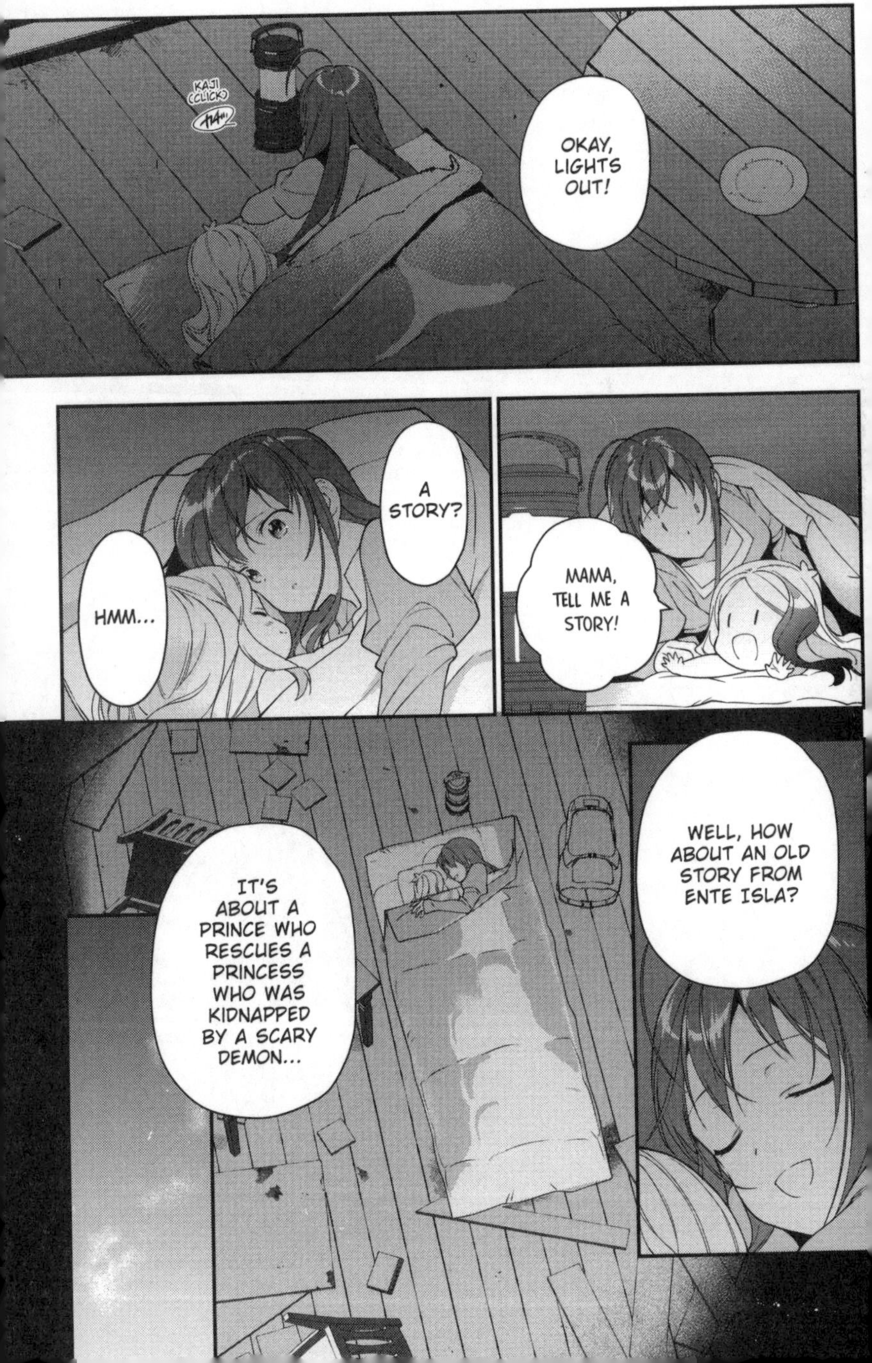
OKAY, LIGHTS OUT!
KAJI (CLICK)
MAMA, TELL ME A STORY!
A STORY?
HMM...
WELL, HOW ABOUT AN OLD STORY FROM ENTE ISLA?
IT'S ABOUT A PRINCE WHO RESCUES A PRINCESS WHO WAS KIDNAPPED BY A SCARY DEMON...

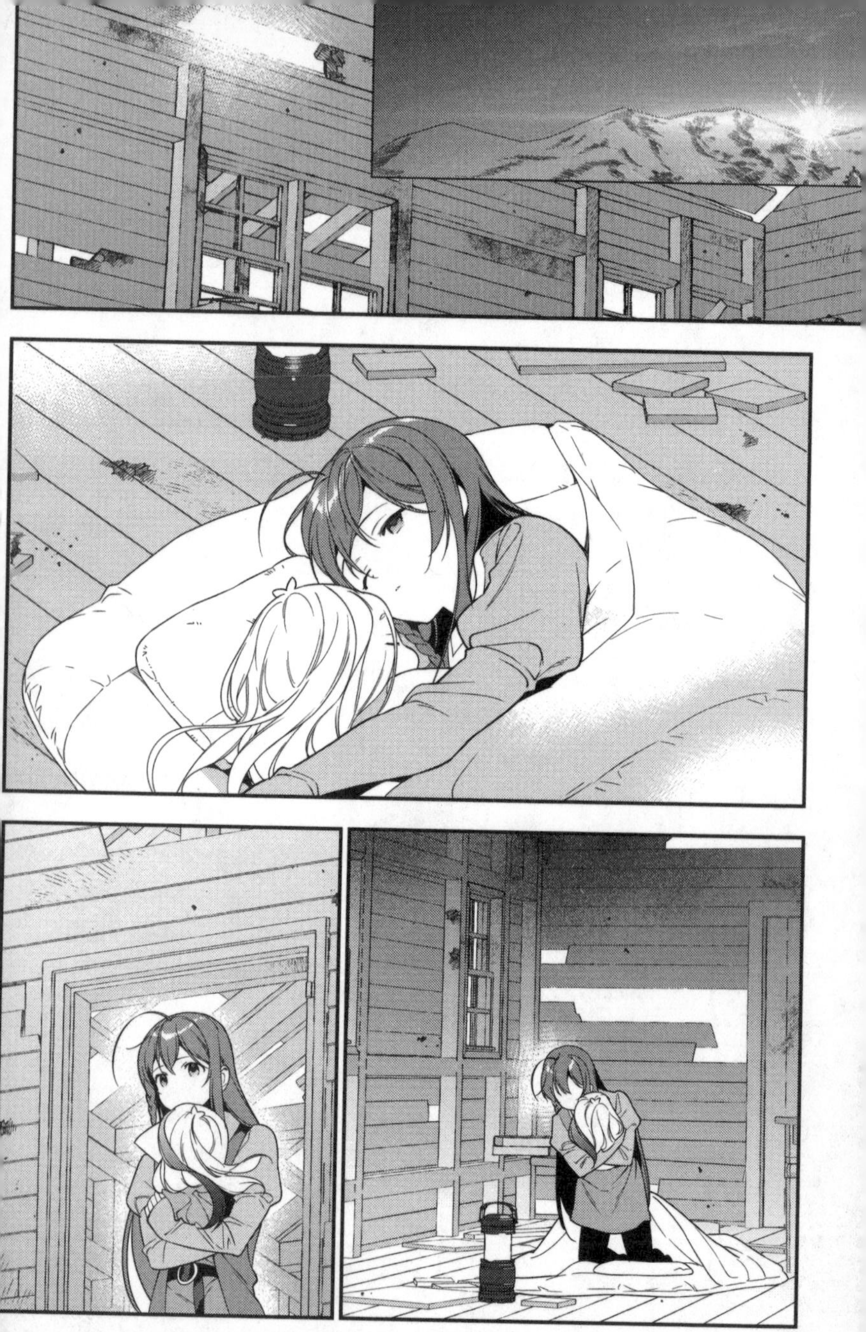

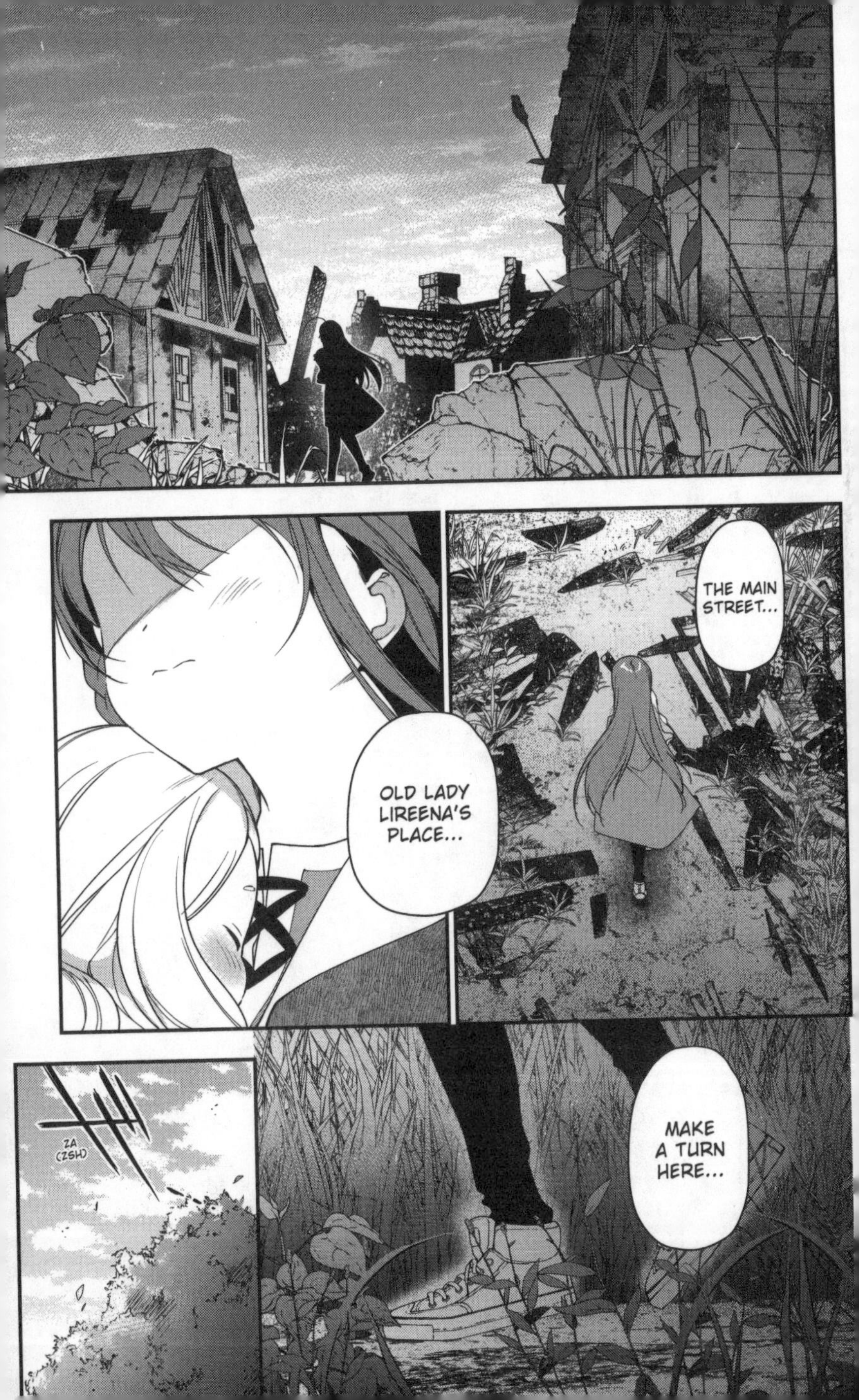
THE MAIN STREET...
OLD LADY LIREENA'S PLACE...
MAKE A TURN HERE...
ZA (ZSH)

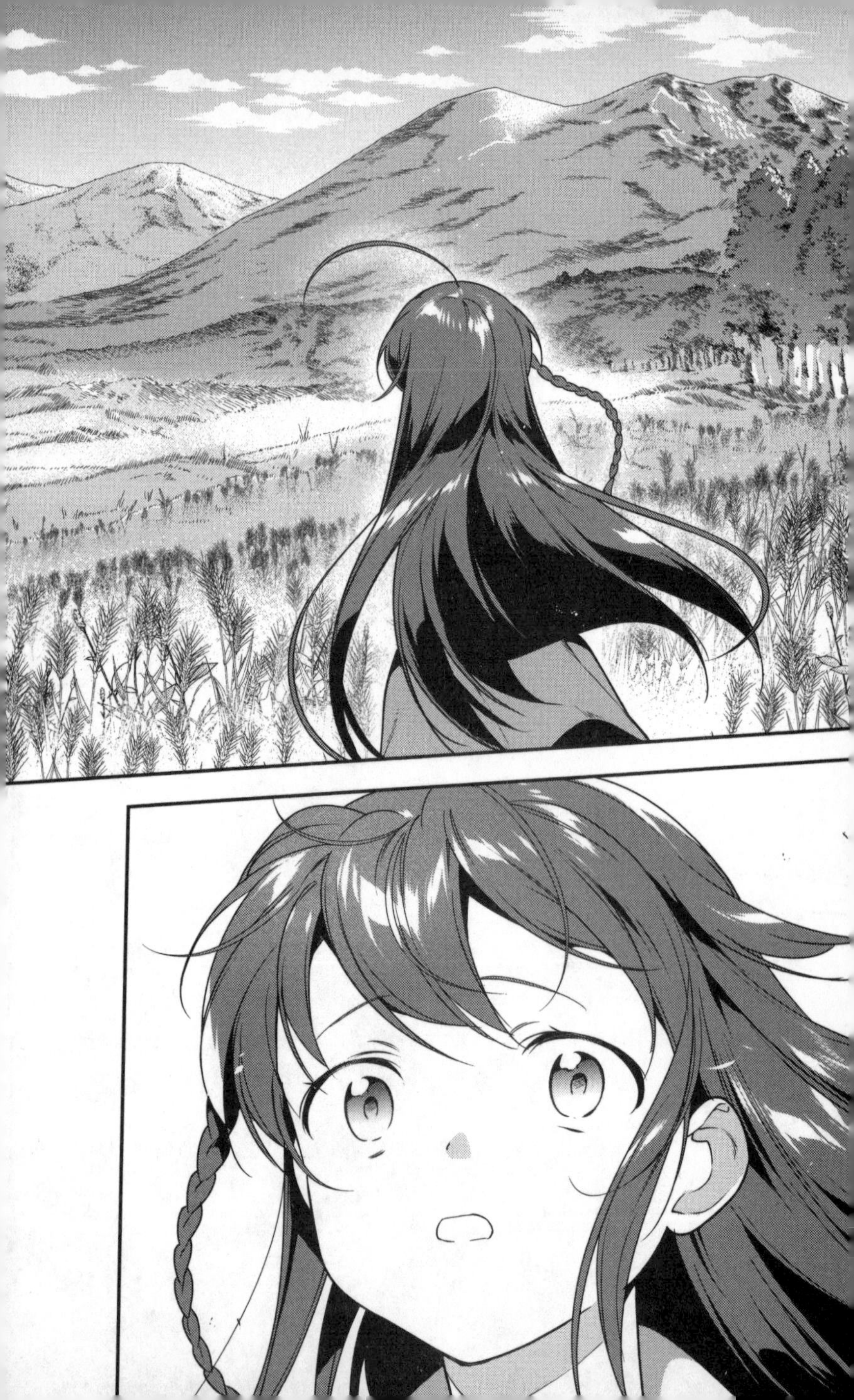

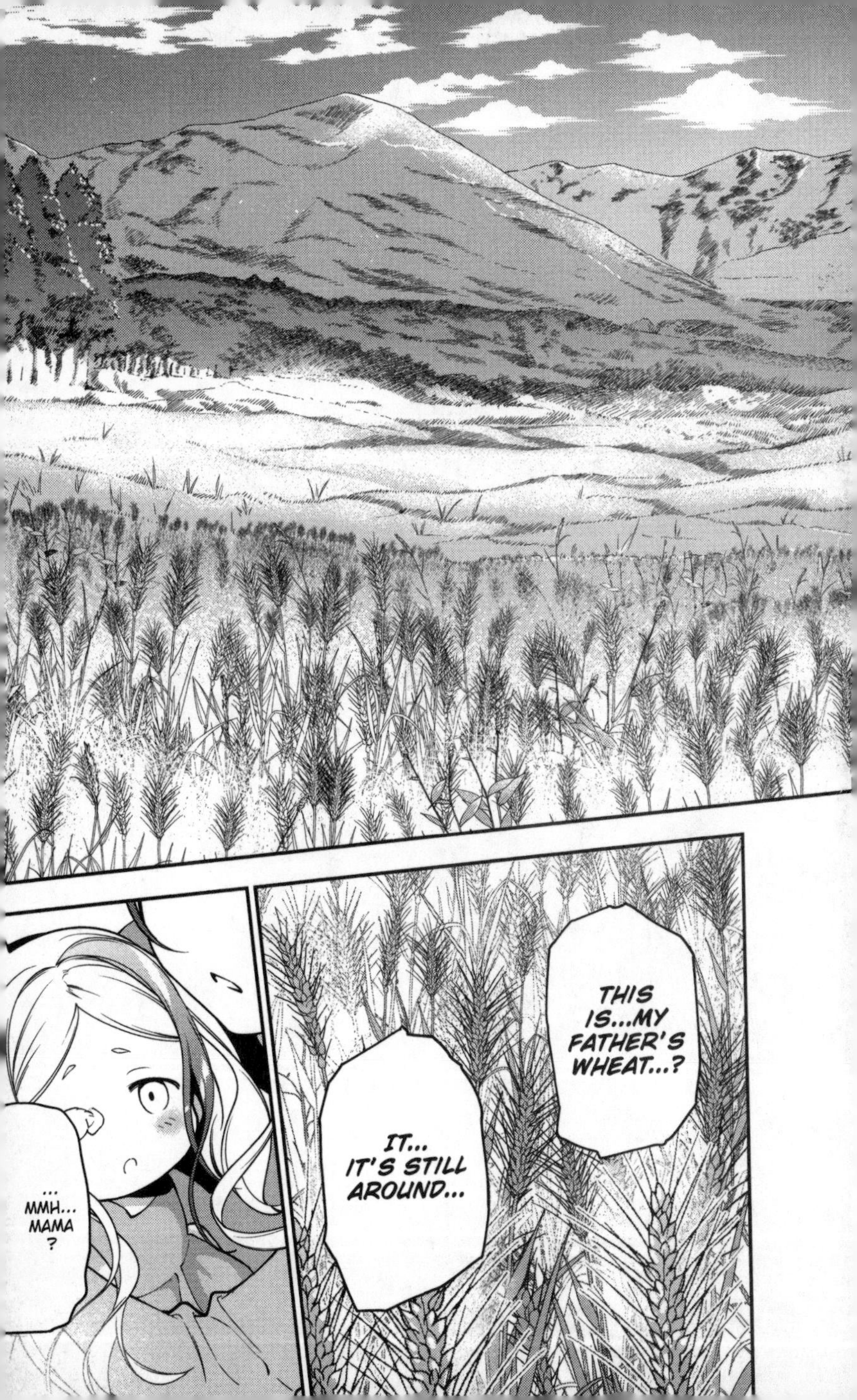
THIS IS...MY FATHER'S WHEAT...?
IT... IT'S STILL AROUND...
... MMH... MAMA ?

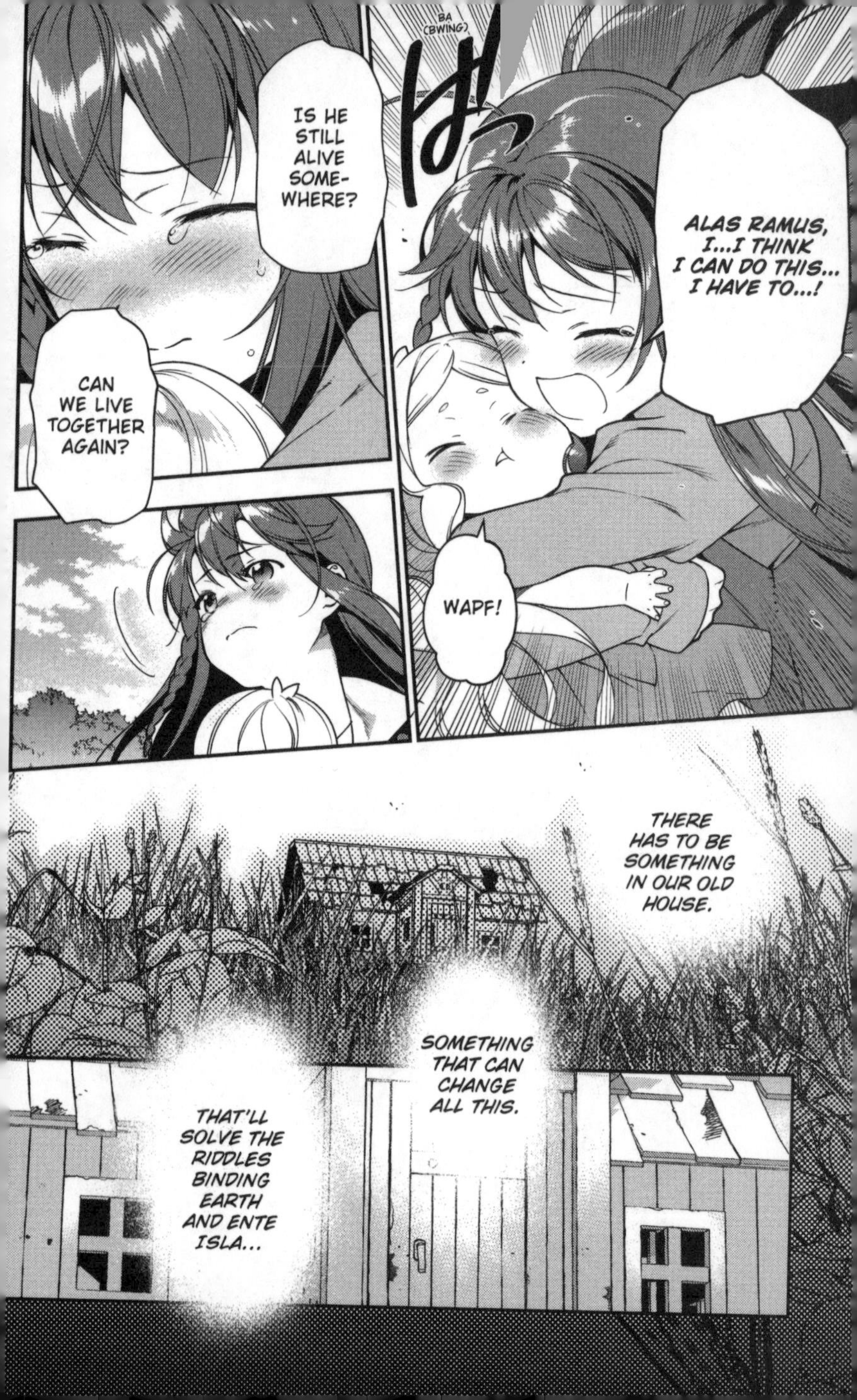
BA (BWING)
ALAS RAMUS, I...I THINK I CAN DO THIS... I HAVE TO...!
WAPF!
IS HE STILL ALIVE SOMEWHERE?
CAN WE LIVE TOGETHER AGAIN?
THERE HAS TO BE SOMETHING IN OUR OLD HOUSE.
SOMETHING THAT CAN CHANGE ALL THIS.
THAT'LL SOLVE THE RIDDLES BINDING EARTH AND ENTE ISLA...

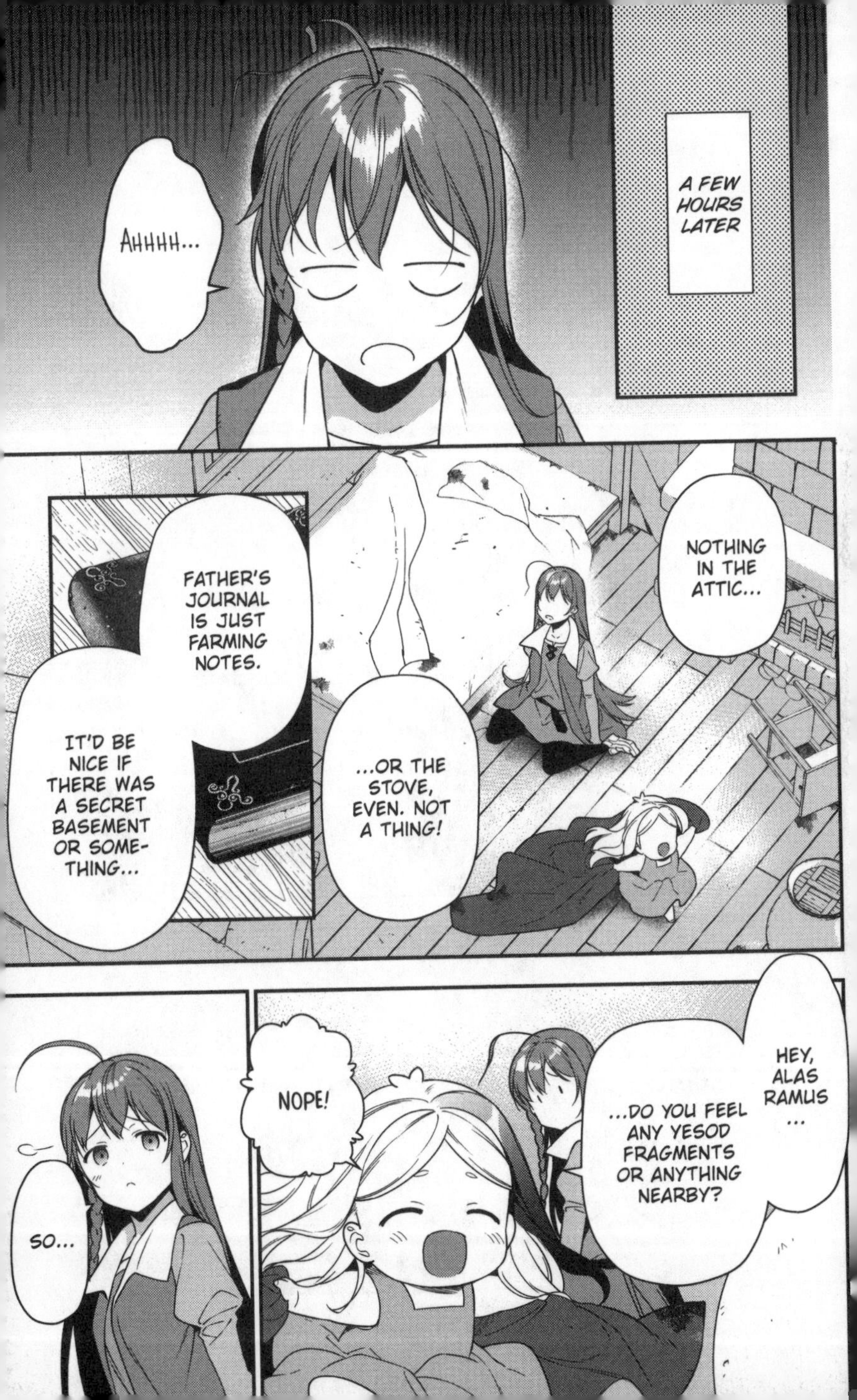

A FEW HOURS LATER
AHHHH...
NOTHING IN THE ATTIC...
...OR THE STOVE, EVEN. NOT A THING!
FATHER'S JOURNAL IS JUST FARMING NOTES.
IT'D BE NICE IF THERE WAS A SECRET BASEMENT OR SOME-THING...
HEY, ALAS RAMUS ...
...DO YOU FEEL ANY YESOD FRAGMENTS OR ANYTHING NEARBY?
NOPE!
SO...

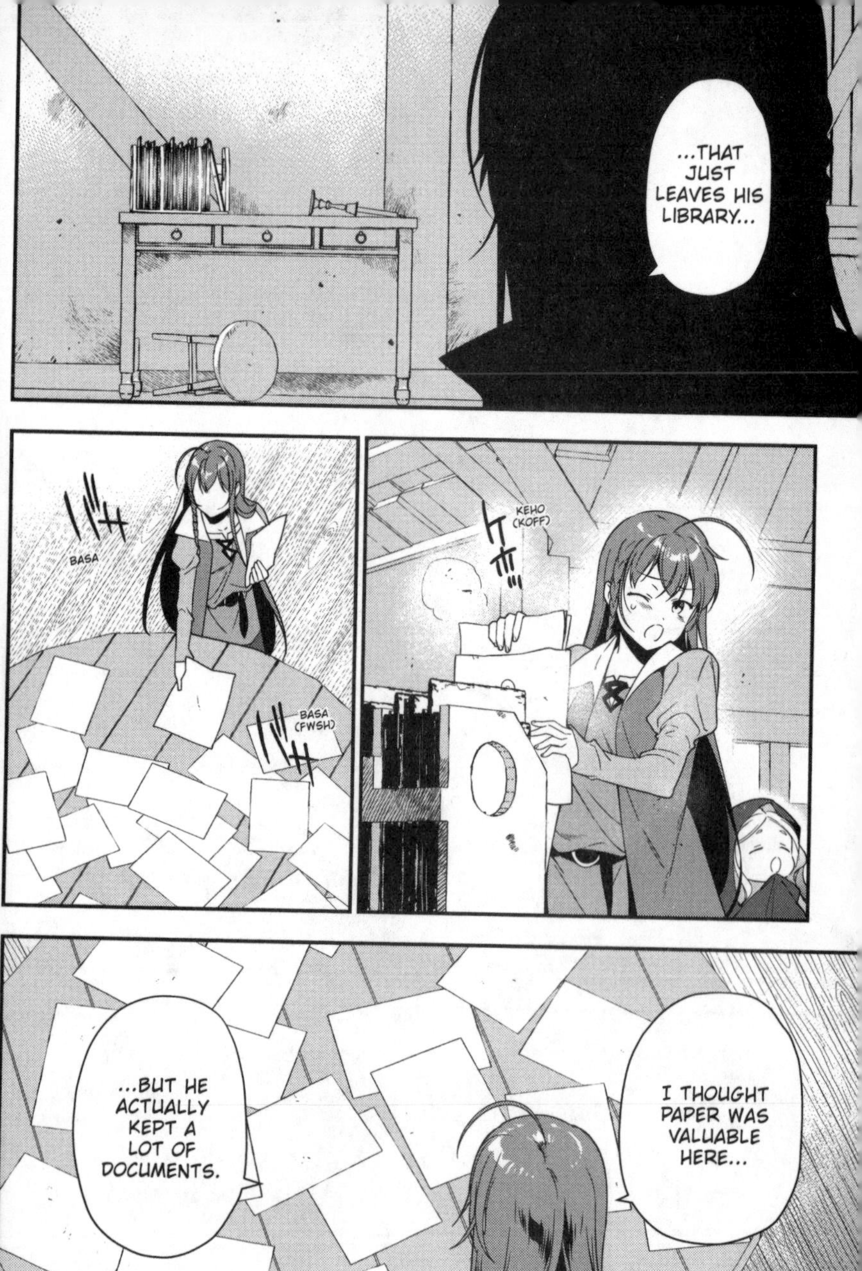
...THAT JUST LEAVES HIS LIBRARY...
KEHO (KOFF)
BASA
BASA (FWSH)
I THOUGHT PAPER WAS VALUABLE HERE...
...BUT HE ACTUALLY KEPT A LOT OF DOCUMENTS.

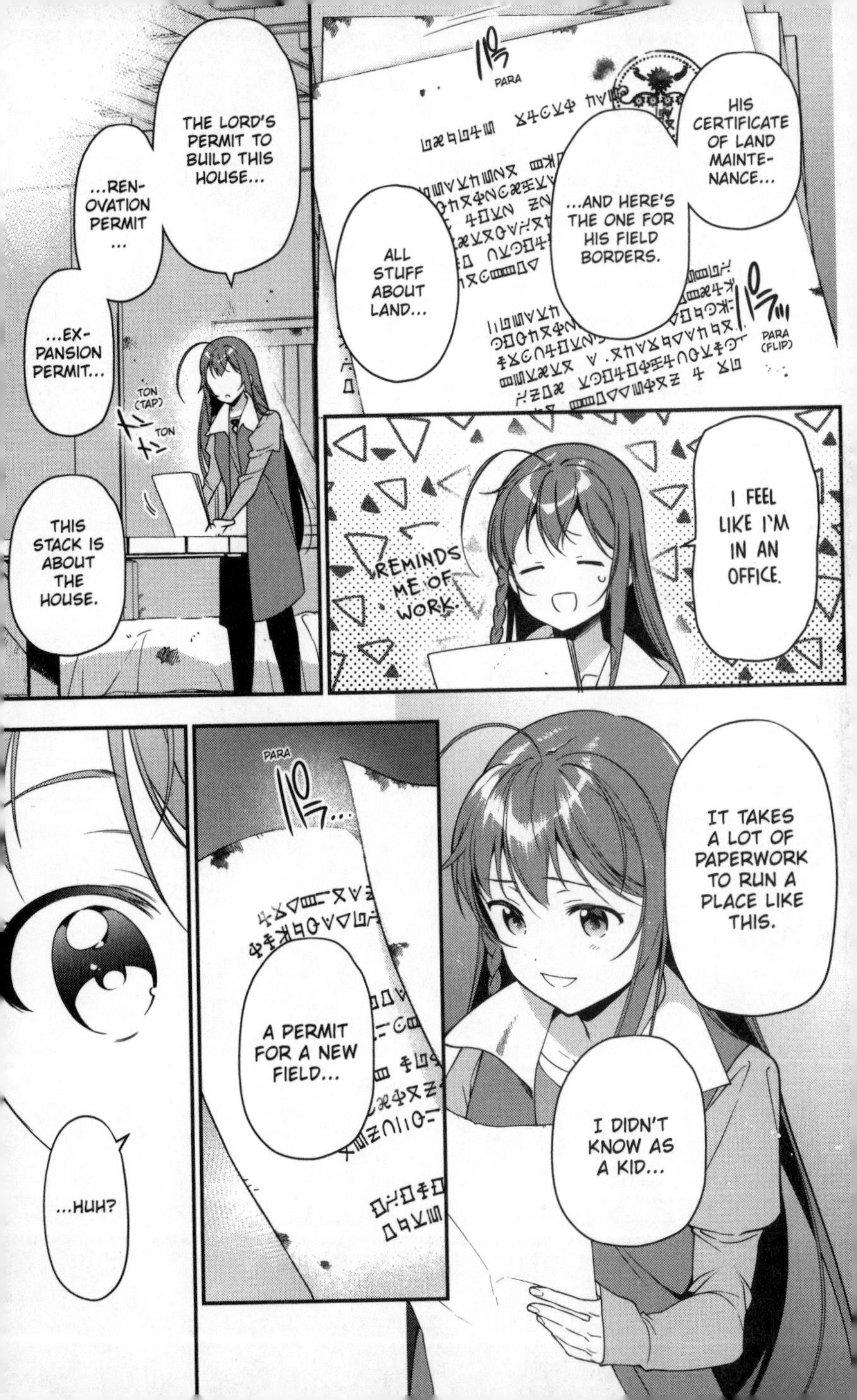
PARA
HIS CERTIFICATE OF LAND MAINTE-NANCE...
...AND HERE'S THE ONE FOR HIS FIELD BORDERS.
ALL STUFF ABOUT LAND...
PARA (FLIP)
I FEEL LIKE I'M IN AN OFFICE.
REMINDS ME OF WORK.
THE LORD'S PERMIT TO BUILD THIS HOUSE...
...REN-OVATION PERMIT...
...EX-PANSION PERMIT...
TON (TAP)
TON
THIS STACK IS ABOUT THE HOUSE.
IT TAKES A LOT OF PAPERWORK TO RUN A PLACE LIKE THIS.
I DIDN'T KNOW AS A KID...
PARA
A PERMIT FOR A NEW FIELD...
...HUH?

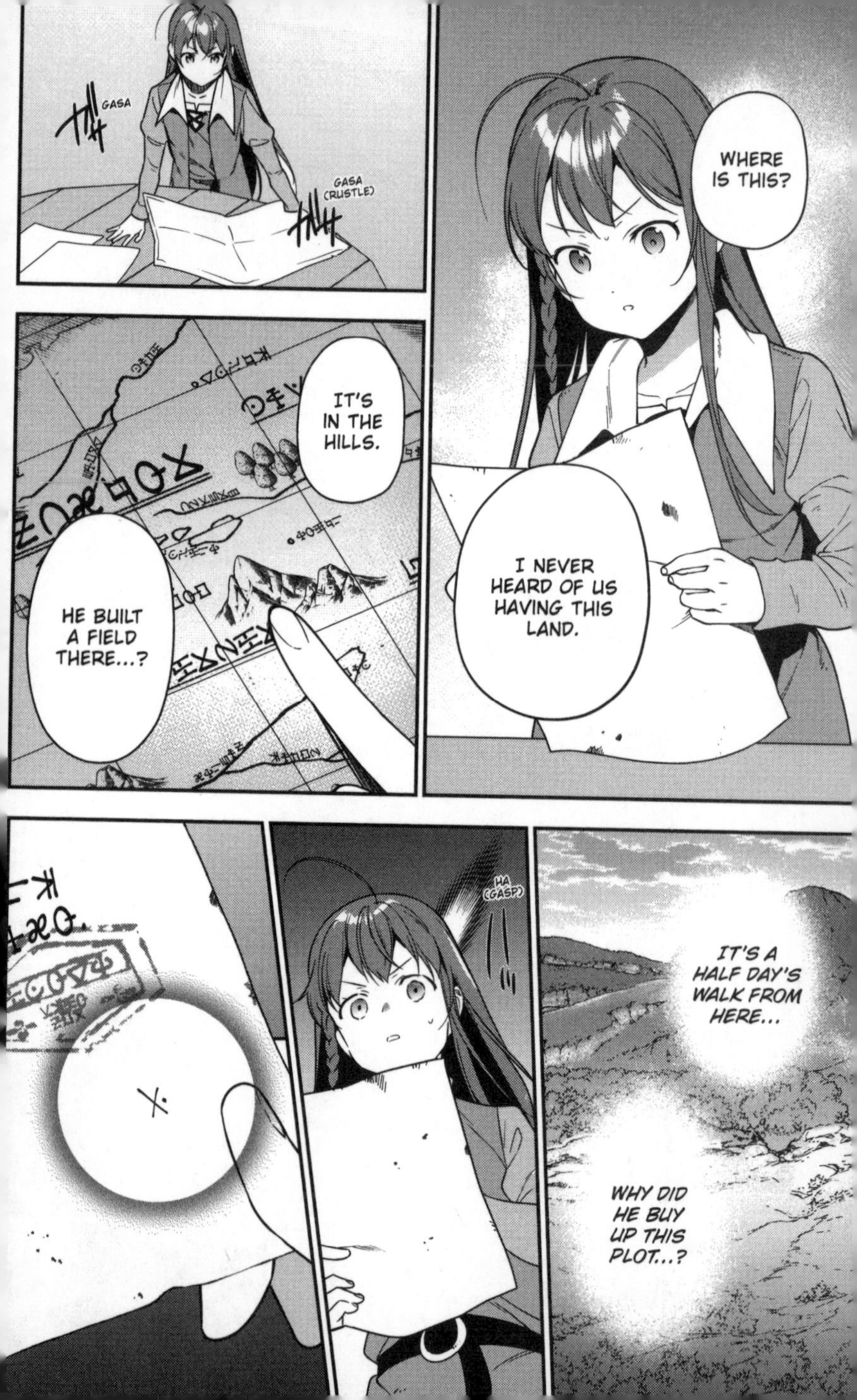
WHERE IS THIS?
I NEVER HEARD OF US HAVING THIS LAND.
GASA
GASA (RUSTLE)
IT'S IN THE HILLS.
HE BUILT A FIELD THERE...?
IT'S A HALF DAY'S WALK FROM HERE...
WHY DID HE BUY UP THIS PLOT...?
HA (GASP)

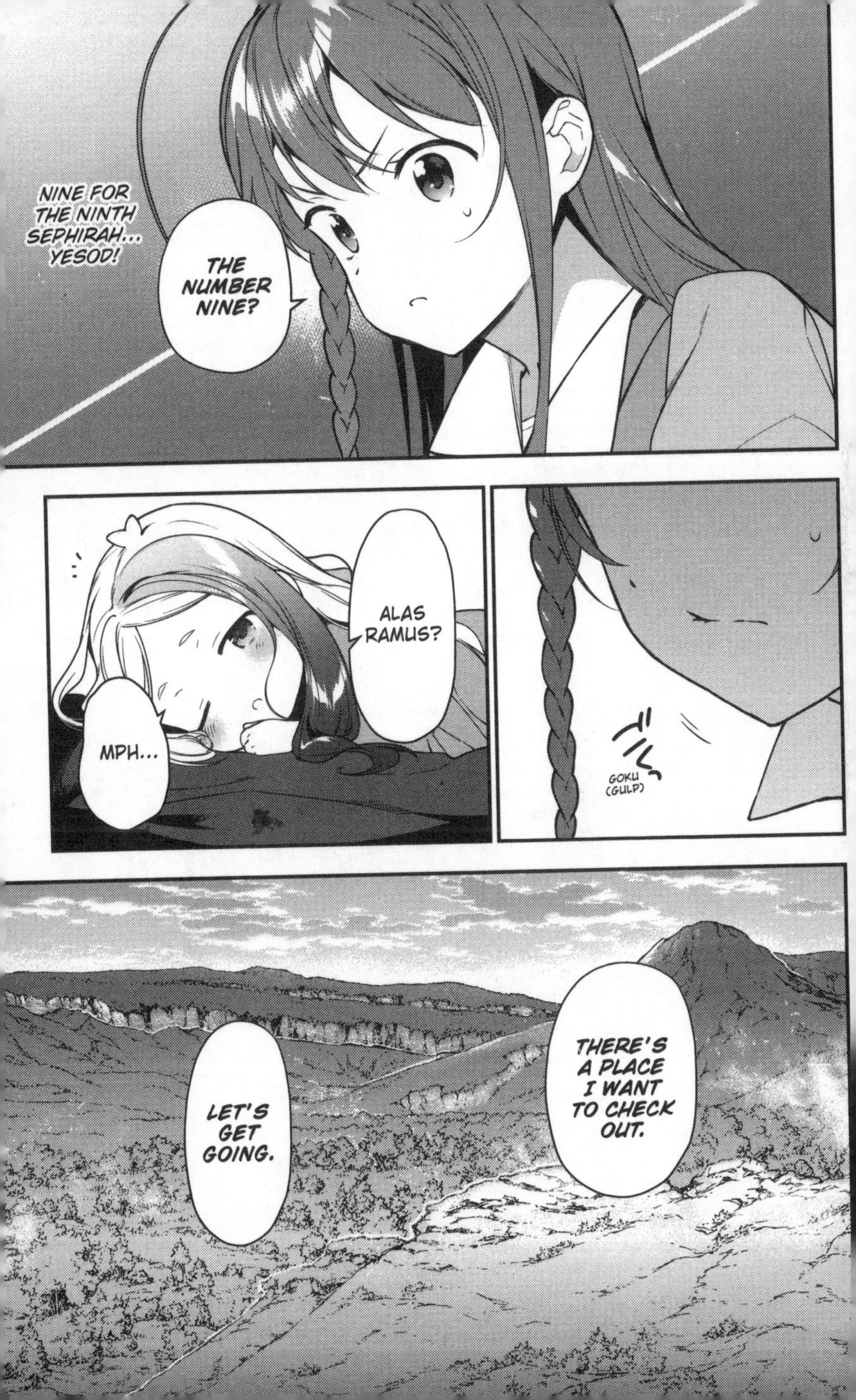
THE NUMBER NINE?
NINE FOR THE NINTH SEPHIRAH... YESOD!
GOKU (GULP)
ALAS RAMUS?
MPH...
THERE'S A PLACE I WANT TO CHECK OUT.
LET'S GET GOING.

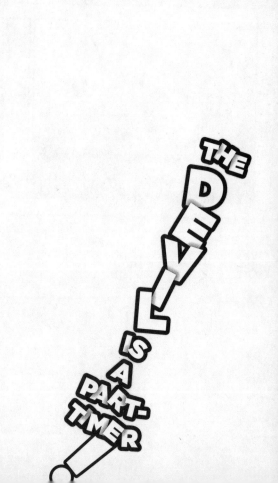

THE DEVIL IS A PART-TIMER

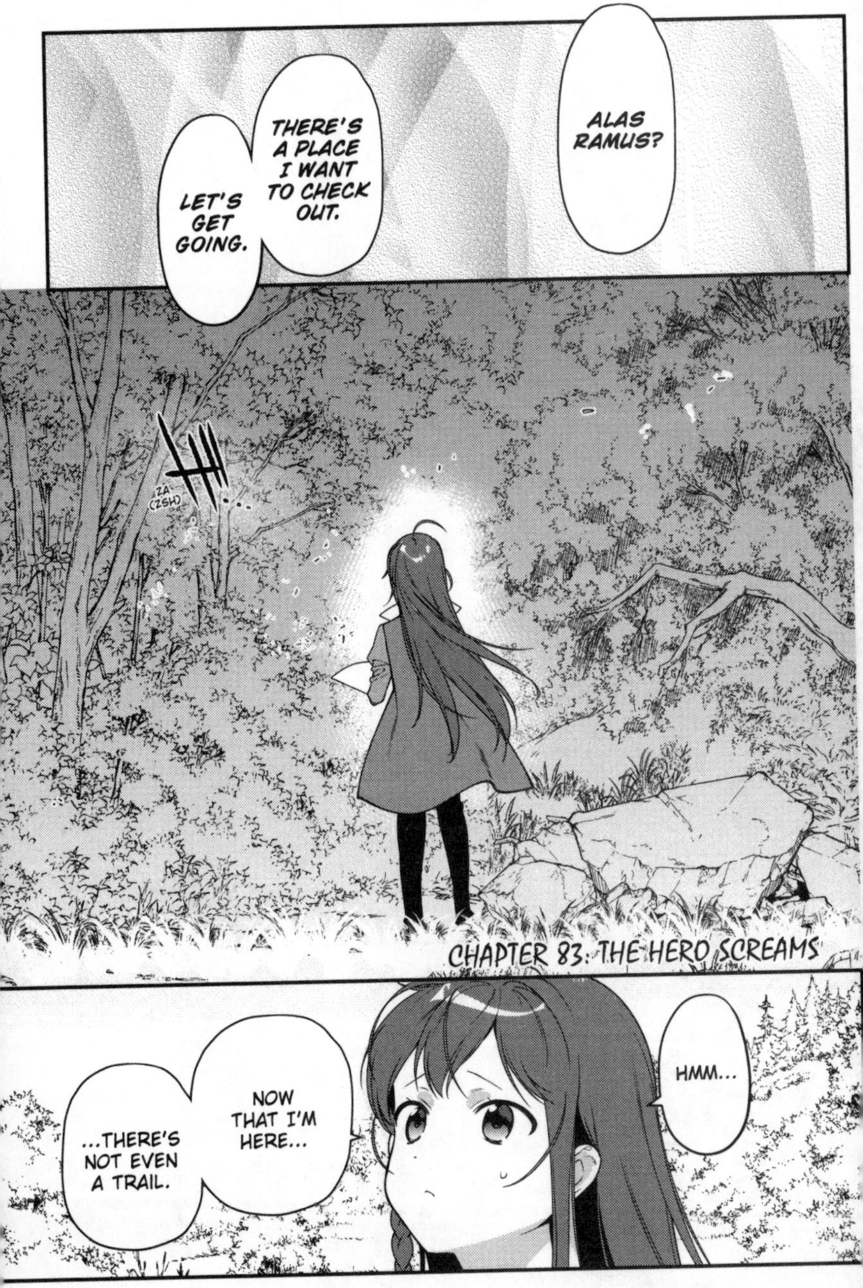
ALAS RAMUS?
THERE'S A PLACE I WANT TO CHECK OUT.
LET'S GET GOING.
ZA (ZSH)
CHAPTER 83: THE HERO SCREAMS
HMM...
NOW THAT I'M HERE...
...THERE'S NOT EVEN A TRAIL.

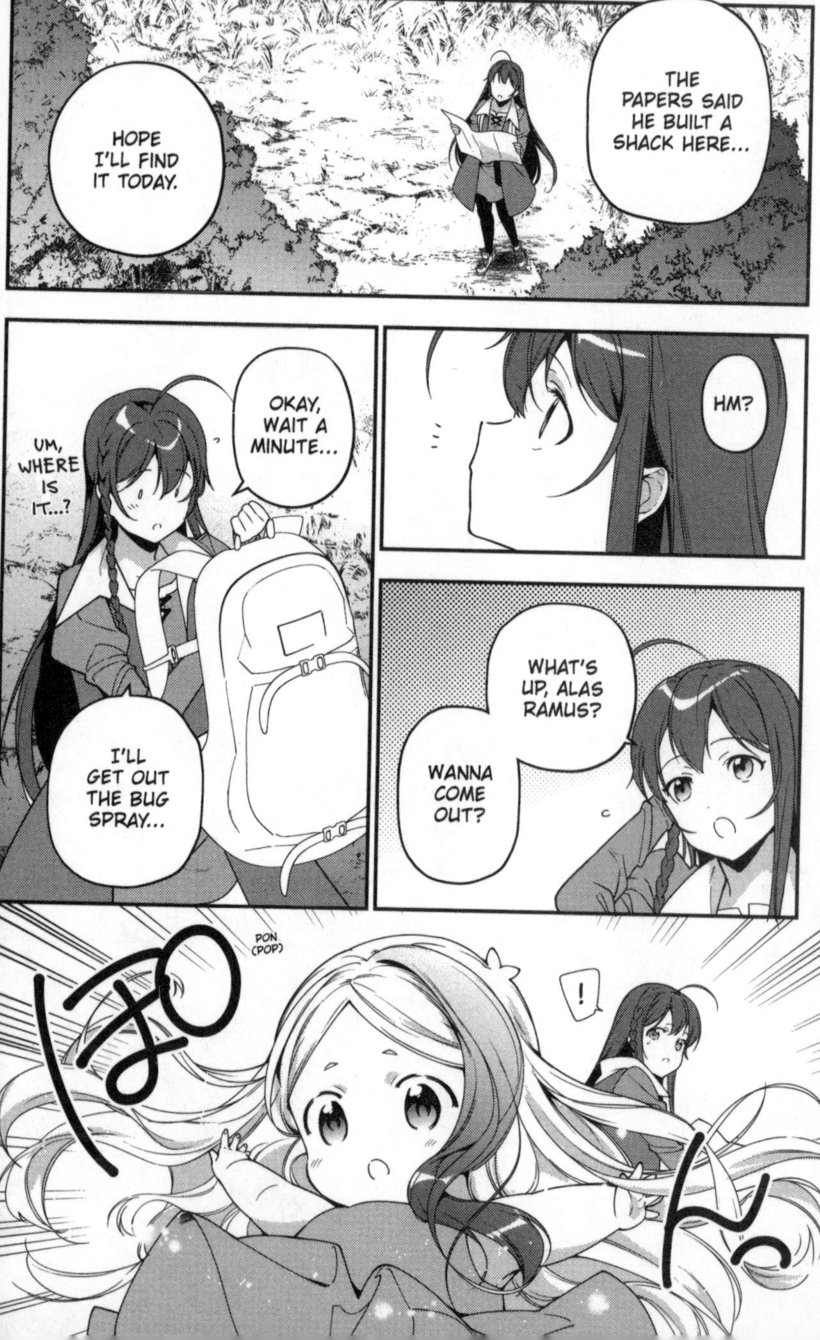
THE PAPERS SAID HE BUILT A SHACK HERE...
HOPE I'LL FIND IT TODAY.
HM?
WHAT'S UP, ALAS RAMUS?
WANNA COME OUT?
OKAY, WAIT A MINUTE...
UM, WHERE IS IT...?
I'LL GET OUT THE BUG SPRAY...
!
PON (POP)

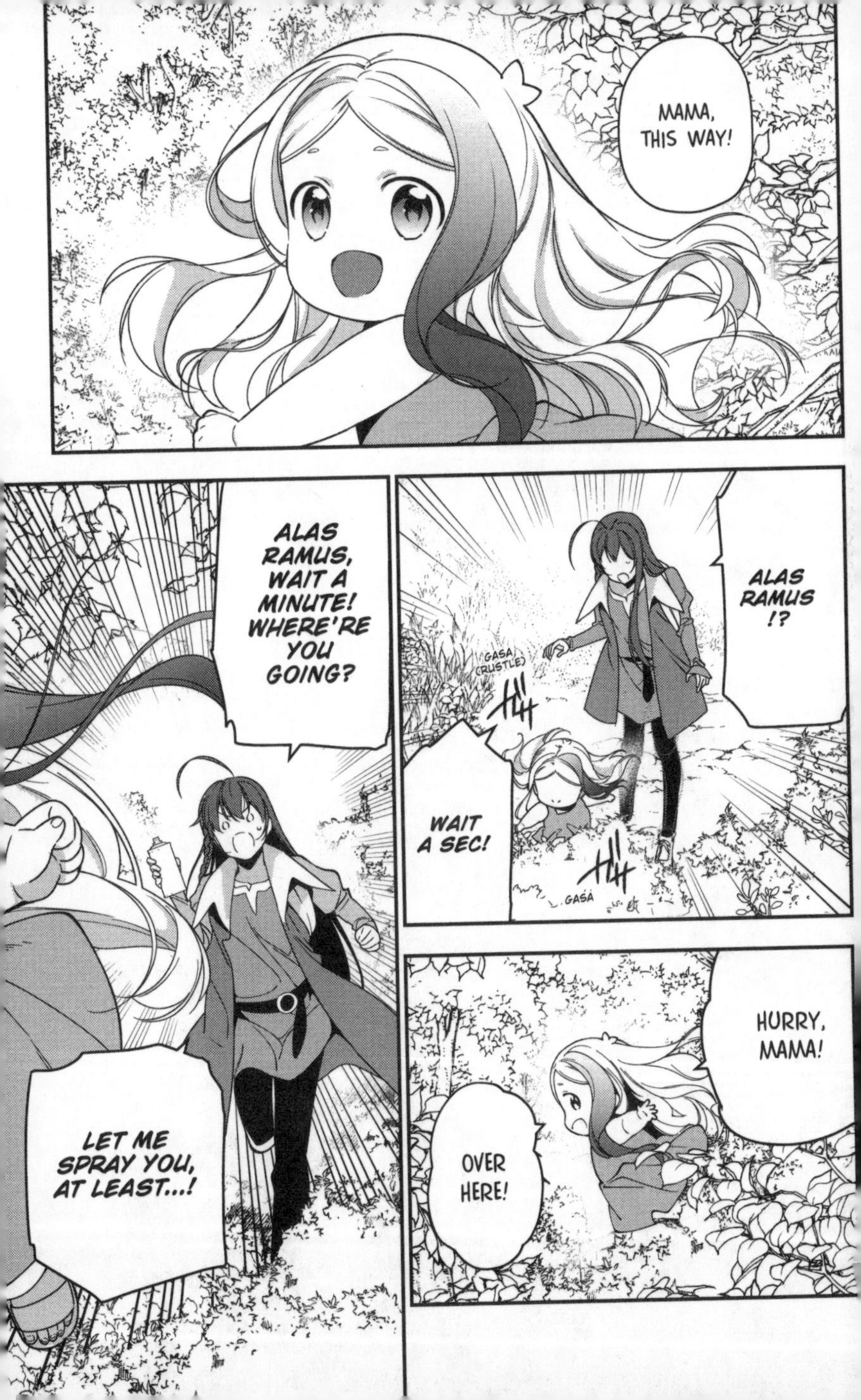
MAMA, THIS WAY!
ALAS RAMUS !?
GASA (RUSTLE)
WAIT A SEC!
GASA
HURRY, MAMA!
OVER HERE!
ALAS RAMUS, WAIT A MINUTE! WHERE'RE YOU GOING?
LET ME SPRAY YOU, AT LEAST...!

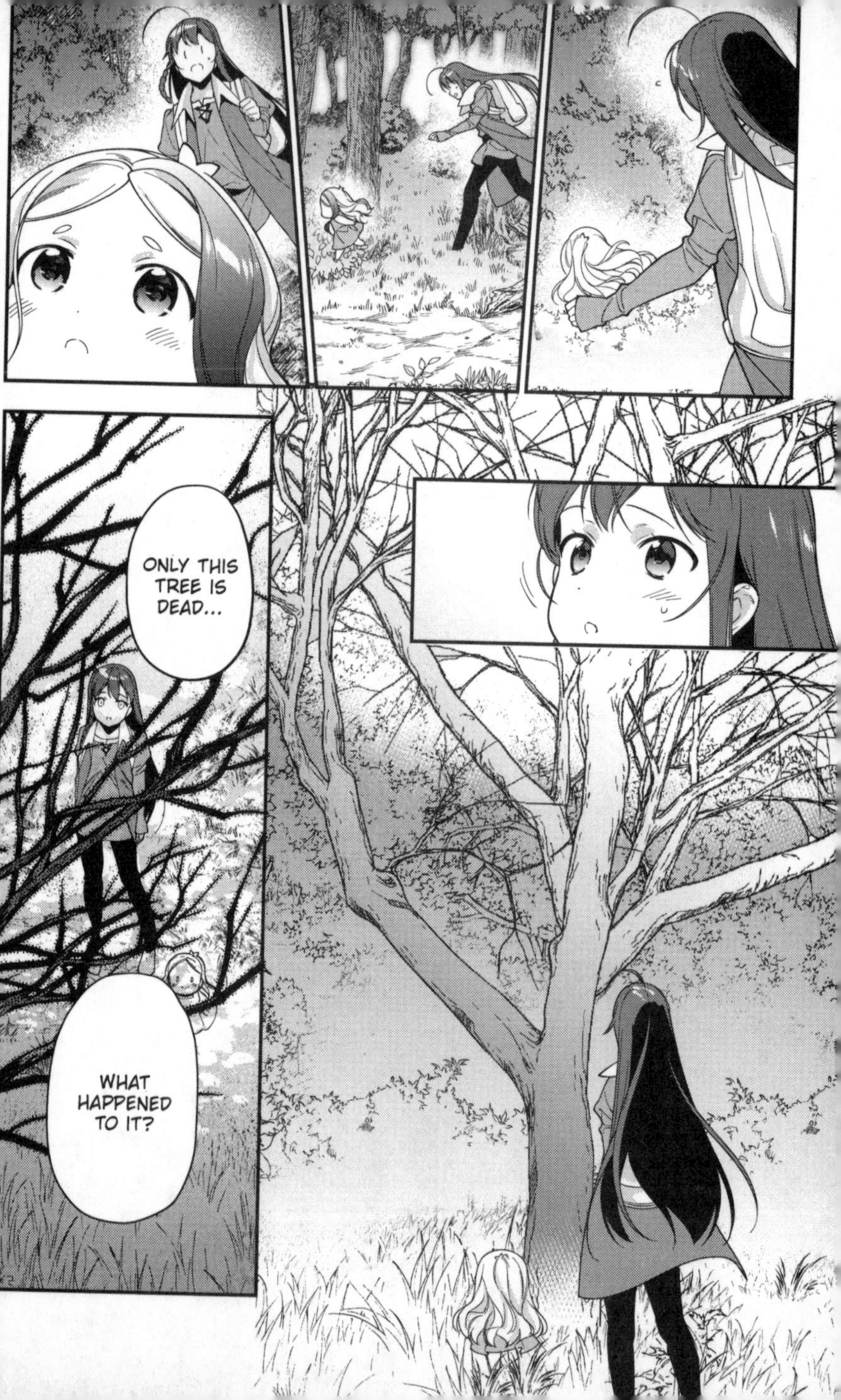
ONLY THIS TREE IS DEAD...
WHAT HAPPENED TO IT?

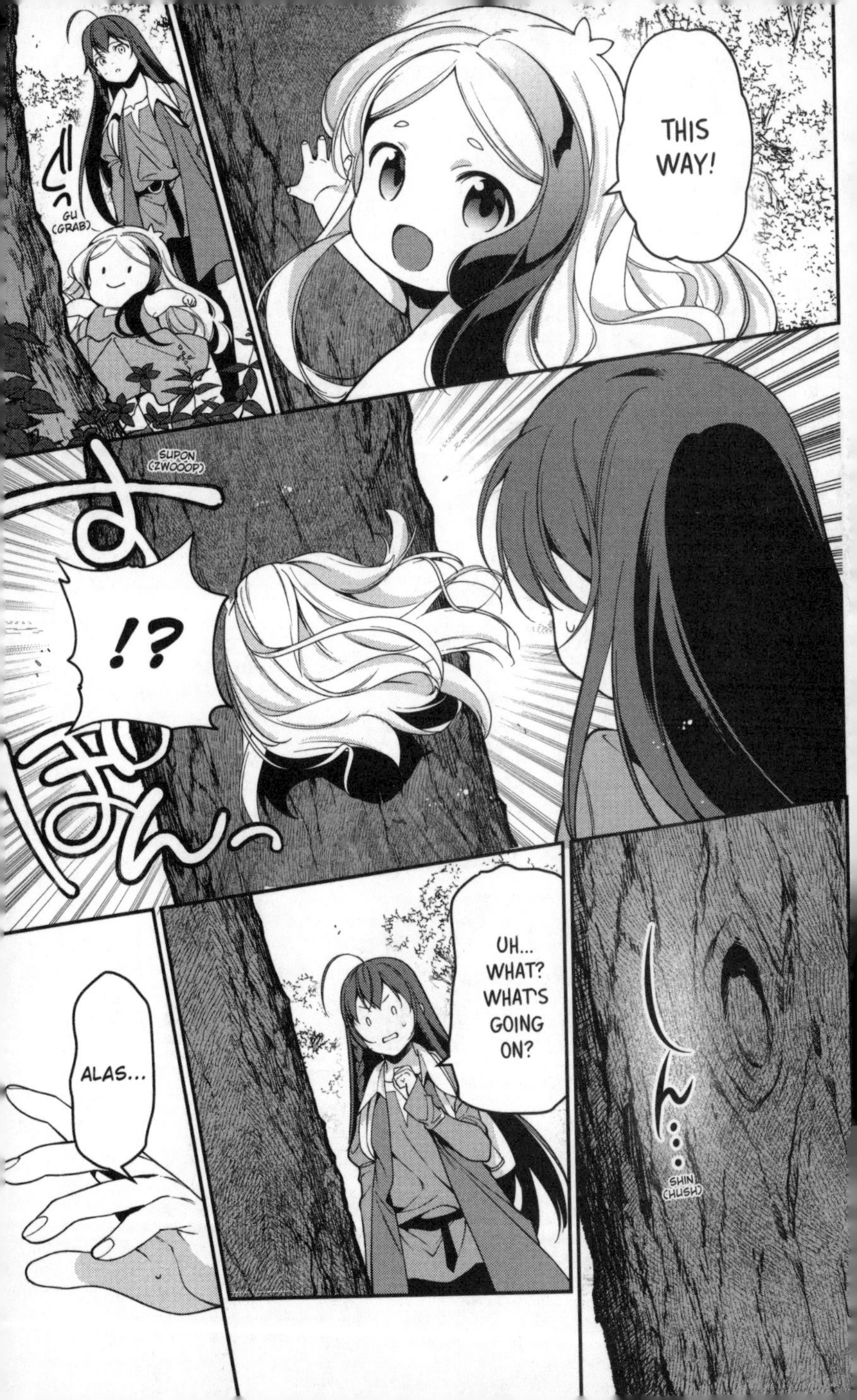
THIS WAY!
GU (GRAB)
SUPON (ZWOOOP)
!?
SHIN (CHUSH)
UH... WHAT? WHAT'S GOING ON?
ALAS...

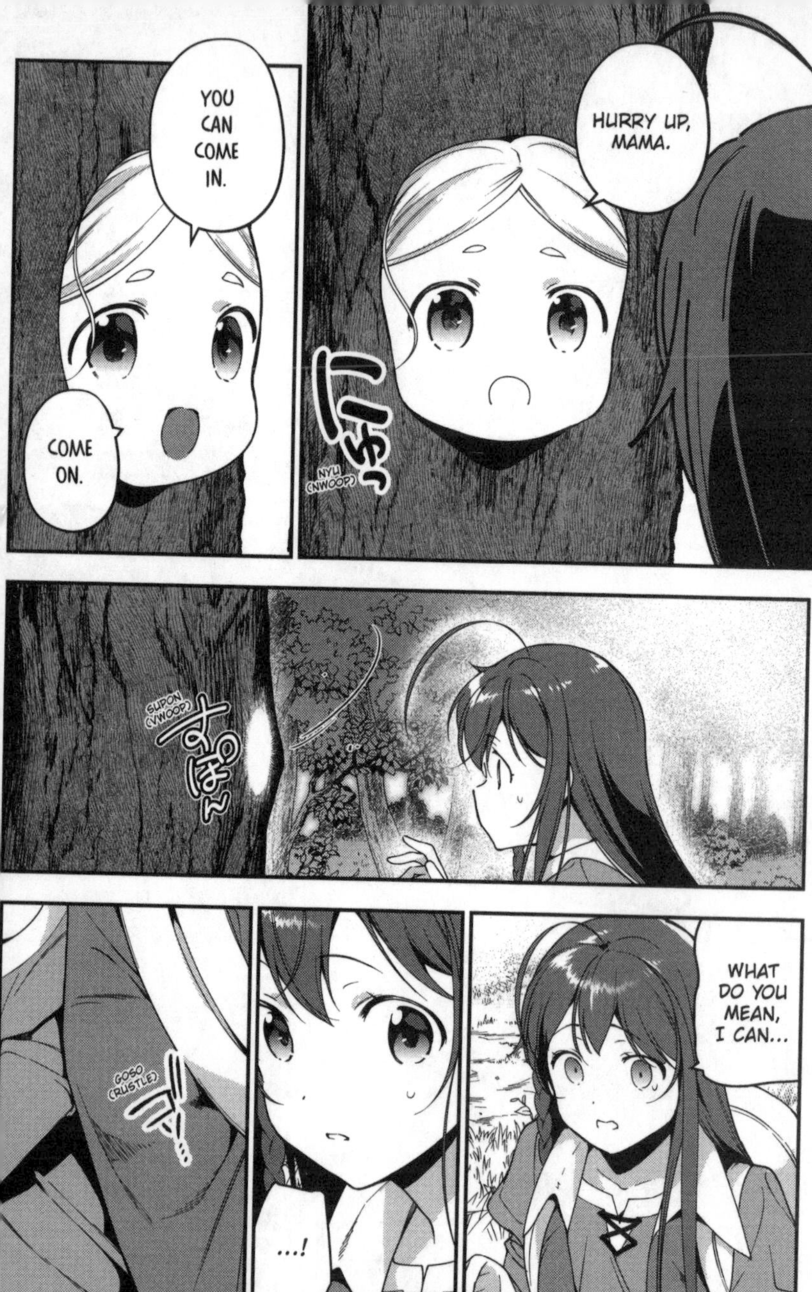
HURRY UP, MAMA.
NYU (NWOOP)
YOU CAN COME IN.
COME ON.
SUPON (VWOOP)
WHAT DO YOU MEAN, I CAN...
...!
GOSO (RUSTLE)

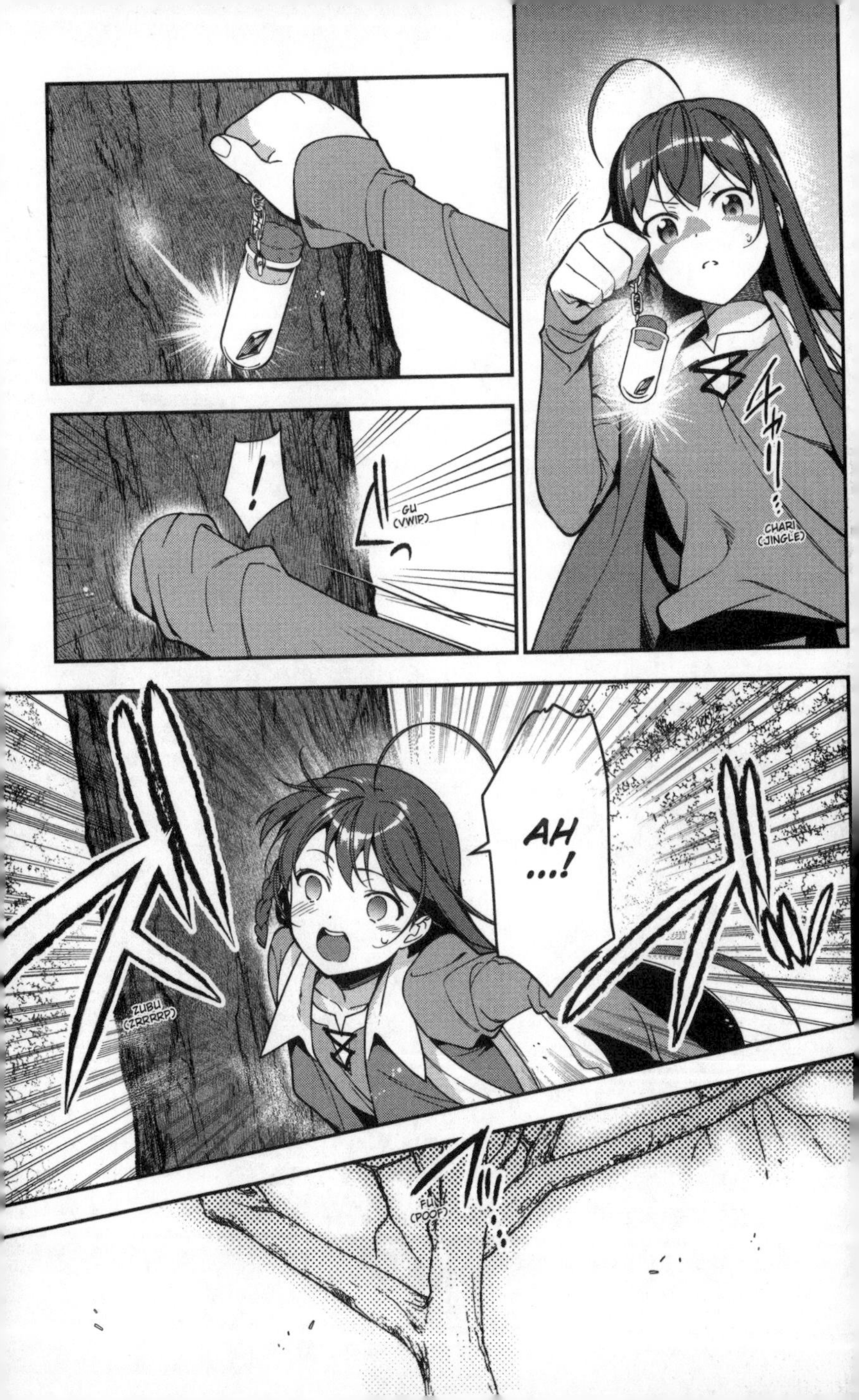
CHARI
(JINGLE)
GU
(VWIP)
!
AH
...!
ZUBU
(ZRRRRP)
FU
(POOF)

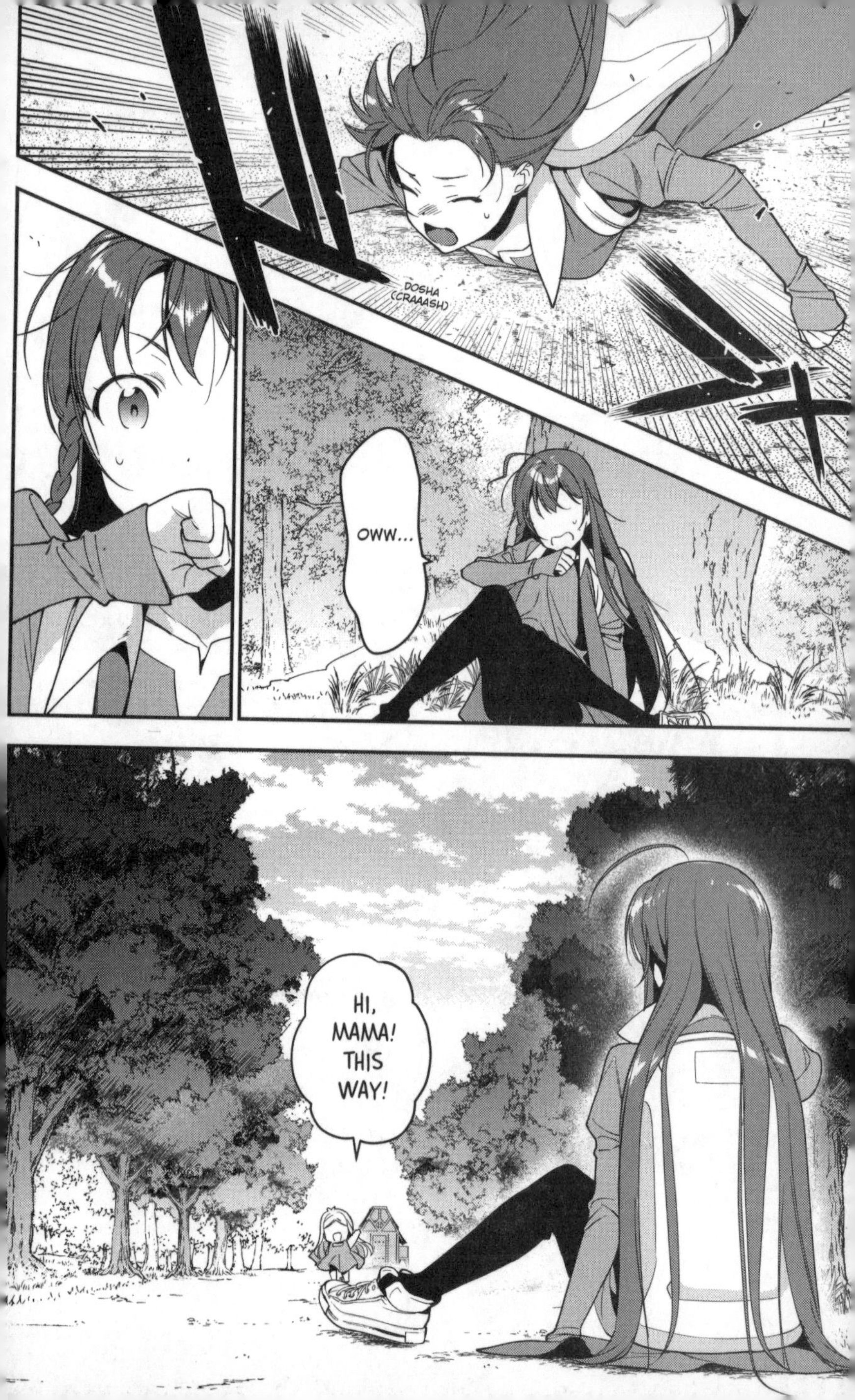
DOSHA (CRAAASH)
OWW...
HI, MAMA! THIS WAY!

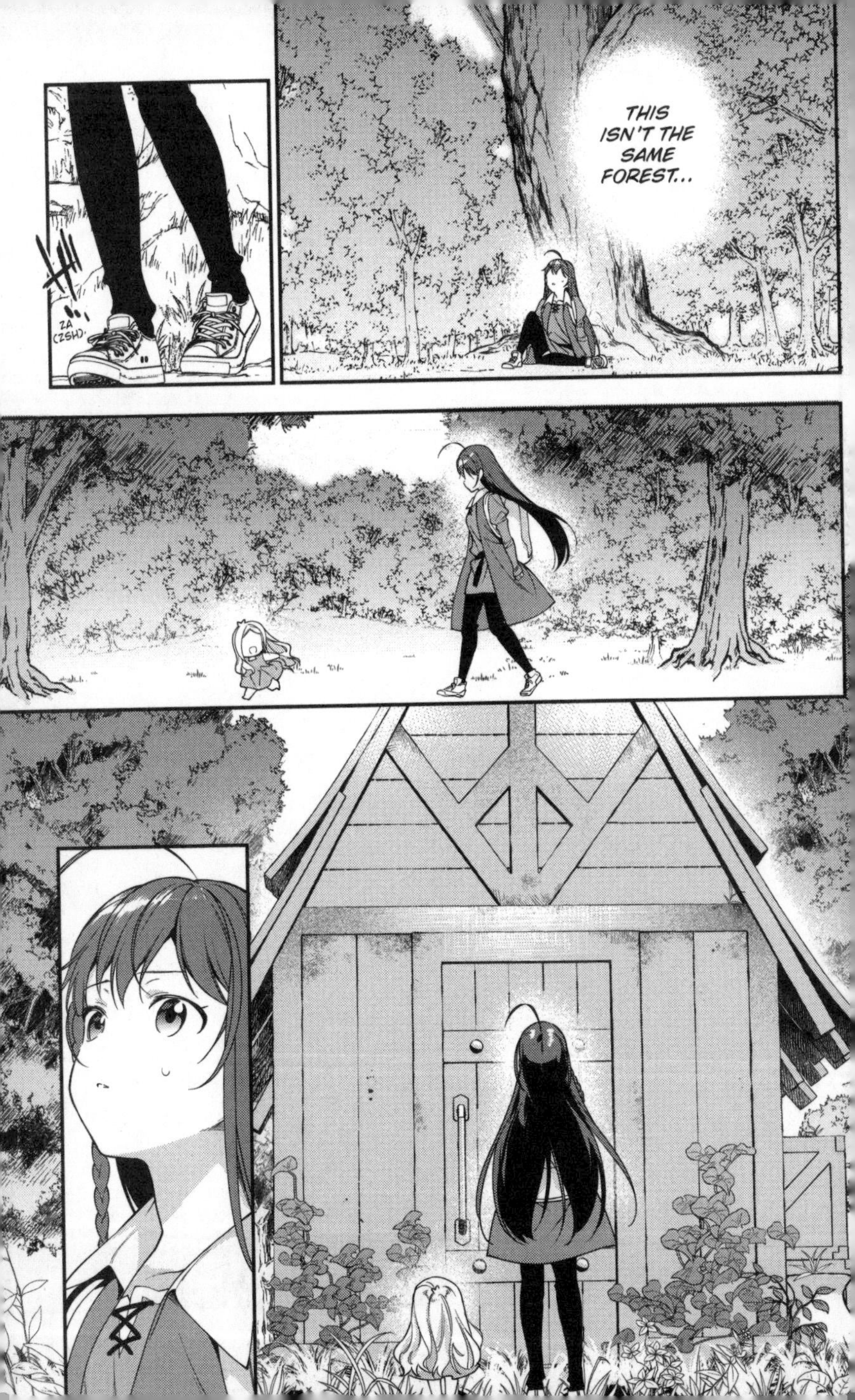
THIS ISN'T THE SAME FOREST...
ZA (ZSH)

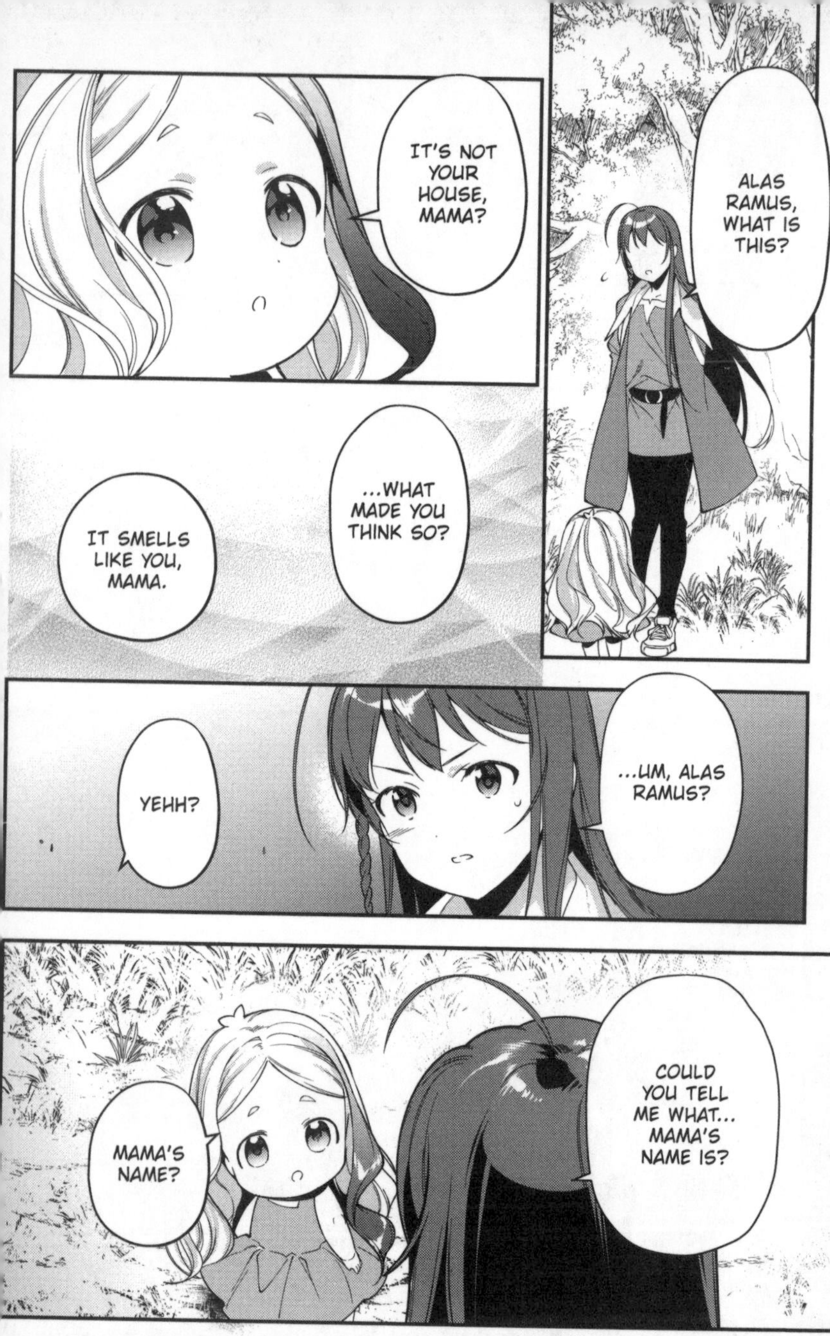
ALAS RAMUS, WHAT IS THIS?
IT'S NOT YOUR HOUSE, MAMA?
...WHAT MADE YOU THINK SO?
IT SMELLS LIKE YOU, MAMA.
...UM, ALAS RAMUS?
YEHH?
COULD YOU TELL ME WHAT... MAMA'S NAME IS?
MAMA'S NAME?

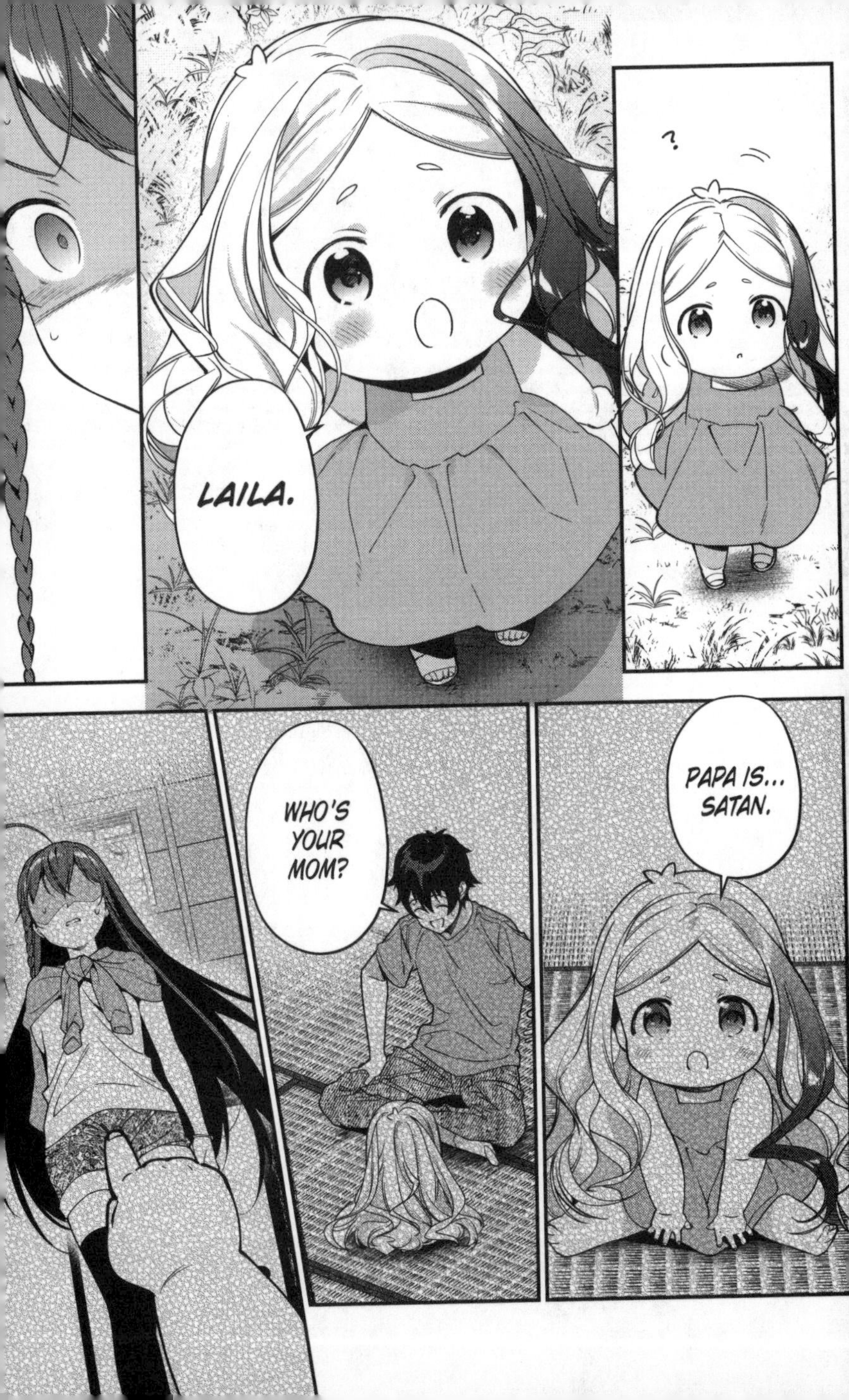
?
LAILA.
PAPA IS... SATAN.
WHO'S YOUR MOM?

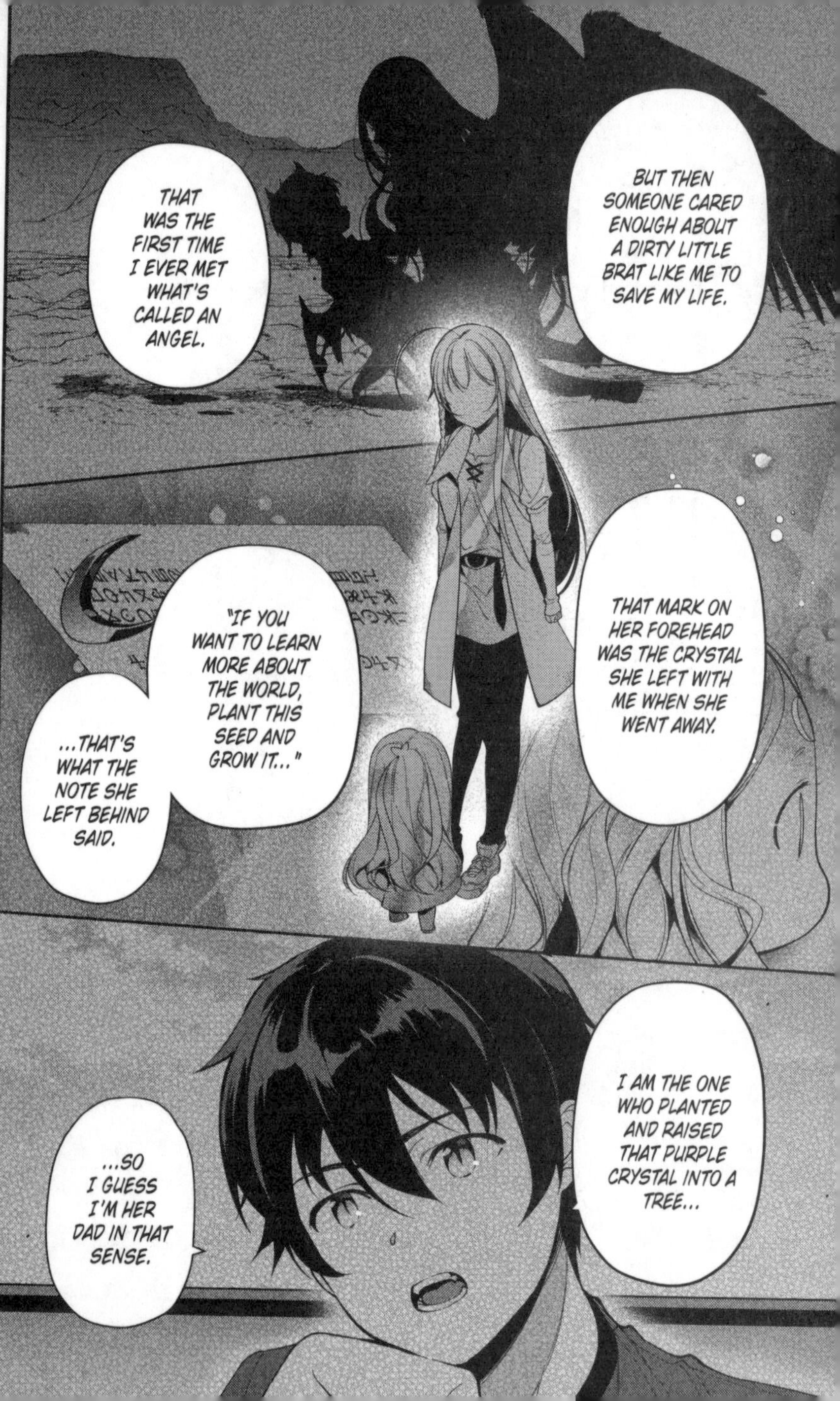
BUT THEN SOMEONE CARED ENOUGH ABOUT A DIRTY LITTLE BRAT LIKE ME TO SAVE MY LIFE.
THAT WAS THE FIRST TIME I EVER MET WHAT'S CALLED AN ANGEL.
THAT MARK ON HER FOREHEAD WAS THE CRYSTAL SHE LEFT WITH ME WHEN SHE WENT AWAY.
"IF YOU WANT TO LEARN MORE ABOUT THE WORLD, PLANT THIS SEED AND GROW IT..."
...THAT'S WHAT THE NOTE SHE LEFT BEHIND SAID.
I AM THE ONE WHO PLANTED AND RAISED THAT PURPLE CRYSTAL INTO A TREE...
...SO I GUESS I'M HER DAD IN THAT SENSE.

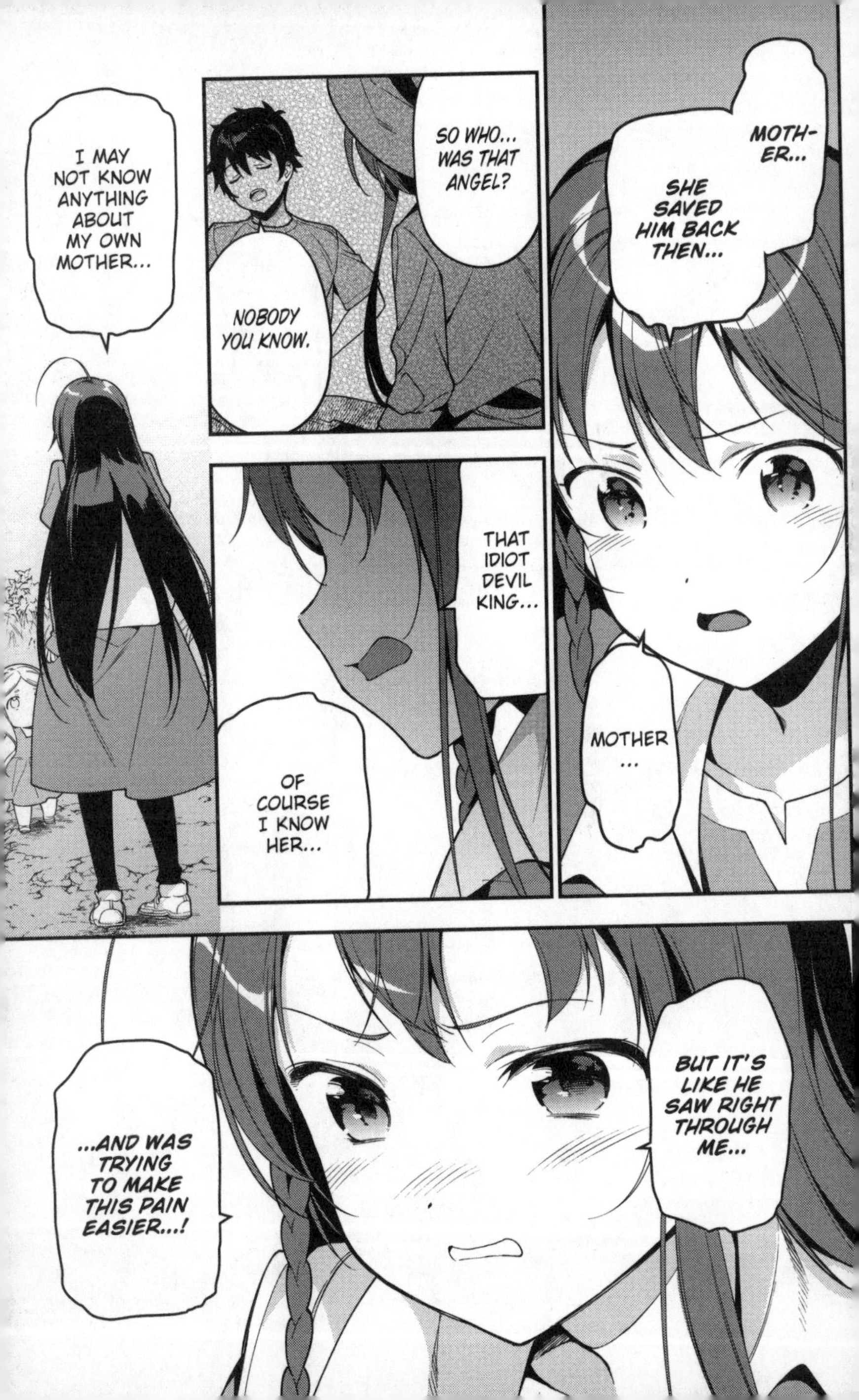
MOTH-ER...
SHE SAVED HIM BACK THEN...
MOTHER...
SO WHO... WAS THAT ANGEL?
NOBODY YOU KNOW.
THAT IDIOT DEVIL KING...
OF COURSE I KNOW HER...
I MAY NOT KNOW ANYTHING ABOUT MY OWN MOTHER...
BUT IT'S LIKE HE SAW RIGHT THROUGH ME...
...AND WAS TRYING TO MAKE THIS PAIN EASIER...!

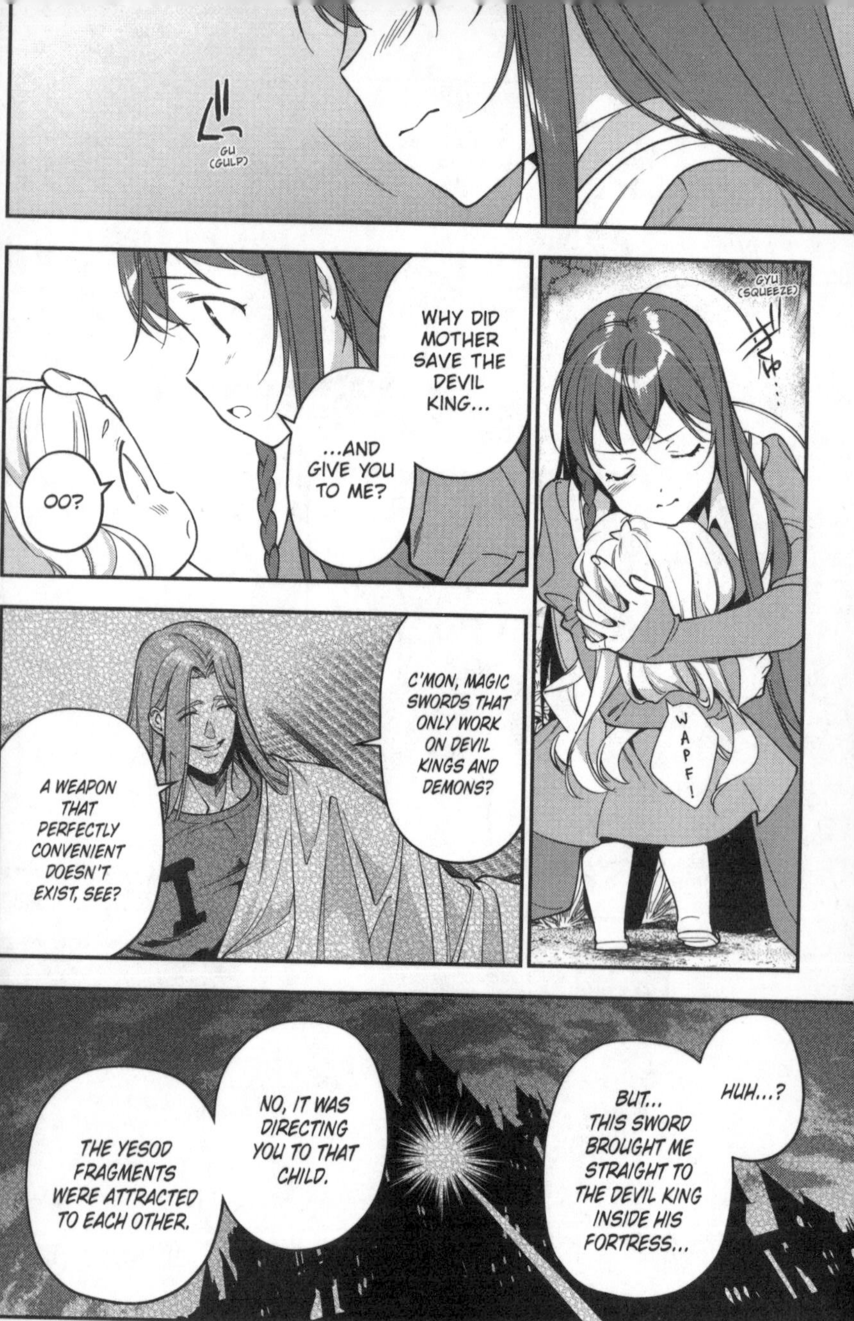
GU (GULP)
GYU (SQUEEZE)
WAPF!
WHY DID MOTHER SAVE THE DEVIL KING...
...AND GIVE YOU TO ME?
OO?
C'MON, MAGIC SWORDS THAT ONLY WORK ON DEVIL KINGS AND DEMONS?
A WEAPON THAT PERFECTLY CONVENIENT DOESN'T EXIST, SEE?
HUH...?
BUT... THIS SWORD BROUGHT ME STRAIGHT TO THE DEVIL KING INSIDE HIS FORTRESS...
NO, IT WAS DIRECTING YOU TO THAT CHILD.
THE YESOD FRAGMENTS WERE ATTRACTED TO EACH OTHER.

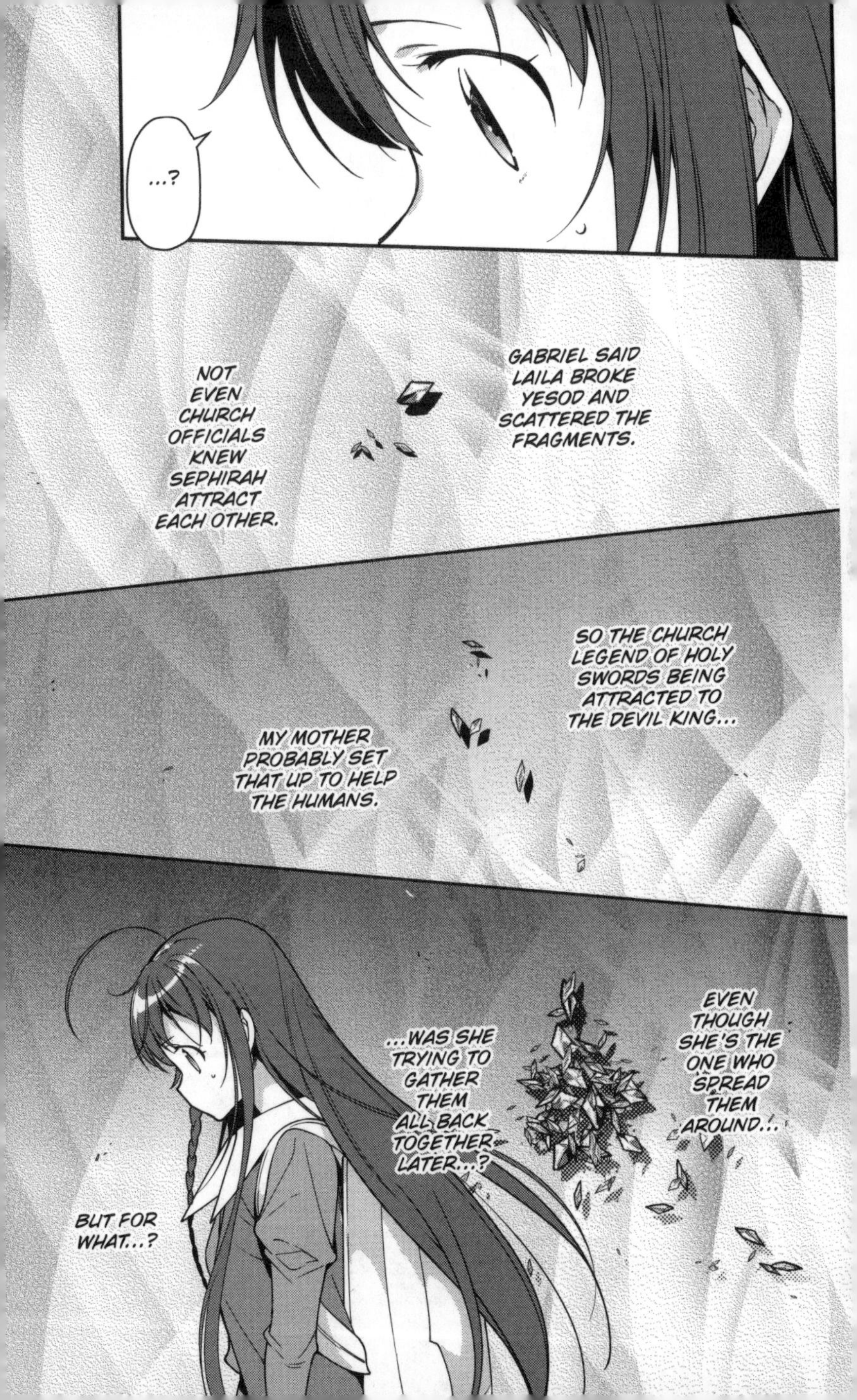
...?
GABRIEL SAID LAILA BROKE YESOD AND SCATTERED THE FRAGMENTS.
NOT EVEN CHURCH OFFICIALS KNEW SEPHIRAH ATTRACT EACH OTHER.
SO THE CHURCH LEGEND OF HOLY SWORDS BEING ATTRACTED TO THE DEVIL KING...
MY MOTHER PROBABLY SET THAT UP TO HELP THE HUMANS.
EVEN THOUGH SHE'S THE ONE WHO SPREAD THEM AROUND...
...WAS SHE TRYING TO GATHER THEM ALL BACK TOGETHER LATER...?
BUT FOR WHAT...?

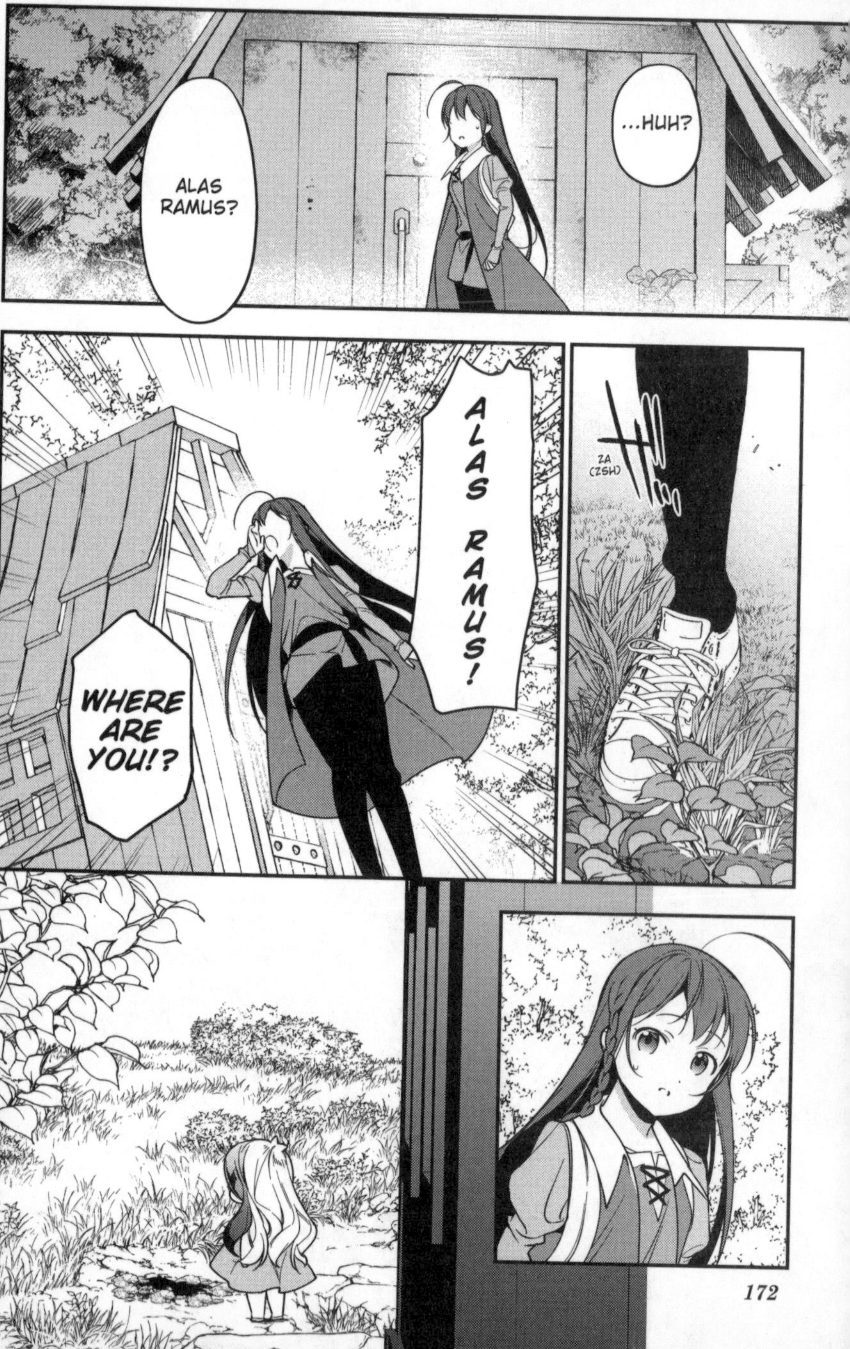
...HUH?
ALAS RAMUS?
ZA (ZSH)
ALAS RAMUS!
WHERE ARE YOU!?

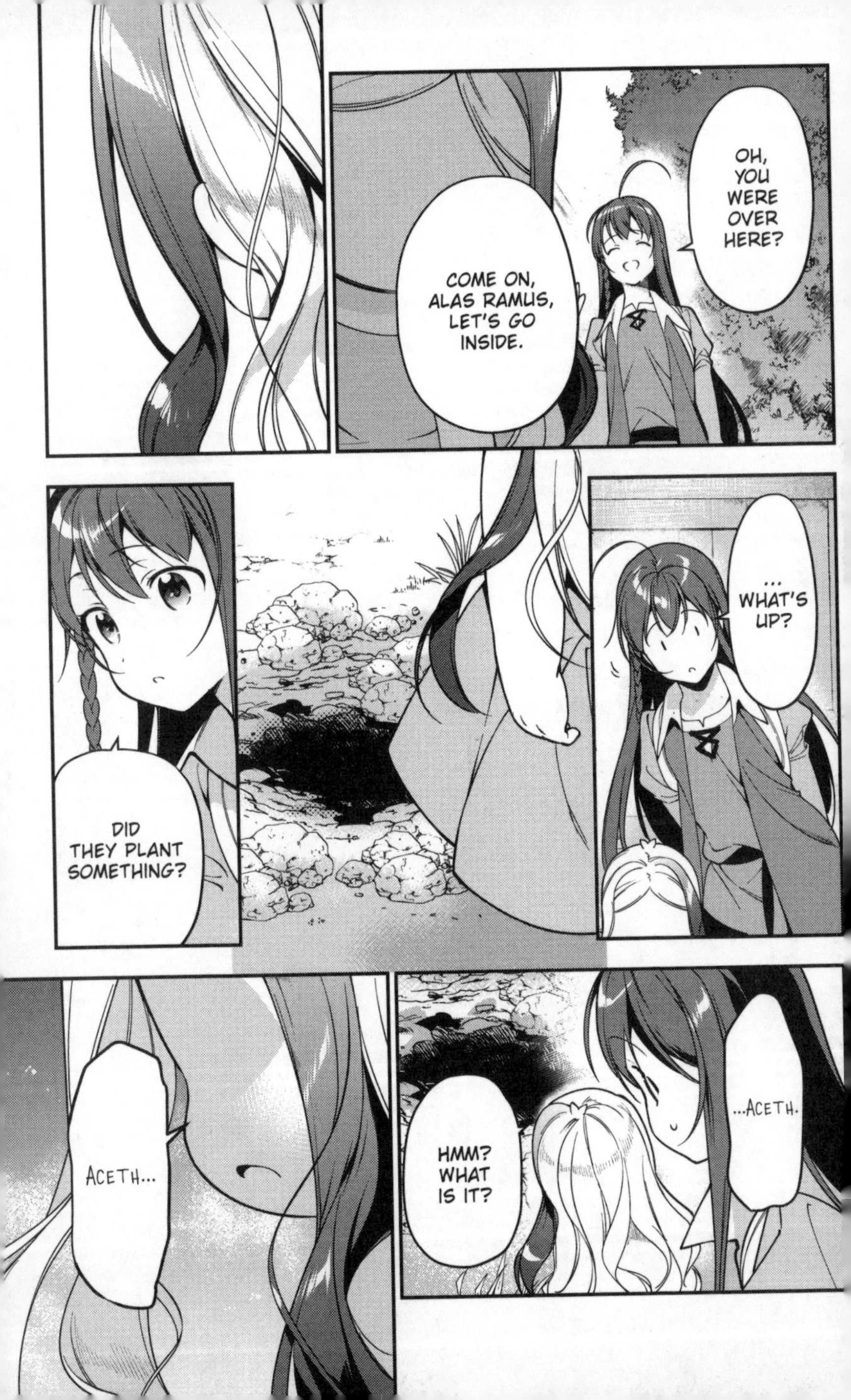
OH, YOU WERE OVER HERE?
COME ON, ALAS RAMUS, LET'S GO INSIDE.
... WHAT'S UP?
DID THEY PLANT SOMETHING?
...ACETH.
HMM? WHAT IS IT?
ACETH...

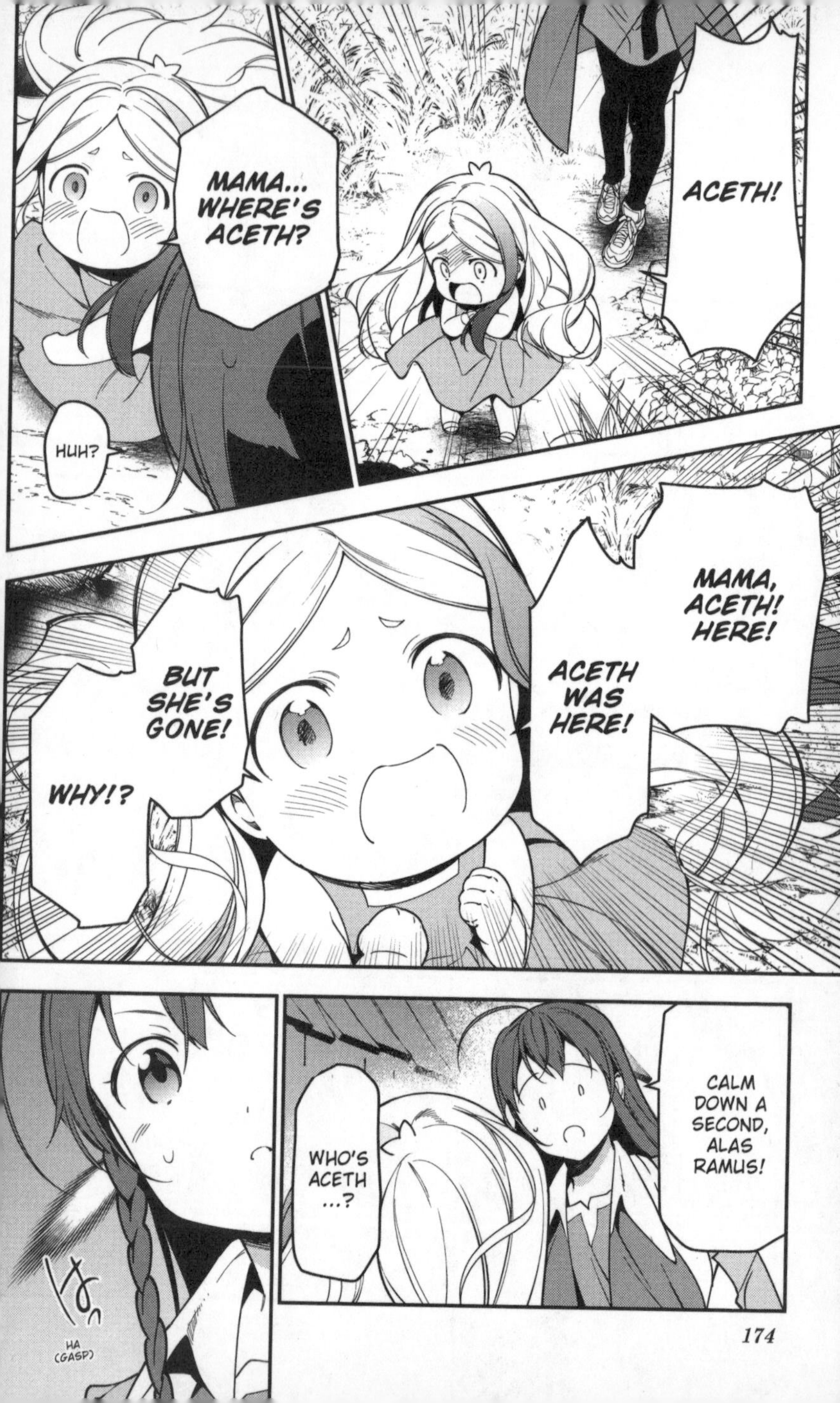

ACETH!
MAMA... WHERE'S ACETH?
HUH?
MAMA, ACETH! HERE!
ACETH WAS HERE!
BUT SHE'S GONE!
WHY!?
CALM DOWN A SECOND, ALAS RAMUS!
WHO'S ACETH ...?
HA (GASP)

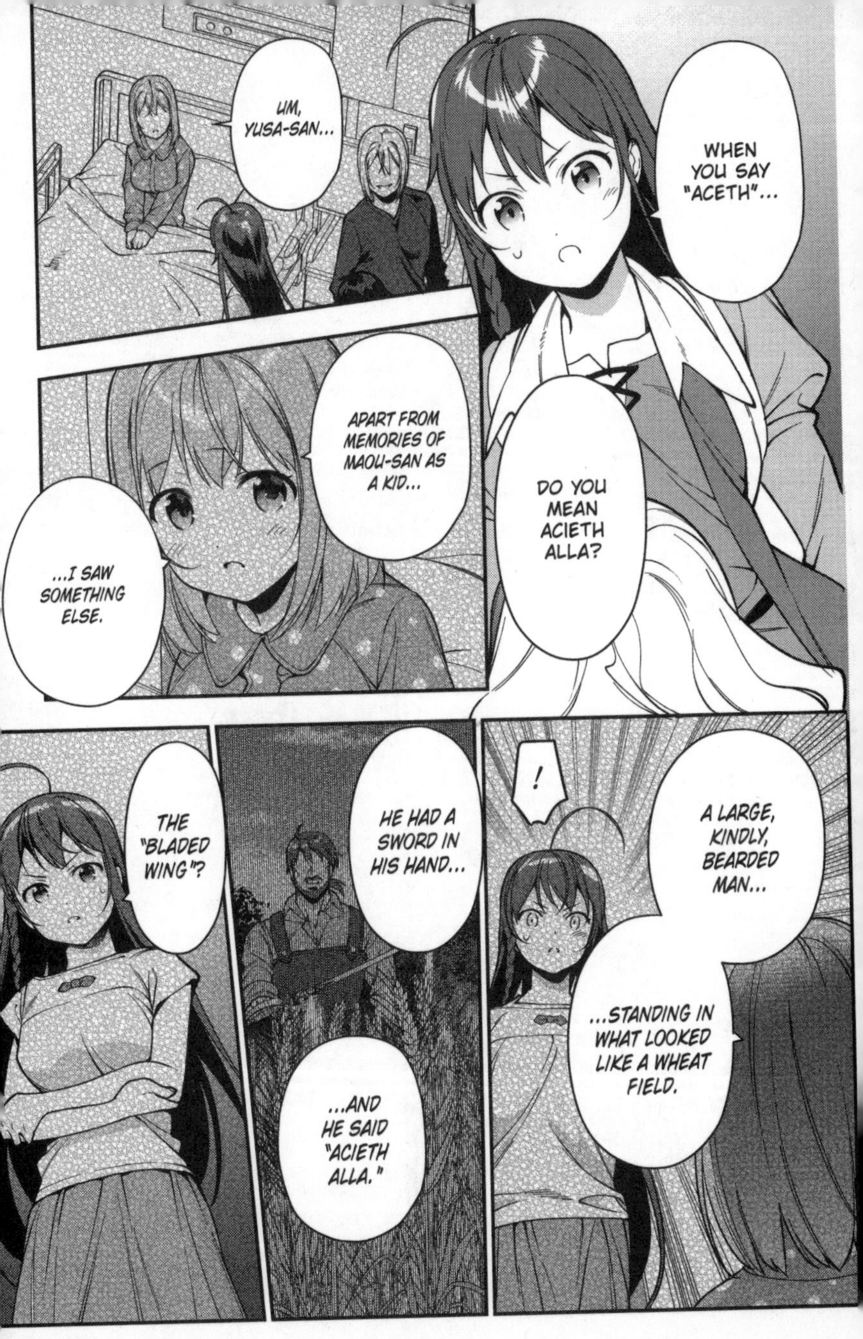
WHEN YOU SAY "ACETH"...
DO YOU MEAN ACIETH ALLA?
UM, YUSA-SAN...
APART FROM MEMORIES OF MAOU-SAN AS A KID...
...I SAW SOMETHING ELSE.
!
A LARGE, KINDLY, BEARDED MAN...
...STANDING IN WHAT LOOKED LIKE A WHEAT FIELD.
HE HAD A SWORD IN HIS HAND...
...AND HE SAID "ACIETH ALLA."
THE "BLADED WING"?

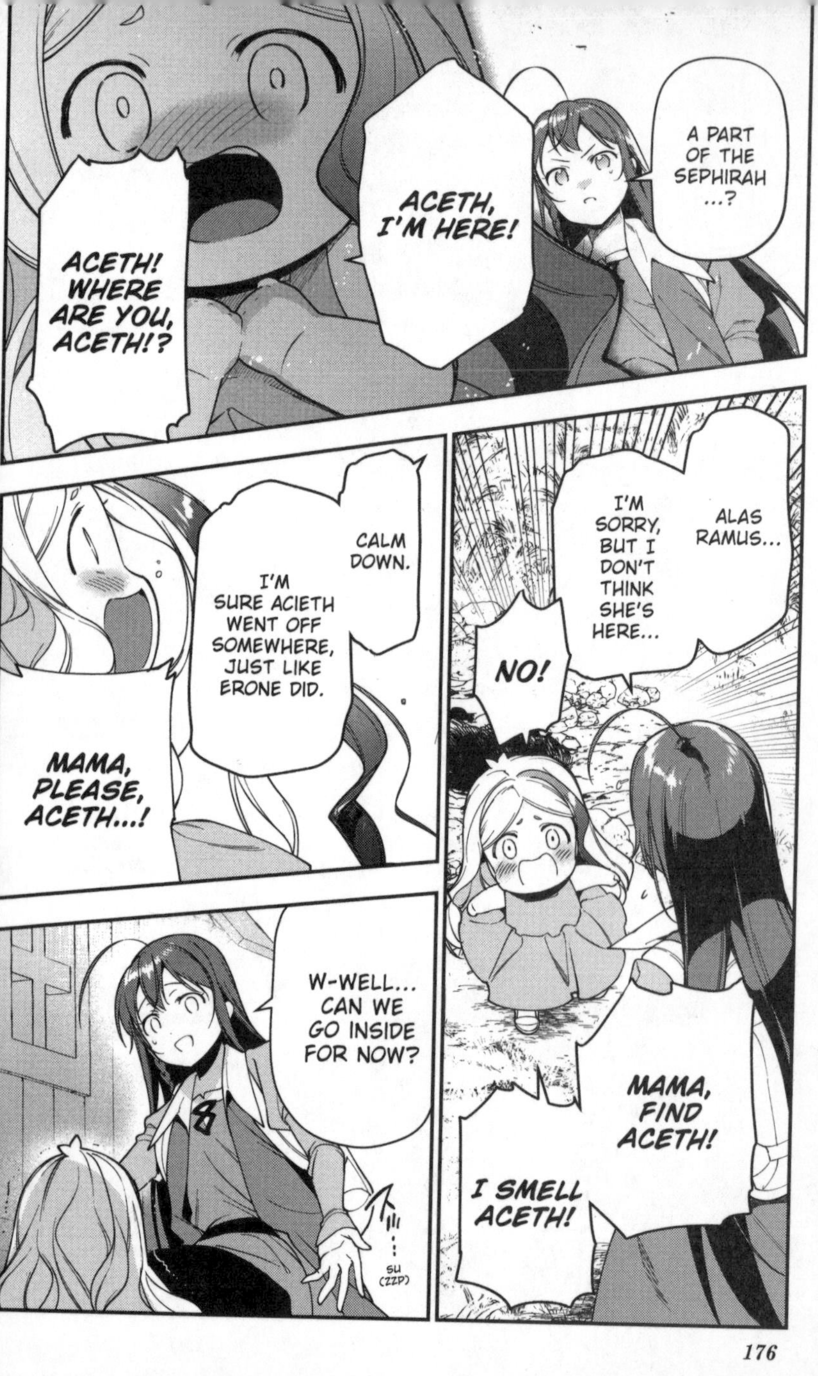
A PART OF THE SEPHIRAH ...?
ACETH, I'M HERE!
ACETH! WHERE ARE YOU, ACETH!?
ALAS RAMUS...
I'M SORRY, BUT I DON'T THINK SHE'S HERE...
NO!
MAMA, FIND ACETH!
I SMELL ACETH!
CALM DOWN.
I'M SURE ACIETH WENT OFF SOMEWHERE, JUST LIKE ERONE DID.
MAMA, PLEASE, ACETH...!
W-WELL... CAN WE GO INSIDE FOR NOW?
SU (ZZP)

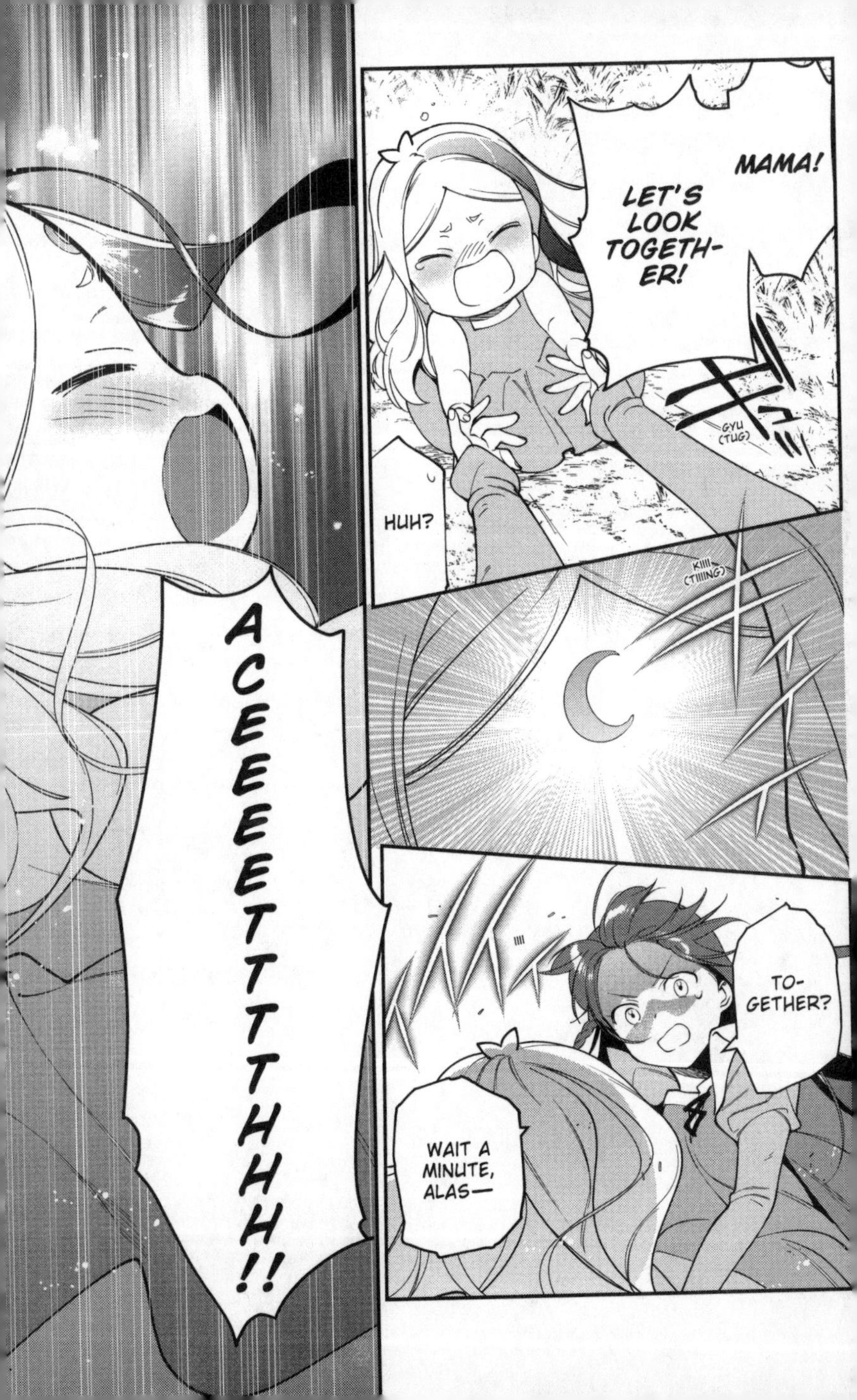
MAMA!
LET'S LOOK TOGETH-ER!
GYU (TUG)
HUH?
KIIII (TIIIING)
TO-GETHER?
WAIT A MINUTE, ALAS—
ACEEEEETTTTTHHHH!!

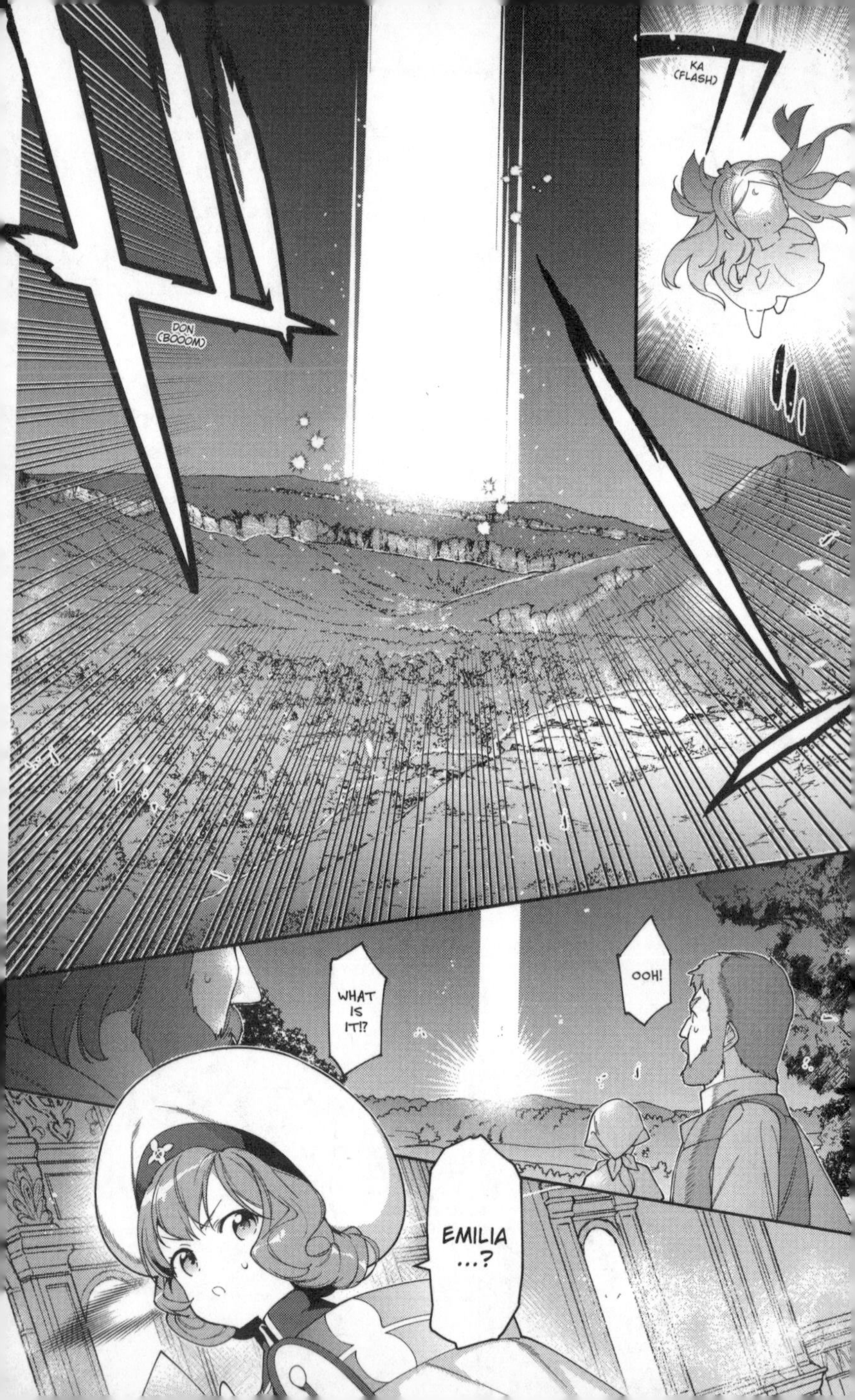
KA (FLASH)
DON (BOOOM)
OOH!
WHAT IS IT!?
EMILIA ...?

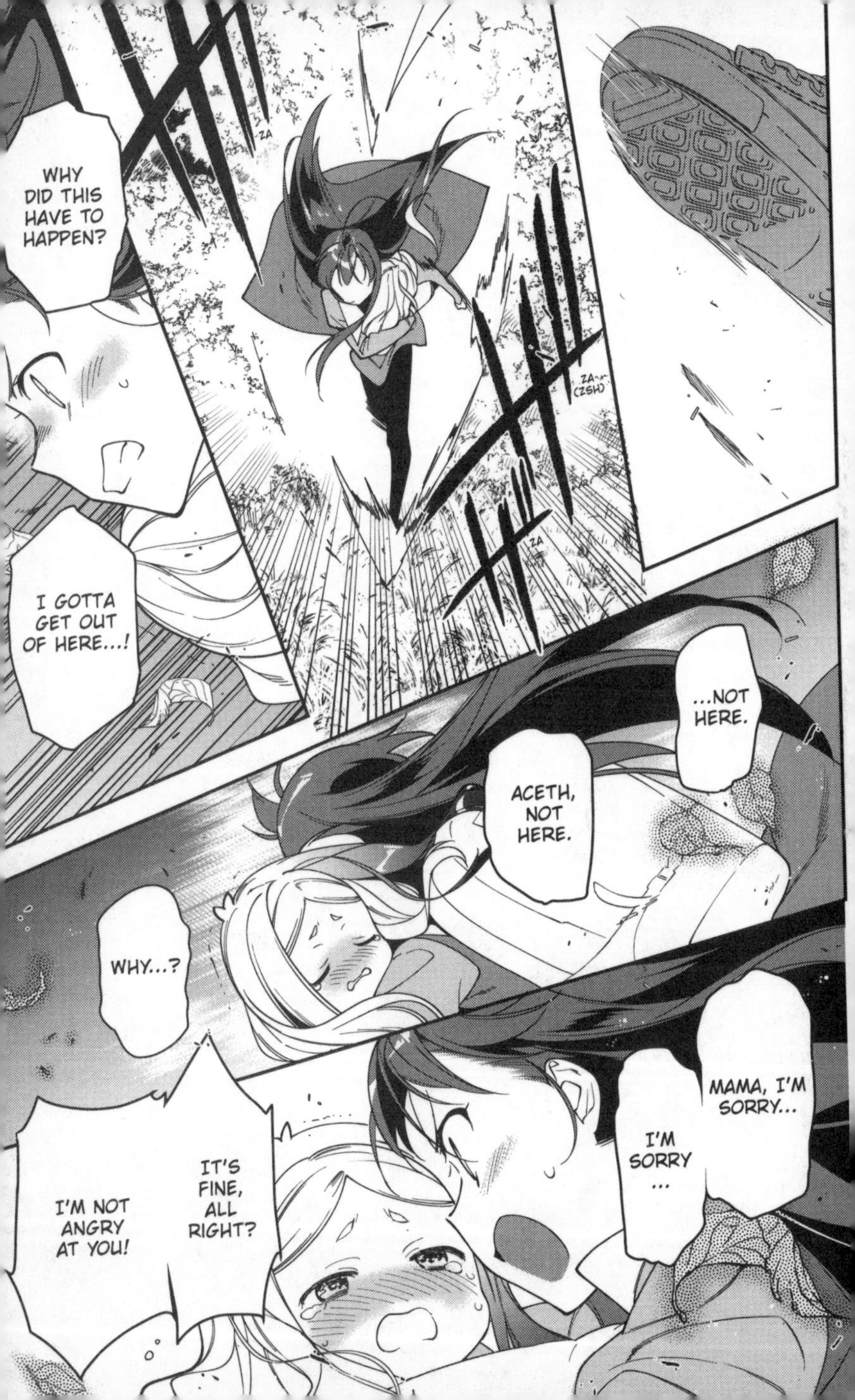
ZA
ZA (ZSH)
ZA
WHY DID THIS HAVE TO HAPPEN?
I GOTTA GET OUT OF HERE...!
...NOT HERE.
ACETH, NOT HERE.
WHY...?
MAMA, I'M SORRY...
I'M SORRY ...
IT'S FINE, ALL RIGHT?
I'M NOT ANGRY AT YOU!

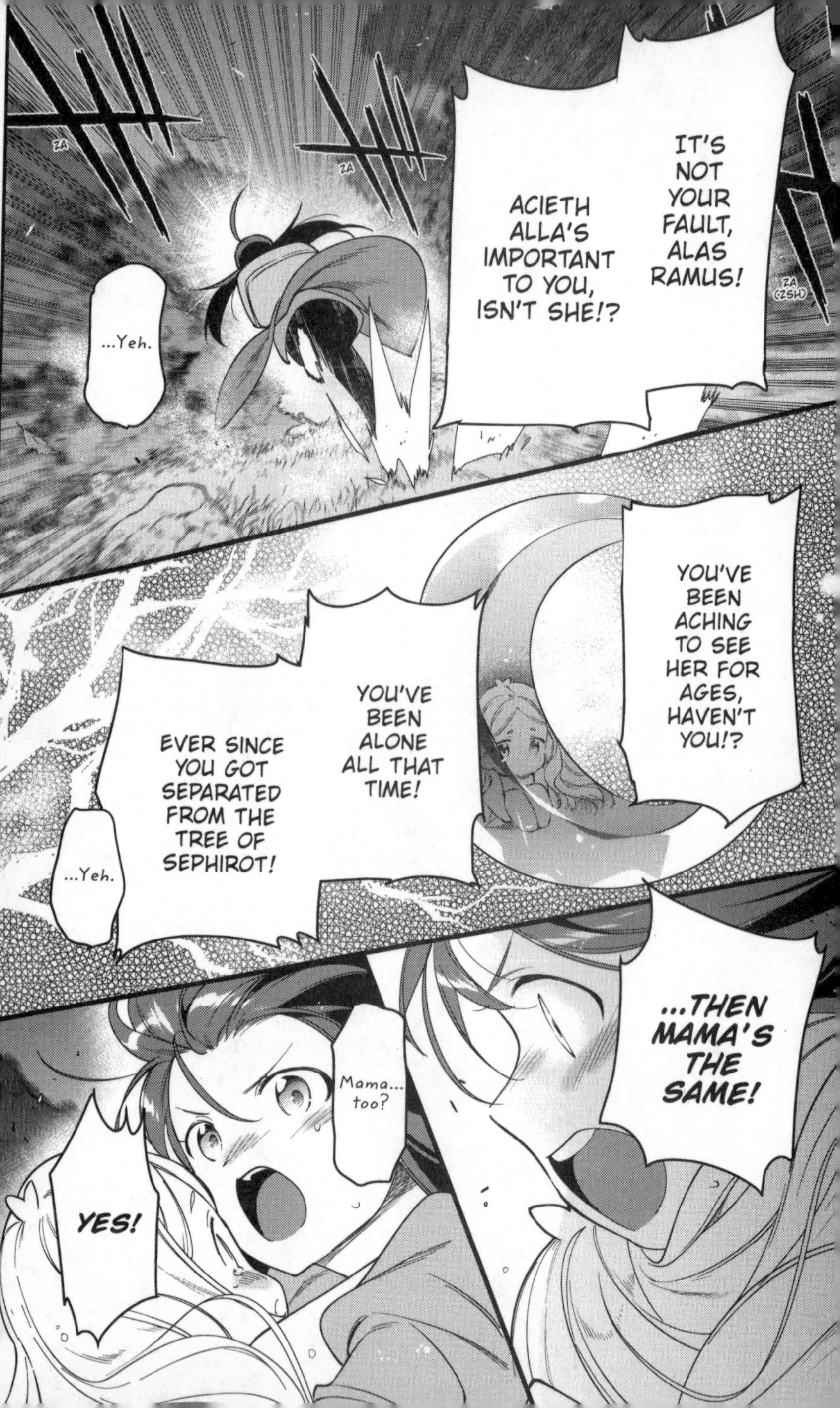
IT'S NOT YOUR FAULT, ALAS RAMUS!
ACIETH ALLA'S IMPORTANT TO YOU, ISN'T SHE!?
ZA (ZSH)
ZA
ZA
...Yeh.
YOU'VE BEEN ACHING TO SEE HER FOR AGES, HAVEN'T YOU!?
YOU'VE BEEN ALONE ALL THAT TIME!
EVER SINCE YOU GOT SEPARATED FROM THE TREE OF SEPHIROT!
...Yeh.
...THEN MAMA'S THE SAME!
Mama... too?
YES!

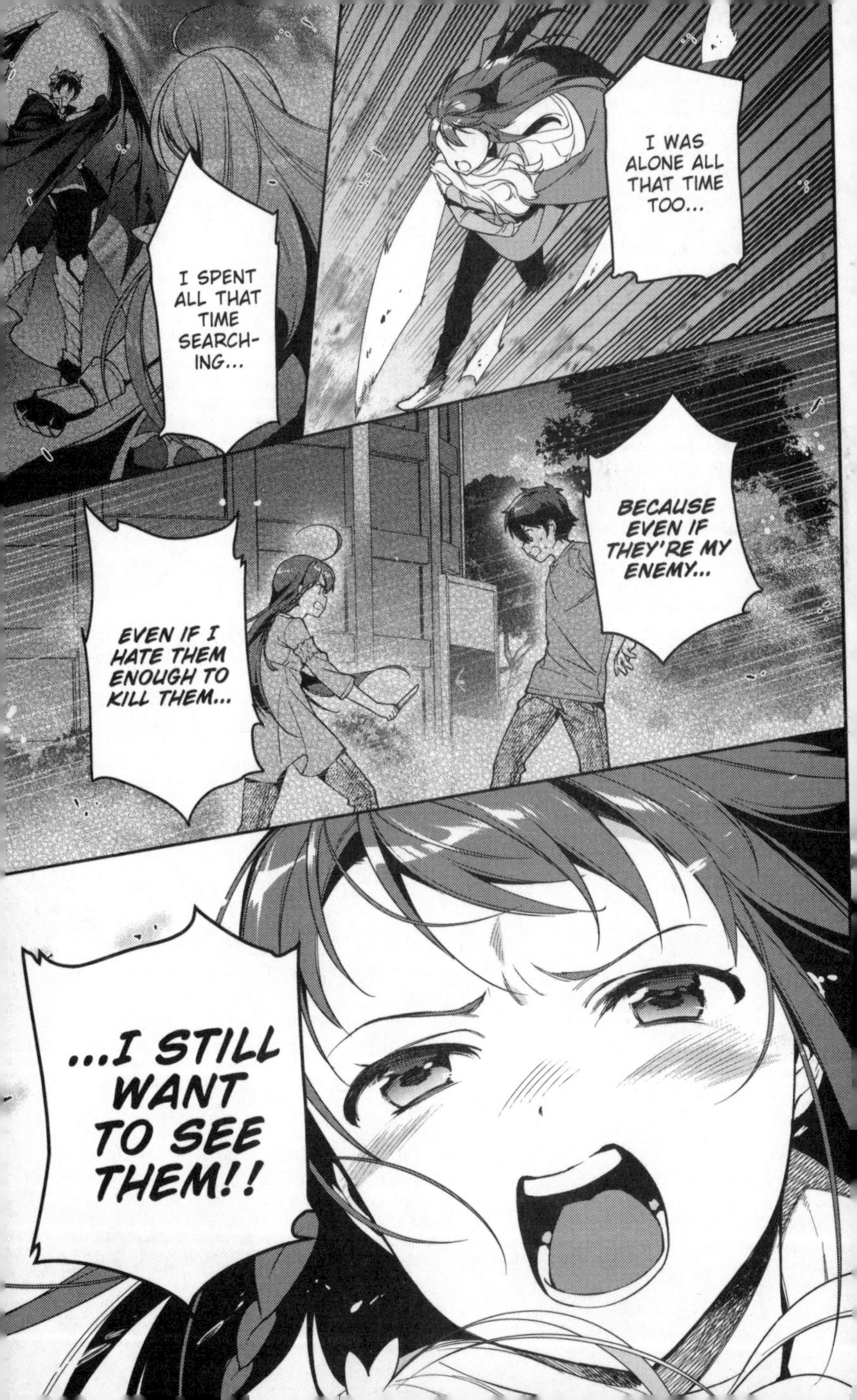
I WAS ALONE ALL THAT TIME TOO...
I SPENT ALL THAT TIME SEARCHING...
BECAUSE EVEN IF THEY'RE MY ENEMY...
EVEN IF I HATE THEM ENOUGH TO KILL THEM...
...I STILL WANT TO SEE THEM!!

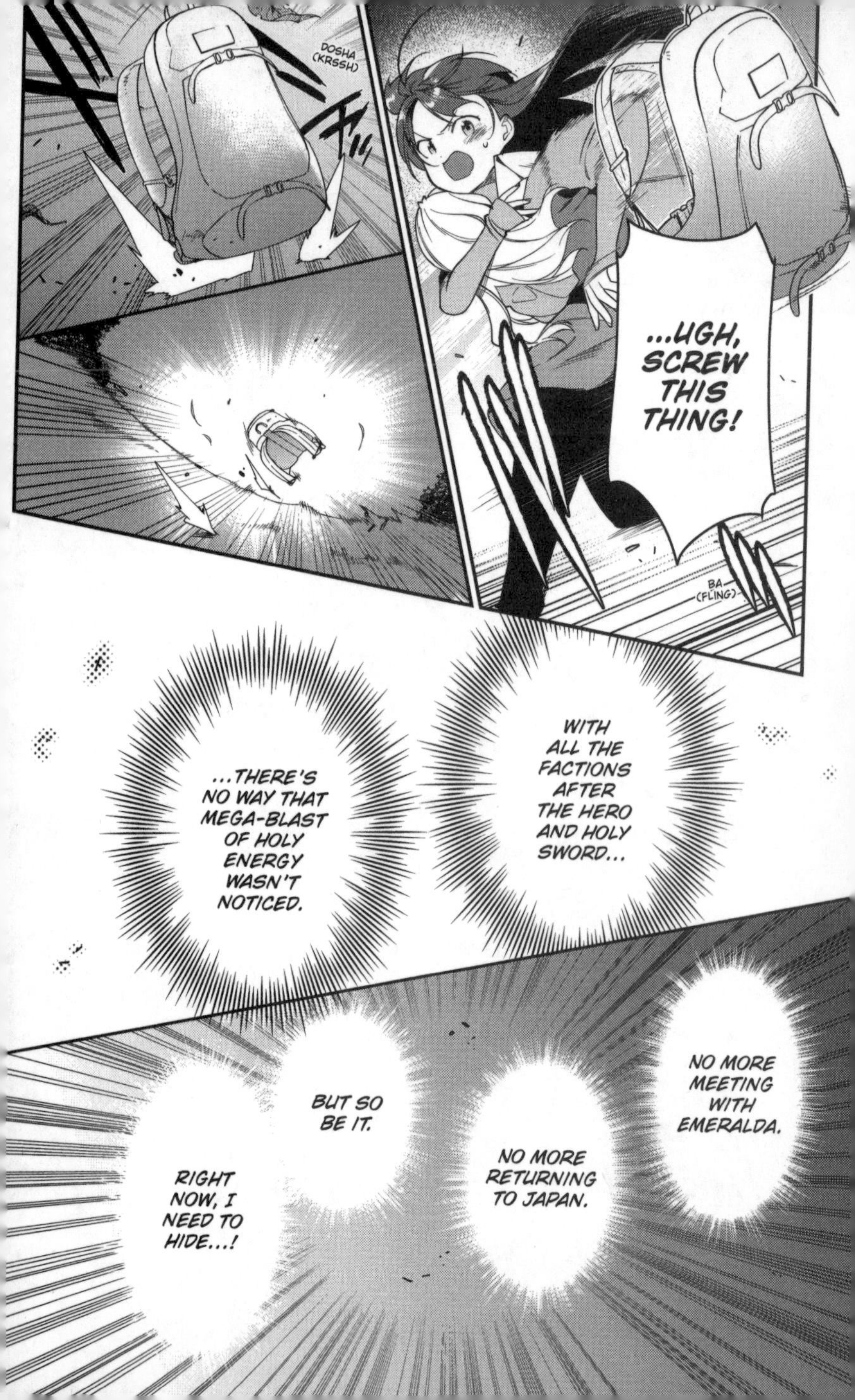
...UGH, SCREW THIS THING!
BA (FLING)
DOSHA (KRSSH)
WITH ALL THE FACTIONS AFTER THE HERO AND HOLY SWORD...
...THERE'S NO WAY THAT MEGA-BLAST OF HOLY ENERGY WASN'T NOTICED.
NO MORE MEETING WITH EMERALDA.
NO MORE RETURNING TO JAPAN.
BUT SO BE IT.
RIGHT NOW, I NEED TO HIDE...!

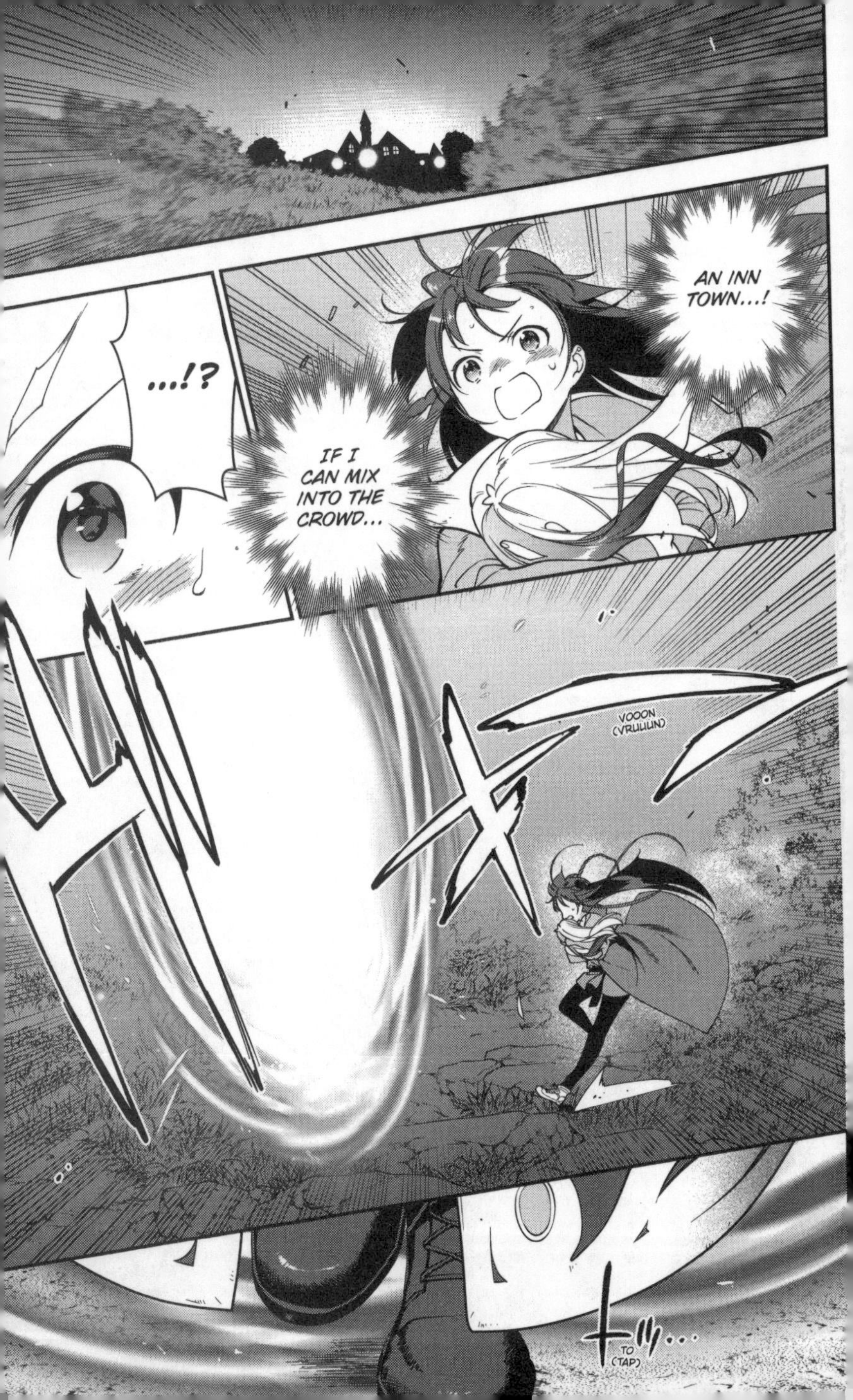
AN INN TOWN...!
IF I CAN MIX INTO THE CROWD...
...!?
VOOON (VRUUUN)
TO (TAP)

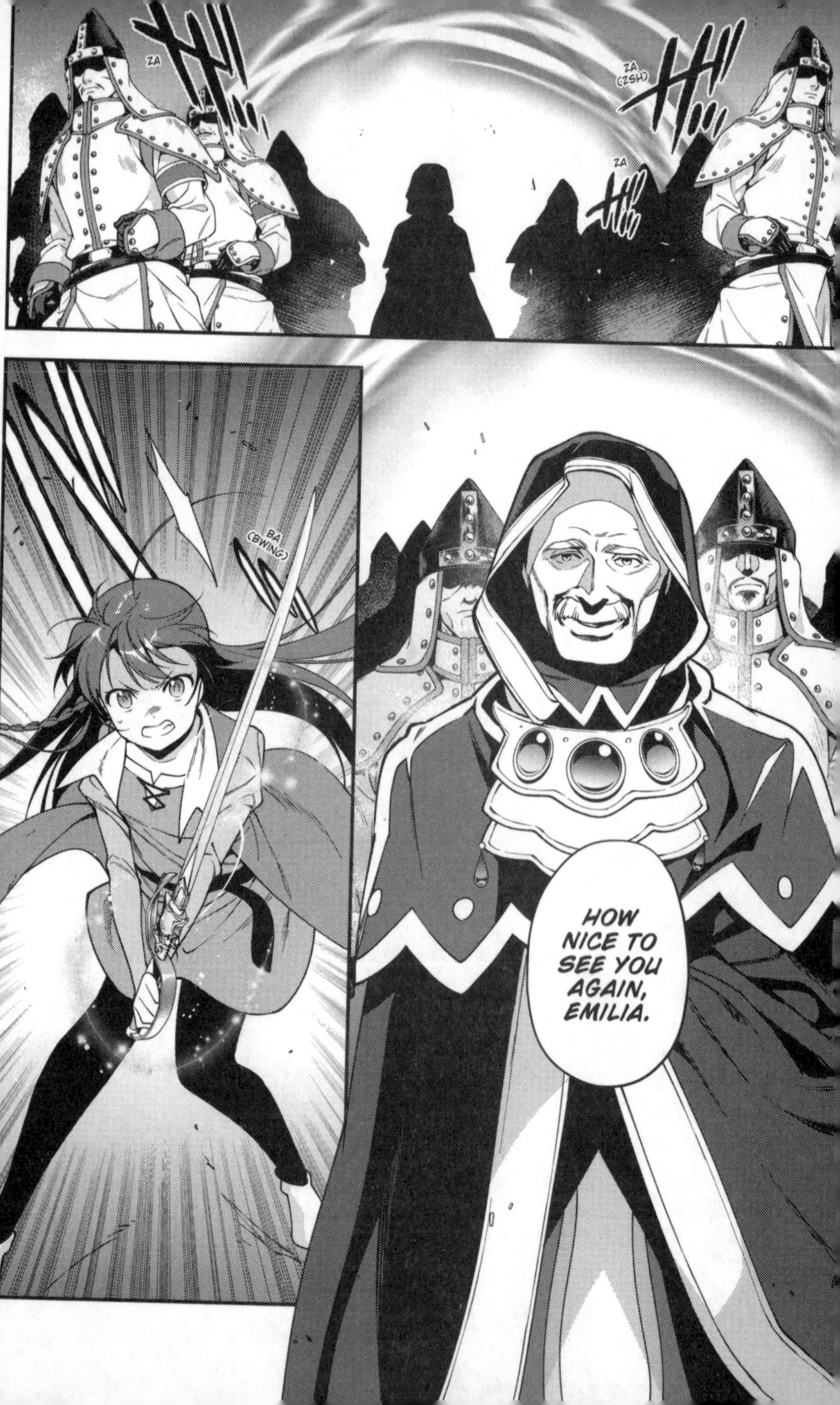
ZA (ZSH)
ZA
ZA
HOW NICE TO SEE YOU AGAIN, EMILIA.
BA (BWING)

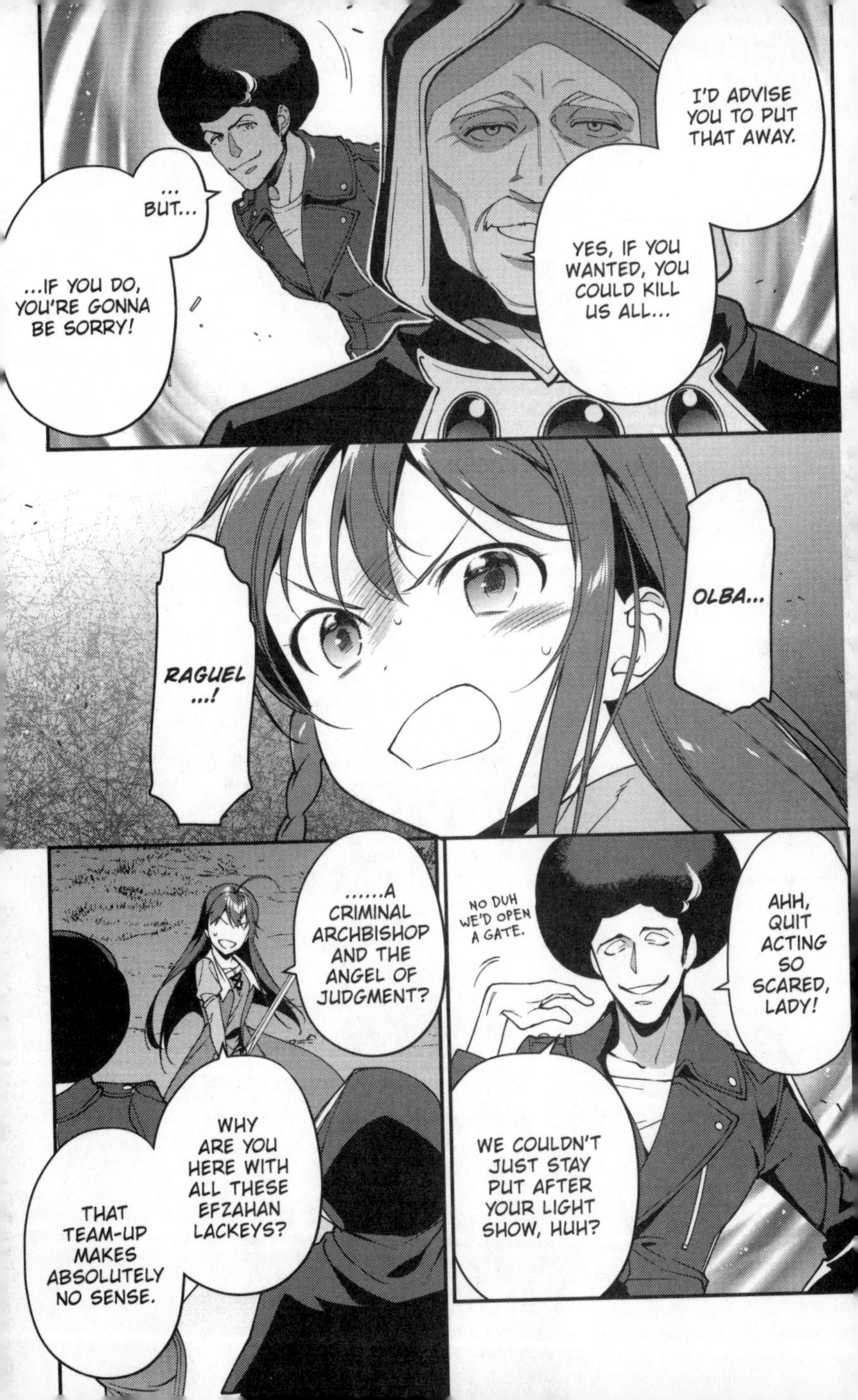
I'D ADVISE YOU TO PUT THAT AWAY.
YES, IF YOU WANTED, YOU COULD KILL US ALL...
... BUT...
...IF YOU DO, YOU'RE GONNA BE SORRY!
OLBA...
RAGUEL ...!
AHH, QUIT ACTING SO SCARED, LADY!
NO DUH WE'D OPEN A GATE.
WE COULDN'T JUST STAY PUT AFTER YOUR LIGHT SHOW, HUH?
......A CRIMINAL ARCHBISHOP AND THE ANGEL OF JUDGMENT?
WHY ARE YOU HERE WITH ALL THESE EFZAHAN LACKEYS?
THAT TEAM-UP MAKES ABSOLUTELY NO SENSE.

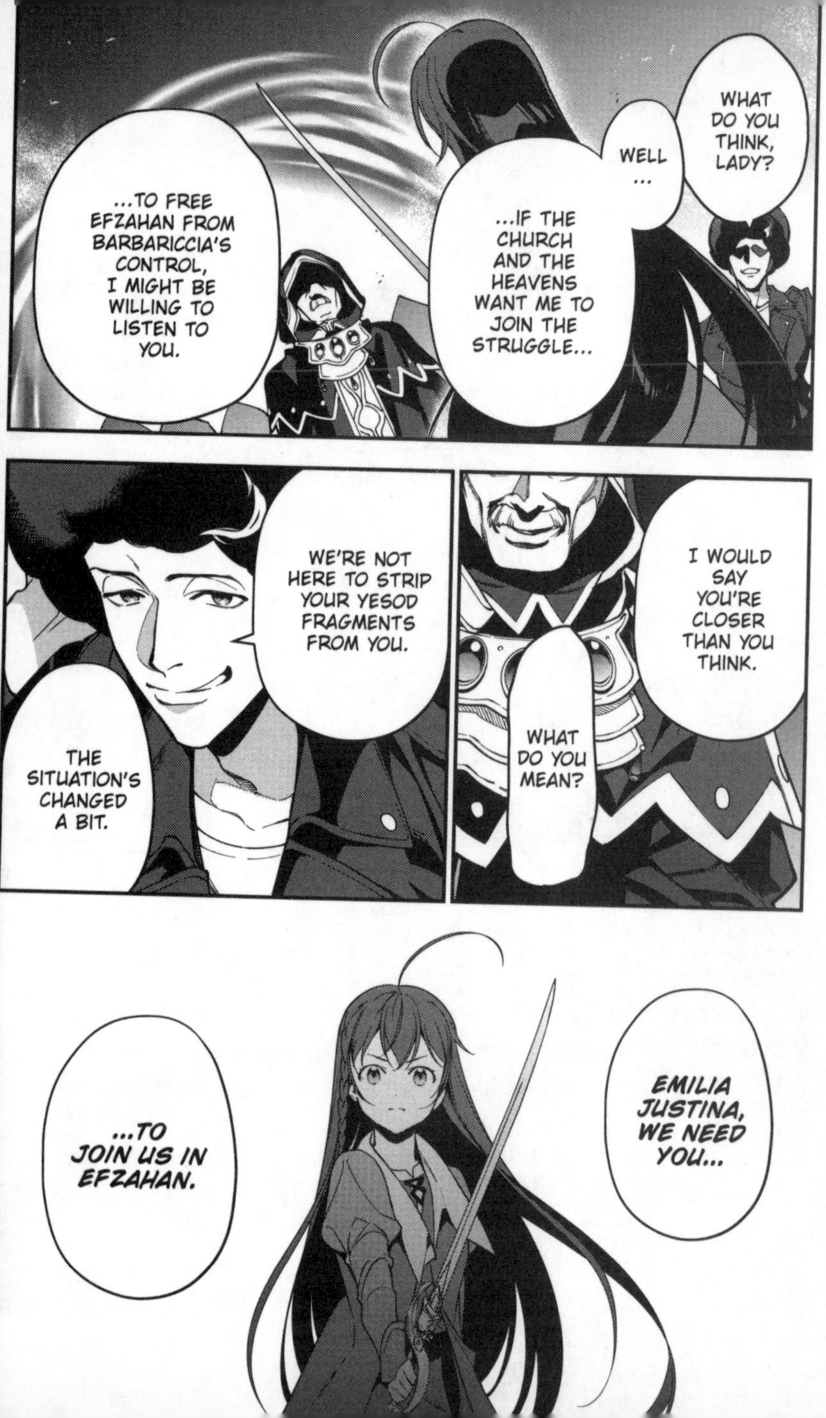
WHAT DO YOU THINK, LADY?
WELL...
...IF THE CHURCH AND THE HEAVENS WANT ME TO JOIN THE STRUGGLE...
...TO FREE EFZAHAN FROM BARBARICCIA'S CONTROL, I MIGHT BE WILLING TO LISTEN TO YOU.
I WOULD SAY YOU'RE CLOSER THAN YOU THINK.
WHAT DO YOU MEAN?
WE'RE NOT HERE TO STRIP YOUR YESOD FRAGMENTS FROM YOU.
THE SITUATION'S CHANGED A BIT.
EMILIA JUSTINA, WE NEED YOU...
...TO JOIN US IN EFZAHAN.

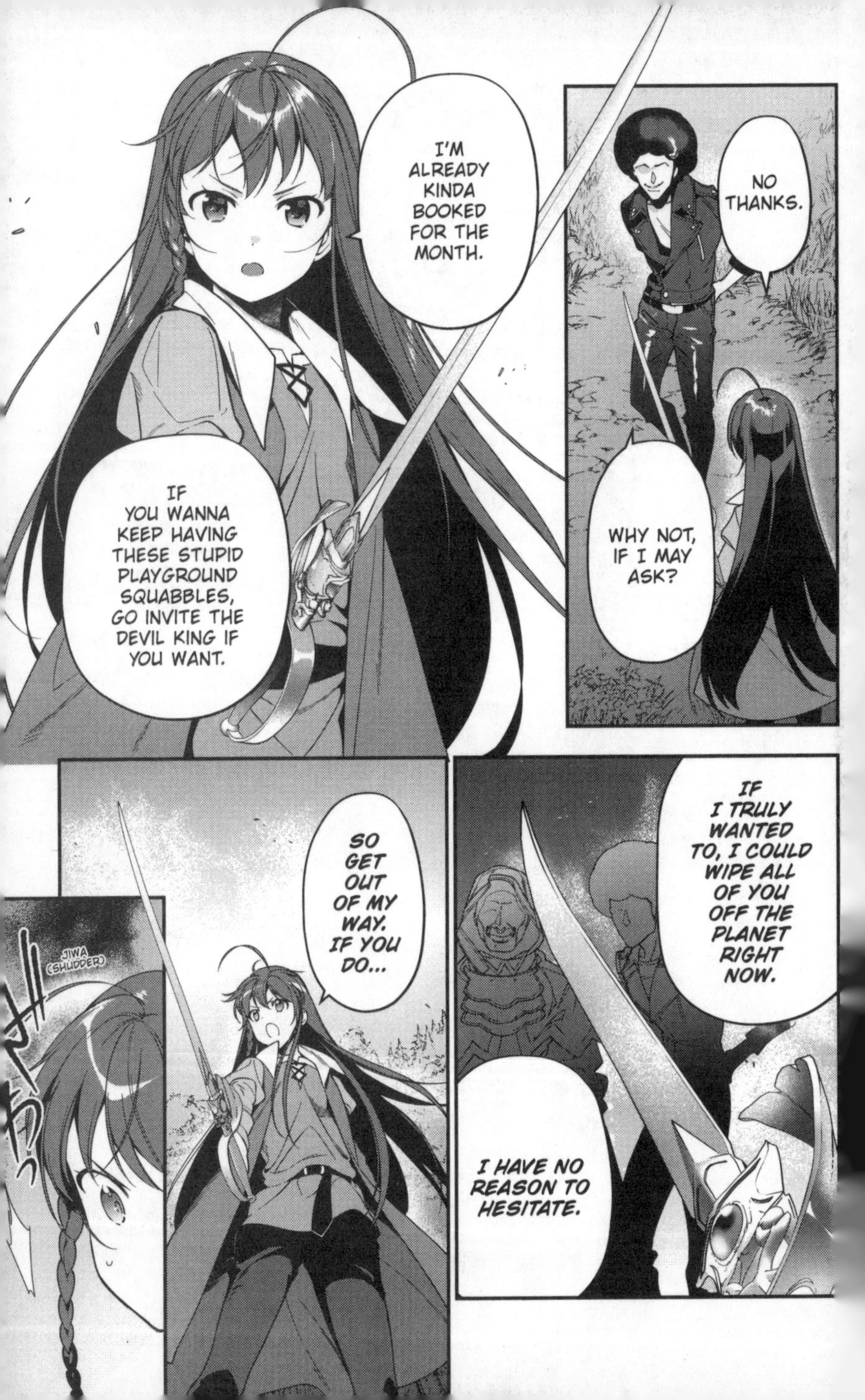
NO THANKS.
WHY NOT, IF I MAY ASK?
I'M ALREADY KINDA BOOKED FOR THE MONTH.
IF YOU WANNA KEEP HAVING THESE STUPID PLAYGROUND SQUABBLES, GO INVITE THE DEVIL KING IF YOU WANT.
IF I TRULY WANTED TO, I COULD WIPE ALL OF YOU OFF THE PLANET RIGHT NOW.
I HAVE NO REASON TO HESITATE.
SO GET OUT OF MY WAY. IF YOU DO...
JIWA (SHUDDER)

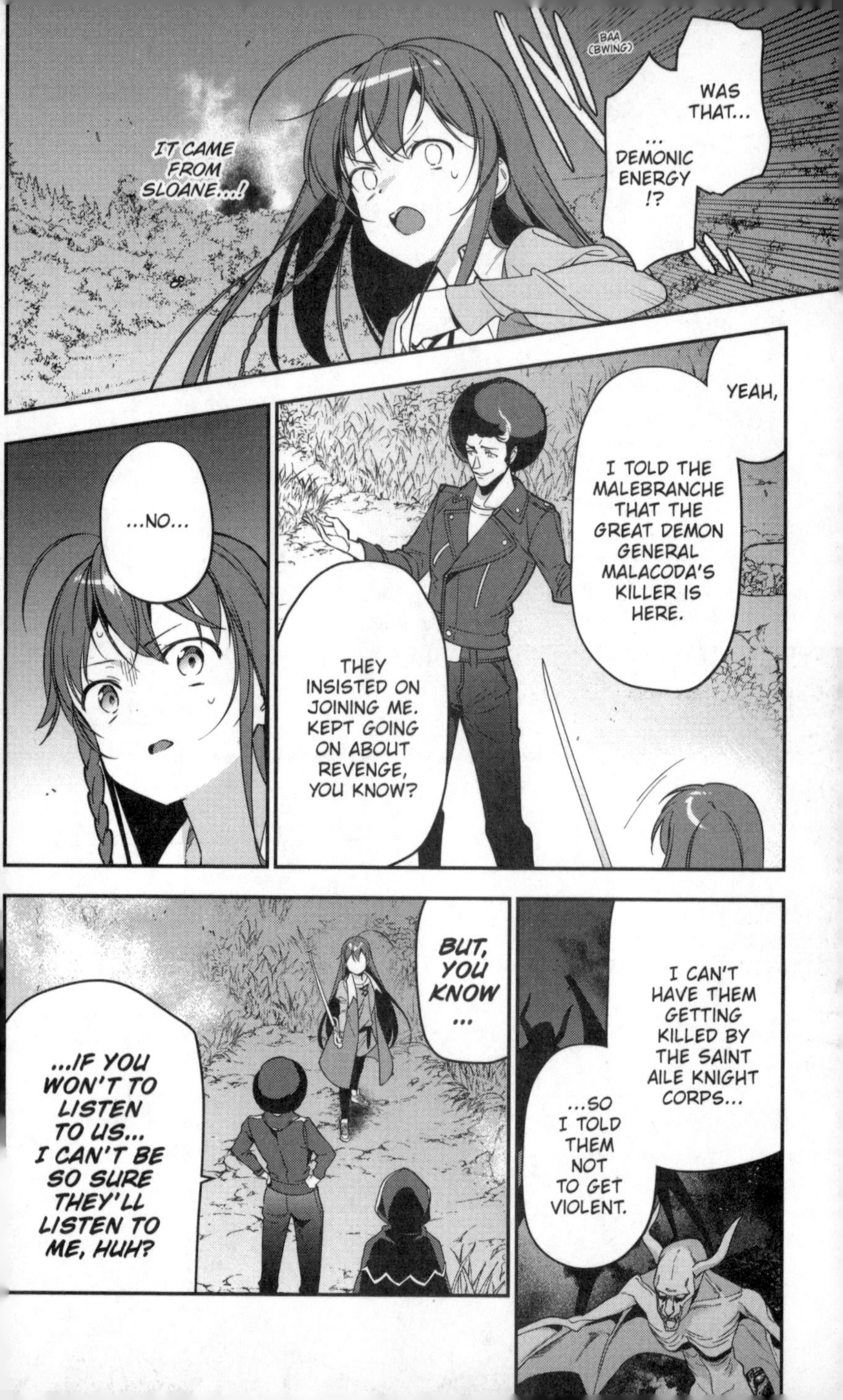
BAA (BWING)
WAS THAT...
...DEMONIC ENERGY !?
IT CAME FROM SLOANE...!
YEAH,
I TOLD THE MALEBRANCHE THAT THE GREAT DEMON GENERAL MALACODA'S KILLER IS HERE.
THEY INSISTED ON JOINING ME. KEPT GOING ON ABOUT REVENGE, YOU KNOW?
...NO...
I CAN'T HAVE THEM GETTING KILLED BY THE SAINT AILE KNIGHT CORPS...
...SO I TOLD THEM NOT TO GET VIOLENT.
BUT, YOU KNOW ...
...IF YOU WON'T TO LISTEN TO US... I CAN'T BE SO SURE THEY'LL LISTEN TO ME, HUH?

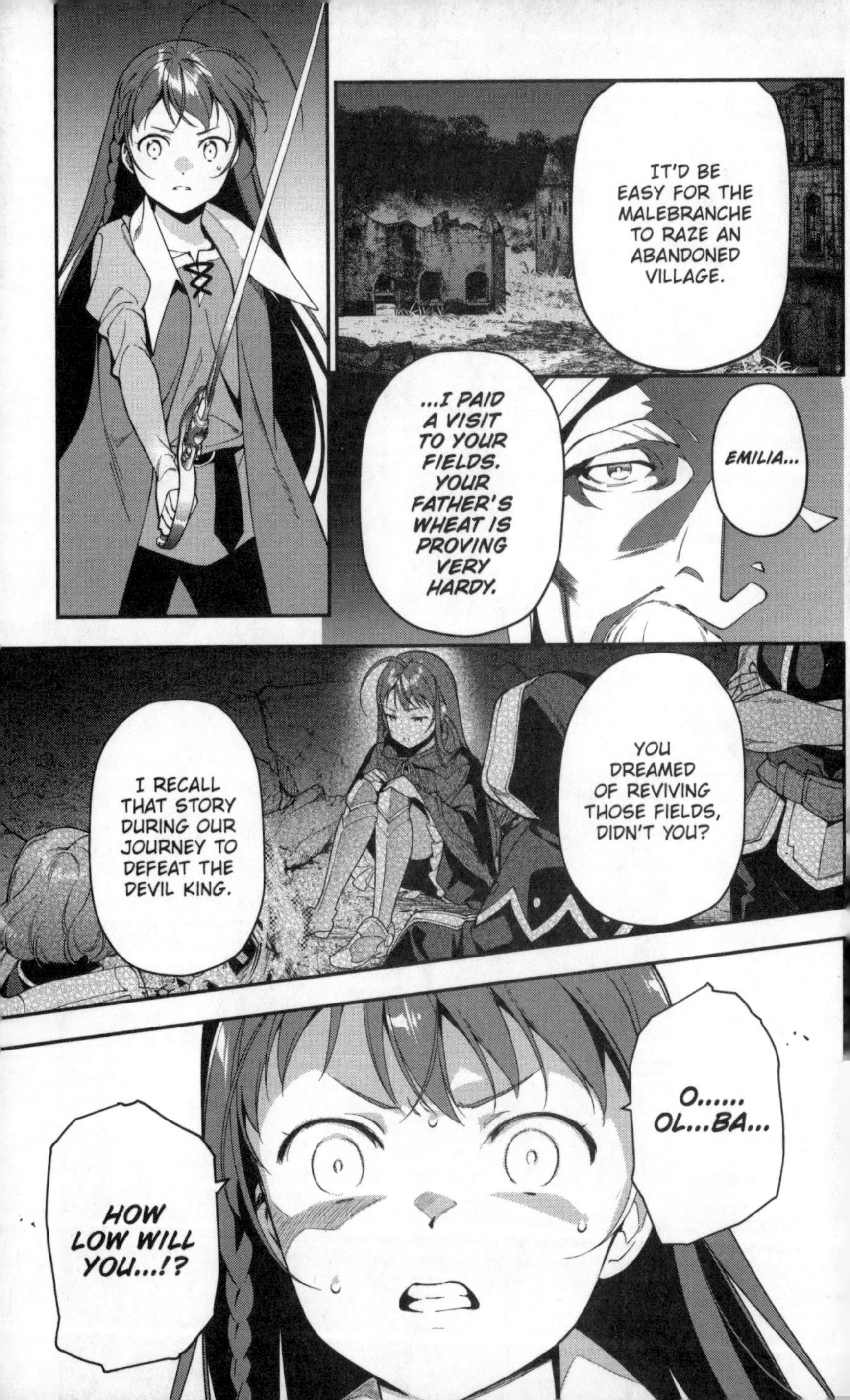
IT'D BE EASY FOR THE MALEBRANCHE TO RAZE AN ABANDONED VILLAGE.
EMILIA...
...I PAID A VISIT TO YOUR FIELDS. YOUR FATHER'S WHEAT IS PROVING VERY HARDY.
YOU DREAMED OF REVIVING THOSE FIELDS, DIDN'T YOU?
I RECALL THAT STORY DURING OUR JOURNEY TO DEFEAT THE DEVIL KING.
O...... OL...BA...
HOW LOW WILL YOU...!?

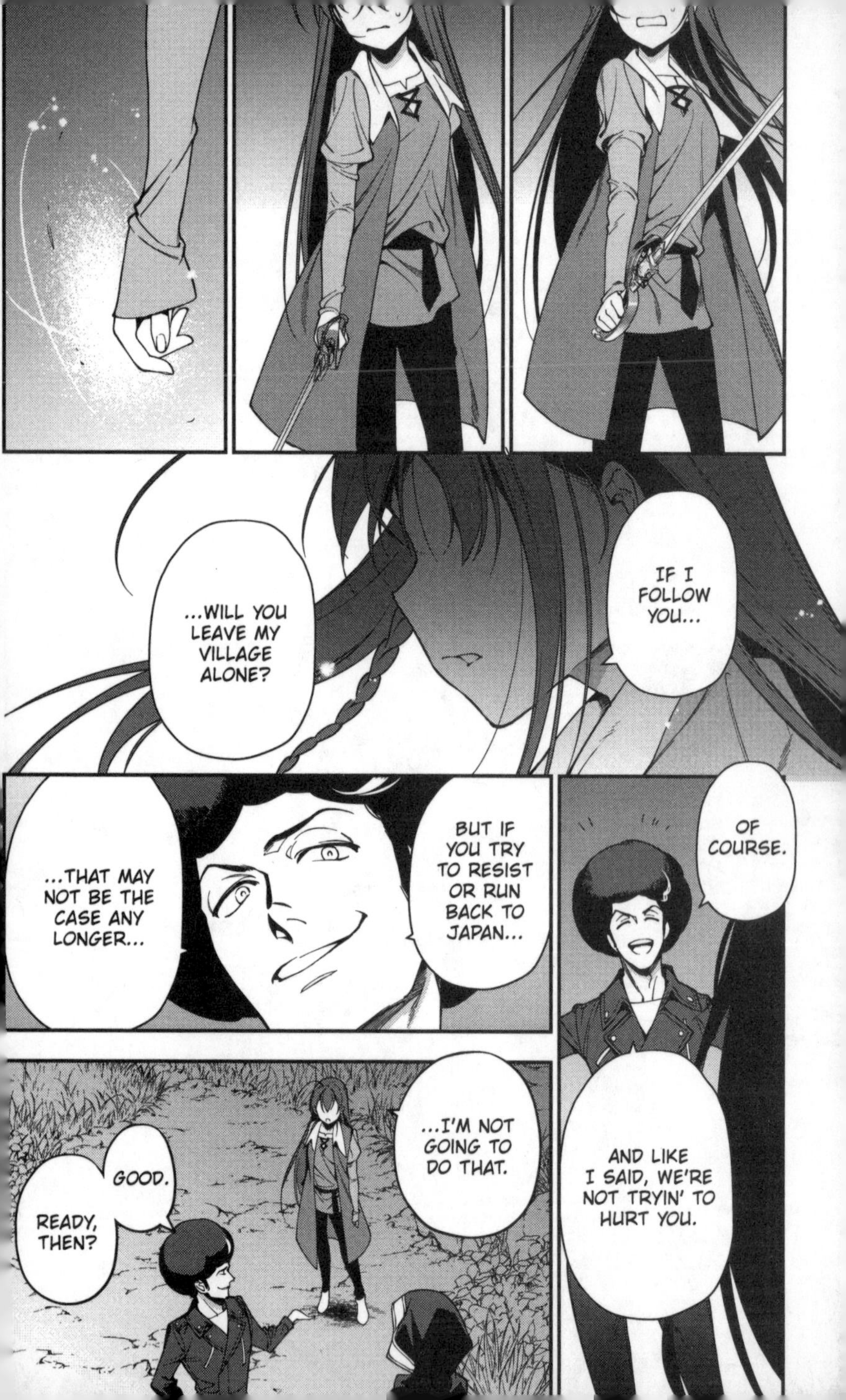
IF I FOLLOW YOU...
...WILL YOU LEAVE MY VILLAGE ALONE?
OF COURSE.
AND LIKE I SAID, WE'RE NOT TRYIN' TO HURT YOU.
BUT IF YOU TRY TO RESIST OR RUN BACK TO JAPAN...
...THAT MAY NOT BE THE CASE ANY LONGER...
...I'M NOT GOING TO DO THAT.
GOOD.
READY, THEN?

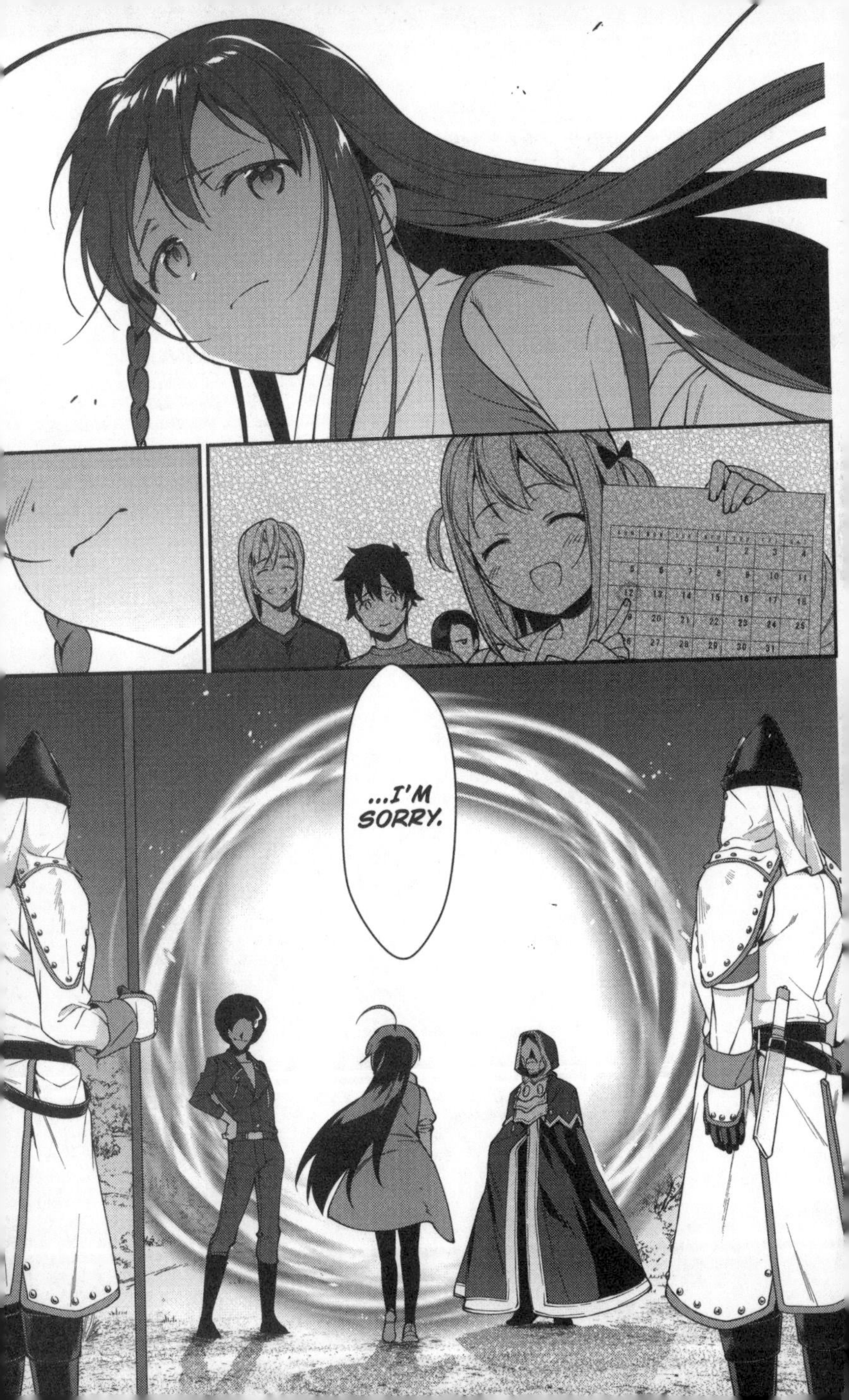
...I'M SORRY.

Thank you for picking up Volume 16 of the comic version of *The Devil Is a Part-Timer!* This series's run began in December 2011, so as I write this in January 2020, I'm entering the ninth year. I know I say this every time, but wow... To Wagahara-sensei, Oniku-sensei, everyone involved with Devil, and most of all the readers, thank you very much as always.

In this volume, Maou and the gang finally head off to Ente Isla. I got to draw a lot of Emi this time, which was great fun.

Now it's my chance to draw tons of otherworld stuff from Ente Isla...! I figure it'll be surprisingly easier than Sasazuka, even as my assistants are working incredibly hard on designing Heavensky, heh... I'm excited about all the tough, yet fun times ahead. I hope you'll keep on supporting us...!

Special thanks:
Akira Hisagi – Rusuke
and you!

2020.03
Akio Hiiragi

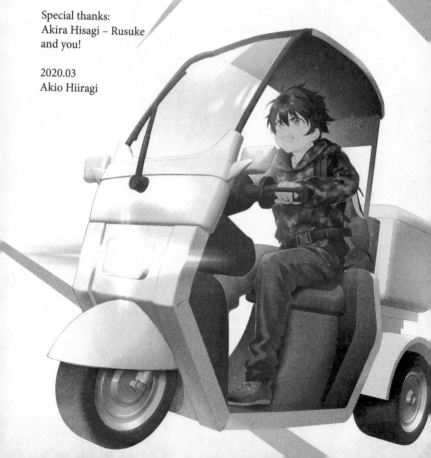

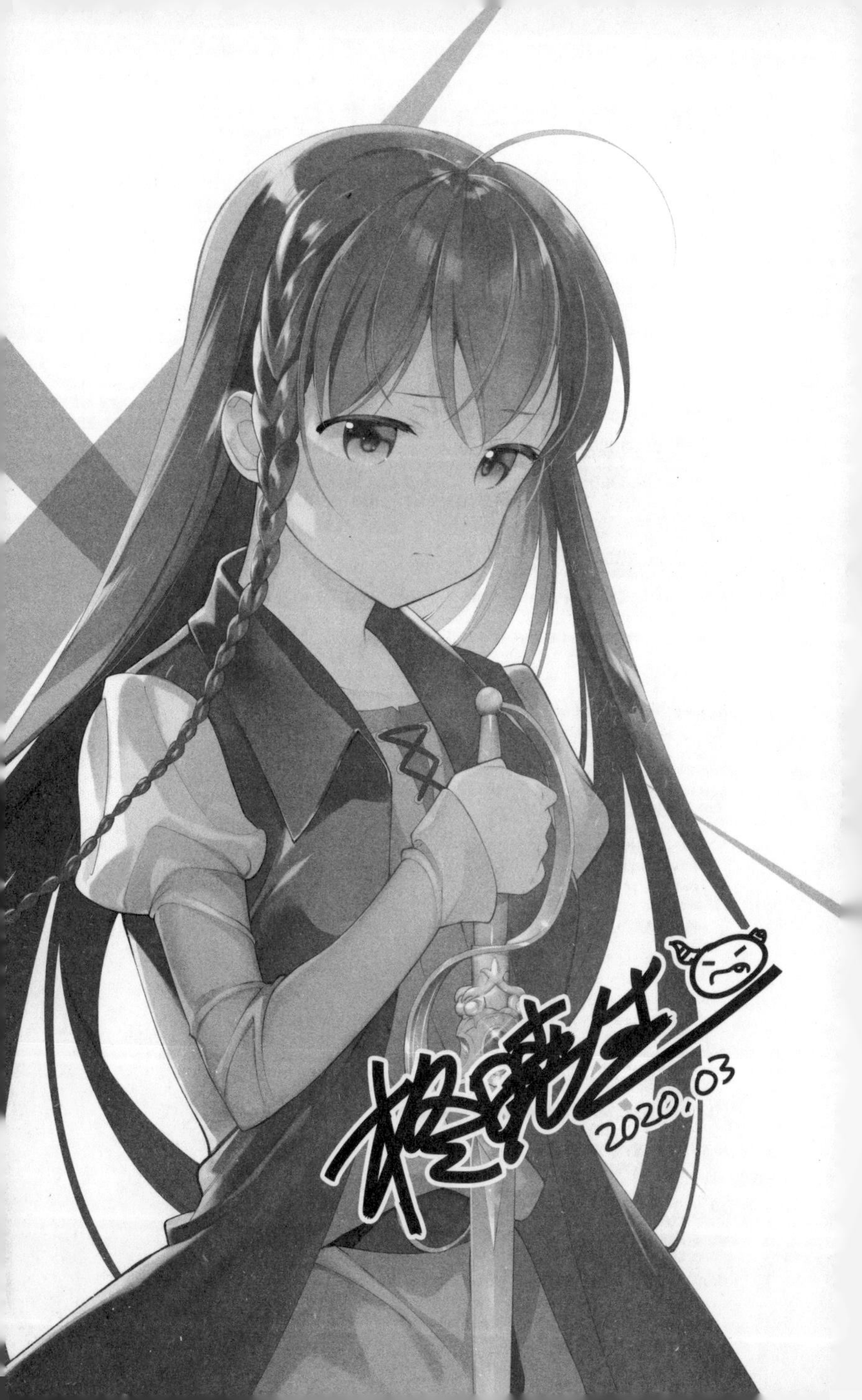
2020.03

THE DEVIL IS A PART-TIMER! ⑯

ART: AKIO HIIRAGI
ORIGINAL STORY: SATOSHI WAGAHARA
CHARACTER DESIGN: 029 (ONIKU)

Translation: Kevin Gifford

Lettering: Liz Kolkman

HATARAKU MAOUSAMA! Vol. 16
© Satoshi Wagahara / Akio Hiiragi 2020
First published in Japan in 2020 by KADOKAWA CORPORATION, Tokyo.
English translation rights arranged with KADOKAWA CORPORATION, Tokyo, through Tuttle-Mori Agency, Inc., Tokyo.

English translation © 2020 by Yen Press, LLC

Yen Press
150 West 30th Street, 19th Floor
New York, NY 10001

Visit us at yenpress.com
facebook.com/yenpress
twitter.com/yenpress
yenpress.tumblr.com
instagram.com/yenpress

First Yen Press Edition: December 2020

Yen Press is an imprint of Yen Press, LLC.
The Yen Press name and logo are trademarks of Yen Press, LLC.

Library of Congress Control Number: 2014504637

ISBNs: 978-1-9753-1871-0 (paperback)
       978-1-9753-1872-7 (ebook)

10 9 8 7 6 5 4 3 2 1

WOR

Printed in the United States of America